NETFLIX

STRANGER THINGS

THE COMPLETE SCRIPTS
SEASON 1

NETFLIX

STRANGER THINGS

THE COMPLETE SCRIPTS
SEASON 1

CREATED BY THE DUFFER BROTHERS

RANDOM HOUSE
WORLDS

NEW YORK

CONTENTS

INTRODUCTION

For as long as we can remember, we wanted to make movies. There was one problem: We lived in Durham, North Carolina, which felt like a galaxy far, far away from Hollywood.

So we came up with a plan.

Step one: Get closer. After graduating high school, we enrolled in film school at Chapman University in Orange County, California—a roughly forty-five-minute drive from Los Angeles. Close enough, we figured. At Chapman, we made a few short films, landed some internships, and made our very first Hollywood connections. We even secured an agent. A real Hollywood agent! Everything was falling into place.

Then we graduated—and the bubble burst. Like so many art graduates, we struggled to find work. The years slipped by. We wrote script after script, pitched countless ideas to glassy-eyed executives . . . but had nothing to show for it. We were broke, burned out, and on the verge of giving up. But we gave ourselves one last Hail Mary. Only this time, we wouldn't chase a big studio paycheck. We'd find independent financing and shoot on the cheap.

We came up with a simple idea: a contained thriller about a family hiding in a bomb shelter from monsters. We called it *Hidden*. Against all odds, our tiny indie script found its way to Warner Bros., and to our disbelief, they bought it. Not only that, they wanted us to direct. It felt like the impossible was finally happening: Our dreams were coming true.

And then everything went wrong.

After we completed *Hidden,* Warner Bros. decided our small film was in fact too small. They pulled its theatrical release and sent it straight to video. In the years before streaming, that was a death sentence. After a stretch of mourning and panic, we dusted ourselves off and started to toss around new movie ideas. One of them was inspired by the Montauk Project—a conspiracy theory involving secret government experiments in the early eighties. These (alleged) experiments touched on just about every supernatural phenomenon imaginable: psionic powers, interdimensional rifts, monsters. In other words, everything we loved. At the time, *Paranormal Activity* was a smash hit, so, in a desperate (and admittedly rather lame) attempt to appeal to the marketplace, we shaped the Montauk Project into a found footage film. There was just one problem: We didn't actually like found footage films. The idea never sparked. So we shoved it in a drawer in our Los Feliz apartment, where it quickly began to gather dust.

Everything changed in the fall of 2013 when we saw the film *Prisoners,* an intense thriller about a young girl who is tragically abducted—and her family and the police chief are determined to find her and bring her home. We liked it so much that we found ourselves wishing it was longer. Perhaps, we thought, there was something to a TV show about a child's kidnapping? It might be cool, if not exactly original.

That next morning, it struck us: What if we took the structure of a child kidnapping storyline and merged it with our old Montauk idea? A child goes missing—but instead of being kidnapped by a serial killer, he's taken by a demonic force, stolen into an alternate dimension. Set in the 1980s, the story would channel the works of Stephen King and Steven Spielberg—the kinds of stories we grew up loving. We still vividly remember the rush of excitement when the idea clicked. We knew it could be special.

We set about writing it the very next day. In our ten-plus years of writing scripts, nothing ever wrote itself faster. We knew these kids, these voices, this world. We called it *Montauk.* We sent the script out to various producers and eventually teamed up with

21 Laps—just the first of many unlikely choices we made in bringing this show to life. Shawn Levy, the founder of the company, was best known for directing family films like *Night at the Museum*. To top it off, he had never produced television before. But unlike other producers, Shawn and his executive Dan Cohen understood *Montauk* in a way no one else did, and they believed in us—not just as writers but also as showrunners and directors. To us, that was everything.

Before we knew it, we found ourselves traipsing around town, enthusiastically pitching the show to studios. Our enthusiasm wasn't exactly mirrored. Instead, we got puzzled looks, polite nods—and concern.

"Period pieces are expensive and no longer popular. Can you set it in the present day?"

"Who is this show for? It's too dark for kids, but it stars kids. Can't you just make it about the troubled small-town detective?"

The noes began to pile up—faster and faster, like a horror montage we couldn't control. We despaired. But then fate—or luck—intervened when our agent had lunch with a young Netflix executive to talk about a completely different project. Almost as an aside, the Netflix exec mentioned they were looking for a supernatural show with young protagonists. "You don't have anything like that, do you?"

Two weeks later, the show had a series greenlight.

We were elated—and terrified. Production was set to begin in the fall, it was already March, and we had one script. While we had a rough idea for the season, there were still so many things we hadn't figured out. Over the next few months in the writers' room, a lot came together: the setting of Hawkins, Indiana; the name and look of the Upside Down; Joyce communicating with Will through Christmas lights; Will's fake "death"; Steve's transformation from jock asshole to unexpected hero; and even a new title for the show, *Stranger Things* (a title that, we might add, wasn't popular right away).

Casting began almost immediately. We found Gaten, Millie, Finn, Caleb, Noah, Joe, Winona, and David. Their personalities began to shape, adding depth and complexity to the characters we had written. Before we knew it—and before we even had all the scripts finished—filming began.

We'd be lying if we said we knew it was going to work. But somehow, the speed and the fear imposed on us worked in our favor. There was no time to procrastinate, no time to overthink. We wrote from the gut, relying on instinct, on memories of our childhoods, and on the movies and stories we'd always loved.

It was fun. It was stressful. It was madness.

In many ways, because of the way it all came together, this first season is scrappier—a little rougher around the edges—than the ones that followed. But we think that's key to its success. There's a simplicity, an honesty, a purity to the storytelling that feels uniquely tied to where we were in that moment in time. We'd never dare compare the quality of the show to *Star Wars*, but in our minds, this season has always been our *A New Hope*. Less polished, more handmade—but perhaps more endearing because of it.

We hope you enjoy looking back on it as much as we did.

Over and out,
Matt and Ross Duffer

NETFLIX

STRANGER THINGS

THE COMPLETE SCRIPTS
SEASON 1

CHAPTER ONE:
THE VANISHING OF WILL BYERS

WRITTEN BY **THE DUFFER BROTHERS**

We HEAR A LOW-END RUMBLE. Like the GROWL OF AN UNSEEN BEAST.

Superimpose titles:

NOVEMBER 6th, 1983

HAWKINS, INDIANA

EXT. HAWKINS - SKY - NIGHT 1

FADE UP on the night sky. Dark clouds swallow the stars.

WE TILT DOWN to find an IMPOSING BUILDING, sitting alone in a dense woods. Superimpose titles:

HAWKINS NATIONAL LABORATORY

U.S. DEPARTMENT OF ENERGY

INT. HAWKINS LABS - SUB-LEVEL CORRIDOR

We are now inside the laboratory... SLOWLY CREEPING down a long windowless corridor toward a STEEL DOOR. Fluorescent lights flicker... a SIREN WARBLES... And we continue to HEAR that LOW-END RUMBLE...

We DRAW CLOSER to the door... and closer... and...

WHOOM! THE DOOR EXPLODES OPEN. THE HINGES SHRIEKING.

A SCIENTIST staggers out. Terrified.

He sprints down the corridor. Running for his life.

Faster, faster, *faster* --

INT. HAWKINS LABS - SUB-LEVEL CORRIDOR & ELEVATOR

He rounds a corner. Up ahead: a FREIGHT ELEVATOR.

He mashes the CALL BUTTON. As he waits for the elevator to arrive, he keeps looking back over his shoulder... down that long corridor. Terrified.

The elevator arrives. The doors grind vertically open.

The scientist leaps inside. He hits the button for the top floor. As he waits for the doors to close, he hears:

A STRANGE RUMBLING NOISE. COMING FROM *ABOVE HIM.*

He looks up at the ceiling. His eyes grow wide and --

WATCH THROUGH THE FLICKERING LIGHTS AS THE SCIENTIST IS
SUCKED UP TOWARD THE CEILING BY *SOMETHING*. HIS LEGS KICK
VIOLENTLY IN MID-AIR AND HE SCREAMS IN HORROR AND THEN --

The elevator doors snap shut.

EXT. SUBURBAN NEIGHBORHOOD - NIGHT

HISS! LAWN SPRINKLERS kick on.

We are now in a 1980s SUBURBAN CUL-DE-SAC. Quiet. Calm.

We HEAR the VOICE OF A YOUNG BOY. Dramatic, intense.

> MIKE (V.O.)
> Do you hear that? Listen...

We FOCUS on a TWO-STORY HOUSE at the end of the cul-de-sac.

The mailbox reads: "THE WHEELERS."

> MIKE (V.O.)
> ... Something is coming...
> something hungry for blood...

INT. WHEELER HOUSE - BASEMENT - NIGHT

A GROUP OF BOYS, 12 years old, play DUNGEONS AND DRAGONS.

They sit around a CARD TABLE. A GRID MAP is spread out on
the table before them, along with a nearly empty pizza box,
canned Cokes, and the all-important DUNGEONS AND DRAGONS
MONSTER MANUAL.

MIKE WHEELER, 12, is the "Dungeon Master" and de facto leader
of our group.

> MIKE (CONT'D)
> ... A shadow grows on the wall
> behind you... swallowing you in
> darkness... *it* is almost here...

The other boys lean forward. Riveted. We survey them:

LUCAS SINCLAIR, 12, playing as a knight. He is very small
but his loud mouth more than makes up for it.

DUSTIN HENDERSON, 12, playing as a dwarf. He is the most
fearful -- and least confident -- of our group.

WILL BYERS, 12, playing as a wizard. He is soft-spoken,
gentle, delicate.

                         WILL
                    ... What is it?

                         DUSTIN
                    What if it's the Demogorgon? We're
                    in deep shit if it's the Demogorgon --

                         LUCAS
                    It's not the Demogorgon --

Mike waits for them to settle down. Then:

                         MIKE
                    An army of Troglodytes charge into
                    the chamber!

He slams SIX WINGED MINIATURES onto the map.

                         MIKE (CONT'D)
                    Their tails drum the floor. Boom!
                    Boom! Boom!

                         DUSTIN
                    Troglodytes?!

                         LUCAS
                    Toldja.

                         DUSTIN
                    Pfff.

Mike looks over his shoulder. His eyes grow wide.

                         MIKE
                    Wait... do you hear that? Boom!
                    Boom! BOOM! That sound... it
                    didn't come from the *Troglodytes*.
                    No. It came from something else...

Mike slams a LARGE TWO-HEADED MONSTER MINIATURE onto the map.

                         MIKE (CONT'D)
                    THE DEMOGORGON.

The boys stare.

                         DUSTIN
                    We're in deep shit.

                         MIKE
                    Will, your action.

Will swallows. God, he wishes it wasn't his turn.

                    WILL
          I -- I don't know --

                    LUCAS
          Fireball him --

                    WILL
          I'd have to roll thirteen or higher --

                    DUSTIN
          Too risky. Cast a protection spell --

                    LUCAS
          Don't be a wimp! Fireball him!

                    DUSTIN
          Protection spell -- !

                    MIKE
          The Demogorgon is tired of your
          silly human bickering. It stomps
          toward you. BOOM!

                    LUCAS
          FIREBALL HIM WILL!

                    MIKE
          Another step. BOOM!

                    DUSTIN
          Cast protection!

                    MIKE
          It roars in anger --

              LUCAS   DUSTIN
          Fireball -- !   Protection --

                    MIKE
          And --

                    WILL
          FIREBALL!

Will rolls the die. Too hard. The die scatters to the
other side of the basement. It lands by the basement steps.

                    LUCAS
          What is it?!

                    WILL
          I don't know!

                    DUSTIN
          Is it a thirteen?

                    WILL
          I DON'T KNOW!

The boys scramble to look at the die when --

WHOOM! The basement door swings open. The boys look up to
find KAREN WHEELER, late 30s, Mike's mom, standing at the top
of the stairs.

                    MIKE
          Mom, we're in the middle of a
          campaign --

                    KAREN
          You mean the *end*.

She taps her watch.

                    KAREN (CONT'D)
          Fifteen after.

INT. WHEELER HOUSE - LIVING ROOM - NIGHT

Mike chases his mom up out of the basement.

                    MIKE
          Just twenty more minutes --

                    KAREN
          It's a school night, Michael, and I
          just put Holly to bed. You can
          finish next weekend --

                    MIKE
          That'll ruin the flow --

                    KAREN
          Michael --

                    MIKE
          I'm serious, Mom! It took two
          weeks to plan. How was I supposed
          to know it'd take ten hours -- ?

                    KAREN
          You've been playing *ten hours*?

Mike's dad, TED, 45, is watching TV. Or *trying* to. The
signal is terrible; a snowstorm of STATIC obscures the image.

He smacks the TV.

8

                    MIKE
          Dad, don't you think -- ?

                    TED
                (not even listening)
          I think you should listen to your
          mother. DAGGUM PIECE OF JUNK!

He smacks the TV again. The static flares.

INT. WHEELER HOUSE - BASEMENT - NIGHT

Lucas, Dustin, and Will stuff belongings into backpacks.

                    WILL
          Does the seven count?

                    LUCAS
                (shit)
          It was a seven?

Will nods.

                    LUCAS (CONT'D)
          Did Mike see it?

Will shakes his head.

                    LUCAS (CONT'D)
          Then it doesn't count.

The boys zip up their backpacks and race up the stairs.

Dustin holds up the pizza box. Still one slice left.

                    DUSTIN
          Hey guys -- anyone want this?!

                    LUCAS/WILL
          No!

Dustin looks back at the pizza. Considers.

INT. WHEELER HOUSE - UPSTAIRS HALLWAY - NIGHT

Dustin heads upstairs, pizza box in arms. He walks up to a
bedroom door. Through a crack in the door, he sees...

NANCY WHEELER. This is Mike's sister, 16, girl-next-door
pretty. She is on her bed in pajamas, a phone in hand,
fingers twisting its cord, slender legs kicked in the air.

                    NANCY
          I know, I know, but -- I don't
          think so -- yeah, he's cute, but --
          Barb -- BARB!   -- listen to me --

Dustin waves, getting her attention. Holds up the pizza box.

                    DUSTIN
          Hey Nancy, there's a slice left if
          you want. Pepperoni and sausage --

                    NANCY
               (into phone)
          Hold on --

Nancy walks over and --

SHUTS THE DOOR in Dustin's face.

EXT./INT. WHEELER GARAGE - NIGHT

WHOOM! Dustin shuts the garage door behind him.

He's in the middle of eating the last pizza slice. The other
three boys are out here already: Lucas and Will are climbing
onto their bikes; Mike is seeing them off.

                    DUSTIN
               (talking with mouth full)
          Something's wrong with your sister.

                    MIKE
          What're you talking about?

                    DUSTIN
          She's got a stick up her butt --

                    LUCAS
          It's 'cause she's seeing that barf
          bag, Steve Harrington --

                    DUSTIN
          Yeah, she's turning into a real
          jerk.

                    MIKE
          She's always been a real jerk --

Dustin climbs onto his bike.

                    DUSTIN
          Nu-uh. She used to be cool. Like
          that time she dressed up as an elf
          for our Eldertree campaign --

                               10

                        MIKE
          Four years ago!

                        DUSTIN
          Just sayin'.

Dustin and Lucas bike off out of the garage.

Will lingers behind a second longer. Turns back to Mike.

                        WILL
          ... It was a seven.

                        MIKE
          What?

                        WILL
          The roll. It was a seven. The
          Demogorgon -- it got me.
                  (shrugs)
          See you tomorrow.

Will smiles at Mike, then bikes away, joining the others.

BZZZZZ. The light in the garage flickers. *Strange.*

Mike switches it off and heads back inside.

EXT. NEIGHBORHOOD - NIGHT

The boys bike home. Their handlebar lights wink in the
night. And good thing, because it's *very* dark out here.

Lucas peels off from the group.

                        LUCAS
          See ya, ladies.

                        DUSTIN
          Kiss your mom 'night for me.

Lucas flips him the bird and bikes up a driveway toward a
TWO-STORY HOUSE. It looks almost identical to Mike's.

Will and Dustin bike on in silence for a beat, then:

                        DUSTIN (CONT'D)
          Race to my place? Winner gets a
          comic?

                        WILL
          Any comic?

                         DUSTIN
          Yeah --

Will has heard enough. He starts pedaling. *Fast.*

                    DUSTIN (CONT'D)
          Hey!

Dustin pedals in pursuit. But he's already behind. And...

EXT. NEIGHBORHOOD - A FEW MINUTES LATER - NIGHT

Will whizzes past a house at the far end of the neighborhood.

He waves at Dustin. Now fifty yards back.

                         WILL
               I'll take your "X-Men" one-three-
               four!

Dustin stops. Out-of-breath.

                         DUSTIN
                    (really bummed)
          ... *Man.*

EXT. FOREST ROAD - LATER - NIGHT

Will is now biking along an empty forest road. All alone.

He lives much further out than the rest of his friends. It
is even darker out here and quiet; unnervingly so. Only the
SOUND of CICADAS and a gentle breeze to keep him company.

He bikes past a LARGE METAL FENCE. A warning sign reads:

                    HAWKINS NATIONAL LABORATORY.
               RESTRICTED AREA. NO TRESPASSING.

His bike's headlight flickers. Will looks down at it. After
a beat, the light returns to normal. He looks back up and --

A TALL FIGURE STANDS IN THE MIDDLE OF THE ROAD.

Will yanks the handlebars -- loses control --

He veers off the road -- explodes into --

EXT. WOODS - CONTINUOUS

And *CRASHES*. Will flies off the bike. He skids, rolls, eats
dirt. As he lies there on the ground, gasping, he hears:

STRANGE GUTTURAL SOUNDS. COMING FROM BEHIND HIM.

He pushes to his feet and turns to the sound. Foliage
shudders. The SOUNDS GROW. Something is *coming*.

Will abandons his bike --

And runs.

EXT. BYERS HOUSE - NIGHT

Will bursts out of the woods. Up ahead: his HOUSE.

It is small, one story, lower class, falling apart.

INT. BYERS HOUSE - NIGHT

Will slams the door shut behind him and bolts the lock.

A shaggy dog, CHESTER THE MUTT, races to greet him.

> WILL
> MOM?! JONATHAN?! MOM?!

He checks his MOM'S BEDROOM. His BROTHER'S BEDROOM.

No one is home. *He is all alone.*

INT. BYERS HOUSE - LIVING ROOM - NIGHT

Will scrambles back to the living room window.

He cups his hands to the glass and peers out into the yard.

It is dark. Murky. Quiet. A gust of wind blows and...

Day-old laundry flutters on a clothes line to REVEAL...

THAT FIGURE AGAIN. JUST STANDING THERE AMONGST THE BILLOWING
LAUNDRY. WE CAN'T MAKE OUT ANY FEATURES, BUT ITS PROPORTIONS
SEEM... OFF. ITS HEAD IS TOO LARGE. ITS ARMS ARE TOO LONG.
ITS BODY IS SWOLLEN AND BENT IN A STRANGE, TWISTED SHAPE.

Another gust of wind. The clothes flutter again and...

The Figure is gone.

Will pales. His heart in his throat.

INT. BYERS HOUSE - KITCHEN - MOMENTS LATER - NIGHT

Will rips the phone receiver off the kitchen wall. Dials
911. But --

It does not ring. Just hums with LOW-END STATIC.

                              WILL
                    Hello?! HELLO -- ?!

Will pauses. He HEARS SOMETHING on the other line. But not
a voice... it is that GUTTURAL SOUND he heard in the woods.
The pitch rises and falls, making a series of strange sounds.
Words? It is as if the figure... whoever... *whatever* it
is... is somehow speaking to him through the phone receiver.

Behind him, Chester begins to GROWL at the front door.

Will lowers the phone. And looks back at the door.

A SHADOW fills the crack at the base of the door.

And then somehow, *impossibly*, the chain bolt begins to slide
open, as if drawn by an invisible hand. The metal SHRIEKS.

Will drops the phone and --

EXT. BYERS HOUSE - BACKYARD - NIGHT

WHOOM! Will explodes out the back screen door.

He sprints into an OLD WOODEN SHED and --

INT. BYERS SHED - MOMENTS LATER - NIGHT

WHAM! He slams the shed doors behind him. Breathing hard.

His eyes dart. Searching for *something*.

The shed is cluttered and dark, lit only by a NAKED LIGHT
BULB, hanging from the ceiling. The bulb buzzes, flickers.

At last he spots it:

AN OLD REMINGTON RIFLE. DUSTY. HANGING ON A WALL MOUNT.

Will yanks it down, retrieves a few AMMO SHELLS from a work
bench, and loads the rifle as fast as he can, which isn't
very fast at all; he is so scared his hands sweat and shake.

Will finishes loading the rifle. He snaps the chamber shut
and aims it at the door. The rifle trembles in his hands.

While Will keeps his eyes trained on the door, we notice a
SHADOWED FIGURE SLOWLY RISE behind him.

Will senses movement. Turns. He doesn't fire.

He just stares. Paralyzed by fear. Shock.

He fights tears.

                         WILL
              ... P-please --

A HIGH-PITCHED SHRIEKING SOUND SUDDENLY FILLS THE SHED.

WE DON'T SEE WHAT HAPPENS TO WILL; WE JUST WATCH THAT NAKED
DANGLING LIGHT BULB. IT GLOWS BRIGHTER AND BRIGHTER AND
BRIGHTER, FILLING THE SHED WITH OVERWHELMING WHITE LIGHT. WE
THINK THE GLASS OF THE BULB IS GOING TO SHATTER BUT THEN --

The TERRIBLE SHRIEKING sound abruptly stops.

The bulb dims. Returning to normal wattage.

We PULL AWAY from the light.

The shed is empty.

Will has vanished.

                    MAIN TITLES

INT. HOPPER'S TRAILER - LIVING ROOM - MORNING 2

We FADE UP on a CHILD'S DRAWING on the wall.

It depicts a perfect family: a MAN, a GIRL, a WOMAN.

WE PAN from the picture and slowly survey this mess of a
trailer. We see, among other things...

A dusty TV from which a LOCAL NEWSWOMAN drones:

                    LOCAL NEWSWOMAN (ON TV)
              ... reports of surges and outages
              across the county... We reached out
              to Public Service and Gas and...

- A CLUTTER OF BEER BOTTLES

- Opened PLASTIC VIALS.

- A scattering of RED AND BLUE PILLS.

- And last but certainly not least:

-- JIM HOPPER, or "HOP," early 40s. He is sprawled out on a
grungy sofa, shirtless, wearing only a pair of worn Levi
jeans and a BLUE BRACELET on his wrist.

A RAY OF SUN slices through blinds. Waking him.

He blinks. Grimaces. *Hungover.*

                          15

EXT. HOPPER'S TRAILER - MORNING

Hopper steps out onto a decrepit porch.

He lights up a HAND-ROLLED CIGARETTE. Drags on it.

His trailer is perched on the shore of a lake. It's a bit
lonely out here. But damn if it isn't beautiful.

Hop rubs his arms. Getting cold. Enough beauty for now.

INT. HOPPER'S TRAILER - BATHROOM - A LITTLE LATER - MORNING

- Hopper showers. So tiny in here his body barely fits.

- Hopper studies his beard in the mirror. Considers shaving.
Doesn't.

- Hopper pops open a PLASTIC VIAL labeled "TUINAL." He
shakes out two capsules. Red and blue. Scoops a mouthful of
water. Washes them down.

INT. HOPPER'S TRAILER - BEDROOM - A LITTLE LATER - MORNING

Hopper dresses. He yanks on a pair of brown pants... a
matching brown collared shirt... a belt with a holster... a
9MM GLOCK... a gray hat... and lastly, he clips on...

A GOLD BADGE. It reads:

                    HAWKINS POLICE.   CHIEF.

Behind him, the TV continues to drone...

                         LOCAL NEWSWOMAN (ON TV)
                    ... In other news, it seems like
                    you may want to stay in tonight --
                    or pack an umbrella. Let's go now
                    to everyone's favorite morning
                    weatherman, Charles. Charles?

Hopper heads out the door. The trailer door RATTLES shut.

EXT. BYERS HOUSE - MORNING

We TILT from the darkening sky to find the Byers house. The
laundry hangs. It billows a bit in the gathering wind...
A storm is coming...

INT. BYERS HOUSE - KITCHEN - MORNING

JONATHAN BYERS, 16, Will's older brother, cooks breakfast.

He is lanky with long hair. Quietly handsome... but he
wouldn't believe it if you told him.

>   JOYCE (O.S.)
>   Where the hell are they?!

His mom, JOYCE BYERS, late 30s, races past, frazzled. She
wears a wrinkled "Melvald's General Store" uniform.

>   JOYCE (CONT'D)
>   Dammit!

>   JONATHAN
>   Check the couch.

Joyce does. She finds her keys under a cushion. *Thank God.*

She snatches them up, gives Jonathan a quick peck on the
cheek, and races for the door, only to pause at the last
second, realizing something. She turns back to Jonathan.

>   JOYCE
>   -- Will? Where's Will?

>   JONATHAN
>   Sleeping, I guess.

>   JOYCE
>   You gotta make sure he's up,
>   Jonathan, how many times -- ?

>   JONATHAN
>   I'm making breakfast --

Joyce shakes her head. Irritated. She hurries down the
hallway. CLAPS HER hands.

>   JOYCE
>   Will -- Will come on, get up.

Joyce throws open the door to Will's room. It's empty.

INT. BYERS HOUSE - KITCHEN - MOMENTS LATER

She strides back over to Jonathan. Worried now.

>   JOYCE
>   He came home last night, right?

>   JONATHAN
>   He's not in his room?

>   JOYCE
>   He come home or not?

                    JONATHAN
          I don't know --

                    JOYCE
          You *don't know*?

                    JONATHAN
          I got back late, I was working --

                    JOYCE
          You were working?

                    JONATHAN
          Eric asked if I could cover for
          him, I said yeah; I figured we
          could use the cash --

                    JOYCE
          We talked about this -- I told you
          not to take shifts on nights I'm
          working, I *specifically* told you --

                    JONATHAN
          He was over at the Wheelers' all
          day. I'm sure he just stayed over.

                    JOYCE
          I can't believe this.

                    JONATHAN
          I'm sorry --

                    JOYCE
          I *can't* believe it.

Joyce grabs the kitchen wall phone. Dials a number.

INT. WHEELER HOUSE - KITCHEN - MORNING - INTERCUT

A WALL PHONE RINGS at the Wheelers. It is chaos over here.

Mike is grabbing syrup from a cabinet; Nancy is eating
scrambled eggs, HOLLY, 3, is crying; Ted is watching the
morning news; and now the phone is ringing. *The fucking
phone.*

Karen answers. Holly squirms in her arms.

                    KAREN
          Hello?

                    JOYCE
          Karen -- it's Joyce.

                    KAREN
          Joyce, hi --

Behind her, Mike pours syrup onto his scrambled eggs.

                    NANCY
          That's *disgusting*.

                    MIKE
          It's good, swear.

Mike squeezes some onto Nancy's eggs.

                    NANCY
          WHAT THE HELL MIKE?!

                    TED
          Hey, language!

Karen puts the phone on her shoulder. She can't hear Joyce.

                    KAREN
               (to kids)
          QUIET!
               (back to phone)
          I'm sorry, one of those mornings --

                    JOYCE
          Was that Will I heard back there?

                    KAREN
          Will? No, no -- just Michael.

                    JOYCE
          Will didn't spend the night?

                    KAREN
          ... No. He, he left here a little
          after eight.
               (worried now)
          He's not home?

INT. BYERS HOUSE - MORNING

Joyce tries to hide her panic.

                    JOYCE
               (into phone)
          I -- I was working late last night.
          I'm sure he just left early for
          school. Thanks... thanks Karen --

Joyce hangs up the phone.

She looks scared. And so does Jonathan.

EXT. HAWKINS MIDDLE SCHOOL - MORNING

Mike, Lucas, and Dustin ride their bikes past the high
school, making their way toward Hawkins Middle School -- a
quaint one-story brick building tucked beneath a WATER TOWER.

EXT. MIDDLE SCHOOL - BACK - MORNING

As the boys slot their wheels into bike racks, they look
around at all the kids streaming in. *Looking for Will.*

>   MIKE
>   ... I don't see him. Weird.

>   LUCAS
>   I'm telling you: his mom's right,
>   he just went to class early again --

>   DUSTIN
>   Yeah -- he's always paranoid
>   Gursky's gonna give him a pop quiz.

Mike nods. Feeling better.

>   TROY (O.S.)
>   Step right up, ladies and
>   gentlemen! Step right up and get
>   your tickets for the freak show!

The boys look to find two kids, JAMES and TROY, 14, headed
toward them. Our boys don't run... they just stand there
like statues. This is clearly a regular occurrence, and this
is how they deal with it: with passivity.

Troy sizes them up.

>   TROY (CONT'D)
>   Who do you think would make more
>   money at a freak show: "Frogface,"
>   "Midnight," or "Toothless?"

>   JAMES
>   Ooof. Tough call, tough call.
>   (eyes Dustin)
>   I'd go with Toothless.

>   DUSTIN
>   My teeth are coming in, I told you
>   a million times, it's called
>   *cleidocranial dysplasia* --

                        JAMES
                   (mocking lisp)
          I told you a *million times* --

                        TROY
          Do the arm thing.

Dustin hesitates.

                        JAMES
          Do it, freak.

Dustin sighs, relents. He pulls his arms across his body.
Because Dustin has no collar bones, his arms stretch all the
way across.

The bullies share disgusted looks, shiver...

                        TROY
          Gets me every time! Every time!

They shove past our boys and head into the school, laughing.

                        LUCAS
                   (under breath)
          Numbskulls.

                        MIKE
                   (to Dustin)
          ... I think it's cool. It's like a
          superpower or something. Like
          Mister Fantastic.

                        DUSTIN
          Yeah, except I can't fight evil
          with it.

The boys pull on their backpacks and head to school.

EXT. HAWKINS HIGH SCHOOL - MORNING

Nancy heads into the high school.

INT. HIGH SCHOOL - HALLWAY - MORNING

Nancy wades through a bustling hallway.

BARBARA, 16, her best friend, a bit dorky, catches up.

                        BARBARA
          So? Did he call?

                        NANCY
          Keep your voice down --

                    BARBARA
          Did he?

Nancy shakes her head. Walks up to her locker.

                    NANCY
          I told you, it's not like that.

Barbara shoots her a look.

                    NANCY (CONT'D)
          Okay, I mean, yes, fine, he likes
          me, you know, but not like *that* --
               (lowers voice)
          We just made out a couple times.

                    BARBARA
               (mocking)
          "We just made out a couple times."
          Jesus, you're gonna be so cool now
          it's ridiculous --

                    NANCY
          No I'm not!

                    BARBARA
          You better still hang out with me,
          that's all I'm saying. If you become
          friends with Carol and Tommy H. --

                    NANCY
          Gross. And I'm telling you, this
          was just a one-time --
               (off Barbara)
          -- *two-time* thing, alright?

Nancy silences. There is a FOLDED NOTE taped to the inside
of her locker, addressed "NANCY." She opens it. It reads:

          MEET ME. BATHROOM. STEVE.

Nancy looks up at Barbara. Speechless.

                    BARBARA
          You were saying?

INT. HIGH SCHOOL - GIRLS' BATHROOM - MORNING

Nancy is now full-on MAKING OUT with --

STEVE HARRINGTON, 17, wealthy, athletic, charm to spare.
Their make-out session gets more and more intense when --

THE BELL RINGS. Nancy crashes back to reality. She pulls
away from Steve. Her cheeks are flushed.

                    NANCY
          Okay -- I -- I have to go --

                    STEVE
          One more minute --

Steve kisses her again. Nancy gives in for a bit, but...

                    NANCY
          Steve --

                    STEVE
             (between kissing)
          Yeah --

                    NANCY
          I really --
             (kiss)
          -- like, seriously ---
             (kiss)
          -- have to go --

She finally tears away from him. Pulls on her backpack.

                    STEVE
          Let's do something tonight, yeah?

                    NANCY
          I-I can't -- I have to study. For
          Kaminsky's chem test --

                    STEVE
          What's your GPA again? Three-point-
          nineninenineninenine-- ?

                    NANCY
          Kaminsky's tests are impossible --

                    STEVE
          So let me help --

                    NANCY
          You *failed* chem.

                    STEVE
          C-minus.

                    NANCY
          Oh, well, in that case...

                    STEVE
          So should I come over, say, eight?

                    NANCY
          Uh, are you crazy? My mom won't
          allow that, no way --

                    STEVE
          Who says she needs to "allow"
          anything? I'll just climb through
          your window -- she won't even know
          I'm there. I'm stealthy -- like a
          ninja.

                    NANCY
          You *are* crazy.

                    STEVE
          Okay, okay, forget your place --
          we'll just chill in my car, find a
          nice quiet place to park --

                    NANCY
          Steve, I have to study -- I'm not
          kidding.

                    STEVE
          Why do you think I want it nice and
          quiet?

Nancy can't help but smile.

                    NANCY
          You're an idiot, Steve Harrington.

Nancy heads for the door. At the last second:

                    NANCY (CONT'D)
          I'll meet you at Dearborn and
          Maple. At eight. To study.

With that -- she's out.

Steve gives a victorious karate chop!

EXT. HAWKINS POLICE STATION - MORNING

An American flag flutters on a flagpole.

We are outside the LOCAL POLICE STATION. It is quaint. As
in, *really* quaint. If the sign out front didn't read
"POLICE," you'd probably mistake it for a gift shop.

Hopper's CHEVY BLAZER POLICE CAR pulls into the lot.

INT. POLICE STATION - ENTRANCE - MORNING

Hopper lumbers inside. Smoking a cigarette.

His secretary, FLORENCE, 61, sits behind a glass partition.

> FLORENCE
> Good of you to show --

> HOPPER
> Mornin' to you too, Flo.

Hopper heads straight into --

INT. POLICE STATION - BULLPEN - MORNING

He makes a beeline for the coffee machine.

OFFICER CALLAHAN and OFFICER POWELL look up from a game of five-card draw, their boots kicked up on their desks.

The mood here is casual, to say the least.

> OFFICER CALLAHAN
> You look like hell, Chief.

> HOPPER
> Your wife looked worse when I left
> her.

Powell cackles at this. *Burn!*

Hopper begins to make himself a cup of coffee. Florence walks up to Hopper, yanks the cigarette out of his mouth, and snubs it out.

> FLORENCE
> While you were drinking or sleeping
> or whatever it is you deem so
> important on Monday mornings, Phil
> Larson called, said some kids stole
> the gnomes out of his garden again --

> HOPPER
> Gnomes again, huh? Yeah, tell Phil
> I'll get right on that.

Hopper heads back through the bullpen with his coffee.

He's already lighting up another cigarette.

Florence nips at his heels.

                    FLORENCE
          A more pressing matter -- Joyce
          Byers can't find her son this
          morning --

                    HOPPER
          Yeah, alright, I'll give her a
          call. Just give me a minute --

                    FLORENCE
          Chief, Joyce is very upset and --

                    HOPPER
          What have we talked about? Morning
          is a time for contemplation and
          coffee.

                    FLORENCE
          Chief, she's --

                    HOPPER
          Contemplation. And coffee.

Hopper heads up to the second floor.

INT. POLICE STATION - UPSTAIRS - MORNING

He crashes to a stop. Almost spilling his coffee. *Shit.*

REVERSE ANGLE:

Joyce is already *in* his office.

She looks back at him. Not happy.

INT. POLICE STATION - HOPPER'S OFFICE - MORNING

WHAP! WHAP! WHAP! Type-hammers slam ink onto a police
report.

A single, ominous word forms one letter at a time: "MISSING."

Hopper looks up from the typewriter. He now has on a pair of
READING GLASSES, which lend him a more earnest look. His
desk, however, shatters the illusion: It's cluttered with
papers and mugs and candy wrappers, like the desk of a child.

Joyce paces. Dragging on a cigarette. She's on edge. So
far out she might just fall right off.

                    JOYCE
          I've been waiting an hour --

                    HOPPER
And I apologize again --

                    JOYCE
-- AN *HOUR* --

                    HOPPER
I understand. But a boy his age,
most likely he's playing hookey --

                    JOYCE
Not my Will, no. He wouldn't do
that. He's not like that --

                    HOPPER
You never know. My mother thought
I was on the debate team, when
really I was screwing Chrissy
Carpenter in the back of my dad's
boat --

                    JOYCE
Will's not like you. He's not like
me. He's not like most.

She takes another drag on her cigarette. Fights tears.

                    JOYCE (CONT'D)
He's got a couple of friends. But
everyone else, they -- they make
fun of him. Call him names, laugh
at him, his clothes --

                    HOPPER
His clothes? What's wrong with his
clothes?

                    JOYCE
I-I don't know. Does it matter?

                    HOPPER
Maybe.

Joyce takes another drag.

                    JOYCE
Lonnie... Lonnie always said he was
queer --

                    HOPPER
Is he?

                    JOYCE
He's missing. That's what he is.

                          27

Hopper scratches his stubble.

                    HOPPER
          You hear from Lonnie lately?

Joyce hesitates. This is an uncomfortable subject.

                    JOYCE
          He was in Indianapolis last I
          heard. That was about a year ago.
          But he's got nothing to do with
          this.

Hopper rummages around his desk. Unearths a pen and a pad.

                    HOPPER
          What's his number?

                    JOYCE
          I told you, he's got nothin' to do
          with this --

                    HOPPER
          Kid goes missing, ninety-nine times
          outta a hundred the kid's with a
          parent or relative --

                    JOYCE
          What about the other time?

                    HOPPER
          What?

                    JOYCE
          You said "ninety-nine outta a
          hundred." What about the other
          time? The one.

Hopper removes his reading glasses. Leans forward.

                    HOPPER
          This is Hawkins, Joyce. In four
          years, you know the worst thing
          I've seen? You know what it was?
               (beat)
          When that owl attacked Eleanor
          Gillepsie. Thought her hair was a
          nest. I mean -- it does look like
          a nest, doesn't it? All that
          frizz?

Hopper chuckles at the memory. Trying to lighten the mood.

Joyce begins to relax a little. But only a *little*.

28

                    JOYCE
          I'll call Lonnie. He'll talk to me
          before he talks to a --

                    HOPPER
          -- pig?

                    JOYCE
          Cop.

Joyce sits down. She snuffs her cigarette in an ashtray.
Then she looks back up at Hopper. Her eyes are bloodshot.
Glassy.

                    JOYCE (CONT'D)
          Find my son, Hop. *Find him.*

Hopper takes this in. All at once he feels burdened with a
responsibility he doesn't want. He finds his composure,
nudges his glasses back on his nose, and resumes typing.

Hammer type SLAMS paper. WHAP! WHAP! WHAP!

EXT. HAWKINS LABS - DAY

Black, unmarked sedans accelerate up to the entrance.

They slam to a stop and --

INT. HAWKINS LABS - CORRIDOR - DAY

WHAP! WHAP! WHAP! Shoes drum on linoleum as...

DR. MARTIN BRENNER, 40s, leads a group of NSA AGENTS through
the corridors of the lab. Dr. Brenner wears a casual suit,
loose tie, stubble. He clearly hasn't slept in some time.

All around them -- chaos. Scientists whipping to and fro.

SCIENTIST #1 turns to the LEAD AGENT.

                    SCIENTIST #1
          We've evacuated the east wing --
          sealed it off, following quarantine
          protocol --

They arrive at a PLASTIC QUARANTINE DOOR.

Brenner ZIPS open the plastic door and --

29

INT. HAWKINS LABS - PREPARATION ROOM

A SERIES of very quick, very CLOSE SHOTS as --

Dr. Brenner, Scientist #1, the agents, and a TRIO OF SOLDIERS silently dress into HAZMAT SUITS. They secure hoods. Gloves. Boots.

PRE-LAP: THE SOUND OF GROANING METAL.

INT. HAWKINS LABS - FREIGHT ELEVATOR

The freight elevator GROANS and SHUDDERS as it carries...

Dr. Brenner, Scientist #1, the agents, the soldiers down into the bowels of the labs. The soldiers are armed with M16-style rifles with barrel-mounted flashlights.

The Lead Agent looks up at the ceiling, uneasy, and...

INT. HAWKINS LABS - SUB-LEVEL CORRIDOR - CONTINUOUS

WHOOM! The elevator CRASHES to a halt. The doors open.

The group exits into the dark corridor.

INT. HAWKINS LABS - SUB-LEVEL CORRIDOR - CONTINUOUS

They retrace the path of the scientist in the opening scene.

As their flashlights sweep around, we see that a few things have changed since our last visit: The fluorescent lights are now completely dead. The atmosphere is dense, clouded in a white fog... spore-like particles dance in the air... there are cracks in the cement... It's like this place is... *dying*.

INT. HAWKINS LABS - MAIN LABORATORY

The group of men enter the lab. Sweep the area.

It's a total nightmare in here. FLESHY MOLD-LIKE GROWTHS cling to the walls, and the atmosphere is even denser, making it difficult to see.

> SCIENTIST #1
> Doctor Shepherd and Doctor Braun
> were over there, Doctor Wilkins and
> Doctor Manning over there...

He motions at an OBSERVATION WINDOW.

                    SCIENTIST #1 (CONT'D)
          ... myself and Doctor Brenner were
          observing.

Lead Agent's flashlight cuts through fog, illuminates...

THE FAR WALL. This is the beating heart of this subterranean
nightmare. Fleshy mold-like growths smother the entire wall,
alive, wet, *throbbing*. In the center of this growth, there is
what appears to be a TWELVE-FOOT-DIAMETER OPENING. This is...

THE RIFT. IT UNDULATES. ALMOST BREATHING. *ALIVE*.

HEAVY BREATHING through gas masks as our men take in this
extraordinary sight.

                    AGENT #1
          ... This is where it came from?

Dr. Brenner nods.

                    LEAD AGENT
               (to Dr. Brenner)
          And the girl...?

                    DR. BRENNER
          She can't have gone far.

We CUT TO A WIDE SHOT of our men staring at this rift. And
then, slowly, we DOLLY TOWARD...

AN UPRIGHT ISOLATION TANK. It has a clear viewing window.

It's filled with water. But no one's in there. *Not anymore*.

EXT. BENNY'S BURGERS AND ICE CREAM - DAY

CLOSE ON: Two bare feet. Stepping onto grass.

WIDEN TO REVEAL: A YOUNG GIRL, 12, standing outside a forest.

She makes an immediate impression on us: Her hair is buzzed
close to the scalp. Her feet are bare. Her skin is pale.
She wears a tattered white hospital gown spattered with MUD.

She is more like a wild animal than a child.

She stares at a RUN-DOWN RESTAURANT. A sign reads:

               "BENNY'S BURGERS AND ICE CREAM."

The side screen door swings open and...

BENNY HAMMOND, late 40s, lumbers out carrying a TRASH BAG. He has sleeve tattoos, a greasy apron wrapped around his waist.

The Young Girl watches him closely as...

He dumps out the trash, then heads back inside.

INT. BENNY'S BURGERS - STORAGE ROOM - DAY

The Young Girl sneaks through the side screen door.

She creeps forward into...

INT. BENNY'S BURGERS - DINING ROOM - DAY

She stops and watches very intently as, in the dining room, Benny drops a plate of burgers and fries off at...

A table of CHAIN-SMOKING REGULARS, including one we'll get to know as EARL.

> EARL
> Benny, how about Kellogg last
> night? Who-ee --

> BENNY
> Oh yeah, oh yeah --

> EARL
> He's gonna win us the championship,
> I just know --

> BENNY
> Eh, if we hadn't traded English --

> EARL
> Don't get me started on that, too
> damn early --

As their idle sports talk continues...

INT. BENNY'S BURGERS - KITCHEN - MOMENTS LATER - DAY

The Young Girl sneaks into the kitchen.

She steps up to a PAN OF FRENCH FRIES. She reaches in and picks one up. It's almost... like she's never seen a french fry in her life.

She tries it. *Loves it.* She starts to eat more when --

                              BENNY
          HEY -- !

She snaps back around --

Benny is headed back into the kitchen.

She grabs the PAN OF FRENCH FRIES and sprints out of the
kitchen. She blows through the swinging doors --

INT. BENNY'S BURGERS - DINING ROOM

... sprints through the dining room...

INT. BENNY'S BURGERS - STORAGE ROOM - DAY

... and races as fast as she can for the back door!

But a split second before she reaches the door --

WHAAM! Benny catches her.

The french fries go SCATTERING across the floor.

Benny whirls her around.

                              BENNY
            Think you can steal from me, boy?

The Girl writhes in his arms, trying to tear free but --

Benny holds her tight. But his expression softens as he
realizes that this is no boy at all. It's also not a girl
either, not exactly, at least not like any he has ever seen.

                         BENNY (CONT'D)
            ... What in the hell?

Finally the Girl stops struggling.

She locks eyes with Benny. Breathing hard. And...

INT. MIDDLE SCHOOL - MR. CLARKE'S SCIENCE CLASS - DAY

EEEEEEE! A BELL BLARES and CHAOS REIGNS as...

A SWARM OF MIDDLE SCHOOLERS grab up their books and backpacks
and hurry out of class, talking loudly amongst themselves.

Their teacher, MR. CLARKE, 30s, calls after them:

                    MR. CLARKE
          Remember: Finish Chapter Twelve,
          and answer twelve-point-three on
          the difference between an
          experiment and other forms of
          science investigation --

Mr. Clarke silences as he realizes he's talking to no one --
everybody is gone. Well, that is, *almost* everybody.

                    MIKE (O.S.)
          Did it come?

Lucas, Mike, and Dustin gather excitedly by his desk.

Mr. Clarke hesitates. Gives the boys a sad look.

                    MR. CLARKE
          Sorry, boys, I hate to be the
          bearer of bad news, but...
               (beat)
          It came.

INT. MIDDLE SCHOOL - A.V. CLUB ROOM - DAY

The door to the A.V. Club bursts open.

Our boys race inside. Mr. Clarke follows close behind.

                    MR. CLARKE
          The Heathkit ham shack. Ain't she
          a beaut?

A BRAND-NEW HAM RADIO sits on a desk amidst a pile of older
equipment. The boys examine it with wide, expectant eyes.

                    DUSTIN
          I bet you can talk to New York on
          this thing --

                    MR. CLARKE
          Think bigger --

                    LUCAS
          California -- ?

                    MR. CLARKE
          Bigger.

                    MIKE
          Australia?

Another nod. *Holllly shit.*

                              LUCAS
                    Oh man. When Will sees this he's
                    going to totally lose his shit --

                              MR. CLARKE
                    Lucas --

                              LUCAS
                    Sorry.

The boys sit down by the radio. As Lucas starts to work the
dials, Mike grabs up the transceiver, practices:

                              MIKE
                         (bad Australian accent)
                    'Ello, this is Mike Wheeler,
                    President of Hawkins Middle A.V.
                    Club --

Dustin takes the receiver. His turn.

                              DUSTIN
                         (worse Australian accent)
                    'Ello, this is Dustin Henderson,
                    Secretary and Treasurer of Hawkins
                    Middle A.V. Club -- Do you eat
                    kangaroos for breakfast -- ?

A SHARP KNOCKING SOUND interrupts the fun. Mr. Clarke turns.

The PRINCIPAL is in the doorway.

                              MIDDLE SCHOOL PRINCIPAL
                    Sorry to interrupt... but may I
                    borrow Michael, Lucas, and Dustin?

Chief Hopper and Officer Callahan now step into view.

Off Mike, Lucas, and Dustin, expressions darkening.

                              HOPPER (PRE-LAP)
                    ... So you were... racing?

INT. MIDDLE SCHOOL - PRINCIPAL'S OFFICE - DAY

Our three boys are now scrunched together on a couch.

Hopper and Callahan sit opposite.

                              DUSTIN
                    It was me and him, actually --

                              LUCAS
                    My house is the first up --

                    MIKE
He takes Mirkwood home --

                    DUSTIN
We were racing on a bet and --

                    HOPPER
Whoa, whoa, whoa. One at a time.
     (points at Mike)
You. You said he takes... what?

                    MIKE
Mirkwood.

                    HOPPER
"Mirkwood?"
     (to Callahan)
You ever hear of a "Mirkwood?"

                    OFFICER CALLAHAN
Sounds made-up.

                    LUCAS
It's from Lord of the Rings --

                    DUSTIN
The Hobbit --

                    LUCAS
It doesn't matter -- !

                    DUSTIN
He asked -- !

                    HOPPER
Hey! What'd I just say? One at a
damn time.

He points at Mike.

                    HOPPER (CONT'D)
You.

                    MIKE
Mirkwood. It's a real road. It's
just the name that's made-up --

                    HOPPER
What's its real name?

                    MIKE
I don't know. It's where
Cornwallis and Kerley meet.

Hop jots this information down onto his pad.

                    HOPPER
          Yeah, I think I know it.

                    MIKE
          We can show you --

                    HOPPER
          I said I know it.

                    MIKE
          We could help look --

Hopper looks up at Mike sharply.

                    HOPPER
          No, after school, you go straight
          home. *All of you.*

He looks at the other boys. Making eye contact with each.

                    HOPPER (CONT'D)
          That means no biking around looking
          for your friend, no investigating,
          no nonsense. This isn't some Lord
          the Rings book --

                    DUSTIN
          The Hobbit.

Hopper bites his tongue.

                    HOPPER
          Do I make myself clear?
                    (firmer)
          I make myself clear?

The boys share looks. Worried. Shaken by his tone.

They nod.

INT. BENNY'S BURGERS - KITCHEN - DAY

SNAP-HISS! A well-seasoned hamburger patty slaps to the
broiler. Benny tends it.

INT. BENNY'S BURGERS - DINING ROOM - DAY

Benny slides a plate of burger and fries to the Young Girl.

She is seated at a table in the dining room. It is just her
now; the regulars are gone.

Her gown has been replaced with a "BENNY'S BURGERS AND ICE CREAM" T-shirt. It droops to her knees like a dress.

The Girl snatches up the burger and begins to *devour* it.

>   BENNY
>   Your parents forget to feed you?

The Girl doesn't respond. Just keeps eating.

>   BENNY (CONT'D)
>   That why you ran away?

Still nothing.

>   BENNY (CONT'D)
>   They... hurt you?

Nothing.

>   BENNY (CONT'D)
>   And... you went to the hospital,
>   that it? But you got scared, ran
>   off, found your way here?

The Girl finally looks up at Benny. *Has he hit close to the mark?* It seems like she is finally going to speak, but then she returns to eating her burger.

Benny has no choice -- he yanks away the plate.

The Girl looks up at him, confused.

>   BENNY (CONT'D)
>   I'll give it back, you can have as
>   much as you like, maybe even some
>   ice cream; but first, you gotta
>   answer a few 'a my questions. We
>   got a deal?

No response.

>   BENNY (CONT'D)
>   We'll start easy. My name's Benny.
>   Benny Hammond.

He holds out his hand. Wraps it around her tiny hand.

>   BENNY (CONT'D)
>   Nice to meet ya. And you are...?

Still no response. Benny sighs. He starts to withdraw his hand when he notices a SMALL TATTOO on the inside of her lower left wrist. It reads in simple black lettering: **011.**

                    BENNY (CONT'D)
          "Eleven"?

The Young Girl yanks her hand away.

                    BENNY (CONT'D)
          What's that mean?

                    YOUNG GIRL
          No.

                    BENNY
          Well *I'll be damned*. She speaks.
               (beat, considers)
          No? No what?

Still nothing.

                    BENNY (CONT'D)
          Alright, guess "no" more food then.

Benny starts to walks with her plate when:

                    YOUNG GIRL
          ... Eleven.

Benny turns back around.

                    BENNY
          Eleven. Yeah. What's it mean?

The Young Girl points to herself. We'll now know her as:

                    YOUNG GIRL/ELEVEN
          Eleven.

INT. BENNY'S BURGERS - KITCHEN - DAY

CLOSE ON: A PHONE BOOK OPEN TO THE SOCIAL SERVICES PAGE.

Benny is now on a corded phone in the kitchen. Voice hushed.

                    BENNY
          ... All I know is, poor thing's
          scared to death... confused...
               (beat)
          I think she's been abused or
          kidnapped or *somethin'*.
               (beat)
          It's 4819 Randolph Lane. Randolph,
          right.
               (beat, starts to spell)
          R-A-N --

                              39

As Benny continues to talk, we return to...

INT. BENNY'S BURGERS - DINING ROOM - CONTINUOUS

Where "Eleven" is finishing off her fries. She becomes aware
of a soft, HIGH-PITCHED NOISE. *Eeeee. Eeee. Eeee.* She
looks up. It's an old and rusty OSCILLATING METAL FAN. It
SQUEAKS with every turn. *Eeeee. Eeee. Eeeee.*

It is incessant. *Annoying.* Eleven narrows her eyes and --

The fan and the blades *stop*. Like they somehow *froze*.

Eleven looks away. Content now.

She continues eating her fries.

EXT. FOREST ROAD - DAY

WHOOSH! TWO POLICE CARS speed down the road.

EXT. WOODS - MIRKWOOD SHORTCUT - MINUTES LATER - DAY

Hopper trudges down the road, searching for signs of Will.

Behind him, we can see Callahan and Powell. They call out:

> OFFICER CALLAHAN
> Will Byers?! WILL BYERS?!

> OFFICER POWELL
> WILL -- ?!

Hopper pulls a vial out of his pocket. Pops two more of
those red-and-blue pills. And... his eyes narrow. Noticing
something off the side of the road.

EXT. WOODS - DAY

Hopper heads into the woods. Calls out to Callahan and
Powell:

> HOPPER
> Hey, I got something here.

Hop kneels down by...

WILL'S BICYCLE. Brushes away some leaves.

Callahan and Powell race over to him.

                    OFFICER CALLAHAN
            That his bike, Chief?

Hopper nods. Notes some SCRAPED BARK.

                    HOPPER
            Looks like he crashed.

                    OFFICER CALLAHAN
            Maybe he got hurt in the fall.

Hopper looks back to the road. Squints in the sun.

                    HOPPER
            Not so hurt he couldn't make it
            home. And a bike to these kids...
            that's like a Cadillac. Doesn't
            make sense he'd leave it out here.
                (beat)
            He'd walk it home.

A beat. Then:

                    HOPPER (CONT'D)
            He was in hurry.

EXT. HAWKINS LABS - DAY

ZOOM IN on a LARGE RADAR DISH.

INT. HAWKINS LABS - RADIO MONITORING ROOM

We SLOWLY DOLLY DOWN A LINE of a HALF-DOZEN AGENTS. They are
seated before bulky radio equipment, all wearing headphones.

As we pass each agent, we can HEAR SNIPPETS of what they're
listening to...

                    PARENT VOICE
                (filtered)
            ... going to the store...

                    TEACHER VOICE
                (filtered)
            ... be home by...

                    OFFICE WORKER VOICE
                (filtered)
            ... meeting with Tom in ten...

And it hits us: they're listening in on the town. *Spying*.

We land on the last agent in the line.

He's listening to a familiar voice:

> JOYCE'S VOICE (OVER PHONE)
> Lonnie. It's Joyce --

> CYNTHIA'S VOICE (OVER PHONE)
> Lonnie isn't here right now --

INT. BYERS HOUSE - KITCHEN - AFTERNOON

Joyce is on the phone. Pacing. Dragging hard on a
cigarette.

> JOYCE
> Who is this? *Cynthia?* This is
> Joyce -- *Joyce,* Lonnie's ex-*wife.*
> I need to speak to him -- This is
> an emergency... no, not later, *now*
> bitch --

CLICK. The phone goes dead. Joyce burns with anger.

IN THE LIVING ROOM, Jonathan works on a MISSING PERSON
POSTER.

> JONATHAN
> Mom, you need to stay calm.

> JOYCE
> I'm calm.

She hangs up, dials the number again. The phone RINGS.

But this time no one answers. It goes to message.

> LONNIE'S VOICE (OVER PHONE)
> (filtered)
> Hey, you've reached Lonnie, I'm not
> here at the moment but...

Joyce's rage rises and rises and... BEEP. Her turn.

> JOYCE
> Lonnie, some teenage whore just
> hung up on me. You don't call me
> back in the next hour I'll report
> you for not paying child support I
> swear to God I will and I'll make
> sure you rot in jail where you
> belong --

WHAM! Joyce slams the phone down.

                    JONATHAN
          Mom.

                     JOYCE
          What?

And that's when we realize: Jonathan isn't looking at her.
He's looking out the window.

                    JONATHAN
          Cops.

EXT. BYERS HOUSE - MOMENTS LATER - AFTERNOON

Joyce explodes out onto the porch. Jonathan follows. It's...

Hopper and the officers, parking in the driveway.

As Hop exits, he pulls Will's bike out of the back.

Joyce and Jonathan fight panic and --

INT. BYERS HOUSE - VARIOUS - LATER - AFTERNOON

Hopper and his officers search the Byers' house.

Joyce and Jonathan trail. On edge.

                    JOYCE
          And it was just sitting there -- ?

                    HOPPER
          Yes --

                    JOYCE
          Was there any blood or -- ?

                    HOPPER
          No --

                    JONATHAN
          If you found his bike out there,
          why're you here?

                    HOPPER
          He's got a key to the house?

                    JONATHAN
          Yeah --

                    HOPPER
          So maybe he came back here.

                         JOYCE
               So -- what? You think I haven't
               checked my own house -- ?!

                         HOPPER
               Never said you didn't.

Hopper inspects the back door. The adjacent wall is dented,
the paint chipped. He opens the door: its handle aligns with
the damaged wall. Someone threw it open. *Hard.*

                         HOPPER (CONT'D)
               This always here?

                         JOYCE
               Probably. I got two boys. Look at
               this place --

                         HOPPER
               But you're not sure?

Joyce hesitates. *Not sure.* Suddenly they HEAR --

WHIMPERING. COMING FROM THE BACK.

EXT. BYERS HOUSE - BACKYARD - AFTERNOON

Hopper and Joyce step outside onto the porch.

They find Chester pacing in front of the shed. WHIMPERING.

                         HOPPER
               This normal?

                         JOYCE
               Just hungry, I'm sure. Come on...

Joyce leads Chester back to the house by his collar.

But Hopper doesn't follow. Not yet.

His eyes turn to the shed. As...

INT. BYERS HOUSE - JONATHAN'S ROOM - DAY

Callahan and Powell inspect Jonathan's room.

Jonathan watches them, arms crossed.

                         JONATHAN
               What're you looking for exactly?

They ignore him. Powell checks under the bed. Nothing.

Callahan eyes an *EVIL DEAD* poster on the wall.

> OFFICER CALLAHAN
> What's going on there?

> JONATHAN
> The tree's possessed. It's...
> going inside her.

> OFFICER CALLAHAN
> Yeeeeeeesh.

> OFFICER POWELL
> Hey kid, you got some water or
> juice or something? Dying here.

Jonathan nods. Exits.

Callahan exhales. Looks at Powell.

> OFFICER CALLAHAN
> You see that?

> OFFICER POWELL
> See what?

> OFFICER CALLAHAN
> Suspect number one. Am I right?

Off Powell...

INT. BYERS SHED - AFTERNOON

EEEEEEE. Wood GROANS as...

Hopper heads into the shed. Still dark in here.

Hop flips a light switch. The naked light bulb hums to life.

He walks up to the rifle wall mount. The rifle is, of
course, missing. He inspects the mount. There are
fingerprints in the dust. Someone was here... recently.

BZZZZ! THE LIGHT BULB BEGINS TO FLICKER.

Hopper turns and looks up at the light. It fluctuates,
growing bright, then dim, then bright, then dim, then --

WHOOM. THE LIGHT CUTS OUT. LEAVING US IN DARKNESS.

WE HEAR A FAINT GUTTURAL SOUND. LIKE SOME KIND OF GROWL.

Hopper looks around. *The hell is that coming from?*

                         HOPPER
              That you, buddy? You hungry?

Hop removes a flashlight from his utility belt, clicks it on,
and slowly sweeps its beam across the darkness. He makes out
nothing. But that sound, whatever the hell it is, persists.

Gets louder. Louder. LOUDER STILL. And then --

The beam illuminates an APPROACHING FIGURE.

Hop reaches for his gun, but --

Officer Callahan steps into the light.

                     OFFICER CALLAHAN
              You deaf? I've been callin' you.

Hopper looks back at the light bulb. It flickers back to
life. Returning to 48 Watts. *Strange.*

Hop shakes it off and --

EXT. BYERS HOUSE - BACKYARD - AFTERNOON

Hopper strides to the Byers house. Moving fast.

Callahan struggles to keep up...

                     OFFICER CALLAHAN
              You sure you're alright, Chief?

                         HOPPER
              I want you to call Florence, have
              her get a search party together, as
              many volunteers as she can muster,
              flashlights too --

                     OFFICER CALLAHAN
              Think we got a problem here?

Hopper doesn't answer. Uncertain.

He heads inside. The door slaps shut.

EXT. NEIGHBORHOOD - NIGHT 2

HISS! A sprinkler kicks on. Night in the suburbs again.

                       MIKE (PRE-LAP)
              We should be out there right now.
              We should be helping look for him.

INT. WHEELER HOUSE - DINING ROOM - NIGHT

The Wheeler family is seated at the dining table.

A home-cooked meal is before them. But Mike isn't eating.

>   KAREN
> We've been over this. The chief
> said --

>   MIKE
> I don't care what the chief said.

>   KAREN
> *Michael* --

>   MIKE
> He's not even real police, Mom. We
> have to do something -- Will could
> be in danger!

>   KAREN
> More reason to stay put.

>   MIKE
> Mom --

>   KAREN
> End of discussion.

Mike looks away, upset. The family resumes eating in
silence. Or, rather, some of them do. Nancy just moves her
food around with a fork. Then, in as casual a tone as she
can summon:

>   NANCY
> So... me and Barb... we're gonna
> study for the chemistry test at her
> house tonight. That's cool, right?

Karen looks up from her meal.

>   KAREN
> No. Not cool.

>   NANCY
> What? Why not?

>   KAREN
> Why do you think? Am I speaking
> Chinese in this house? Until we
> know Will's okay, no one leaves.

                    NANCY
So we're under *house arrest?*

                    KAREN
Don't be dramatic, Nancy.

                    NANCY
This is such bullshit!

                    TED
Language!

                    NANCY
Barb lives two minutes away, just
because Mike's friend got lost on
his way home --

                    MIKE
This is Will's fault -- ?!

                    KAREN
Nancy, take that back --

                    NANCY
No!

                    MIKE
You're just pissed because you
wanna hang out with Steve --

                    TED
Steve?

                    KAREN
Who is Steve?

                    MIKE
Her new boyfriend --

                    NANCY
YOU'RE SUCH A DOUCHE MIKE --

                    TED
LANGUAGE!!!

Nancy shoves out of her chair. Storms off.

                    KAREN
Nancy! Come back! NANCY!

But Nancy is already bounding up the stairs to her bedroom.

Karen wants to follow her but can't; the argument has caused
Holly to cry. Karen picks her up and rocks her in her arms.

                    48

                    KAREN (CONT'D)
          There, there, shhhh...

                    TED
          See, Michael: This is what happens.

                    MIKE
          What happens when what? I'm the
          only one acting normal here -- I'm
          the only who cares about Will!

Ted takes a bite out of a chicken drum. Chews.

                    TED
          That's not fair, Michael. We care.

Mike stares at his dad. He can't take his apathy, not
tonight. He stands up from the table and hurries off.

Holly cries louder. Ted continues to chew.

Karen shoots daggers at him.

                    KAREN
          I hope you're enjoying your
          chicken, Ted.

She carries Holly out of the room.

EXT. WOODS - NIGHT

A constellation of flashlights glimmers in the night.

Over two dozen SEARCH AND RESCUE VOLUNTEERS are scouring the
woods for Will. They wear orange vests, grave expressions.

We FIND Hopper. Mr. Clarke walks at his side.

                    MR. CLARKE
          He's a good student.

Hopper turns. Surprised this man is speaking to him.

                    HOPPER
          What's that?

                    MR. CLARKE
          Will. He's a good student. A
          great one, actually. I can't
          fathom him getting into any kind of
          trouble.

Hopper nods. Looks away.

Mr. Clarke offers his hand.

                    MR. CLARKE (CONT'D)
          I don't think we've met. Scott
          Clarke. I teach at Hawkins Middle.
          Earth and Biology --

Hopper shakes his hand. Then averts his gaze.

                    HOPPER
          Always had a distaste for science.

                    MR. CLARKE
          Maybe you had a bad teacher.

                    HOPPER
          Ms. Ratliff was a nasty piece of
          work.

                    MR. CLARKE
          Ratliff? You bet. She's still
          kicking around, believe it or not --

                    HOPPER
          Oh I believe it. Mummies don't
          die, or so they tell me.

Mr. Clarke smiles softly.

                    MR. CLARKE
          So you're local?

                    HOPPER
          Class of fifty-eight.

                    MR. CLARKE
          Sixty-two. Just missed each other.

They walk for another beat. Hopper seems lost in thought.

                    HOPPER
          Sara, my daughter. Galaxies, the
          universe, whatnot: She always
          understood that stuff. Maybe she
          got it from her mother, I dunno.
          There's enough down here, I don't
          need to go lookin' elsewhere.

                    MR. CLARKE
          Your daughter. What grade is she?
          Maybe I'll get her in my class.

                         HOPPER
          She lives in the city. With her
          mother.

                         MR. CLARKE
          Oh.

Hopper slaps Mr. Clarke on the back.

                         HOPPER
          Thanks for coming out, teach.
          Appreciate it.

Hopper picks up his pace, leaving Mr. Clarke behind.

A nearby VOLUNTEER whispers to Mr. Clarke:

                         VOLUNTEER
          She passed a few years back.

                         MR. CLARKE
          Sorry?

                         VOLUNTEER
          His kid.

Mr. Clarke darkens. He looks back at Hopper.

He is a distant silhouette now.

INT. WHEELER HOUSE - BASEMENT - NIGHT

The Demogorgon gazes at us. Four angry eyes.

Mike is lying down by the Dungeons and Dragons map. He looks
worried and restless. He examines the field of miniatures.
The Troglodytes... the knight... the dwarf... and the wizard.

He picks up the wizard. Studies it. Considering.

                         MIKE (PRE-LAP)
          Lucas? It's Mike. You copy?
          Lucas?

INT. WHEELER HOUSE - BASEMENT - MOMENTS LATER - NIGHT

Mike is now at the table. Calling into a walkie-talkie.

Lucas finally answers. His voice crackles.

                         LUCAS'S VOICE (OVER WALKIE)
          Hey, it's Lucas.

                              MIKE
          I know it's you. And say "over"
          when you're done talking or I don't
          know you're done. Over.

                         LUCAS'S VOICE
          I'm done. Over.

                              MIKE
          I'm worried about Will. Over.

                         LUCAS'S VOICE
          Yeah. This is crazy. Over.

                              MIKE
          I was thinking... Will could've
          cast Protection last night. But he
          didn't. He cast Fireball. Over.

                         LUCAS'S VOICE
          What's your point? Over.

                              MIKE
          My point is... he could've played
          it safe. But he didn't. He put
          himself in danger to help the
          party. Over.

A very long beat. Then:

                         LUCAS'S VOICE
          Meet me in ten. Over and out.

INT. WHEELER HOUSE - BASEMENT - LATER STILL - NIGHT

Mike jams a few flashlights into his backpack.

EXT. WHEELER HOUSE - NIGHT

Mike wheels his bike out of the garage.

He starts down the driveway when he suddenly notices --

Steve. He's attempting to climb up to Nancy's room. He
locks eyes with Mike. A *very* awkward beat.

Steve holds up a hand. *Hey.*

Mike just stares. *Unbelievable.* Then, without saying a
word, he climbs on his bike... and pedals off into the night.

INT. WHEELER HOUSE - NANCY'S ROOM - NIGHT

Nancy sits at her desk, morosely studying her CHEM BOOK, when she hears a dull sound: TAP TAP TAP. She turns to find...

Steve outside her window. Nancy stares in shock, tries to wave him away, but he just knocks again, more urgently.

Nancy hurries over and opens the window.

> NANCY
> (whispers urgently)
> What're you doing? I told you I
> have to stay in tonight --

> STEVE
> I know, so we'll study here --

> NANCY
> No, I told you, absolutely not, go
> away -- !

> STEVE
> I don't want you failing tomorrow --

Steve climbs in anyway...

Or tries to. His foot catches on the window frame and he stumbles, nearly toppling over a bedside lamp. He catches himself, turns back to Nancy, and strikes a pose.

> STEVE (CONT'D)
> What'd I tell you? A ninja.

Nancy shakes her head. Unbelievable.

She shuts the window. Closes the blinds. WHOOSH!

INT. BENNY'S BURGERS - KITCHEN - NIGHT

WHOOSH! Water rushes out of a faucet as Benny cleans dishes.

Eleven sits on a counter. She eats STRAWBERRY ICE CREAM out of a pint-sized container.

> BENNY
> You like that ice cream, huh?

Eleven looks at him, smiles. For the first time this day, she seems like an actual kid. Benny knocks off the faucet.

> BENNY (CONT'D)
> Hey. A smile looks good on ya.

Eleven stares at him. Confused.

                    BENNY (CONT'D)
          A smile.

Benny gives a big smile. Eleven smiles back.

But her smile fades when she hears --

THE SOUND OF KNOCKING. *Someone's at the front door.*

Eleven tenses. Nervous.

                    BENNY (CONT'D)
          Just... stay put. Whoever it is,
          I'll turn 'em away, a'ight?

Eleven watches while eating ice cream as...

INT. BENNY'S BURGERS - DINING ROOM - NIGHT

Benny lumbers to the front door. He swings it open to find --

A FRIENDLY WOMAN, 40s. She smiles.

                    FRIENDLY WOMAN
          You must be Mister Hammond?

                    BENNY
          'fraid so. Also 'fraid we've
          closed shop. Why don't you try
          back tomorrow --

Benny starts to shut the door, but the woman extends a hand.

                    FRIENDLY WOMAN/CONNIE
          Connie Frazier. Social Services.

Benny stops. Opens the door back up. Embarrassed.

                    BENNY
          Social Services. Apologies.

He takes her hand. His grip is firm.

                    BENNY (CONT'D)
          Didn't think you were gonna make it
          here so quick. That's a heckuva
          drive.

                    CONNIE
          Not too bad this time of night.

Benny nods, lowers his voice.

> BENNY
> Listen. I still haven't told her
> about you. I didn't want her
> runnin' off again. She's a tad
> skittish.

> CONNIE
> Children I work with usually are.
> (smiles)
> Where is she now?

> BENNY
> In the back. Come on. I'll
> introduce ya.

Benny turns and lumbers toward the kitchen.

> BENNY (CONT'D)
> Apologies again for trying to turn
> you away. It's funny, your voice,
> it sounded different on the phone --

> CONNIE
> Mister Hammond?

> BENNY
> Yeah -- ?

As Benny turns...

Connie raises a SILENCED PISTOL and --

POP! SHE SHOOTS HIM IN THE SIDE OF THE HEAD. HIS BODY GOES
LIMP AND HE CRASHES TO THE GROUND WITH A HEAVY THUD.

HIS BODY TWITCHES. THEN STILLS. HE IS DEAD.

INT. BENNY'S BURGERS - KITCHEN - NIGHT

Eleven watches in wide-eyed horror. She drops the ice cream,
turns around, and sprints back through the kitchen.

INT. BENNY'S BURGERS - DINING ROOM

Eleven blows through the double doors as --

INT. BENNY'S BURGERS - DINING ROOM/KITCHEN - NIGHT

THE AGENTS we met earlier sweep into the kitchen.

They are followed closely by Dr. Brenner.

INT. BENNY'S BURGERS - STORAGE ROOM - NIGHT

Eleven sprints for the back screen door. But she crashes to a halt as --

TWO MORE AGENTS sweep through from the back door.

She is *trapped*.

AS THE AGENTS RAISE ELECTRICAL SHOCK STICKS ...

WE DOLLY IN FAST ON ELEVEN --

AND --

INT. BENNY'S BURGERS - KITCHEN - NIGHT

LOUD NOISES ECHO FROM THE STORAGE ROOM. SCREAMING. CHAOS.

Dr. Brenner and the agents exchange looks and --

INT. BENNY'S BURGERS - DINING ROOM - NIGHT

Dr. Brenner and the agents blow through the double doors and race into --

INT. BENNY'S BURGERS - STORAGE ROOM - MOMENTS LATER - NIGHT

They find BOTH AGENTS unconscious on the ground.

Bones twisted. Heads bleeding.

EXT. BENNY'S BURGERS - BACK - NIGHT

Dr. Brenner explodes out the back door.

He looks around. Desperate. But --

He sees only darkness.

Eleven is gone.

EXT. FOREST ROAD - NIGHT

Silence as our kids bike down "Mirkwood" road.

Mike leads the way. He slows to stop.

Lucas and Dustin pull up beside him.

> LUCAS
> Why are we stopping?

Mike doesn't answer. He just looks off into the woods.

Dustin and Lucas follow his gaze to find a LINE OF POLICE TAPE, wrapped around a row of trees along the side of the road.

The reality of what happened hits our boys right here. This isn't some make-believe D&D campaign. This is... *real*.

BOOM! HEAVY RUMBLE SHATTERS THE SILENCE.

They boys look up. Sheet LIGHTNING flashes the sky, illuminating dark STORM CLOUDS.

A PLOP OF WATER hits Dustin in the face.

>   DUSTIN
>   Oh man. You guys feel that?

Dustin holds out a hand. Watches water strike his palm.

It's raining.

>   DUSTIN (CONT'D)
>   Maybe we should go back.

Mike isn't listening. Or if he is, he doesn't care. He removes a walkie from his backpack, hands it to Dustin.

>   MIKE
>   No splitting up or anything stupid
>   like that, but stay on channel six.
>   Just in case.

With that, Mike heads into the woods, ducking under the caution tape. Lucas follows.

Dustin is now all alone.

BOOM! Another thunder crash! It scares the shit out of him.

>   DUSTIN
>   Hey, guys, wait up! WAIT UP!

He races after his friends as ANOTHER BOOM rattles us and --

INT. WHEELER HOUSE - NANCY'S ROOM - NIGHT

Steve and Nancy now sit on her bed. A few feet apart.

Steve reads homemade flash cards, while Nancy answers the questions. MUSIC PLAYS on a boombox ("Sweet Dreams" by The Eurythmics) loud enough that their voices don't carry out of the room...

STEVE
"... Which polymers occur
naturally?"

NANCY
... Starch and cellulose.

STEVE
(yup, switches cards)
"In a molecule of CH4, the hydrogen
atoms are spatially oriented toward
the centers of a regular -- "

NANCY
Tetrahedron.

STEVE
(switches card)
Jesus, how many of these did you
make?

NANCY
You said you wanted to help!

STEVE
How 'bout this: Every time you get
something right, I have to take off
an item of clothing. Every time
you get something wrong...

NANCY
Uh, pass.

STEVE
Come on, it'll be fun --

NANCY
No!

STEVE
(next card)
"During fractional distillation,
hydrocarbons are separated
according to their -- "

NANCY
Melting points.

STEVE
EEEEEE! Boiling points.

NANCY
That's what I meant --

58

                    STEVE
          But it's not what you said.

He mimes unbuttoning a shirt.

                    NANCY
          No. NO!

                    STEVE
          No? You need help?

Steve pushes down on the bed, and kisses her. Soon they're
going at it, hot and heavy. After a moment of making out,
Steve begins to unbutton her top but --

Nancy stops him.

                    NANCY
          Steve, come on --

                    STEVE
          What?

                    NANCY
          Are you crazy? My *parents* are here --

                    STEVE
               (looking around)
          Weird. I don't see them.

Nancy slides away.

                    NANCY
          Was this your plan all along? Get
          in my room, then... get another
          notch on your belt?

                    STEVE
          What -- no! Jesus, no.

                    NANCY
          I'm not like Laurie. Or Amy. Or --
          or Becky --

                    STEVE
          You mean you're not a slut.

                    NANCY
          That's not what I'm saying.

                    STEVE
          You're cute when you lie.

                              NANCY
                    Shut up.

Steve smiles. He picks up a Holly Hobbie doll and makes it
shake its head in disapproval, speaks in a squeaky voice:

                              STEVE
                    "Bad Steve, bad; stay away from
                    Miss Nancy!"

Nancy can't help but laugh.

                              NANCY
                    You're an idiot, Steve Harrington.

                              STEVE
                    You're beautiful, Nancy Wheeler.

Nancy blushes.

Steve picks up the flash cards. Clears his throat. And...

                              STEVE (CONT'D)
                    "Compared to the rate of inorganic
                    reactions, the rate of organic
                    reactions generally is..."

Off Nancy, falling for this guy...

INT. BYERS HOUSE - LIVING ROOM - NIGHT

Jonathan and Joyce sit around the coffee table.

They are working on the MISSING PERSON POSTER for Will.
Bold red letters at the top read: "HAVE YOU SEEN ME?"

There is an EMPTY SPACE for a photo in the middle.

They flip through the portfolio, looking for a photo. There
are many photos of Joyce and Will, as well as the town, and
the people who live here. All artfully taken by Jonathan.

                              JOYCE
                    Wow. Jonathan. These are great...

Jonathan doesn't say anything, embarrassed by the compliment.

She flips through more pages.

                                 60

                    JOYCE (CONT'D)
          I've been working so much lately...
          I feel like I barely know what's
          going on with you anymore...

She looks up. Notices Jonathan is fighting tears.

                    JOYCE (CONT'D)
          What is it, baby?

                    JONATHAN
          Nothing.

                    JOYCE
          What is it?

Joyce takes his hand.

                    JONATHAN
          It's just... last night... I
          just... I should've been here --

Joyce squeezes his hand.

                    JOYCE
          Hey. This wasn't your fault, baby,
          you hear me? You *hear me?*

Jonathan averts his gaze.

                    JOYCE (CONT'D)
          He's gonna come home soon. I know
          it. I know it... because I feel
          him. I *feel him* in my heart. He's
          close. *He's close.* You believe
          me, Jonathan, right?

Jonathan finally looks at his mom. And nods.

Joyce smiles faintly. She then returns to looking at the
pictures. She finds one of Will at the park, smiling big.

                    JOYCE (CONT'D)
          Oh this one -- I... I always liked
          this one.

She holds it up. Jonathan smiles softly.

                    JONATHAN
          ... Me too.

An emotional beat. Then:

The KITCHEN PHONE BLARES TO LIFE.

Joyce and Jonathan look up sharply. *News.*

INT. BYERS HOUSE - KITCHEN - MOMENTS LATER - NIGHT

Joyce grabs up the phone. Her voice tense, strained.

> JOYCE
> Yes -- hel-hello?

There is no answer. But she can HEAR the SOUND of LOW
BREATHING on the other end.

> JOYCE (CONT'D)
> Lonnie...? Hopper...?

Still no answer.

> JOYCE (CONT'D)
> Who is this?

Jonathan stands up. Getting worried now.

The SOUND OF BREATHING grows louder. It sounds... like the
breathing of a *child*. Joyce pales. Tears rush to her eyes.

> JOYCE (CONT'D)
> Will?!! *Will*?!!

Jonathan races over to his mom.

> JOYCE (CONT'D)
> Where are you, baby?! Talk to me!
> WILL?! *WILL*?!

But Will's breathing is now gone. In its place...

ANOTHER SOUND. GUTTURAL. INHUMAN. Shifting in pitch.

> JOYCE (CONT'D)
> WHO IS THIS? WHAT HAVE DONE WITH
> MY BABY?! WHAT HAVE YOU DONE?!!

Silence. Then --

A HIGH-PITCHED SHRIEK ERUPTS FROM THE RECEIVER.

Joyce gasps in pain and drops the phone. She looks at her
hand. Her palm is SEARED. She backs away from the phone.
Her eyes wide with dread.

Jonathan grabs up phone. His voice shakes.

> JONATHAN
> Who is this?! WHO IS THIS?!

But the phone line is now dead.

Joyce slumps down to the floor. And begins to sob.

EXT. WOODS - NIGHT

BOOM! Another CRASH OF THUNDER.

Our boys are deep in woods. Soaked now.

Their flashlights illuminate the rain.

>   MIKE
>   Will? WILL???

>   LUCAS
>   BYERS?!

>   DUSTIN
>   I've got your "X-Men!" One-thirty-
>   four!

No response. Only silence.

They march for a little bit longer.

>   DUSTIN (CONT'D)
>   Guys, I really think we should turn
>   back --

>   LUCAS
>   Seriously, Dustin, if you want to
>   be a baby, just go home already.

>   DUSTIN
>   I'm just being *realistic,* Lucas --

>   LUCAS
>   No, you're being a sissy --

>   DUSTIN
>   You ever think Will went missing
>   because, you know, he ran into
>   someone bad? And now we're going to
>   the place where he was last seen,
>   and we don't even have weapons or
>   anything --

>   MIKE
>   -- Dustin shut up --

>   DUSTIN
>   -- I'm just sayin', does that seem
>   smart to you -- ?!

                         MIKE
               Shut up!

Dustin silences. Everyone turns to Mike.

He's not mad. He's -- *listening*...

                         MIKE (CONT'D)
                    (low)
               You guys hear that?

The boys listen. Hear RUSTLING FOLIAGE. Everyone tenses.

Mike slowly swings his flashlight around the dark woods. Ten
degrees, twenty, thirty, forty, fifty, sixty --

WHOOSH! A SHADOWED FIGURE DARTS BEHIND THEM.

They whirl around. Startled. Their flashlights illuminate --

ELEVEN. Bald head. Wild eyes. Benny's T-shirt.

Mike looks at her. She looks at Mike.

Their gaze holds.

THUNDER BOOMS.

And...

                    <u>END EPISODE</u>

CHAPTER TWO:
THE WEIRDO ON MAPLE STREET

WRITTEN BY **THE DUFFER BROTHERS**

EXT. WHEELER HOUSE - NIGHT 2 - ESTABLISHING

BOOOM! Thunder CRASHES outside the Wheeler house.

INT. WHEELER HOUSE - BASEMENT - NIGHT

Rain POUNDS the basement window.

WIDE TO REVEAL: our soaking wet BOYS huddled around...

ELEVEN. She shivers on the couch, Mike's jacket wrapped around her like a blanket. She seems like a rescued puppy.

>   MIKE
> Is there a number we can call? For your parents?

No answer.

>   DUSTIN
> Where's your hair? Do you have cancer?

No answer.

>   LUCAS
> Did you run away?

No answer.

>   MIKE
> Are you in some kind of trouble?

No answer.

>   LUCAS
> Is that blood?!

Lucas reaches out and touches a spot of dried blood on the side of her face. She flinches. Mike bats his hand away.

>   MIKE
> You're freaking her out!

>   LUCAS
> She's freaking me out!

>   DUSTIN
> I bet she's deaf.

Dustin CLAPS his hands. Eleven startles.

                    DUSTIN (CONT'D)
          Not deaf.

                    MIKE
          That's enough! Leave her alone!
          She's just scared. And cold.

Mike grabs DRY CLOTHES from a LAUNDRY BASKET.

                    MIKE (CONT'D)
          Here. These are clean. Okay?

He passes them to Eleven. She takes one look at the clothes,
then promptly begins to remove her wet shirt -- changing
right in front of our boys! They *freak out*.

                    DUSTIN
          Oh my God oh my God --

                    LUCAS
          WHOA -- !!

                    MIKE
          No no -- !

Eleven pauses. Confused.

                    MIKE (CONT'D)
          Not *here*. In there.
               (points at bathroom)
          That's the bathroom. Privacy. Get
          it?

Eleven looks at the bathroom. Considers. And...

INT. WHEELER HOUSE - BASEMENT BATHROOM - LATER - NIGHT

Eleven pads into the bathroom. She looks around the small
space. Uncertain. Mike closes the door behind her but --

Eleven stops it with an outstretched hand.

                    MIKE
          You don't want it closed?

                    ELEVEN
          ... No.

                    MIKE
          Oh. So you *can* speak?

Eleven nods. Mike takes this in. *Well, that's a start.*

He closes the door again, but this time leaves it cracked.

                         MIKE (CONT'D)
          How's this? Okay?

A beat. Then a nod from Eleven.

                         ELEVEN
          Yes.

INT. WHEELER HOUSE - BASEMENT - A FEW MINUTES LATER

Mike and the boys huddle in the basement corner.

They speak in low voices.

                         DUSTIN
          This is *mental*.

                         MIKE
          At least she can talk.

                         LUCAS
          She said "no" and "yes." Your
          three-year-old sister says more --

                         DUSTIN
          She almost got *naked* --

                         LUCAS
          Something's seriously wrong with
          her, like wrong in the head.

                         DUSTIN
          She just went like --

Dustin mimes taking off his shirt.

                         LUCAS
          I bet she escaped from Pennhurst --

                         MIKE
          From *where?*

                         LUCAS
          Pennhurst. That nuthouse out in
          Kerley County.

                         DUSTIN
          You have a lot of family there?

                         LUCAS
          Bite me. Seriously, though, think
          about it. That would explain her
          shaved hair and why she's so crazy --

                    DUSTIN
          -- and why she tried to --

Dustin mimes the shirt removal again.

                    LUCAS
          She's an *escapee* is the point.
          She's probably a psycho --

                    DUSTIN
                (realizing)
          Like Michael Myers --

                    LUCAS
          Exactly. We never should've
          brought her back here --

                    MIKE
          You wanted to just leave her out
          there in the storm?

                    LUCAS
          Yes! We went out to find Will, not
          another problem --

                    DUSTIN
                (to Mike)
          We should tell your mom.

                    LUCAS
          I second that.

                    MIKE
          Who's crazy now?

                    LUCAS
          How is that crazy?

                    MIKE
          We weren't supposed to be out
          tonight, remember?

                    LUCAS
          So?

                    MIKE
          So if I tell my mom about this,
          she'll tell your mom, and your mom --

                    DUSTIN
          Oh man --

                    LUCAS
          Our houses will become like
          Alcatraz.

                    MIKE
          Exactly. We'll never find Will.

Mike drifts to a SLEEPING BAG, rolled up in the basement
corner. *Light bulb.* He turns back to his friends.

                    MIKE (CONT'D)
          Alright, here's the plan: She
          sleeps here tonight --

                    DUSTIN
          You're letting *a girl* -- ?!

                    MIKE
          Just listen! In the morning, she
          walks around to the front door and
          rings the doorbell. My mom'll know
          exactly what to do -- she'll get
          her back to Pennhurst or wherever
          she comes from. We'll be totally
          in the clear. And tomorrow night,
          we go back out.
               (beat)
          And this time, *we find Will.*

Lucas and Dustin share looks. *Damn, Mike's good.*

INT. WHEELER HOUSE - BASEMENT - MOMENTS LATER - NIGHT

Lucas and Dustin walk back up the basement stairs. Lucas
pauses at the top and looks back into the basement.

He sees Mike helping Eleven into a MAKESHIFT TENT made out of
sheets hanging on clothes pins. A sleeping bag rests inside.

His expression betrays a hint of jealousy.

                    DUSTIN
               (low)
          You really think she's psycho?

                    LUCAS
          Wouldn't want her in my house.

Lucas heads out the door, but Dustin hangs back an extra
second, watching Mike get into the tent. He shakes his head.

                    DUSTIN
          ... Mental.

He follows Lucas out of the basement.

Eleven gets into the sleeping bag. Mike passes her a pillow.

> MIKE
> Hey... I never asked you your name.

Eleven holds up her wrist. Showing him the "**011**" TATTOO.

> MIKE (CONT'D)
> Is that real??

Mike reaches out to touch the tattoo, but Eleven yanks her hand away.

> MIKE (CONT'D)
> Sorry -- I just... I've never seen
> a kid with a tattoo before. What's
> it mean? Eleven?

Eleven points at herself.

> MIKE (CONT'D)
> Eleven... is your... *name*?

She nods. Mike tries to wrap his head around this.

> MIKE (CONT'D)
> Eleven. *Eleven*. Okay... well.
> I'm... Mike. Short for Michael.
> (beat)
> Maybe you could be "El." Short for
> Eleven.

Eleven considers. Likes it. Nods.

> MIKE (CONT'D)
> Okay, well. Uh... 'Night. *El*.

> ELEVEN
> Night. *Mike.*

Mike smiles softly, climbs out of the tent, and removes a clothes pin, causing a sheet to fall over the tent "door."

Eleven is now left alone in near darkness, save for the reflection of rain water on her frightened face.

BOOM! Thunder cracks. She nearly jumps out of her skin. Frightened, she pulls the sleeping bag to her chin.

And then she shuts her eyes. And tries to sleep.

MAIN TITLES

EXT. DOWNTOWN - MORNING 3 - ESTABLISHING

The sun rises over Hawkins. The town is waking up.

EXT. BYERS HOUSE - MORNING

The crane of a UTILITY TRUCK whines as it lifts a REPAIR MAN to the top of a UTILITY POLE.

INT. BYERS HOUSE - MORNING

JOYCE watches the Repair Man from the window. A CIGARETTE trembles in her hand, and her eyes are bloodshot, ringed with darkness. She clearly hasn't slept all night.

Behind her, JONATHAN scrapes eggs onto plates. He sets the plates on the dining table -- right alongside the completed MISSING PERSON POSTER.

                    JONATHAN
        Mom, ready --

Joyce glances at the food. Not interested.

                    JOYCE
        No -- that's okay. Careful of the
        poster, alright?

                    JONATHAN
        You need to try to eat, Mom.

But Joyce isn't listening. She snuffs out her cigarette. Digs through her purse.

                    JOYCE
        Listen, the Copy Mart'll be open
        soon. You mind going -- ?

                    JONATHAN
        Mom --

                    JOYCE
        We should make, what -- two hundred
        copies? Three hundred?

                    JONATHAN
        You have to try to eat.

                    JOYCE
        How much is a copy? Ten cents?
        How much is that if we get three --

                    JONATHAN
        <u>Mom</u>.

Joyce finally looks over Jonathan. He pleads with his eyes.

> JONATHAN (CONT'D)
> You can't get like this. Not now.
>> (beat)
> <u>Please</u>.

Joyce hesitates. She sees that her anxiety is feeding
Jonathan's and it pains her. She is about to say something
when she hears...

A KNOCKING ON THE DOOR.

INT. BYERS HOUSE - LIVING ROOM - MOMENTS LATER - MORNING

The front door swings open.

Joyce glares at Hopper, dragging on a cigarette. *Not happy.*

> JOYCE
> I called six hours ago.

Hopper gives a tired nod.

> HOPPER
> Came as soon as I could.

Hopper takes off his hat, heads inside. She shuts the door.

> JOYCE
> *Six hours --*

> HOPPER
> A little trust here. We were
> searching through the night. Made
> it all the way out to Cartersville.

> JOYCE
> And?

Hopper takes a breath. The answer clearly "nothing."

INT. BYERS HOUSE - MOMENTS LATER - MORNING

Hopper studies the phone. The receiver is MELTED.

Joyce paces behind him. JONATHAN is silent in the kitchen.

> HOPPER
> Storm barbecued it real good.

> JOYCE
> The storm?

                    HOPPER
          What else, then?

                    JOYCE
          You're saying that's not weird?

                    HOPPER
          No. It's weird.

Joyce reins in her frustration.

                    JONATHAN
          Can you trace who made the call?
          Call the phone company or --

                    HOPPER
          It doesn't work like that.
               (back to Joyce)
          You sure it was Will? Flo said you
          just heard breathing.

                    JOYCE
               (certain)
          It was him. It was Will. He
          was... scared... and then...
               (how to put this?)
          There was something else...
          I don't know.

Joyce's eyes tear up. She's still shaken.

Hopper places the dead phone back on the counter.

                    HOPPER
          Probably just a prank call.
          Someone trying to scare you.

                    JONATHAN
          Who would do that?

                    HOPPER
          This is on the TV now, brings out
          the crazies like you wouldn't
          believe. False leads, pranks --

                    JOYCE
               (firm)
          It wasn't a prank. It was *him*.

                    HOPPER
          Joyce.

                    JOYCE
          How about some trust *here*. You think
          <u>what</u>? I'm -- I'm *making this up*?

                    HOPPER
          Just saying this is an emotional
          time --

                    JOYCE
          You think I don't know my own son's
          breathing, is that it? You
          wouldn't know your daughter's?

This hits Hopper like a <u>gut punch</u>. He tries to mask it.

                    HOPPER
          What about Lonnie? You hear from
          him yet?

Joyce hesitates. Obviously not. Hopper shakes his head.

                    HOPPER (CONT'D)
          It's been long enough. I'm having
          him checked out.

Hopper heads for the door.

EXT. BYERS HOUSE - DAY

Hopper trudges back to his car. Just as he's about to get in --

                    JONATHAN (O.S.)
          Let me go.

Hopper turns to find Jonathan approaching.

                    HOPPER
          Sorry?

                    JONATHAN
          To Lonnie's. If Will's there, it
          means he ran away. If he sees
          cops, he'll think he's in trouble.
          He'll hide.
               (beat)
          He's... good at hiding.

                    HOPPER
          And cops are good at finding. Your
          mom needs you here, kid. Stay put.

Hopper climbs into his car. Slams the door.

INT. WHEELER HOUSE - KITCHEN - DAY

POP! THREE EGGOS leap out of a toaster. Mike slides two on his plate... and tucks the third into his jacket pocket.

INT. WHEELER HOUSE - DINING ROOM - A FEW MINUTES LATER

Mike eats breakfast with his family. The scene is a familiar one: KAREN is feeding HOLLY, TED is watching the news, and NANCY pokes at her food, clearly distracted.

Mike eats noticeably fast. Shoveling down his waffle.

> NANCY
> Mike, slow down, that's disgusting.

Mike gives her an annoyed look.

> MIKE
> (mouth full)
> You do a lot of studying last
> night?

> NANCY
> Yeah, I did, actually.

> MIKE
> What's your test on again? Human
> anatomy?

Nancy KICKS Mike under the table. Mike KICKS her back.

> KAREN
> Hey, what's going on?

> MIKE/NANCY
> Nothing.

The kids return to eating. Like everything is normal.

INT. WHEELER HOUSE - BASEMENT - DAY

HISSSS! A RADIO CRACKLES WITH STATIC.

Eleven is awake in her "tent." She is sitting cross-legged on her sleeping bag, fidgeting with Mike's walkie-talkie.

> MIKE (O.S.)
> Hey. You found my supercomm.

She looks up to find Mike approaching.

                    MIKE (CONT'D)
          Pretty cool, huh?

Eleven, nods. Promptly resumes fidgeting.

                    MIKE (CONT'D)
          I talk to my friends with it,
          mostly Lucas, 'cause he lives so
          close. The signal's pretty weak.

Mike sits beside her. Removes the Eggo from his jacket.

                    MIKE (CONT'D)
          I got you breakfast.

The Eggo is pretty mashed up from being in his jacket. Mike
tries his best to flatten it out, then hands it to Eleven.

She begins to eat it.

                    MIKE (CONT'D)
          So, listen. This is gonna sound
          weird.

Mike points to the basement door. Eleven clocks it.

                    MIKE (CONT'D)
          I need you to go out there, then
          just walk around to the front of the
          house and ring the doorbell and my
          mom'll answer and you'll tell her
          that you're lost and need help but
          whatever you do you *can't* mention
          last night or that you know me.
                (beat)
          Understand?

Eleven has stopped eating her Eggo. Unsettled by this plan.

                    MIKE (CONT'D)
          Really, it's no big deal, okay?
          We'll just pretend to meet each
          other again. And my mom, she'll
          know who to call --

                    ELEVEN
          No.

                    MIKE
          No?

                    ELEVEN
          No.

                         MIKE
          No...   You don't want my mom to get
          help?

Eleven shakes her head again. Her eyes well with tears.
She's not just upset. She's actually... *scared*.

                         MIKE (CONT'D)
                    (low, understanding)
          You're in trouble. Aren't you?

A long beat. Eleven nods.

                         MIKE (CONT'D)
          Who -- who are you in trouble with?

Another beat.

                         ELEVEN
          Bad...

                         MIKE
          Bad? Bad people...?

She nods.

                         MIKE (CONT'D)
          They want to hurt you? The bad
          people?

Eleven nods. "Yes." She aims a finger at herself: *Bang.*

Then at Mike: *Bang.*

                         ELEVEN
          ... Understand?

Mike's face goes pale. He understands, but he wishes he
didn't. Before he can find the words to respond --

                         KAREN (O.S.)
          MICHAEL!! WHERE ARE YOU?! YOU'RE
          GOING TO BE LATE! LET'S GO!

Mike's mind races. *What the hell should he do???* He looks
up the stairs. Then back to Eleven. And...

                         MIKE
          I'll be right back. Just -- stay
          here. *Stay here.*

Eleven gives a timid nod.

INT. HAWKINS LABS - HALLWAY

CONNIE, the LEAD AGENT, and DR. BRENNER stride down a
hallway.

>   DR. BRENNER
>   When was this?

>   CONNIE
>   Last night. Less than two miles
>   away.

>   DR. BRENNER
>   And the boy?

>   LEAD AGENT
>   Still missing.

**INT. HAWKINS LABS - RADIO MONITORING ROOM - A LITTLE LATER -
DAY**

Brenner wears headphones in the radio monitor room.

He is listening to the recording of a familiar voice...

>   JOYCE'S VOICE (RECORDING)
>   -- it was my son, I know it, and...
>   I heard something else...

>   FLORENCE'S VOICE (RECORDING)
>   (filtered)
>   Something else?

>   JOYCE'S VOICE (RECORDING)
>   It was... like some kind of
>   animal... I-I don't know -- please
>   just tell Hop to hurry --

Off Brenner, his concern growing...

EXT. FIELD - DAY

Hopper wades through an ocean of weeds.

There are dozens of VOLUNTEERS fanned out here, continuing
their search for Will. A few SEARCH DOGS sniff the area.

Hop sidles up to OFFICERS CALLAHAN and POWELL.

                    HOPPER
Anything?

                    OFFICER CALLAHAN
             (shakes head, "no")
You?

                    HOPPER
Nothing but a dead phone.

                    OFFICER CALLAHAN
Joyce?

                    HOPPER
About one step from falling right
off the edge.

                    OFFICER POWELL
She's been a few steps for awhile
now, hasn't she?

                    HOPPER
Her kid's missing. Show some class.

Hopper pushes forward through the weeds. Claps his hands.

                    HOPPER (CONT'D)
OKAY, PEOPLE, LET'S KEEP IT MOVING!
LET'S GO!

Powell leans over to Callahan, whispers:

                    OFFICER POWELL
The chief and her, they've screwed
before, huh?

Off Callahan, not going there...

EXT. HIGH SCHOOL - DAY - ESTABLISHING

The hustle and bustle of high school.

INT. HIGH SCHOOL - HALLWAY - DAY

Nancy and Barbara move quickly through the hallways.

Barbara is reading the FLASH CARDS. Nancy answers.

                    BARBARA
          When alpha particles go through
          gold foil, they become...?

                    NANCY
          Unoccupied space.

                    BARBARA
          And a molecule that contains only
          non-metal ions will --

The flash cards are suddenly ripped away by STEVE. He's with
his two friends: TOMMY H. (sloppy) and CAROL (smacking gum).

                    NANCY
          HEY!

Nancy reaches for the flash cards, but Steve holds them away.

                    STEVE
          You've studied enough.

                    NANCY
          Steve -- !

                    STEVE
          I'm telling you, you got this.

He stuffs the cards into his back pocket.

                    STEVE (CONT'D)
          Now -- on to more important matters.
          My dad's left for a conference in
          Cleveland. My mom went with him
          'cause she doesn't trust him --

                    TOMMY H.
          Good call.

                    STEVE
          So... you in?

                    NANCY
          In? For what?

                    CAROL
               (uhhh)
          No parents. Big house...

                    NANCY
          A party?

                         CAROL
          Ding-ding-ding!

                         NANCY
          ... It's Tuesday.

                         TOMMY H.
                    (mocking)
          "It's Tuesday!"

Carol laughs.

                         STEVE
          Come on, it'll be low key, just us.
          What do you say? You in or out?

Before Nancy can respond --

                         CAROL
          Oh God. Look.

Everyone follows Carol's gaze. ACROSS THE HALLWAY, Jonathan
is hanging up a MISSING PERSON POSTER OF WILL on a bulletin
board. None of the passing students are even talking to him;
a few throw uncomfortable glances in his direction.

Nancy feels awful.

                         STEVE
          That is... really depressing.

                         NANCY
          Should we say something?

                         CAROL
          Uh, I don't think he speaks.

                         TOMMY H.
          How much you want to bet he killed
          him?

Nancy suddenly heads over to Jonathan.

Steve and the others watch her go. Carol smacks her gum.

                         CAROL
          She really is Little Miss Perfect,
          isn't she?

ACROSS THE HALL, we're now with Jonathan as he finishes
hanging up the poster.

                         NANCY (O.S.)
          Hey.

                              82

He turns to find Nancy. Surprised.

                    JONATHAN
          Hey.

                    NANCY
          I -- I just wanted to say... you
          know... I'm sorry about everything.
               (motions to group)
          Everyone's... thinking about you.
               (beat)
          It sucks.

                    JONATHAN
          Yeah.

Nancy searches for better words.

                    NANCY
          I'm sure he's okay...

A seemingly never-ending beat before...

BRRRRRING! The bell SCREAMS.

                    NANCY (CONT'D)
          I -- I gotta go. Chemistry test...
          Good luck?

Nancy gives an awkward smile, then races back to the others.

Jonathan watches her go for a beat, then stuffs the remaining
flyers into his backpack and walks the opposite direction.

As students around him vanish into classrooms, an
ANNOUNCEMENT drones over the speakers:

                    PRINCIPAL P.A. VOICE (O.S.)
               (filtered)
          ... At eight PM tonight, there will
          be an assembly on the field in
          support of Will Byers and his
          family. Missus Robertson will be...

INT. MIDDLE SCHOOL - MR. CLARKE'S CLASSROOM - DAY

WHUMP! A TEXTBOOK hits a desk as --

Dustin plops into his seat. Lucas drops next to him. Their
eyes move to the empty seat next to him. *Mike's seat.*

                    DUSTIN
          Okay, this is weird, he's never
          this late --

                    LUCAS
          I'm telling you, his stupid plan
          failed.

                    DUSTIN
          I thought you liked his plan.

                    LUCAS
          Yeah, but obviously it was stupid
          or he would be here, wouldn't he?

Dustin considers this logic. Finds it solid.

                    DUSTIN
          If his mom found out a girl spent
          the night --

                    LUCAS
          He's in deep shit right about now.

                    DUSTIN
          What if she slept naked?
               (suddenly realizing)
          Oh man, if Missus Wheeler tells my
          parents...

                    LUCAS
          No way. Mike would never rat us out.

                    DUSTIN
          I don't know --

                    LUCAS
          Don't worry. All that matters is
          that by the time school's over, the
          freak will be back in the looney
          bin, and we can focus on what
          really matters.
               (beat)
          Finding Will.

EXT. WHEELER HOUSE - DAY

Karen's Country Squire station wagon reverses out of the
driveway.

WE PAN TO REVEAL: Mike watching from behind a tree, his bike
on the ground beside him. *He never left for school.* As soon
as she is gone, Mike wheels his bike back to the house.

INT. WHEELER HOUSE - DAY

Mike leads Eleven out of the basement.

                    MIKE
          ... You want something to drink?
          We have o.j. and skim milk and --

Eleven ignores him, looking around, taking it all in.

                    MIKE (CONT'D)
          This is my living room. It's
          really just for watching TV.

Eleven walks up to the TV. Twists the dials.

                    MIKE (CONT'D)
          Nice, right? It's a twenty-two
          inch. That's like ten times bigger
          than Dustin's --

Eleven doesn't care. She crosses to the fireplace. Various
photos line the mantle -- including a WHEELER FAMILY PORTRAIT.

She seems particularly interested in Nancy.

                    ELEVEN
          Pretty.

                    MIKE
          I guess. That's my sister, Nancy.
          And those are my parents.
                    (beat, fishing)
          What are your parents like? Do
          they live close?

No answer. Eleven's attention is now onto something else:

The LA-Z-BOY. She eyes its LEVER. A little scared by it.

                    MIKE (CONT'D)
          That's a La-Z-Boy. You've never
          seen one? It's where my dad sleeps.

Eleven approaches, hesitant.

                    MIKE (CONT'D)
          Here -- try it. Sit!

Eleven hesitates. Mike finds this amusing.

                    MIKE (CONT'D)
          It's not gonna hurt you!

Eleven sits down. Her tiny body sinks into the fat cushion.

Mike grabs the lever. Eleven tenses.

                        ELEVEN
        No --

                         MIKE
            Just... trust me? Okay?

Eleven hesitates. Then gives a small nod.

Mike yanks back the lever and --

FWOOM! The chair drops! Eleven gasps... and then LAUGHS!

                         MIKE (CONT'D)
            See, fun, right? You try it.

Eleven yanks the lever on her own. FWOOM! The chair jerks
upright. She laughs. She pulls the lever again and --

INT./EXT. JONATHAN'S CAR & COUNTRY ROAD - DAY

VROOOM! Jonathan shifts gears as --

His car RIPS down a country road. The Clash blasts on the
radio, "Should I Stay or Should I Go." As Jonathan listens
to the SONG, we slowly ZOOM IN on the radio and...

INT. BYERS HOUSE - JONATHAN'S ROOM - DAY (FLASHBACK)

We ZOOM OUT of another cassette tape PLAYING the <u>same song</u>.

*Jonathan sits on the bed next to his kid brother, WILL. They
listen to the song together. Feet tapping. Will bobs his
head. A little awkward, but getting into it.*

                         JONATHAN
            Like it?

                         WILL
            Yeah... it's cool.

                         JONATHAN
            You can keep my mix if you want.

                         WILL
            Really?

                         JONATHAN
            *Really. All the best stuff's on
            there. Joy Division, Bowie,
            Television, The Smiths -- it'll
            totally change your life.*

                         WILL
            Yeah, totally.

We can tell Will really looks up to his brother. This is
like... the coolest thing ever. But this intimate brother
moment is shattered by SHOUTING FROM THE OTHER ROOM.

Will turns. THROUGH A CRACKED DOOR he sees Joyce on the
phone, upset, angry. We catch a snippet of the argument:

> JOYCE
> Where the hell are you?! No, no, I
> don't care about your -- !

Jonathan shuts the door. The shouting drops in volume.

But Will heard enough. His face darkens.

> WILL
> ... He's not coming. Is he?

Jonathan shrugs it off.

> JONATHAN
> Do you even like baseball?

> WILL
> ... No. But... I don't know. It's
> fun to go with him sometimes --

> JONATHAN
> Come on. Has he ever done anything
> with you that you actually like?
> Like the arcade or something?

> WILL
> I... I don't know.

> JONATHAN
> No. He hasn't. He's trying to
> force you to like normal things.
> And you shouldn't like things just
> because people tell you you're
> supposed to like them, okay?
> (beat)
> Especially not him.

Will gives a small nod.

> JONATHAN (CONT'D)
> But you like The Clash? For real?

> WILL
> For real. Definitely.

Jonathan smiles. He cranks up the volume. And --

INT./EXT. JONATHAN'S CAR & COUNTRY ROAD - DAY

The Clash BLASTS as Jonathan HAMMERS the accelerator.

SHARP WHIP PAN AS: His car races past a "YOU ARE NOW LEAVING HAWKINS" SIGN.

EXT. DOWNTOWN - MELVALD'S GENERAL STORE AND PHARMACY - DAY

Joyce's car speeds through downtown. She crashes to a stop in front of MELVALD'S GENERAL STORE AND PHARMACY.

INT. MELVALD'S GENERAL STORE - MOMENTS LATER - DAY

DOORS CHIME as Joyce bursts in. She moves at a fast clip.

MR. MELVALD, 60s, the owner, is stocking shelves. He clocks Joyce -- and looks surprised to see her. As is JEFFREY, 20, the pimple-faced assistant working the pharmacy counter.

> MR. MELVALD
> Joyce... I... I didn't expect you
> today, I asked Jeffrey to cover --

> JOYCE
> I'm actually -- I'm not here to
> work. The storm last night, it --
> (how to explain?)
> I need a new phone.

INT. MELVALD'S GENERAL STORE - FRONT COUNTER - MINUTES LATER

CLOSE ON: A BELL ROTARY PHONE drops on the counter.

Mr. Melvald calculates the tax.

> MR. MELVALD
> Let's see... that comes to twenty-
> two dollars, fifty-six cents.

A friendly smile. Joyce makes a show of riffling through her purse, then looks back up at Mr. Melvald.

> JOYCE
> Mr. Melvald. I was wondering... I
> gave Jonathan some money to make
> copies this morning, for posters --
> (beat)
> I need an advance.

Mr. Melvald glances at Jeffrey. Then back at Joyce.

> MR. MELVALD
> ... Yes. Of course. *Of course.*

He begins to fill out a check. Joyce eyes the number.

>   JOYCE
>   I was thinking -- two weeks.
>   (off his hesitation)
>   I'll be back to work soon. As soon
>   as they find Will --

>   MR. MELVALD
>   I understand. It's only -- I have
>   to pay Jeffrey here, and --

>   JOYCE
>   I've been here ten years, Donald.
>   Have I ever called in sick once?
>   Missed a shift? I've worked New
>   Years and Thanksgiving and
>   Christmas Eve and my son is gone
>   and I don't know where he is or if
>   he's hurt or if I'll ever see him
>   again and I'd just...
>   (beat, gathers composure)
>   ... I'd like this phone and a two-
>   week advance.
>   (beat, fuck it)
>   And a pack of Camels.

Off Mr. Melvald...

EXT. BYERS HOUSE - FRONT - DAY

A "REPAIR MAN" KNOCKS on the Byers' door.

He waits a beat. When there's no answer, he looks back at a
Power & Light VAN parked out in the driveway. Gives a small
nod.

The door slides open and --

WHOMP. A pair of heavy boots hits the ground.

EXT. BYERS HOUSE - BACKYARD - DAY

Dr. Brenner and a PAIR OF SCIENTISTS (wearing HAZMAT SUITS)
move through the backyard. Dr. Brenner carries a DEVICE
that measures EMF and RADIATION LEVELS.

The needle slowly rises as he nears the shed.

INT. BYERS SHED - CONTINUOUS

Dr. Brenner enters the shed.

He slowly walks up to THE BACK WALL. Several of the wood
planks are, ever so subtly, undulating. It's almost as if
this wall of the shed is... *alive.*

The needle rises and rises...

>   DR. BRENNER
>   ... Extraordinary.

Another scientist steps up to him.

Dr. Brenner turns to him.

>   DR. BRENNER (CONT'D)
>   It was here.

INT. WHEELER HOUSE - MIKE'S ROOM - DAY

WHAM! A YODA ACTION FIGURE is slammed into frame.

>   MIKE
>   (in Yoda voice)
>   "Ready are you? What know you of
>   ready?"

Mike is showing his toys off to Eleven.

She stares at this strange green man.

>   MIKE (CONT'D)
>   ... His name's Yoda. He can use
>   the Force to move things with his
>   mind, like this...

Mike makes a WHOOSHING sound and then knocks over an army of
D&D MINIATURES with his hand. He looks at Eleven to see what
she thinks of his act... but she's not there anymore.

She has wandered to his shelf. Entranced by...

A ROW OF SHINY TROPHIES.

Mike goes to her side.

>   MIKE (CONT'D)
>   Those are from the science fair.
>   We got first every year except last
>   year when we got third. Mister Clarke
>   said it was totally political...

Eleven's not listening. Her eyes have shifted to something
behind the trophies. A PHOTOGRAPH OF OUR FOUR BOYS. Her gaze
is fixed on the small boy in the center of the group: Will.

TIME SLOWS DOWN as we SLOWLY ZOOM IN on the picture of Will.

Mike follows her gaze. Realizing now who she is looking at.
Will. She slowly lifts her finger. And points at Will.

She then looks back at Mike. Eyes wide with fear.

Mike's heart goes in his throat.

>   MIKE (CONT'D)
>   You know Will?

Eleven doesn't respond. Doesn't need to. The answer is "yes."

>   MIKE (CONT'D)
>   ... Did you see him? Last night?
>   On the road?

Before Eleven has a chance to respond...

WE HEAR THE SOUND OF AN APPROACHING CAR ENGINE.

Mike races to the window and throws open the blinds.

MIKE'S POV: His mom's car is pulling into the driveway.

>   MIKE (CONT'D)
>   We gotta go...

INT. WHEELER HOUSE - STAIRS - MOMENTS LATER - DAY

Mike drags Eleven down the stairs. But they're too late --

Karen opens up the front door. She carries GROCERIES in one
hand, Holly in the other.

Mike does a 180, dragging Eleven back up the stairs.

Karen doesn't see them. But she *HEARS* them.

>   KAREN
>   Ted? Is that you? Hello?!

INT. WHEELER HOUSE - UPSTAIRS HALLWAY - MOMENTS LATER - DAY

Mike drags Eleven back into his room. Shouts to his mom:

>   MIKE
>   It's just me, Mom!

>   KAREN (O.S.)
>   Mike?! What are you doing home?!

                              MIKE
                  One -- one second!

Mike shuts the door behind him.

INT. WHEELER HOUSE - MIKE'S ROOM - MOMENTS LATER

Mike pushes Eleven toward the closet.

                              MIKE
                  In here -- I'll be right back, okay?!

Eleven stares into the closet. Anxiety growing...

                         MIKE (CONT'D)
                  Please, you have to get in, <u>or my</u>
                  <u>mom will find you</u>, understand?

Eleven's gaze snaps back to Mike. Her eyes narrowing...

                         MIKE (CONT'D)
                  I *won't* tell her about you. *I*
                  promise.

                            ELEVEN
                     (softening, confused)
                  ... "Promise?"

                              MIKE
                  It means something you can't break --
                  ever.

                         KAREN (O.S.)
                     (louder, closer)
                  Michael???

Mike looks back at Eleven. Pleading desperately with his
eyes. Finally... reluctantly... she steps into the closet.

Mike shuts the door and...

INT. WHEELER HOUSE - MIKE'S CLOSET - CONTINUOUS

Eleven is swallowed in darkness. We MOVE IN TIGHT ON her as her
eyes dart around the space. It's dark, claustrophobic, scary.
She panics: Her breathing quickens... her heart pounds...

As her panic grows, the SOUNDSCAPE is overtaken by a HIGH-
PITCHED TINNITUS-LIKE SOUND. It grows LOUDER and LOUDER and --

INT. HAWKINS LABS - SUB-LEVEL CORRIDOR (FLASHBACK)

WHOOM! ELEVEN is dragged down a corridor by TWO MEN IN LAB
COATS.

                               92

She struggles against them, trying to tear free, but they are too strong. As she flails, she catches a fleeting glimpse of --

Dr. Brenner. He watches from a hallway. She screams to him through tears. Her voice echoes. Distant and hollow.

> ELEVEN
> Papa!! PAPA!!!

Dr. Brenner makes no move to help.

Her head whips back around as she is thrown into...

INT. HAWKINS LABS - THE BOX - CONTINUOUS (FLASHBACK)

"The box" is a claustrophobic, windowless cell.

Eleven lands on hands and knees. Hard. She doesn't waste a beat. She spins around and scrambles back to the door but --

WHOOOM! It SLAMS SHUT just as she reaches it.

We are now left in almost total darkness. We can make out just a faint outline of Eleven. She pounds on the door.

> ELEVEN
> PAPA!! PAPPPAAA!!!

Her voice is overtaken by that terrible TINNITUS SOUND.

It grows LOUDER and LOUDER and --

INT. WHEELER HOUSE - MIKE'S CLOSET - DAY

Eleven shuts her eyes. Clearly in pain.

> MIKE (PRE-LAP)
> ... I just... I don't feel good...

INT. WHEELER HOUSE - LIVING ROOM - DAY

Mike is sitting on the sofa across from his mom.

Karen looks at him with grave concern.

> MIKE
> ... I just, I woke up, and my head --
> it hurt really bad and my throat was
> all scratchy and I wanted to tell you
> but last time I said I was sick you
> made me go to school anyway and --

                    KAREN
          Michael.

                    MIKE
          ... Yeah?

                    KAREN
          I'm not mad.

                    MIKE
          No?

                    KAREN
          No! Of course not.

Karen slides closer to him. Takes his hand.

                    KAREN (CONT'D)
          All this that's been going on...
          with Will. I can't imagine what
          it's been like for you.

Mike relaxes. *Relieved this is about Will, not Eleven.*

                    KAREN (CONT'D)
          I just... I want you to feel like
          you can talk to me. About anything.
          I don't ever want you to ever feel
          like you have to hide anything from
          me. I'm here for you. Okay?

Mike is about to respond, when we HEAR a SOFT WHUMP UPSTAIRS.

                    KAREN (CONT'D)
          Is someone else here?

Mike considers. *Should he tell her?*

                    MIKE
          ... No.

INT. WHEELER HOUSE - MIKE'S ROOM - DAY

Mike shuts the door behind him. Locks it.

                    MIKE
          Eleven. You okay?? El??

Mike crosses to the closet and throws open the door.

He finds Eleven curled up in the corner of the closet. A
pile of clothes and shoes and books have toppled to the
floor. This place is a giant mess!

                         94

She looks up at Mike. Fills with relief when she sees him.

> MIKE (CONT'D)
> Is everything... okay?

She nods. Smiles softly.

> ELEVEN
> Promise.

Off Eleven, her trust in Mike growing...

INT. BYERS HOUSE - LIVING ROOM & KITCHEN - DAY

Joyce strides into her house.

She drops a new phone, a check, and Camels onto the counter.

We move through a frantic series of QUICK CUTS as Joyce tears open the new phone box... removes the phone... plugs in the cord... shoves the receiver to her ear... and finally...

She gets a DIAL TONE. She is flooded with relief.

She carries the phone over to her sofa. Or, rather, she *tries to*. The phone cord is short by at least five feet.

She grabs the sofa and -- SCREEECH! -- drags it across the floor as Joyce hauls the sofa closer to the phone. She sits... places the phone in her lap. And then she waits...

We SLOWLY DRIFT AWAY FROM HER...

She seems small in this house. And very, very alone.

EXT. QUARRY TOP - DAY

WHAM! Boots SMASH dirt as...

Hopper leads his search to THE TOP OF A MAJESTIC QUARRY.
Callahan approaches the edge of the ridge and peers down.
The walls drop precipitously into a pool of water below.

Hopper pulls Callahan back from the edge.

> HOPPER
> Careful. Need you alive -- for a
> few days more, at least.

> OFFICER CALLAHAN
> Oh, I could survive that.

Hopper gives him a look.

                    OFFICER CALLAHAN (CONT'D)
          George Burness made the jump.
          Drunk as a skunk, did it on a ten-
          dollar bet.

                    HOPPER
          George is a liar. You jump this,
          that water hits you like a ton of
          bricks. Break about every damn
          bone in your body.

Callahan looks back down. Considers for a beat.

                    OFFICER CALLAHAN
          ... Nah.

CHHHH! Hopper's RADIO SQUAWKS to life.

                    FLORENCE'S VOICE (OVER RADIO)
               (filtered)
          Chief -- you copy?

Hopper draws the radio to his mouth.

                    HOPPER
          Yessum. Talk to me, Flo.

WE CUT TO A VERY WIDE SHOT of Hopper standing atop this
massive quarry. We CAN'T HEAR FLORENCE anymore, not from
this distance, but we can make out Hopper's expression, which
just gets bleaker and bleaker.

PRE-LAP: THE SOUND OF SIRENS.

EXT. BENNY'S BURGERS - DAY

A SWARM OF EMERGENCY LIGHTS FLASH outside Benny's Burgers.

WIDEN TO REVEAL: a CLUSTER OF EMERGENCY VEHICLES (POLICE,
FIRE, AMBULANCE), including Hop's, parked outside Benny's.

INT. BENNY'S BURGERS - DINING ROOM - DAY

Hopper, POWELL, and CALLAHAN move into the restaurant.

                    OFFICER CALLAHAN
          Ahhh Jesus...

Callahan covers his mouth and nose. Powell grimaces.

REVERSE ANGLE TO REVEAL: BENNY. Or what's left of him. He's slumped at a booth, head lolled back, a hole in the side of his head. A dark cloud of blowflies hovers around him.

Hopper walks up to the corpse. Not bothered by it in the least. He examines the head wounds closely. Then clocks:

A REVOLVER on the table.

                    OFFICER POWELL
          Suicide?

                    HOPPER
          Mm.

Hopper inspects the back wall. A bullet is stuck in it. He glances back at Benny. Gauging the trajectory. *Seems right.*

                    OFFICER CALLAHAN
          Missing kid... suicide... must feel
          like you're a big-city cop again,
          huh, Chief?

                    HOPPER
          Dealt with strangers then.
               (beat)
          Benny, hell. He was my friend.

INT./EXT. JONATHAN'S CAR & BLUE-COLLAR STREET (INDIANAPOLIS) DAY

Jonathan drives down a blue-collar street. Slows down.

He watches the house numbers pass by. His eyes lock onto a shitty little house, screen door, porch, overgrown lawn.

He pulls over, parks.

EXT. LONNIE'S HOUSE & STREET (INDIANAPOLIS) - DAY

Jonathan knocks on the door. No answer.

He tries knocking again. Louder. The door finally opens to reveal CYNTHIA, 30s. She wears a too-small tank top and acid-washed jeans.

                    CYNTHIA
          -- I help you?

                    JONATHAN
          Is Lonnie around?

                    CYNTHIA
          He's out back -- what do you want?

                    JONATHAN
          To look around. I'll be fast.

Jonathan brushes past Cynthia into...

INT. LONNIE'S HOUSE - CONTINUOUS - DAY

Cynthia trails after him.

                    CYNTHIA
          Hey -- what do you think you're
          doing?! Hey -- !

Jonathan ignores her and keeps moving, looking around. It's
a mess in here; looks like a tornado swept through. Empty
beer bottles, dirty plates, cigarette butts, a blaring TV.

                    JONATHAN
          Will? You here? Will?!

Jonathan continues into the bedroom. He flings open the
closet door. Checks the bathroom.

                    JONATHAN (CONT'D)
          Will -- ?

WHAM! SOMEONE SUDDENLY SLAMS HIM UP AGAINST THE WALL.

Meet LONNIE, 40s, Jonathan's dad.

Cynthia stands behind him.

                    JONATHAN (CONT'D)
          Get off --

Jonathan shoves Lonnie away. Lonnie grins.

                    LONNIE
          Damn. You've gotten stronger.

                    CYNTHIA
          Someone want to explain what the
          hell is going on?

                    LONNIE
          Jonathan, meet Cynthia. Cynthia,
          Jonathan.
               (beat)
          My oldest.

EXT. WHEELER HOUSE - DAY

Lucas and Dustin bike up to the Wheeler house.

INT. WHEELER HOUSE - MIKE'S ROOM - DAY

Lucas and Dustin stare off-camera with wide eyes.

                    LUCAS
          Are you out of your mind??

REVERSE ANGLE TO REVEAL: <u>Eleven is on Mike's bed</u>.

                    MIKE
          Just listen to me.

                    LUCAS
          You <u>are</u> out of your mind --

                    MIKE
          She knows about Will.

This shuts Lucas up.

                    DUSTIN
          What do you mean "she knows about
          Will?"

Mike goes to the trophy case. Removes the photo.

                    MIKE
          She pointed at him. At his
          picture. She knew he was missing --
          I could tell.

                    LUCAS
          You could *tell?*

                    MIKE
          Just think about it! You really
          think it's a coincidence we found
          her on Mirkwood -- exactly where
          Will disappeared?

                    DUSTIN
          That is weird.

                    MIKE
          She said bad people are after her --
          I think maybe these bad people are
          the same ones who took Will.
                    (beat)
          I think she knows what happened to him.

                    LUCAS
          Then why doesn't she tell us!

Lucas marches over to Eleven. She startles back.

                    LUCAS (CONT'D)
          Do you know where he is? Do you
          know where Will is??

                    MIKE
          Stop it -- you're scaring her!

                    LUCAS
          She should be scared!
               (back to Eleven)
          If you know where he is, tell us!

Eleven fights back tears. Lucas is losing patience.

                    LUCAS (CONT'D)
          This is nuts, we have to take her
          to your mom --

                    MIKE
          No -- Eleven said telling any
          adults will put us in danger.

                    DUSTIN
          Danger? What kind of danger?

                    LUCAS
          Her name is Eleven?

                    MIKE
          El for short --

                    DUSTIN
          Mike! What kind of danger?!

                    MIKE
          Danger danger.

Mike aims a finger at Lucas. *Bang.* Then at Dustin. *Bang.*

Dustin goes pale. But Lucas isn't buying it.

                    LUCAS
          No. No no no no. We're going back
          to plan A. We're telling your mom --

Lucas heads for the door. He throws it open when --

WHOOM! THE DOOR VIOLENTLY SUCKS CLOSED. Startled, confused,
Lucas tries to open it again, but --

WHOOM! IT YANKS SHUT AGAIN. POP! The lock snaps.

                    ELEVEN (O.S.)
          No.

Mike and Lucas slowly look at Eleven. Their eyes wide.

Her gaze is fierce. FRESH BLOOD slips down her nose.

We PUSH IN on our stunned boys and...

EXT. LONNIE'S HOUSE - BACKYARD - DAY

Lonnie whips off a TARP revealing a GLEAMING, REFURBISHED
CLASSIC CAR.

>   LONNIE
>   Take a look at this beaut.
>   Should've seen it when I got it.
>   Took me a year, but almost done --

But Jonathan isn't even listening to Lonnie. He could give a
shit about his car. He's looking for signs of Will.

He opens the trunk. Empty.

>   LONNIE (CONT'D)
>   Really? You want to check up my
>   ass too? I told you, same as I
>   told those cops, he isn't here and
>   never has been here --

Jonathan shuts the trunk. Hard. He's pissed.

>   JONATHAN
>   Then why didn't you call Mom back?

>   LONNIE
>   I assumed she just forgot where he
>   was. Or he got lost or something.
>   That boy never could take care of
>   himself.

>   JONATHAN
>   This isn't <u>some joke</u>. There are
>   search parties, reporters --

>   LONNIE
>   Hopper's not still chief, is he?

Jonathan doesn't answer. Doesn't have to.

>   LONNIE (CONT'D)
>   (shakes head)
>   I tell your mother, she's gotta get
>   you out of that hellhole. Come out
>   here to the city. It's more real
>   here, you know? And I could see
>   you more.

Jonathan scoffs. *Give me a fucking break.*

> LONNIE (CONT'D)
> You think I don't want to see you?

> JONATHAN
> I know you don't.

> LONNIE
> See that's your mom talkin' right
> there. Word of advice, kiddo:
> Don't listen to everything your
> mother tells you.
> (beat, realizing)
> Does she even know you're here?

Jonathan doesn't answer. The answer is clear: no.

Lonnie can't help but scoff a bit.

> LONNIE (CONT'D)
> So one kid goes missing, she lets
> the other run wild? That is some
> real *fine* parenting right there.
> (beat)
> All I'm saying is... maybe I'm not
> the asshole, alright?

Jonathan takes this in for a beat. There's something in his
dad's words that ring true... but he refuses to admit it.

> JONATHAN
> Next time -- answer the damn phone.

He turns and strides away.

Cynthia walks up and wraps her arms around Lonnie.

> CYNTHIA
> He's kinda cute. Maybe I trade you
> in for the younger model?

Lonnie smiles. But as he watches Jonathan climb into his
car, his smiles fades with what looks like a hint of concern.

INT. POLICE STATION - BULLPEN - DUSK

EARL SUMNER, one of the regulars from Benny's, is being
questioned. He seems a bit shell-shocked.

> EARL
> It just don't add up, Chief.

Earl struggles to light a cigarette. The lighter trembles
too much in his hand.

Hopper lights it for him. His hand is steady.

Earl nods "thanks," takes a drag.

>   HOPPER
>   Notice anything off about him these
>   past weeks?

>   EARL
>   Nah. Hell -- we was goin' fishing
>   down in Etowah on Sunday. He was
>   lookin' forward, I know that.

>   HOPPER
>   He have any enemies you know about?
>   Maybe'd want him gone?

Earl considers.

>   EARL
>   Well. His exes don't like him
>   much, but... nuh-uh.

>   HOPPER
>   When'd you last see him?

>   EARL
>   Yesterday, lunch. Same as always.

>   HOPPER
>   Just you and the boys?

>   EARL
>   Yessir, just me and Henry and --
>   (remembering)
>   There was that kid, I guess. But a
>   kid didn't do this.

Hopper stares.

>   HOPPER
>   A kid? What're you talking about?

>   EARL
>   Yesterday -- some... boy tried to
>   steal some food from his kitchen.

Hopper shoots a glance to Callahan. *Holy shit.* Callahan
hurries off. Hopper flips open a note pad, pulls out a pen.

                    HOPPER
          This boy? What'd he look like?

Earl shrugs. Holds up his hands to about five feet.

                    EARL
          Like this maybe, real tiny like. I
          didn't get a good look, he was back
          in the kitchen.

Callahan returns with a MISSING POSTER. He hands it to Earl.

                    OFFICER CALLAHAN
          Like this?

Earl takes one look. Shakes his head.

                    EARL
          That's Lonnie's missin' kid. Yeah.
          Not the same kid. This kid had short
          hair. Buzzed, right down to scalp.

                    HOPPER
          Forget the hair. Could it have
          been Lonnie's kid? If his hair was
          buzzed?

                    EARL
          I really didn't get much of a look.

Earl takes another look at the poster. Considers.

                    EARL (CONT'D)
          I guess he's about the same size.
          Coulda been 'im, I s'pose. Yeah.
               (beat)
          Coulda been.

Hopper looks at Callahan. And...

INT. WHEELER HOUSE - NANCY'S ROOM - DUSK

Nancy is on her bed, on the phone with Barb.

                    NANCY
          ... Because I don't want to go by
          myself!
               (beat)
          Barb, Barb. This isn't rocket
          science -- just tell your parents
          you're staying over at my house
          afterwards --
               (listens)
          No, say we have to study --

Downstairs, her mom calls:

                    KAREN (O.S.)
          NANCY!! DINNER!

                    NANCY
          COMING!
              (back to phone)
          I gotta go. I'll see you in an
          hour.

Nancy hangs up the phone. CLICK!

INT. WHEELER HOUSE - DINING ROOM - DUSK

CLOSE ON: A pot roast sizzles. A knife cuts through the meat.

PULL OUT TO REVEAL: Lucas and Dustin have joined the Wheelers
for dinner. They (along with Mike) try to act normal, but
they're clearly freaked by their Eleven encounter. They've
barely touched their food. Karen, of course, clocks this.

                    KAREN
          Something wrong with the pot roast?

                    DUSTIN
          I ate two bologna sandwiches for
          lunch. I don't know why.

                    LUCAS
          Me too.

                    NANCY
              (sucking up)
          It's delicious, Mommy.

                    KAREN
          Thank you, sweetie.

A beat. The kids poke at their food.

                    NANCY
          So, Mom, there's this... special
          assembly thing tonight, for Will. At
          the school field. Barb's driving.

                    KAREN
          Why am I just hearing about this?

                    NANCY
          I thought you knew.

                              KAREN
              How would I know?
                  (Nancy shrugs)
              What time?

                              NANCY
              Eight.

                              KAREN
              I told you, I don't want you out
              after dark, not until Will is found --

                              NANCY
              I know, I know. But I just think
              it'd be super weird if I wasn't
              there. I mean, everyone's going...

                              KAREN
              Just... be back by ten. And why
              don't you take the boys too --

                              NANCY/MIKE
              No!

Karen looks at Mike. Surprised.

                              KAREN
              You don't you think you should be
              there? For Will?

Mike shakes his head. "Nope." He takes another sip of milk --
and nearly spits it back out as (behind his mom) he spots:

Eleven. She's sneaking back down into the basement. Dustin
and Lucas see her too. Karen quickly realizes the boys are
looking at something and starts to follow their gaze when --

BAM! Dustin pounds the table, startling everyone.

                              DUSTIN
              Sorry. Spasm.

Holly giggles. And starts to POUND the table too!

                              KAREN
              Holly -- *no!*

Nancy looks at Dustin.

                              NANCY
              Nice.

EXT. BENNY'S BURGERS - NIGHT 3

A CLUSTER OF CITIZENS' CARS are now parked in the gravel lot, and we see a flurry of volunteers are searching the field behind Benny's with flashlights.

EXT. WOODS - NIGHT

Hopper, Callahan, and Powell search the nearby woods.

A DOZEN VOLUNTEERS around them, flashlights in hand.

> OFFICER CALLAHAN
> You honestly think Earl saw *Will?* I mean, what's Will doin' with a shaved head? Stealin' food from Benny?

> HOPPER
> When we find him, we'll ask.

> OFFICER POWELL
> Can't ask a corpse questions.

Hopper shoots Powell a look.

A WHISTLE interrupts. Their heads snap. And...

EXT. WOODS - BY STREAM - NIGHT

Hopper and his officers hurry over to the source of the whistle. They find Mr. Clarke and a few other searchers kneeling down by a dirty stream. They are peering into...

A SMALL OPEN PIPE.

> HOPPER
> Whatchya got, teach?

> MR. CLARKE
> Not sure. Maybe nothing. But...

Mr. Clarke holds up a SCRAP OF WHITE CLOTH.

> MR. CLARKE (CONT'D)
> I found this. In there.

Hopper takes the cloth. It's wet, grimy. Looks like a gown.

He kneels down by the creek and shines the beam of his flashlight into the pipe. It's small in there. *Really small.*

> OFFICER POWELL
> No way a kid crawls through there.

                    HOPPER
          Scared-enough one might... Will's
          brother said he was good at hiding.

Hopper stands, dusts off his pants, and walks briskly in the
direction the pipe travels. His officers follow.

EXT. WOODS - FENCE - A LITTLE LATER - NIGHT

Hopper reaches a dead end: A LARGE BARBED-WIRE FENCE. It
stretches in either direction for what seems like miles. On
it, a familiar sign:

               RESTRICTED AREA. NO TRESPASSING.
               U.S. GOVERNMENT PROPERTY.

The officers join his side. Out-of-breath. As the three men
stand there, blocked by this fence, we SLOWLY CRANE UP OVER
THEM TO REVEAL A WIDE VIEW OF HAWKINS NATIONAL LABORATORY.
LARGE BUILDINGS AND POWER LINES, ALL BORDERED BY THIS MASSIVE
STEEL FENCE. It looks somehow ominous. Somehow... *evil.*

INT. WHEELER HOUSE - BASEMENT - NIGHT

CHHHH!!! STATIC blasts.

Eleven is by herself, fidgeting with the radio dials,
seemingly entranced by it. Just like this morning.

                    MIKE (O.S.)
          El?

She looks up to find Mike, Dustin, and Lucas coming down the
stairs. Mike carries a TV tray with a plate of leftovers.
An offering of peace.

Dustin and Lucas follow close behind him. They look...
scared of Eleven. Eleven eyes them. Equally scared.

                    MIKE (CONT'D)
          No adults. Just us. And... some
          pot roast.

Mike places the TV tray down in front of Eleven. But she
doesn't touch it. *Doesn't even look at it.* She keeps her
eyes locked on Lucas and Dustin. *Doesn't trust them.*

                    MIKE (CONT'D)
          Don't worry -- they won't tell
          anyone about you. They promised.
               (to Lucas and Dustin)
          Right?

Dustin and Lucas nod. "Right."

                            108

                    DUSTIN
          We never would've upset you if we
          knew you had superpowers --

Mike punches him.

                    MIKE
          What Dustin is trying to say is,
          they were just... upset, earlier,
          that's all.

                    LUCAS
          We just want to find our friend.

Eleven looks confused.

                    ELEVEN
             "Friend"?

                    LUCAS
          Friend, yeah. Will.

                    ELEVEN
          What... is "friend"?

Lucas looks at the others. Whispers:

                    LUCAS
             Is she serious?

They shrug. "I guess."

                    LUCAS (CONT'D)
          Uh... a friend...

                    MIKE
          Is someone you'd do anything for --

                    DUSTIN
          You lend them your cool stuff, like
          comic books and trading cards --

                    MIKE
          And they never break a promise --

                    LUCAS
          Especially if there's spit.

                    ELEVEN
             Spit?

Lucas spits into his hand. Demonstrating.

                    LUCAS
          A "spit swear" means you never
          break your word. It's a bond.

                    MIKE
          That's super important, because
          friends, they tell each other
          things. Things parents don't know.

Off Eleven, considering this...

EXT. FORESTED ROAD - NIGHT

WHOOM! Barbara's car zips down a dark street.

                    NANCY (O.S.)
          Pull over --

                    BARBARA (O.S.)
          What?

                    NANCY (O.S.)
          Pull over!

The car pulls off to the side of the road.

INT./EXT. BARBARA'S CAR - WOODS - NIGHT

Barbara stares at Nancy, who is busy applying make-up.

                    BARBARA
          His house is three blocks away --

                    NANCY
          I know -- we're not supposed to
          park in the driveway.

                    BARBARA
          Are you serious?

                    NANCY
          Calm down.

                    BARBARA
          This is so stupid. I'll just drop
          you off --

                    NANCY
          Barbara, come on. You promised
          you'd come, you're coming --

                    BARBARA
          He just wants to get in your pants --

                    NANCY
          No, he doesn't -- !

                    BARBARA
          Nance, seriously? He invited you
          to *his house.* His parents are
          gone. You are _not_ this stupid.

Nancy blushes. She's actually a bit flattered by the idea.

                    NANCY
          Tommy H. and Carol will be there --

                    BARBARA
          Tommy and Carol were having sex in
          like, seventh grade! It'll probably
          just be just like a big orgy --

                    NANCY
          GROSS!

                    BARBARA
          I'm serious!

                    NANCY
          You'll be my guardian, alright?
          Make sure I don't get drunk and do
          anything stupid.

Nancy reaches into her purse and pulls out a sexy top. She
pulls off her sweater. She's wearing a SEXY BRA underneath.

                    BARBARA
          ... Is that a new bra?

                    NANCY
                (yes)
          No.

Nancy slips on the top.

EXT. WOODS & STEVE'S HOUSE - NIGHT

Nancy and Barb head down a driveway toward Steve's home.

It's a somewhat sprawling '70s-style house, with big windows
and a pool in the back. Steve clearly comes from wealth.

Nancy steps up to the door and rings the DOORBELL. As they
wait for someone to answer, Nancy glances back at Barbara.

                    NANCY
          You should probably unbutton your
          sweater a bit.

                            111

Barbara rolls her eyes. Undoes a single button.

The door swings open. It's Steve. He grins.

> STEVE
> Ladies. Welcome.

INT. HOPPER'S TRAILER - NIGHT

EMPTY BEER BOTTLES are scattered across the dining table. We
MOVE PAST the bottles to find Hopper in bed. He's not
alone... a blonde woman, SANDRA, sleeps at his side.

Hopper slides out of bed. Pulls on his jeans.

EXT. HOPPER'S TRAILER - NIGHT

Hopper steps out onto his porch. Looks out at the lake.

He lights up a hand-rolled cigarette.

> SANDRA (O.S.)
> Whatya doin'?

Sandra joins him on the porch, wearing only a T-shirt. It's
not enough. She shivers, draws her arms around Hop.

> SANDRA (CONT'D)
> It's freezing.

> HOPPER
> (doesn't care)
> You ever feel cursed?

She looks at him like he's nuts.

> HOPPER (CONT'D)
> You know the last person went
> missing here? Summer of '23.
> (beat)
> The last suicide? Fall of '61.

Hop shakes his head in disbelief.

> SANDRA
> And when'd the last person freeze
> to death?
> (no answer)
> Come back to bed, huh? Warm me up.

> HOPPER
> Yeah. One minute.

Sandra nods, then heads back inside.

As Hopper takes another drag of his cigarette, we FOCUS on his left hand. He is twirling the blue bracelet around his wrist.

INT. WHEELER HOUSE - BASEMENT - NIGHT

Eleven sits down at the card table by the D&D board. Studies it. Her eyes close for a second. Then snap back open --

> LUCAS
> (low)
> What's the weirdo doing?

She picks up the WIZARD MINIATURE. *This is Will's miniature.*

> ELEVEN
> ... Will.

The boys share looks. *Holy shit.*

> DUSTIN
> (low)
> Superpowers.

Mike sits down by Eleven. He points at the miniature.

> MIKE
> Did you see him out there? On
> Mirkwood? Do you know where he is?

A beat. Eleven flips the gridded D&D game board upside down, then places "Will" atop it. Mike stares. Confused.

> MIKE (CONT'D)
> I... I don't understand.

> ELEVEN
> Hiding.

> MIKE
> Will's... hiding...?

Eleven nods. "Yes."

> MIKE (CONT'D)
> From... the bad men?

Another beat. Then Eleven shakes her head. "No."

> MIKE (CONT'D)
> Then... from who?

Eleven picks up the DEMOGORGON MONSTER MINIATURE...

And places it on the board right next to "Will."

The boys look at one another. *Terrified.*

EXT. BYERS HOUSE - NIGHT

Outside the Byers'. It's quiet. Too quiet.

INT. BYERS HOUSE - LIVING ROOM - NIGHT

WE CREEP TOWARD Joyce. Asleep on the couch.

BRRRRRRRING! The Bell telephone SCREAMS to life.

Joyce jolts awake on the couch. It takes her a confused
moment to realize that she drifted off. BRRRRRING --

She rips the receiver off the cradle.

                    JOYCE
          He-hello? Hello??

There is nothing on the other end.

                    JOYCE (CONT'D)
          Who -- who is this? Hello?

Finally she hears something -- THE SOUND OF A CHILD'S
BREATHING. Same as other night. Only now the breathing
sounds raspier, more labored.

She stands up sharply. Her voice catches in her throat.

                    JOYCE (CONT'D)
          Will...??

The BREATHING continues.

                    JOYCE (CONT'D)
          I... I know it's you, baby.
          Just... talk to me -- *please...*

The BREATHING continues. Then, very low, buried beneath a
wall of shifting ELECTRIC STATIC, we hear one simple word:

                    WILL'S VOICE (OVER PHONE)
          ... M...o...m...

Tears rush to Joyce's eyes. *Hope.*

                    JOYCE
          Where are you, baby?! Talk to me!
          Talk to me!

A HIGH-PITCHED SHRIEK SUDDENLY ERUPTS FROM THE RECEIVER.

Joyce gasps in pain and drops the phone. *She was shocked!*

She drops to her knees and grabs the receiver back up.

                    JOYCE (CONT'D)
          Will?! WILL?! Are you there?? WILL?!

There is no answer. The phone is dead. *Again.*

                    JOYCE (CONT'D)
          No no no no NO!

Joyce flings the broken phone across the room. It shatters.

Her frustration, anger, anxiety, fear -- it's all finally too
much for her to take. Her knees buckle and...

She sags to the floor. Fighting tears. Behind her, the
hallway lights flicker on and off. But Joyce doesn't notice.
Not at first. But then...

The lights flicker again.

Joyce notices.

INT. BYERS HOUSE - HALLWAY - NIGHT

Joyce pads into the hallway. It's quiet.

                    JOYCE
          Jonathan...?

WHUMP! ALL OF THE LIGHTS IN THE HOUSE SUDDENLY CUT OFF.

Joyce nearly jumps out of her skin. *What the hell?*

A moment of DARKNESS... and then a DIM LIGHT glows to life
under the door at the end of the hall. A chill runs down her
spine. This is WILL'S ROOM. THE LIGHT PULSES EVER SO GENTLY.

And then: a SONG kicks on loudly, startling Joyce. A familiar
one: "Should I Stay or Should I Go" by The Clash.

Joyce slowly, hesitantly, approaches the door.

A poster reads: "DO NOT ENTER! OR ELSE!"

She turns the handle and...

INT. BYERS HOUSE - WILL'S ROOM - CONTINUOUS - NIGHT

Joyce steps into the room.

The cassette tape spins. But the room is empty.

                    JOYCE
              (whispers)
          Will...?

The lamp flickers, as if in response.

                    JOYCE (CONT'D)
          Will?

Another flicker. The light seems to be... communicating.

Joyce's eyes fill with tears. *Could it really be? It seems
impossible. Yet...*

She walks up to the lamp. Reaches out a hand.

                    JOYCE (CONT'D)
          Will... baby...?

The light grows brighter. And brighter. And...

THE LIGHT ABRUPTLY CUTS OUT AT THE SAME TIME AS THE MUSIC.

Everything is dead now. Dark. A long beat of silence.

                    JOYCE (CONT'D)
          Will --

WHUUUUUMP! THE WALL BEHIND THE LAMP LEAPS OUTWARD AS IF IT
WERE ALIVE. THE WALLPAPER SEEMS TO FORM AROUND THE OUTLINE
OF LONG GNARLED HANDS AND A DEFORMED EYELESS FACE.

Joyce startles back with a SCREAM and --

EXT. BYERS HOUSE - NIGHT

Joyce races out of her house. Leaps into --

INT. JOYCE'S CAR - CONTINUOUS - NIGHT

Her hands shake so much that she struggles getting the keys
in the ignition. Finally she succeeds. The ENGINE COUGHS to
life. She is about to hammer the gas when...

Her eyes lock onto something in the rearview mirror.

A LIGHT IS FLICKERING IN THE BEDROOM WINDOW. *Will.*

Her eyes harden. She turns off the car.

EXT. BYERS HOUSE - NIGHT

We cut to a WIDE SHOT as Joyce steps out of her car. She looks out at the house. Gauging it for a beat. Then she heads back inside. And closes the door behind her.

EXT. FOREST ROAD - NIGHT

VROOM! Jonathan's car speeds down "Mirkwood" road.

He pulls off onto the side of the road and steps out. He looks into the woods. We recognize this as the area where Will disappeared; crime-scene tape is tied to a row of trees.

Jonathan pops the trunk. Removes his 35mm camera.

EXT. WOODS - NIGHT

Jonathan ducks under the tape and heads into the woods.

He surveys the area with his camera lens. We cut to VARIOUS CLOSE-UP SHOTS as he photographs details of the crime scene:

He snaps a few shots of the muddy earth.

A few more of a snapped branch.

A few of the road.

And...

A SCREAM SHATTERS THE SILENCE.

Jonathan tenses. Lowers the camera. *What was that?*

EXT. WOODS - DEEPER - NIGHT

Jonathan moves through the dark forest. He's headed toward the sound of the scream. Another SCREAM. Closer this time.

Jonathan quickens his pace. Moving at a sprint now. He leaps over a fallen branch. Shoves through foliage. And --

Crashes to a stop.

REVERSE ANGLE TO REVEAL the screams are coming from...

EXT. STEVE'S HOUSE - BACKYARD POOL - NIGHT

A drunken Tommy H. holds Carol in his arms, swinging her over the lip of the pool. She SHRIEKS.

> TOMMY H.
> One... two... three --

                         CAROL
        STOP IT, TOMMY!! DON'T!! DON'T!!!

Tommy H. finally lets her down. Laughing. She shoves him.

                      CAROL (CONT'D)
        YOU'RE SUCH AN ASSHOLE TOMMY!

Behind them, we find Nancy, Steve, and Barbara -- the awkward
fifth wheel. She sits on a pool chair, looking miserable.

Steve slices open a beer can with a switchblade.

He shotguns it. Perfectly. Grins at Nancy. A little drunk.

                         NANCY
        That supposed to impress me?

                         STEVE
        You're not?

                         NANCY
        You're a cliché, you do realize that.

                         STEVE
        You're a cliché. With your straight
        A's and your band practice --

                         NANCY
        So not in band.

                         STEVE
        Okay, partygirl. Show us how it's
        done.

Steve hands her the switchblade, a new beer can. Nancy grins.
Up to the challenge. She opens her beer a bit. Air HISSES.

                      STEVE (CONT'D)
        Now make an opening at the bottom --

                         NANCY
        I got it.

                       TOMMY H.
        Yeah, she's smart, you douche!

More LAUGHTER. Nancy cuts the hole. Not perfect but does a
nice job. We can tell Steve and the others are impressed.
She places the hole to her mouth, opens the top.

                   STEVE/TOMMY H./CAROL
        CHUG CHUG CHUG CHUG --

Nancy chugs, and chugs, and... finishes! She tosses the can.
Gives a little curtsey. Everyone CHEERS. Everyone but Barb.

Nancy notices. Feels a pang of guilt.

                    NANCY
          Barb, come on, you try now!

                    BARBARA
          No... it's fine. I don't want to --

                    NANCY
          Yes you do! It's fun --

Barbara can't help but smile, happy to be included.

                    BARBARA
          Okay...

She takes a beer and the switchblade. She starts to cut an
opening when the blade slips in her hand. She gasps.

She's cut her thumb. Blood runs down her palm.

                    NANCY
          You okay?!

                    TOMMY H.
          Gnarly!!!

                    BARBARA
          Yeah, I'm... I'm fine -- I just...
               (to Steve)
          Where's your bathroom?

                    STEVE
          Past the kitchen, to the left.

Barbara bolts back inside, holding her bleeding thumb.

Everyone shares looks, fighting laughs. *That was, well,
interesting.* The silence is violently shattered when --

Tommy H. shoves Carol into the pool.

                    CAROL
          Oh my God -- oh my God -- it's
          f-freezing!!

She tries to scramble out of the pool, but Tommy H. leaps
into the pool after her, dunking her back under the cold
water. Nancy laughs. But her laughter abruptly ends when --

WHOOM! Steve pushes Nancy in! He leaps in after.

EXT. STEVE'S HOUSE - ADJACENT WOODS - NIGHT

Jonathan watches the teens play from afar. He raises his camera to get a closer view. His lens drifts over to Nancy. He seems very transfixed by her. She's striking. *Different.*

EXT. STEVE'S HOUSE - BACKYARD POOL - NIGHT

Carol starts to climb out of the pool.

>   TOMMY H.
> Where you goin'??

>   CAROL
> To escape death --

>   STEVE
> Go under, you'll get used to it!

>   CAROL
> No thanks!

>   NANCY
> Yeah, no thanks!

The girls scramble out of the pool, jumping, laughing, freezing, clutching their sopping wet, sagging clothes.

EXT. STEVE'S HOUSE - ADJACENT WOODS - CONTINUOUS

Jonathan watches as Steve and Tommy H. follow them inside.

INT. STEVE'S HOUSE - HALLWAY - A LITTLE LATER - NIGHT

Nancy, Steve, Tommy H., and Carol dry off with towels.

>   CAROL
> I have hypothermia --

>   TOMMY H.
> His parents' room has a fireplace --

He pulls her in that direction. Steve calls after them:

>   STEVE
> Are you serious?? You're washing the
> sheets after!

Steve gives "the bird," then turns back to Nancy. She's drier but still shivering. He walks up to her, rubs her shoulders a bit to keep her warm.

                    STEVE (CONT'D)
        You alright?

                    NANCY
        Yeah.

                    STEVE
        Let's get something dry. Come on.

INT. STEVE'S HOUSE - STAIRWAY - NIGHT

Steve heads up the stairs. Nancy starts to follow him when --

                    BARBARA (O.S.)
        Nancy.

Nancy stops midway up the stairs and turns around. Barbara
is standing below in the hallway. A BLOOD-STAINED PAPER
TOWEL is wrapped around her finger. She looks miserable.

                    BARBARA (CONT'D)
        Where're you going?

                    NANCY
        Nowhere. Just -- changing.
            (looks at herself)
        I fell in the pool.

Nancy smiles at this. Barbara doesn't.

                    NANCY (CONT'D)
        Why don't you just go ahead home.
        I'll just walk back or get a ride
        or something --

Barbara gives her a look.

                    BARBARA
        Nance.

                    NANCY
        Baaarrb...

                    BARBARA
        This isn't you.

                    NANCY
        Just go home. I'll be fine.
            (off Barb's look)
        I'm *fine.*

Nancy turns, heads up the stairs.

Barbara watches her go. Alone. Fighting tears.

EXT. STEVE'S HOUSE - ADJACENT WOODS - NIGHT

Jonathan watches Barbara hurry outside, upset.

Jonathan TILTS his camera up. He finds Steve leading Nancy
into his BEDROOM. As Steve goes to retrieve dry clothes...

Nancy walks over to the window, gazing outside.

Jonathan snaps a picture.

INT. STEVE'S HOUSE - STEVE'S BEDROOM - NIGHT

Steve tosses Nancy some fresh clothes.

                    NANCY
          Thanks.

She waits for him to go. But Steve doesn't budge. She grins.

                    NANCY (CONT'D)
          Some... privacy maybe?

Steve nods. *Right, right.* He starts to leave.

                    NANCY (O.S.) (CONT'D)
          Hey... Steve?

Steve turns back. Nancy looks at him. Her heart is POUNDING
in her chest. Her cheeks are flush. We HOLD ON A TIGHT
CLOSE UP OF NANCY as she slowly reaches down, grabs the
bottom of her shirt... and pulls it up over her head.

                    STEVE
          ... Damn.

                    NANCY
          ... Shut up.

Steve walks over to her. They begin to make out.

EXT. STEVE'S HOUSE - ADJACENT WOODS - NIGHT

Jonathan instinctively lowers his camera.

A moment later the lights go out in Steve's room.

Jonathan returns the gaze of his camera to the pool, where he
finds Barbara sitting on the diving board, all alone, feet
dangling over the water. She holds her cut thumb, fighting
back tears. The image is evocative.

Jonathan snaps a picture of her. Another. And --

CLICK. His film roll is out. *Shit.*

He begins to reload the camera.

EXT. STEVE'S HOUSE - BACKYARD POOL - CONTINUOUS

Barbara's legs swing back and forth on the diving board.

CLOSE ON: A droplet of blood from her finger splashes into
the water. The pool ripples gently. And that's when Barbara
notices something:

A REFLECTION IN THE WATER. *A FIGURE.* Something is off about
its face. Almost human. But... *not.* Whatever it is...

It's standing right behind her.

Barbara turns. The rest happens so fast it's a blur:

THERE IS A HIGH PIERCING SCREAM --

THE POOL LIGHTS FLICKER WILDLY --

PALE FLESH OPENS UP --

AND --

EXT. STEVE'S HOUSE - ADJACENT WOODS - NIGHT

Jonathan hears a MUFFLED SCREAM. A REAL SCREAM this time.
But it sounds like it's coming from... underwater. *The hell?*

He aims his camera back at the pool. The area is quiet.
Empty. The water is still.

Barbara is gone.

EXT. STEVE'S HOUSE - BACKYARD POOL - NIGHT

We focus on the diving board where Barbara just sat.

The board bounces gently up and down.

Up and down.

                                              BLACK OUT.

                          END EPISODE

CHAPTER THREE:
HOLLY, JOLLY

WRITTEN BY **JESSICA MECKLENBURG**

DARKNESS. A STRANGE RUMBLING SOUND. Then...

EXT. STEVE'S HOUSE (NETHER) - POOL - NIGHT

BARBARA's eyes SNAP OPEN.

She coughs out a MUCUS-LIKE SUBSTANCE. Gasps for air.

Something has happened to her. *Something terrible.* Her skin
is pale... blood drips from her nose, ears, mouth... and
she's lying at the bottom of Steve's pool... which means...

THERE IS NO WATER IN THE POOL. IT IS EMPTY EXCEPT FOR THOSE
NOW-FAMILIAR MOLDY GROWTHS, WHICH CLING TO THE CEMENT WALLS
OF THE POOL. STRANGE SPORE-LIKE PARTICLES DANCE IN THE AIR.

Barbara doesn't know it -- but she's in the Nether.

Barbara staggers to her feet. Weak. Crying. Terrified.

>   BARBARA
>   (choked)
>   Help... some -- body --

BOOM! Lightning SCARS the sky. Illuminating...

A DISFIGURED FIGURE INSIDE THIS NIGHTMARISH WORLD WITH HER.

Barbara screams, stumbles away. She tries to scramble up the
wall, but her hands slip on the wet fleshy growths and --

She collapses back into the pool.

INT. STEVE'S HOUSE - STEVE'S BEDROOM - NIGHT 3

STEVE and NANCY fall back onto his bed.

They are making out. Hot and heavy now.

Steve pulls off his shirt. He's clearly done this before.

Nancy is nervous and awkward, her breaths shaky, but she's
getting into it.

>   STEVE
>   (low)
>   ... You alright?

Nancy nods. Her face flush.

>   NANCY
>   (low)
>   Yeah...

Her head suddenly snaps toward the window. She heard something. *So did we.* It sounded almost like a SCREAM.

Only... *very far away.*

> STEVE
> What's the matter?

> NANCY
> ... Nothing.

She turns back to Steve. Kisses him.

EXT. STEVE'S HOUSE (NETHER) - POOL - NIGHT

Barbara SCREAMS.

> BARBARA
> HELP, PLEASE! NANCY!

She can hear a HORRIBLE GUTTURAL SOUND nearby. That thing, *whatever* it is, is close. And it's drawing closer...

Whimpering with fear, Barbara feels along fleshy walls of the pool, until at last her hands seize onto THE POOL LADDER.

She scrambles up the rungs and drags herself up...

OVER THE LIP OF THE POOL.

BOOM! Another flash of lightning illuminates...

STEVE'S HOUSE. Only, it's not the Steve's house we know. It is empty. Dark. Looks long abandoned. And it's covered in those awful growths. Barbara stares in shock and confusion as...

INT. STEVE'S HOUSE - STEVE'S BEDROOM - NIGHT

Steve kisses Nancy's neck. Whispers in her ear.

> STEVE
> You're so beautiful.

Nancy flushes. Kisses him again, hard, and --

EXT. STEVE'S HOUSE (NETHER) - POOL - SAME TIME

WHOOSH! Barb is suddenly pulled by something OFF-SCREEN.

She JERKS BACKWARD, but she grabs onto the ladder railing, screaming, holding on for dear life as --

INT. STEVE'S HOUSE - STEVE'S BEDROOM - NIGHT

Nancy clasps Steve's hand. Tighter and tighter and --

EXT. STEVE'S HOUSE (NETHER) - POOL - SAME TIME

Barbara can't hold on any longer. Her fingers TEAR FREE and --

FWOOM! She is sucked down into the empty pool.

<u>DARKNESS SWALLOWS HER BODY.</u>

Her screams echo.

And then...

Silence.

MAIN TITLES

INT. STEVE'S HOUSE - STEVE'S BEDROOM - NIGHT

Nancy dresses on the edge of the bed. She slips on one of
Steve's sweatshirts. Looks back at him. He's fast asleep.

> NANCY
> ... Steve? Hey, Steve.

She shakes him. He grumbles. Conscious, but only barely.

> NANCY (CONT'D)
> I'll see you... tomorrow. Okay?

Steve grumbles again, then rolls away from Nancy. Nancy
hesitates. This isn't how she wanted this night to end.

She stands off the bed and zips up her jeans.

EXT. STEVE'S HOUSE - BACKYARD - NIGHT

Nancy steps outside. The pool is normal, filled with water.

Whatever Barb experienced, there's no sign it ever happened.

Trees RUSTLE behind Nancy. She turns, spooked. *Nothing.*

She hugs her arms and hurries away.

INT. WHEELER HOUSE - FRONT DOOR/LIVING ROOM - NIGHT

Nancy enters her house. Quietly closes the door behind her.

CLICK! A light turns on. She turns, startled, to find --

KAREN. She's on the couch in a white robe. Needless to say,
she doesn't look happy.

                    NANCY
          Jesus. You scared me.

                    KAREN
          ... I scared you?

                    NANCY
          ... I'm sorry, I know, I should've
          called --

                    KAREN
          Where have you been? We agreed on
          ten --

                    NANCY
          After the assembly, some friends
          wanted to grab something to eat --

                    KAREN
          And you didn't think to call me and
          let me know? With everything
          that's happened?

                    NANCY
          I just -- I didn't realize it was
          so late. I said I'm sorry --

                    KAREN
          Whose sweatshirt is that?

Nancy looks down at her sweatshirt. Totally forgot. *Shit.*

                    NANCY
          ... Steve's.

Everything starts to click to Karen now.

                    KAREN
          Steve's. So... Steve, is he your
          boyfriend now?

                    NANCY
          What? No. It was just cold so I
          borrowed his sweater. It's not a
          big deal.

Nancy hurries past her mom, desperate to get out of here but --

                    KAREN
          Nancy.

Nancy stops, turns to her mom.

> NANCY
> What?

> KAREN
> I know it's hard to believe -- but
> I was a teenager once, too. You
> can talk to me, okay? Whatever
> happened --

> NANCY
> Mom. Nothing happened.

Karen stares down her daughter. She knows she's lying, but
she has no idea what to do about it. And it crushes her.

> NANCY (CONT'D)
> Can I please go?

A beat. Karen gives a small nod. Nancy heads up the stairs.

Off Karen, feeling like she's losing her daughter...

EXT. BYERS HOUSE - DAY 4 - ESTABLISHING

Morning outside the Byers'.

INT. BYERS HOUSE - JONATHAN'S ROOM - DAY

JONATHAN stirs awake to the sound of:

> JOYCE (O.S.)
> (distant)
> ... Will? Will, can you hear me?

He sits up, listens. *Is his mom... talking to his brother?*

> JOYCE (O.S.) (CONT'D)
> ... Will? Will??

He throws off his covers and...

INT. BYERS HOUSE - WILL'S ROOM - DAY

Jonathan opens the door. Stares in disbelief.

JOYCE is sitting on the edge of Will's bed. Around her are a
COLLECTION OF LAMPS. She has gathered every single lamp in
the house and placed them in a semi-circle.

Stranger still, she seems to be... *speaking* to the lamps.

                         JOYCE
          Will? Will?? Come on baby, talk
          to me.

She waits for a response from the lamps. It never comes.

Jonathan finally speaks up.

                         JONATHAN
          ... Mom?

Joyce turns. Her face is pale, her eyes red, her sockets very
dark. She has clearly gone another full night without sleep.

                         JOYCE
          Jonathan... hey. Come over here.
          Come over --

She drags Jonathan over to the lamps.

                         JONATHAN
          What is this...?

                         JOYCE
          Will... he's... talking to me.

                         JONATHAN
          He's... talking to you?

                         JOYCE
          Through the lights.

                         JONATHAN
          ... Mom --

                         JOYCE
          I know it -- I know. Just -- just
          watch...

Jonathan sees the desperation in his mom's eyes. *She needs
this from him.* He takes a breath. Then nods. *Okay.*

Joyce turns to the lamps.

                         JOYCE (CONT'D)
          Will... your brother's here now...
          Can you -- show him? Show him what
          you showed me, baby?

She waits. And waits... and waits... and...

A LIGHT BULB'S FILAMENT FLICKERS EVER SO SLIGHTLY.

Joyce tears up. Joy, relief!

                    JOYCE (CONT'D)
          There -- there! Did you see?!

It destroys Jonathan to see his mom like this.

                    JONATHAN
          The electricity, it's been acting
          up, same thing that fried the
          phone. That's all it is.

She takes his hands. Squeezes.

                    JOYCE
          No, no, it's not just the
          electricity. Something's going
          on... Yesterday -- that wall --
          it...

Joyce trails off.

                    JONATHAN
          What about the wall?

Joyce turns back to Jonathan. She takes his hand.

                    JOYCE
          I just... I know Will's here.
          He's here with us right now. So
          close.
               (pleading)
          Can't you *feel him?*

She really wants Jonathan to answer "yes." She *needs* him
to. And while a part of Jonathan wants to tell her what she
wants to hear... he just can't. He can't fuel her delusions.

                    JONATHAN
          No, Mom. I don't feel him. I'm
          sorry.

This crushes Joyce. She looks away, hurt.

                    JOYCE
          Maybe if I get more lights...

                    JONATHAN
               (getting angry)
          Mom. You don't need more lights.
          You need to stop this, okay? He's
          just <u>lost</u>. But *everyone's* looking,
          and they're going to find him.
               (motions to lights)
          But this -- this isn't helping.
                    (MORE)

                              JONATHAN (CONT'D)
                    It's not helping me, or you -- or
                    Will.

Joyce fights tears. Jonathan suddenly sees how much he's
wounded his mom, regrets it -- and pulls back a little.

                              JONATHAN (CONT'D)
                    I'm sorry... it's just...
                         (beat)
                    Can you just... try and get some
                    sleep. For me. *Please, Mom.*

Joyce looks at him, realizing how scared she is.

                              JOYCE
                    ... I will. Soon. I promise.

INT. WHEELER HOUSE - BASEMENT - DAY

ELEVEN is curled on the couch, playing with Mike's supercomm.

We PAN OVER to find MIKE, LUCAS, and DUSTIN huddled around
the table.

                              MIKE
                    ... We just tell our parents we
                    have A.V. Club after school. That
                    gives us at least few hours for
                    Operation Mirkwood --

Lucas looks back at Eleven. She's still playing with the
supercomm. She seems totally out of it. And *totally weird*.

                              LUCAS
                    You seriously think the weirdo
                    knows where Will is?

                              MIKE
                    Just... trust me on this, alright?
                         (beat)
                    Did you bring the supplies?

Lucas nods. Unzips his backpack. Removes:

                              LUCAS
                    Binoculars from 'Nam, army knife,
                    also from 'Nam, slingshot, hammer,
                    camouflaged bandana, and...
                         (beat)
                    The Wrist-Rocket.

He takes out a WRIST-ROCKET SLINGSHOT.

                    DUSTIN
          You're going to take the Demogorgon
          out with a slingshot?

                    LUCAS
          First of all, it's a Wrist-Rocket.
          Second of all, the Demogorgon's not
          real, it's made up. But if there
          is something out there... I'll
          shoot it in the eye. Blind it.

Lucas aims the Wrist-Rocket at Dustin's eye. Snaps the band.

Dustin flinches.

                    MIKE
          Dustin, what'd you get?

Dustin unzips his backpack, dumps out:

                    DUSTIN
          Nutty Bars, Pez, Smarties,
          Pringles, Bazooka, Nilla Wafers,
          apples, bananas, trail mix --

Lucas and Dustin share looks. *Umm...*

                    LUCAS
          Seriously?

                    DUSTIN
          We need energy for our travels. For
          stamina! And what do we need
          weapons for, anyway? We've got her.

All eyes turn to Eleven. She shrinks, embarrassed.

                    LUCAS
          She shut one door --

                    DUSTIN
          With her mind. Are you kidding?!
          That's *insane.* I bet she can do
          all kinds of stuff.

Dustin walks over and picks up a *MILLENNIUM FALCON* TOY.

                    DUSTIN (CONT'D)
          Like I bet she can make this fly.

Dustin raises the toy above Eleven... and then drops it. The
toy falls to the floor at Eleven's feet. Needless to say,
this is anticlimactic. Eleven stares blankly at the toy.

Dustin tries again. The *Falcon* falls to the floor. *Again.*

Mike grabs the toy away from Dustin.

                    MIKE
          She's not a dog --

                    DUSTIN
          I'm telling you --

                    KAREN (O.S.)
          BOYS, TIME FOR SCHOOL!!!

The boys share looks. *Shit.* They quickly repack their
supplies. As Dustin and Lucas bound up the stairs...

Mike crouches by Eleven. His voice urgent, hushed.

                    MIKE
          ... Stay down here, don't make any
          noise, and don't leave. If you get
          hungry, eat Dustin's snacks. Okay?

                    KAREN (O.S.)
          MICHAEL!!

                    MIKE
          COMING! *Jesus.*
             (back to Eleven)
          You know those power lines --

                    ELEVEN
          -- power lines --

                    MIKE
          The ones behind my house?

                    ELEVEN
          Yes.

                    MIKE
          Meet us there after school.

                    ELEVEN
          After... school?

                    MIKE
          Yeah, three-fifteen.

Eleven's still confused. Mike removes his DIGITAL WATCH and
slips the watch onto her wrist. Acutely aware of their
physical contact, he quickly pulls his hand away.

                    MIKE (CONT'D)
          When the numbers read three-one-
          five. Meet us there. Got it?

Eleven gives a small nod.

                    ELEVEN
          Three-one-five.

INT. HIGH SCHOOL - HALLWAY - DAY

Nancy heads into the school, clutching her backpack close.

She looks around. Everything in her school now feels
somehow... different. Heightened. It's like somehow
everyone knows she's not a virgin anymore. People laugh,
cast a few glances her way... *are they laughing at her??*

She hurries to her locker, throws open her locker, and --

                    STEVE

          Hey...

She turns. Flustered. It's Steve. He clocks her anxiety.

                    STEVE (CONT'D)
          Everything alright?

                    NANCY
          Yeah, yeah, totally.
              (lowers voice)
          It's just -- I dunno -- I feel like
          everyone's staring at me --

                    STEVE
              (defensive)
          I didn't tell anyone --

                    NANCY
          No, no, I know. Of course not.
              (beat)
          But what about Tommy and Carol --

                    STEVE
          You're being paranoid --

                    NANCY
          Sorry --

                         STEVE
              Nah, it's cute.
                  (grins)
              Hey. I had a good time.

Nancy blushes.

                         NANCY
              Yeah. Yeah. Me too.

EEEEE! THE BELL RINGS.

Steve leans in and kisses her. In public. *Whoa.*

Off Nancy, flushed...

INT. HIGH SCHOOL - ENGLISH CLASS - DAY

Nancy plops down into her seat. Still high from her talk
with Steve. But her excitement fades when she sees that...

The desk beside her is unoccupied.

She turns to a FRIEND.

                         NANCY
              Hey, Ally, where's Barb?

                         FRIEND
              Um... shouldn't *you* know?

Nancy hesitates.

                         NANCY
              You haven't seen her -- at all?

The Friend shakes her head.

Off Nancy, concerned now...

EXT. COUNTRY ROAD - DAY

Hopper's Chevy Blazer speeds down a country road.

Ahead, HAWKINS NATIONAL LABORATORY. The familiar sign reads:

                RESTRICTED AREA. NO TRESPASSING.
                   U.S. GOVERNMENT PROPERTY

INT./EXT. HOPPER'S BLAZER - DAY

HOPPER drives. Hungover from last night.

POWELL rides passenger, CALLAHAN in the back.

                    OFFICER POWELL
          There she is. Emerald City...

                    OFFICER CALLAHAN
          I heard they build space weapons.

                    OFFICER POWELL
          Space weapons?

                    OFFICER CALLAHAN
          Yeah, man: Reagan's Star Wars. Gonna
          blow the Ruskies to smithereens.

EXT. HAWKINS LABS - GATED ENTRANCE - DAY

Hopper pulls up to the main Hawkins Labs gate.

He rolls down his window as an M.P. OFFICER approaches.

                    M.P. OFFICER
          Can I help you?

Hopper flashes his badge.

                    HOPPER
          Yeah, we'd like a quick tour --

                    M.P. OFFICER
          We don't give tours --

                    HOPPER
          A look around, then.

                    M.P. OFFICER
          You'll have to get clearance first.
          You should contact Rick Schaeffer at
          the Department of Energy --

                    HOPPER
          Maybe you saw on TV, local kid's
          gone missing. We've got reason to
          believe he might've snuck in here --

                    M.P. OFFICER
          Like I said, you'll have to speak
          to Mister Schaeffer --

                    HOPPER
          What's your name?

                    M.P. OFFICER
          ... Patrick.

                         HOPPER
          Patrick.

Hopper leans out the window. Puts on a very friendly tone.

                         HOPPER (CONT'D)
               Listen, Patrick. I've got a
               panicked mayor and reporters all
               over my ass, an upset mom... I
               know the kid's not in here, I just
               gotta check off this box, you know
               what I'm saying? So why don't you
               call your boss, see what you can
               swing.
                    (beat)
               We're talking ten minutes, *tops*.

Off the M.P. Officer, softening...

INT. WHEELER HOUSE - BASEMENT - DAY

We DOLLY PAST a pile of half-eaten "Dustin snacks" to find...

Eleven. She is sitting cross-legged on the carpet. Her eyes
are focused intently on something above her. We slowly
FOLLOW her gaze up to find...

The *Millennium Falcon* floating in mid-air. It's magical.

But Eleven finds it boring. She looks away.

The toy crashes to the floor.

INT. WHEELER HOUSE - TELEVISION ROOM - DAY

The basement door creaks open as...

Eleven enters the upstairs floor. And begins to explore.

- She sits on the La-Z-Boy. She yanks the lever, moving
herself up and down. But it isn't as fun without Mike.

- She walks up to the television. A massive 22 inches!

She fidgets with the dials until finally it BURSTS TO LIFE.

A NEWS PROGRAM plays a RONALD REAGAN speech:

                         RONALD REAGAN (ON TV)
               ... Today, Syria has become a home
               for seven thousand Soviet advisers
               and technicians --

Eleven, bored, turns the dial. She sees HE-MAN RAISING HIS
SWORD... *THE PRICE IS RIGHT... WHEEL OF FORTUNE... GOOD
MORNING AMERICA...* until her surfing crashes to a stop on:

A COCA-COLA ADVERTISEMENT. Teenagers are chasing a giant
Coke can into the ocean while a jingle plays:

                    JINGLE (ON TV)
          ... COKE IS IT, THE ONE THAT LETS
          YOU DOWN, COKE IS IT...!

We SLOWLY PUSH IN on Eleven and --

INT. HAWKINS LABS - SMALL LABORATORY (FLASHBACK)

We PULL AWAY from Eleven. We are back in time.

*Eleven is now sitting at a table in a white-tiled laboratory
room. A tangle of electrodes droops from her head. On the
table in front of her: AN EMPTY CAN OF COCA-COLA.*

*FIVE SCIENTISTS, including DR. BRENNER, observe from behind a
glass partition. An EEG monitoring machine hums and whirs.*

Eleven keeps her eyes trained on the can. Intense. Focused.

*At first, nothing happens. But then the EEG needle starts to
shudder, then climb. Brenner and the scientists exchange
looks.*

Blood drips from Eleven's nostrils...

The aluminum can slowly crumples... and then...

CLAP!! THE CAN VIOLENTLY FOLDS INTO A TINY SQUARE.

INT. WHEELER HOUSE - TELEVISION ROOM - DAY

CHHHHH! The TV image stutters wildly.

                    AD NARRATOR (ON TV)
               (garbled)
          ... C--oke i -- s -- i --- t !!!

Eleven switches off the television. It ZAPS to black.

INT. BYERS HOUSE - LIVING ROOM - DAY

WHOOM! Joyce drags a cardboard box into the living room.

The top of the box is labeled "X-MAS."

She opens it and removes --

A TANGLE OF CHRISTMAS LIGHTS.

INT. BYERS HOUSE - LIVING ROOM - MOMENTS LATER - DAY

We move into a MONTAGE as Joyce strings Christmas lights across the living room.

- She hammers dozens of nails into the living room walls.

- Then hammers nails in the kitchen.

- Then in the hallway.

- Then she hangs lights from those nails.

- Zigzagging them up and down the house.

- Putting them anywhere and *everywhere*.

CHESTER THE MUTT watches her with a cocked head. Even *he* seems concerned by her behavior.

Joyce eventually runs out of lights. *Shit.*

Off Joyce, considering...

INT. MELVALD'S GENERAL STORE - DAY

MR. MELVALD stocks shelves in an aisle near the register.

We slowly PUSH DOWN an empty aisle toward the GLASS DOOR...

Joyce's car SQUEALS to a stop outside. She climbs out and moves for the entrance...

DING! The door chimes as she barges in.

Mr. Melvald looks up. Surprised.

                    MR. MELVALD
          Joyce?

Joyce ignores him. Heads straight for the Christmas aisle.

INT. MELVALD'S GENERAL STORE - MOMENTS LATER - DAY

Joyce drops a LARGE BOX OF CHRISTMAS LIGHTS onto the front counter. Then another box. Then another. Then *another*.

She tops it all off with a NEW CORDLESS PHONE.

Mr. Melvald starts to say something, but --

                    JOYCE
          Just ring me up, Donald.

Off Mr. Melvald...

EXT. HAWKINS LABS - GROUNDS BEHIND BUILDING - DAY

A FLASHLIGHT BEAM slices through a dark pipe.

Hopper and his officers are crouched in shallow water outside
a SMALL CULVERT around the back of the lab, while the HAWKINS
LABS SECURITY HEAD calmly observes.

                    SECURITY HEAD
          ... And you think this missing boy,
          he may have crawled through there?

                    HOPPER
          That was the thought.

                    SECURITY HEAD
          Yeah. I just don't see how that'd
          be possible. We've got over a
          hundred cameras. Every square inch
          covered. Plus all my guys. No one
          breaks in here. Certainly not some
          kid.

Hopper stands up. Wipes mud off his jeans.

Hopper clocks a few security cameras on the fence.

                    HOPPER
          Those cameras? You keep the tapes?

INT. HAWKINS LABS - CORRIDOR - DAY

CLOSE ON: SHOES DRUMMING LINOLEUM as...

The Security Head leads Hop and his men through the upper
level of facility. There are lots of people buzzing about.

They pass by the QUARANTINED AREA. Hopper clocks it.

                    HOPPER
          If you don't mind me asking, what
          exactly is it you all do here?

                    SECURITY HEAD
          You're asking the wrong guy.

                    HOPPER
          Just staying one step ahead of the
          Russians?

                    SECURITY HEAD
          I expect something like that.

                         HOPPER
               Who's in charge?

                    SECURITY HEAD
          That'd be Doctor Brenner.

                    OFFICER CALLAHAN
          He build the space lasers?

                    SECURITY HEAD
          Space lasers?

                         HOPPER
               Ignore him.

INT. HAWKINS LABS - SECURITY ROOM - DAY

VWWWWWOP! A SURVEILLANCE TAPE zips backward as...

The engineer rewinds surveillance footage of the culvert.

Hopper, his officers, and the Security Head watch. But
there's not much to see. Nothing is happening. No one is
coming out of that culvert. It looks like a frozen image, if
it weren't for the fast-moving foliage behind the culvert.

                         HOPPER
               And this is the sixth and seventh
               of this month we're seeing here?

                    SECURITY HEAD
          That's correct.

The tape comes to an end. Static.

                         HOPPER
               Is that it?

                    SECURITY HEAD
          Like I said -- we'd have seen him.

EXT. HAWKINS LABS PARKING LOT - DAY

Hopper, Callahan, and Powell exit Hawkins Labs.

They head into the parking lot.

                         HOPPER
               The night of the seventh, we had a
               search party out for Will.
               Remember anything about that?

                    OFFICER CALLAHAN
                (shrugs)
        Not much to remember. Called it
        off --

                    OFFICER POWELL
                (realizing)
        -- 'cause the storm.

                    HOPPER
        Lotta rain that night. You see
        rain on that tape?

Powell and Callahan share looks. "No."

Hopper looks back at the facility. His mind racing.

                    OFFICER POWELL
        What are you thinking?

                    HOPPER
        ... I don't know. But they're
        lying.

Hopper climbs into his car. Slams the door.

EXT. HAWKINS LABS PARKING LOT & GROUNDS - MOMENTS LATER - DAY

Hopper's Blazer speeds away from the facility. But we don't
follow it. Instead, we PAN OVER to a small VENTILATION
SHAFT. The grass around the vent is brown and wilted. <u>Dead.</u>

We SLOWLY ZOOM IN on the shaft... the SOUNDSCAPE is overtaken
by a low GUTTURAL GRUMBLE... DARKNESS swallows us... and...

INT. HAWKINS LABS - RIFT LABORATORY

We ZOOM OUT of a VENTILATION GRATE and find ourselves...

In the underground laboratory. WORK LIGHTS have been set up,
cutting through the fog, illuminating a HALF-DOZEN MEN IN
HAZMAT SUITS. They are studying the GROWTH around the Rift
with analogue equipment. It has spread since the last time
we saw it. It's like some kind of awful paranormal cancer.

DR. BRENNER (also in hazmat) supervises a PAIR OF TECHNICIANS
IN HAZMAT SUITS as they lower...

A LARGE METAL POWER WINCH ONTO THE LAB FLOOR.

They DRILL the base of the winch to the floor.

BZZZZZZ!

EXT. WHEELER HOUSE - DAY

All quiet outside the Wheeler house.

INT. WHEELER HOUSE - STAIRS - DAY

CLOSE ON: DELICATE BARE FEET CLIMBING UP STEPS as...

Eleven heads upstairs.

INT. WHEELER HOUSE - UPSTAIRS HALLWAY - DAY

She walks to Nancy's closed door. And --

INT. WHEELER HOUSE - NANCY'S ROOM - DAY

Eleven inches open the door. Her eyes go wide.

It's a little girl's dream in here.

- She sits on the fluffy bed. Bounces a bit.

- Lifts up Nancy's corded phone.

                ELEVEN
    ... Hello?

- Turns on a music box. A gentle LULLABY twinkles.

- Picks up Nancy's diary and begins to flip through. She
reads some words to herself in her typical stilted fashion:

                ELEVEN (CONT'D)
    "Steve Steve Steve -- ugh -- I'm --
    pathetic -- what's wrong with me" --

And then she sees something even better:

A BULLETIN BOARD. SMOTHERED END-TO-END IN PHOTOGRAPHS.

She walks over to the bulletin board.

Eleven traces a finger along the photos, journeying through
Nancy's life: We see Nancy and Barbara dressed as witches at
Halloween... Nancy in her pajamas opening Christmas presents
with her family... Nancy at a 7th grade dance... Laughing
with Barb... It seems like such a full life. A *happy life*...

As Eleven's eyes glisten with tears, CUT TO:

INT. HIGH SCHOOL - CAFETERIA - DAY

Nancy, looking anxious as she moves through the cafeteria.

She sits down by Steve. Squeezing between him and TOMMY H.

CAROL has her ankle on the table. There's a BLISTER on it.

> CAROL
> I swear, look at this, *totally*
> frostbite --

> TOMMY H.
> Get outta here, you were in there
> about thirty seconds--

> CAROL
> Then what is that?

> STEVE
> A disgusting blister, get that off
> the table! We're eating here!!

LAUGHTER. Nancy forces a smile. Then...

> NANCY
> Hey, Tommy. Last night, when you
> left, did you see Barb?

> TOMMY H.
> ... What?

> NANCY
> Barbara. She's not in school
> today.

> TOMMY H.
> I seriously have no idea who you're
> talking about.

Carol laughs. Nancy doesn't find this funny at all.

> STEVE
> Come on, don't be an ass, man. You
> see her leave last night or not?

> TOMMY H.
> No. She was gone when we left.

> CAROL
> Probably couldn't stand listening
> to all that moaning... Ooooh...
> Ohhhh! OHHH Steve!! OH STEVE!

Carol laughs at her own antics, as does Tommy H.

But Nancy does not join in. She can't. She's too worried.

Steve notices. He reaches out, gently touches her leg.

                    STEVE
               (just to Nancy)
          I'm sure she's fine. She's just --
          skipping or something, you know?

                    NANCY
          Yeah. Yeah. Probably.

Off Nancy, trying to mask her growing concern...

INT. HIGH SCHOOL - HALLWAY OUTSIDE CAFETERIA - DAY

Jonathan heads down the hallway, alone, camera bag slung over
his shoulder.

He slows a bit as he passes the cafeteria. He clocks Nancy
with her new friends. She seems lost, out of place somehow.

She suddenly looks up, makes eye contact with Jonathan.

Jonathan quickly averts his gaze and hurries down the hall.

EXT. MIDDLE SCHOOL - RECESS - DAY

CRACK! A BAT collides with a baseball.

MIDDLE SCHOOL KIDS play baseball at recess.

By the bleachers, Mike, Dustin, and Lucas collect rocks for
Lucas's sling.

Mike picks one up. Shows it to Lucas.

                    MIKE
          How about this?

                    DUSTIN
          Too big for the sling.

Mike tosses his rock, and the search continues.

                    DUSTIN (CONT'D)
          You think Eleven was born with her
          powers, like the X-Men, or she
          acquired them, like Green Lantern?

                    LUCAS
          She's not a superhero. She's just
          a weirdo.

                    MIKE
What does that matter? The X-Men
are weirdos.

                    LUCAS
You love her so much, why don't you
marry her?

                    MIKE
What are you talking about?

                    LUCAS
Mike... seriously?

                    MIKE
What?

                    LUCAS
You look at her all like this...

Lucas makes googly eyes.

                    LUCAS (CONT'D)
"Hi El, hi El! El El El El EL!"

                    MIKE
Shut up, Lucas --

                    TROY (O.S.)
Yeah "shut up Lucas"!

Our boys look up to find --

TROY and JAMES striding over to them.

                    TROY (CONT'D)
What are you losers doing back
here?

                    JAMES
Probably looking for their missing
friend.

                    DUSTIN
That's not funny. It's really
serious. He's in danger --

                    TROY
I hate to break it to you,
toothless, but he's not in danger.
He's dead. That's what my dad
says. Said he was probably killed
by some other queer.

Our bullies chuckle at this. Mike's anger rises. He wants
to do something. He wants to punch this shithead in the
face. But... he just doesn't find the courage. *Not today.*

> MIKE
> (to friends, low)
> Come on. Ignore them.

Our boys just walk past the bullies, or try to, but --

Troy sticks out his foot and trips Mike.

Mike flips onto the ground, hard. He SCRAPES his chin.

> TROY
> Watch where you're going, Frogface.

With that, Troy and James chuckle and continue on their way.

Lucas and Dustin help Mike back to his feet.

> LUCAS
> You alright?

> MIKE
> (shaking it off)
> Yeah...

Mike notices something. Plucks a rock off the ground.

> MIKE (CONT'D)
> ... How about this?

Lucas bounces it in his hand, tests the weight.

> LUCAS
> Oh yeah... oh yeah. This is it.
> (beat)
> The monster killer.

Mike smiles through his pain.

INT. HIGH SCHOOL - DARKROOM - DAY

THROUGH LIQUID, AN IMAGE SLOWLY FORMS: Nancy, standing in her
soaking wet shirt, staring out of Steve's upstairs window.

Jonathan's hand enters the frame.

He stirs the photo in a developing tray, then hangs the photo
on a drying rack alongside OTHER IMAGES:

- CRIME-SCENE TAPE marks a cluster of trees.

- A COUPLE OF TEENS hang outside Steve's.

- Another picture of Nancy at the window.

- BARBARA, sitting alone on the diving board.

Suddenly the darkroom door opens behind him and...

A GIRL comes in with her things. She clocks Jonathan.

> GIRL
> Hey.

> JONATHAN
> Hey...

Jonathan quickly pulls his photos down off the drying rack.
But he's a moment too late -- the girl clocks the photo of
Nancy *just* before he removes it.

She places her things down at her developer. Pretending she
didn't see it. But her eyes are wide with disbelief. *Holy
shit.*

Jonathan gathers his things and hurries out of the room.

As the door CLANGS shut behind, we TILT UP to...

THE RED BULB GLOWING ABOVE THE DOOR.

INT. BYERS HOUSE - KITCHEN - DAY

A tiny bulb GLOWS RED as...

Joyce plugs in a final string of Christmas lights. She then
switches off the power and slowly steps back into the middle
off the room. We WIDEN OUT with her to REVEAL that...

THE HOUSE IS NOW COVERED FROM END-TO-END IN CHRISTMAS LIGHTS.
SHE'S ALSO COVERED THE WINDOWS WITH NEWSPAPERS. KEEPING THE
HOUSE DARK. *VERY DARK.*

She takes a beat to gather her breath. Then...

> JOYCE
> ... Will? Are you there?

She slowly looks around the room. Scanning the lights...
waiting for something to happen... waiting for one of those
little lights to flicker on... And waiting... And...

RAP RAP RAP! A HEAVY THUDDING. Joyce startles.

RAP RAP RAP! It's... *knocking.*

150

<u>Someone's at the door.</u>

INT. BYERS HOUSE - FRONT DOOR - MOMENTS LATER - DAY

Joyce cracks open the door to find...

Karen. She carries HOLLY in one hand, a TIN-FOIL-WRAPPED TRAY OF CASSEROLE in the other.

> KAREN
> Hey... we brought you a casserole.

Karen holds up the casserole. Flashes a smile.

Off Joyce, *really* not wanting to deal with this...

EXT. DOWNTOWN - HAWKINS PUBLIC LIBRARY - PARKING LOT - DAY

Hopper and Powell stride up toward the HAWKINS PUBLIC LIBRARY -- a beautiful building in the heart of Main Street.

INT. PUBLIC LIBRARY - FRONT ROOM - DAY

Hop and Powell walk up to a librarian, MARISSA, at the front desk. She's cute, in a mousey kinda way. She looks annoyed at the sight of Hopper.

Hop plays it cool. Rests an arm on her desk.

> HOPPER
> Hey... Marissa. How you doing?

She gives him a loaded look.

> MARISSA
> You have a lotta nerve showing up
> here.

> HOPPER
> What?

> MARISSA
> You could've at least called.
> Said, "Marissa, hey, it's not gonna
> work out, I'm sorry I wasted your
> time, I'm a dick."

Powell smirks at this. Loves it.

> HOPPER
> Right, yeah. Sorry. Maybe we go
> out again next week?

Marissa stares. Hop quickly changes the subject:

151

                    HOPPER (CONT'D)
          Newspapers -- you have newspapers
          here, right?

INT. PUBLIC LIBRARY - FRONT ROOM - MOMENTS LATER - DAY

Marissa leads Hop and Powell to...

A MASSIVE CARD CATALOGUE. Hop opens a few drawers.

Inside each drawer: HUNDREDS OF INDEX CARDS.

                    MARISSA
          We have *New York Times,* the *Post,*
          all the big ones. They're
          organized by year and topic. You
          can find the corresponding
          microfiche right over there.

She motions to ANOTHER massive filing cabinet.

                    HOPPER
          I'm looking for anything on Hawkins
          National Laboratory.

                    MARISSA
          Shouldn't you be looking for that
          missing kid?

                    HOPPER
          Yeah. We are.

Marissa stares. *Sure...*

                    HOPPER (CONT'D)
          You wanna search the *Times,* we'll
          start with the *Post*?

She gives him a look. *Um, no.* She strides away, leaving
Hopper and Powell on their own. Powell looks at Hopper.

                    OFFICER POWELL
          The librarian? Really?

Hopper shrugs.

We now move into a MONTAGE as...

INT. PUBLIC LIBRARY - RESEARCH AREA - LATER

Hopper and Powell rummage for microfiche.

INT. PUBLIC LIBRARY - RESEARCH AREA - LATER STILL

Hopper sits before an ENORMOUS MICROFICHE READER MACHINE. As
he scrolls through a SERIES OF ARTICLES, zooming in and out,
we focus on relevant words:

- "HAWKINS LABS BLOCKS INQUIRY"

- "DR. MARTIN BRENNER NAMED IN LAWSUIT"

- "ALLEGED EXPERIMENTS, ABUSE"

- "TERRY IVES, SUING."

Hopper hits PRINT. The microfiche spits out the last
article. It features...

A PHOTO of TERRY IVES. Looks like a hippy activist. Below, a
quote:

"THEY TOOK MY DAUGHTER..."

                    JOYCE (PRE-LAP)
          Will. He always loved Christmas.

INT. BYERS HOUSE - KITCHEN - DAY

The oven heats up. Timer counting down.

Joyce and Karen are on the sofa. Karen stares at the Christmas
lights and newspaper-covered walls with obvious concern.

                    JOYCE
          So I guess putting these up... it
          makes me feel like he's here.
          Somehow.
              (shakes head)
          It's silly. I know.

Karen reaches out. Takes Joyce's hand.

                    KAREN
          No... it's not silly. Not at all.
              (awkward beat)
          ... And how is Jonathan holding up?

                    JOYCE
          Oh -- he always takes care of
          himself. He's good that way. I
          mean, he thinks I'm losing my mind --

Joyce laughs a bit at this. Karen forces a smile.

Joyce's eyes go back to the lights... *Did one of them flicker?* Karen follows her gaze. Doesn't see anything.

> KAREN
> Is something the matter?

> JOYCE
> No, no, it's just...

Should she tell the truth?

> JOYCE (CONT'D)
> ... We're having electrical problems.

As the women continue to talk, we find...

Holly. She sees the Christmas lights flicker down the length of the hallway, one after the next. It's like a light show!

Holly giggles, very pleased by this.

She follows the lights.

INT. BYERS HOUSE - HALLWAY - CONTINUOUS

We TRACK with Holly as she waddles down the carpeted hallway.

She walks up to the door to Will's room. The sign on it reads: "NO TRESPASSING." But Holly pays it no heed.

She pushes open the door and heads in.

INT. BYERS HOUSE - WILL'S ROOM - DAY

Holly waddles over to the CIRCLE OF LAMPS in Will's room.

As she approaches the circle of lamps, one of the lamp's filaments glows. Then another lamp glows. Then another.

The lamps begin to light up, one after the next, zipping in a circle, faster and faster, much to Holly's delight, when --

WHUMP. THE LIGHTS ABRUPTLY CUT OUT.

A silent beat. Then...

A LOW RUMBLE reverberates out of the wall.

Holly, curious, totters up to the wall.

The SOUND grows louder and LOUDER --

INT. BYERS HOUSE - KITCHEN - DAY

BEEEEEEEEEEEEP! The OVEN TIMER goes off. *Ready.*

Karen lets go of Joyce's hand. Smiles softly.

>   KAREN
>   Let me just throw in that
>   casserole, okay?

She heads for the kitchen, when she suddenly realizes:

>   KAREN (CONT'D)
>   Where's Holly?

INT. BYERS HOUSE - WILL'S ROOM - DAY

Holly holds out a hand. Touches the rumbling wall.

It bends inward a bit, sinking around her hand, like it was
made of Play-Doh. Holly pulls her hand away and the wall
MORPHS BACK TO ITS NORMAL SHAPE. She giggles. Pleased by
this. She presses into the wall again. Again. And then...

OOOMP! THE WALL BULGES OUTWARD. REACHING FOR HOLLY. AND --

WHOOMP! Holly is suddenly yanked up into the air.

It's Joyce. She passes her to Karen.

>   JOYCE
>   She shouldn't be in here.

>   KAREN
>   I'm sorry -- she's quite the
>   explorer these days...

Karen looks at all the lamps in here.

>   KAREN (CONT'D)
>   What's all this?

>   JOYCE
>   I told you -- electrical problems.

Holly squirms in Karen's arms. Points at the wall.

Joyce notices. Follows her gaze.

>   JOYCE (CONT'D)
>   (to Holly)
>   You see something there? In the
>   wall? Did you?

155

Holly just giggles.

Karen stares. *Why is Joyce talking to a toddler?*

> KAREN
> Joyce... I'm really... I'm worried
> about you. Maybe --

> JOYCE
> Karen.

> KAREN
> Yes?

> JOYCE
> Thank you for the casserole.
> (beat)
> But I need you to leave.

Off Karen...

EXT. HIGH SCHOOL - DAY

Nancy slots change into a pay phone, dials a number.

Students stream past her. Classes are clearly over.

> NANCY
> Come on, come on...

She waits anxiously as it RINGS, RINGS, RINGS...

INT. BARBARA'S HOUSE - KITCHEN - DAY - INTERCUT

The phone RINGS in Barbara's house.

MRS. HOLLAND (Barb's mom) is the middle of cooking dinner.

She picks up the phone -- finally.

> MRS. HOLLAND
> -- Hello...?

Nancy is relieved. But also -- nervous.

> NANCY
> Hi -- hi Mrs. Holland -- it's
> Nancy.

> MRS. HOLLAND
> Nancy, how are you?

                    NANCY
          Yeah, good. I'm good. I was just
          wondering -- is Barb there?

                    MRS. HOLLAND
          No, she's not home yet --

Nancy blanches. *Shit.*

                    NANCY
          She came home though, right, after
          the vigil?

Mrs. Holland stops cooking. Getting worried now.

                    MRS. HOLLAND
          No. She said she was staying with
          you last night -- ?

                    NANCY
                (quickly covering)
          Yeah, yeah. She did. Sorry. I
          meant, did she get home this
          morning? I think she forgot some
          textbooks --

                    MRS. HOLLAND
          Oh, no, I haven't seen her --

                    NANCY
          You know what, I just remembered --
          she's at the library --

                    MRS. HOLLAND
          Nancy, will you please have her
          call me as soon as you find her --

                    NANCY
          Yeah, yeah. I will. Sorry to
          bother you.

Nancy hangs up. *CLICK.*

Her worry has now grown significantly.

EXT. HIGH SCHOOL - PARKING LOT - DAY

Jonathan heads to the parking lot. Camera bag in hand.

He suddenly freezes in his tracks.

REVERSE ANGLE TO REVEAL: Steve, Tommy H., Carol, and the
female from the dark room (NICOLE) all sitting on his car
like a pack of vultures. Carol smacks her gum loudly.

Steve slides off the hood, walks up to Jonathan.

                    STEVE
          Hey man.

                    JONATHAN
          What's going on?

                    STEVE
          Nicole here told us about your work.

                    CAROL
          We've heard great things.

                    TOMMY H.
          Yeah, it sounds cool.

                    STEVE
          And we'd just love to take a look.
          You know -- as connoisseurs of art.

                    JONATHAN
          I don't know what the hell you're
          talking about.

                    STEVE
          No?

Tommy H. rips Jonathan's bag away from behind. *Sneak attack.*

Jonathan tries to grab it back, but Tommy passes it to Steve.

Steve rummages through. Clocks the effect he's having on
Jonathan.

                    STEVE (CONT'D)
          Man, you're like totally trembling.
          You must really have something to
          hide.

Steve removes a FOLDER OF PHOTOGRAPHS. *Gold mine.*

                    STEVE (CONT'D)
          Ah here we are...

Steve starts to flip through the photos. As we know, many of
them feature Nancy... laughing in the pool... climbing out of
the pool... standing at the upstairs window in her wet clothes.

                    STEVE (CONT'D)
          Oh man. *Oh man.*

                    TOMMY H.
          Lemme see -- lemme see.

EXT. HIGH SCHOOL - ENTRANCE - DAY

Nancy heads toward the parking lot. She spots what's going on with Steve and the others. Concerned, she heads toward it.

EXT. HIGH SCHOOL - PARKING LOT - DAY

Steve distributes the photos to his friends.

>   TOMMY H.
>   Dude.

>   CAROL
>   Yeah, this isn't creepy at all.

>   JONATHAN
>   I was looking for my brother --

>   STEVE
>   Um, no. This is called *stalking*.

>   NANCY (O.S.)
>   What's going on?

Nancy reaches the group.

>   TOMMY H.
>   Here's the starring lady --

>   NANCY
>   What?

>   CAROL
>   This creep was spying on us last
>   night. Bet he was gonna keep this
>   one for later...

Carol passes a photograph to Nancy. It's --

THE PHOTO OF NANCY IN STEVE'S BEDROOM WINDOW. A VERY PRIVATE, VULNERABLE MOMENT.

Nancy looks from the photo to Jonathan. Shocked. Hurt.

Jonathan looks away -- ashamed.

>   STEVE
>   See, you can tell he knows it was
>   wrong. But that's the thing about
>   perverts -- it's hardwired into
>   them. They just can't help
>   themselves.

Steve begins to TEAR UP the photos. Carol and Tommy H. follow
suit. Shredded photos fall to the ground like confetti.

                    STEVE (CONT'D)
          So we'll just take away his toy.

Steve removes Jonathan's 35MM CAMERA from the bag.

Hikes it above his head. And...

                    JONATHAN
          Don't. Just -- not the camera,
          alright?

Steve lowers the camera. It seems like he's going to relent.
But then... *Whoops.* He casually drops the camera.

SMASH! IT SHATTERS AGAINST THE PAVEMENT.

Laughter from everyone but Nancy.

Jonathan drops to the ground, collects the pieces.

                    STEVE
          Let's go, game's about to start...

The gang starts to head back toward the school.

Nancy hangs behind a moment. Looks down at Jonathan
collecting the broken pieces of his camera. Part of her
feels absolutely terrible about this. But she has no words.

And that's when she notices ANOTHER PHOTO. Partially torn.

THE PHOTO OF BARBARA ON THE DIVING BOARD.

She grabs it up.

Then hurries after her friends.

EXT. FIELD WITH POWER LINES - DAY

Power lines stretch for the open sky.

Eleven waits for Mike here, as instructed. She checks her
new watch. Three-fifteen. Mike should be here any minute.

                    ELEVEN
          Three-one-five. Three-one-five.

Something suddenly HISSES at her. *Angry.*

Eleven turns, startled, to find...

A CAT. Staring right at her.

Eleven tenses as its hissing gets louder and LOUDER and --

INT. HAWKINS LABS - SMALL LABORATORY (FLASHBACK)

HISSSSS!! A DIFFERENT CAT hisses at Eleven.

She is seated at a table across from the cat, electrodes affixed to her head. It's identical to the Coca-Cola experiment, except with a cat in place of the Coke can.

Dr. Brenner and the scientists observe from behind the glass.

Eleven keeps her eyes trained on the cat. Intense. Focused.

The EEG needle shudders. Climbing. The same as before. Blood drips out of Eleven's nostrils... Then out of her ears... The cat SHRIEKS... Clearly in awful pain... And...

Eleven looks away from the cat. She can't do this.

She rips off the electrodes and looks at Brenner, tearful.

She shakes her head in defiance. "No."

INT. HAWKINS LABS - SUB-LEVEL CORRIDOR (FLASHBACK)

WHOOM! ELEVEN is dragged down a corridor by...

TWO MEN IN LAB COATS. She struggles against them, trying to tear free, but they are too strong.

Dr. Brenner watches coldly from afar.

> ELEVEN
> Papa!! No! PAPA!!!

The men throw her into The Box.

INT. HAWKINS LABS - THE BOX - CONTINUOUS (FLASHBACK)

The men go to slam the door on Eleven, but this time --

She SCREAMS at the top of her lungs and --

FWOOM! THE DOOR EXPLODES BACK ON ITS HINGES -- POWERFUL -- FLINGING ONE OF THE MEN BACK WITH GREAT FORCE -- HIS BACK SLAMS INTO THE BACK WALL -- SPINE SNAPPING ON IMPACT --

The other man reaches for his baton but --

CRACK! His head turns 90 degrees, BREAKING.

He slumps to the ground. Dead.

Eleven stares. She has paid a cost for her exertion: her face has gone deadly white, the veins in her forehead bulge, blood spills from her ears and nose, and a painful TINNITUS SOUND rings in her ears, getting louder and LOUDER and --

She weakens at knees. She is about to crash to the floor --

But Dr. Brenner catches her in his arms.

He looks at Eleven. His eyes are filled with awe. She has shown more ability than he could have ever imagined.

> DR. BRENNER
> (low)
> Incredible...

He gently wipes the blood from her face. And...

> MIKE (PRE-LAP)
> Are you okay?

EXT. FIELD WITH POWER LINES - DAY

Eleven snaps out of the memory, turns to find...

Mike, Dustin, Lucas, approaching on their bikes.

> ELEVEN
> ... Yes.

Mike taps the back of his banana seat.

> MIKE
> Hop on. We only have a few hours.

Eleven hesitates. Then climbs onto Mike's banana seat, wraps her arms around his waist, and --

The boys are off. Racing away under the power lines.

EXT. HIGH SCHOOL - REAR ENTRANCE - DAY

Steve, Nancy, Tommy H., and Carol hang out after school.

They smoke cigarettes and pass around a flask, mid-conversation. Nancy is not paying attention as they talk, her mind racing.

> CAROL
> ... So I told Mister Mundy -- the
> solution of ten plus Y equals:
> "blow me" --

                    STEVE
          Bull, you'd be in detention right
          now --

                    CAROL
          Saturday.

Tommy H. laughs.

Steve offers Nancy the flask, but she doesn't take it.

                    TOMMY H.
          I bet Mundy's still a virgin --

                    CAROL
          He's *so* a virgin --

                    TOMMY H.
          Maybe you should blow *him*, Carol,
          help your grades --

Finally, Nancy can't take it anymore.

She stands up and starts to walk away.

                    STEVE
          Whoa, Nancy, where're you going?

                    NANCY
          I just -- I forgot. I told my mom
          I'd... do something with her.

                    STEVE
          What're you talking about? The
          game's about to start.

                    NANCY
          Sorry --

She hurries away.

Steve watches her go. Dumbfounded. He sits back down.

                    STEVE
          What the hell is wrong with her?

                    TOMMY H.
          You probably freaked her out when
          you went all psycho on the psycho.

                    STEVE
          Oh, give me a break --

                        CAROL
              What'd you expect, dating Miss
              Perfect?

Carol blows a bubble. Bigger, bigger -- POP!

EXT. WOODS - MIRKWOOD - DAY

A canopy of trees. Rustling quietly in the wind.

We CRANE DOWN TO FIND...

Our kids walking their bikes through the rugged terrain.

Mike and Eleven lead the way, walking side by side, while
Lucas and Dustin trail a bit further behind, out of earshot.

                        ELEVEN
              Why do they hurt you?

                        MIKE
              What?

Eleven points to the SCRAPE ON HIS CHIN. Mike looks away.

                        MIKE (CONT'D)
              Oh. That. I just... I fell at
              recess. Playing baseball.

Eleven stares. *Knows he's lying.*

                        ELEVEN
              Mike.

                        MIKE
              What?

                        ELEVEN
              Friends tell the truth.

Mike sighs. Hesitates. Finally spills it:

                        MIKE
              ... I was tripped by this
              mouth breather, Troy, okay?

                        ELEVEN
              "Mouth breather?"

                        MIKE
              Yeah, a dumb person. A
              knucklehead.

                            164

                        ELEVEN
          Knuckle, head.

                        MIKE
          I don't know why I didn't just tell
          you that. Everyone at school
          knows. I guess I just -- I don't
          know. I liked that you didn't know
          I was such a... wasteoid, you know?

                        ELEVEN
          Mike.

                        MIKE
          Yeah?

                        ELEVEN
          I understand.

                        MIKE
          Oh. Okay. Cool.

                        ELEVEN
          "Cool."

Mike and Eleven share a gentle smile.

TWENTY YARDS BEHIND THEM,

Lucas observes Mike and Eleven's smile. He is clearly
annoyed by it.

                        LUCAS
          What do you think happens when we
          find Will?

                        DUSTIN
          Uh, we celebrate?

                        LUCAS
          No, I mean -- what happens to the
          weirdo? Does she just stay in
          Mike's basement forever or what?

                        DUSTIN
          Oh, I don't know. That'd be kinda
          crazy... She'd be like his new
          sister or something --

                        LUCAS
          More like wife --

                        DUSTIN
          They'd have mutant kids!

                    LUCAS
          Gross.
               (beat)
          I think she should go back to
          Pennhurst.

Dustin considers this. Shrugs.

EXT. FORESTED ROAD - DAY

Nancy walks fast. Down an empty road.

BARB'S CAR appears around the bend up ahead.

It's still parked along the side of the road. Hasn't moved.

Nancy's heart pounds. This is not a good sign.

She hurries up to the side of the car. She cups her hands to
the windows, peering inside.

She sees her clothes from last night. But no sign of Barb.

Her panic grows. Her eyes dart around.

                    NANCY
          Barb?! BARB?!

Her voice echoes across the empty road.

EXT. STEVE'S HOUSE - BACKYARD - DAY

Nancy hurries into Steve's backyard. Breathing hard.

She surveys the area. Clocks the empty pool... the shadowy
trees... the eerie quiet. Sees nothing back here. *Wait.*

There's SOMETHING floating in the water.

She kneels down for a closer look. It's...

BARB'S BLOODY BANDAGE. FLOATING GENTLY ON THE SURFACE. And
below it... there is something else. Some kind of STRANGE
FLESHY MOLD... Growing *up* out of the bottom of the pool.

FOLIAGE RUSTLES BEHIND NANCY.

She spins around. Listens for a beat. More RUSTLING.

EXT. STEVE'S HOUSE - ADJACENT WOODS - MOMENTS LATER - DAY

Nancy cautiously steps out into the edge of the forest.

She looks out. Scans the area. More foliage sways.

                        NANCY
          Barb?

We cut to a VERY LONG LENS WIDE SHOT of Nancy as she
continues to scan the forest line for her friend. Then --

A BLURRED FIGURE WIPES FRAME WITH A GUTTURAL SHRIEK.

Nancy startles, tripping over a root, flipping onto the
ground. Her elbow knocks a rock, hitting it <u>hard</u>...

Nancy doesn't even seem to feel it. She's too scared.

Her eyes dart back to the area she saw the figure.

It's not there anymore.

But she hears something. That awful GUTTURAL SOUND.

Getting closer... LOUDER...

She scrambles to her feet.

<u>And runs</u>.

EXT. BYERS HOUSE - DUSK

Quiet outside the Byers. The sun is dropping. Night is
near.

INT. BYERS HOUSE - KITCHEN/LIVING ROOM - DUSK

Candles illuminate the space in moody light...

Joyce scrubs a dish in the sink when...

Chester BARKS behind her.

Joyce turns back to the living room. Her eyes go wide.

One of the Christmas lights is now GLOWING -- like a single
star in the night. She drops the plate into the sink and...

INT. BYERS HOUSE - LIVING ROOM - CONTINUOUS

Strides back into the living room.

                        JOYCE
          Will...?

Another Christmas light suddenly glows with life, and then
another, and then another.

Until, one by one, the Christmas lights turn on, blazing a bright trail across the walls of her house, zipping down over the sofa and then...

THE LIGHTS STOP BY THE BOOKCASE.   THEN GO DARK AGAIN.

Joyce races over to the bookcase.

                    JOYCE (CONT'D)
          Will? Will? Are you there?!

There is no response. *Wait.* Joyce remembers something.

She shoves the bookcase away from the wall to REVEAL...

A SMALL DOOR.   A CRAWL SPACE.

INT. BYERS HOUSE - CRAWL SPACE - CONTINUOUS

Joyce throws open the door to the crawl space.

She ducks in. She cradles a TANGLE OF CHRISTMAS LIGHTS.

                    JOYCE
               (low)
          Will, baby...? Are you here?

A beat... then the COIL OF LIGHTS COMES TO LIFE on her lap, filling this small space with a white light. The light pulsates ever so gently... the rhythm almost like a heartbeat.

Joyce wells up. She can hardly breathe. He's here, *right here.* She feels as though she can nearly touch him.

                    JOYCE (CONT'D)
               (through tears)
          You're here... I knew you were
          here...

Then... the lights dim. Leaving us in darkness once more.

                    JOYCE (CONT'D)
          Okay, okay... one blink for "yes."
          Two for "no," okay?

The lights pulsates again. "Yes."

Joyce chokes back her tears. Gathers her courage. And then finally asks the questions she's been terrified to ask:

                    JOYCE (CONT'D)
          I need to know...
               (beat)
          Are you... alive?

She tenses as she waits for an answer. And...

THE LIGHTS FLICKER ON AND OFF AGAIN. *"Yes."*

She surrenders to the moment. Smiling, weeping.

                    JOYCE (CONT'D)
          ... Are... are you safe?

The lights flicker on and off... then on and off again.

"No."

Joyce fills with terror.

                    JOYCE (CONT'D)
          Baby -- I just -- I need to know.
          Where are you? Where can I find you?

No answer.

INT. BYERS HOUSE - LIVING ROOM - MINUTES LATER - DUSK

POP! Joyce pries open the can of paint with a screwdriver.

She then stands on the sofa and begins to hastily, messily paint on the space of the wall above the Christmas lights.

She paints the letter "**A**."

Then next to it, a "**B**"...

Then a "**C**."

She's painting the alphabet...

INT. WHEELER HOUSE - KITCHEN - DUSK

CLOSE ON: A spoon stirs rice in a bowl as...

Karen cooks in the kitchen.

The door opens behind her. She turns to find --

Nancy. She's breathing hard.

                    KAREN
          Hey. You're back early.
               (beat)
          How was the game?

Nancy doesn't answer. *She looks traumatized.*

169

                         KAREN (CONT'D)
          Nance? What's the matter?

Nancy fights an onrush of tears. Shaking.

                         NANCY
          ... It's Barb. I think... something
          happened. Something *terrible*.

The tears start to flow.

Off Karen, scared now too...

                         OFFICER POWELL (PRE-LAP)
          I don't know, Chief --

INT. PUBLIC LIBRARY - RESEARCH AREA - DUSK

Hopper and Powell read the MICROFICHE ARTICLES.

Powell is skimming the article on Terry Ives.

                         HOPPER
          Don't know what?

                         OFFICER POWELL
          This lady sounds like a real nut to
          me. Her kid was taken for LSD *mind
          control* experiments? She's been
          discredited, claim was thrown out --

                         HOPPER
          Forget her. Look at this.

Hopper slides over an articles titled "MKULTRA EXPOSED."

It features a grainy photograph of SCIENTISTS and COLLEGE-
AGED EXPERIMENTAL PARTICIPANTS. One of the scientists in the
photo is --

A YOUNG DR. BRENNER. Hopper taps him.

                         HOPPER (CONT'D)
          Doctor Martin Brenner.

                         OFFICER POWELL
          Who?

                         HOPPER
          Brenner. Runs Hawkins Lab,
          remember?

                         OFFICER POWELL
          Okay --

                    HOPPER
          You don't find that interesting?

                    OFFICER POWELL
          Not really. He was involved in
          some hippie crap back in the day,
          so what?

                    HOPPER
          It's not hippie crap. This is all
          C.I.A.-sanctioned research.

                    OFFICER POWELL
          Doesn't mean he had anything to do
          with our kid.

                    HOPPER
          Come on. Just look at that. *Look.*

He taps the participants in the photo.

                    HOPPER (CONT'D)
          Hospital gowns. All of 'em. That
          fabric the teacher found by the
          pipe sure looked like a hospital
          gown to me. Am I wrong?

                    OFFICER POWELL
          I don't know, Chief.

                    HOPPER
          Come on. Work with me, man. I'm
          not saying there's some grand
          conspiracy. Just saying maybe
          something happened there. Maybe
          Will was in the wrong place, wrong
          time. Saw something he shouldn't
          have.

                    OFFICER POWELL
          It's a reach.

                    HOPPER
          It's a start.

CHHHHH! Hopper's RADIO blasts to life.

                    OFFICER CALLAHAN'S VOICE (OVER RADIO)
          Chief? You there?

Hop answers up the radio.

                    HOPPER
          Yeah. Talk to me.

EXT. PUBLIC LIBRARY - PARKING LOT - DUSK

Hopper and Powell explode out of the library. Moving fast.

Whatever news they got -- it can't have been good.

They leap in their car and squeal away.

SIRENS BLARE.

EXT. WOODS & BYERS HOUSE - NIGHT 4

Silence as... Eleven and the boys continue their journey.

They emerge out of the woods -- only to find themselves...

Outside the Byers house.

Eleven stops. Points at it.

>   ELEVEN
>   Here.

Mike turns to Eleven, confused.

>   MIKE
>   Yeah, this is where Will lives --

>   ELEVEN
>   Hiding.

>   MIKE
>   No. No. He's not hiding here.
>   This is where he *lives*. He's
>   missing from here. Understand?

Lucas and Dustin catch up. Breathing hard.

>   LUCAS
>   What are we doing here?

>   MIKE
>   She said he's hiding here.

>   LUCAS
>   Um... no.

>   DUSTIN
>   (through heavy breathing)
>   I swear if we walked all this way
>   for nothing --

                    LUCAS
          That's _exactly_ what we did.
               (to Mike)
          I told _you_ she didn't know what the
          hell she was talking about --

Mike turns to Eleven.

                    MIKE
          Why did you take us here?

Eleven hesitates --

                    LUCAS
          Mike, _stop_ wasting your time with
          her!

                    MIKE
          What do you want to do then??

                    LUCAS
          Call the cops -- like we should
          have done yesterday!

                    MIKE
          We're NOT calling the cops --

                    DUSTIN
          Hey, you guys -- !

                    LUCAS
          What other choice do we have -- !

                    DUSTIN
          GUYS!!!

Mike and Lucas turn to Dustin. And then they hear it...

THE SOUND OF APPROACHING SIRENS. Quiet at first. But
getting louder... and louder... _fast approaching._

Emergency vehicles soon appear around a bend in the road.

A FEW POLICE CARS... AN AMBULANCE... TWO FIRE TRUCKS...

Our boys step off the road as the vehicles blow past.

They share looks.

                    DUSTIN (CONT'D)
          ... You don't think...?

But everyone is thinking _the exact_ same thing.

                        MIKE
            Will...

They leap on their bikes and race after the vehicles.

INT. BYERS HOUSE - LIVING ROOM - NIGHT

BLACK PAINT *slashes* right, diagonal, right, making a "**Z**."

Joyce backs away from the wall. Breathing hard. We now
realize that she has painted the entire alphabet on the wall,
effectively turning the living room into...

A GIANT MAKESHIFT OUIJA BOARD.

                        JOYCE
            Okay, baby. Talk to me...
                (beat)
            Where are you?

A long beat. Then, at last...

The light near the "**R**" lights up:

                        JOYCE (CONT'D)
            R! That's good.
                (as another lights)
            I... G... H... T... H... E...

Her eyes go wide as the final letters light up.

                        JOYCE (CONT'D)
            "Righthere..." Right here...

Joyce tries to keep the fear out of her voice.

It's impossible. Her voice cracks.

                        JOYCE (CONT'D)
            I don't know -- what that means...
                (beat)
            Where can I find you? Just tell me
            how... how can I get to you? What
            should I do?

Another letter lights up. "**R**." Followed almost immediately
by "**U**"... Joyce's eyes go wide with a realization as...

Beside her, out of focus, another light goes on. Joyce senses
it. She turns to look. And now we see: the "**N**" is lit up.

Joyce's stomach drops. She backs away from the wall as...

THE WALL <u>BEHIND HER</u> *DISTENDS.* FORMING THE OUTLINE OF OUR MONSTER.

THE CHRISTMAS LIGHTS GO BERSERK, BLINKING RAPIDLY ON AND OFF, ON AND OFF, LENDING THE SEQUENCE A STROBE-LIKE EFFECT AS THE WALL CONTINUES TO EXTEND... THEN *THE WALL TEARS* LIKE SHORN FLESH AND... THE MONSTER BREAKS THROUGH INTO OUR WORLD!

ITS GROTESQUE HANDS SLAMS ONTO THE GROUND... THEN ITS EYELESS, FLESHY FACE PEERS IN. ITS FLESH PEELS OPEN...

Joyce is too scared to speak. Too scared to scream.

So she just turns. <u>And runs</u>.

EXT. DIRT ROAD THROUGH WOODS - NIGHT

The boys bike through the woods. Fast as they can.

INT./EXT. HOPPER'S BLAZER/DIRT ROAD THROUGH WOODS - NIGHT

Hopper and Powell SPEED down a country road. Fast as they can.

EXT. CLEARING - NIGHT

The boys bike through a field. Whipping through tall grass.

INT./EXT. HOPPER'S BLAZER - QUARRY ROAD - NIGHT

Hopper speeds down the quarry road. Taking dangerous turns.

EXT. QUARRY BOTTOM - EDGE OF WATER - MOMENTS LATER - NIGHT

SCREECH! Hop's car SLAMS to a stop at the base of the quarry.

He explodes out of the car. Powell is close behind; Callahan is already there. It's a circus down here. There are STATE TROOPERS, AMBULANCES, two FIRE TRUCKS.

Everyone is gathered around the shore of the quarry, where a few state troopers are knee-deep in the water. They appear to be pulling something... or *someone*... out of the water.

Hop stares at this in a daze.

> HOPPER
> Tell me it's not the kid...

Neither officer answers. They just watch numbly as...

The STATE TROOPERS haul what appears to be a SMALL BODY out of the water.

EXT. QUARRY BOTTOM - NIGHT

The boys race to the bottom of the quarry. Out of breath.

As they round a corner, they now see the horrifying scene.

The boys dump their bikes. Unnoticed, they walk up behind the State Troopers who continue to work by the water's edge.

The boys take refuge behind a fire truck. They watch in stunned silence as, eighty feet away, the State Troopers continue to drag this SMALL BODY out of the water.

>   MIKE
>   (low)
>   It's not Will... It can't be...

EXT. QUARRY BOTTOM - EDGE OF THE WATER - NIGHT

The Troopers drag the body out onto shore.

And that's when Hop sees it:

THE CORPSE IS WEARING A RED JACKET. *WILL'S* RED JACKET.

EXT. QUARRY BOTTOM - NIGHT

>   LUCAS
>   (low)
>   It's him. It's Will.

>   DUSTIN
>   I don't understand...

Mike fights tears. Just totally numb. He can't believe it.

Eleven places a hand on his arm. Trying to comfort him.

He pulls away in anger.

>   ELEVEN
>   Mike...

>   MIKE
>   "Mike?!" "Mike" what??! You were
>   supposed to help us find him *alive*.
>   You said he was alive!

Eleven fights tears. Upset to see Mike like this.

>   MIKE (CONT'D)
>   Why did you lie to us?! What's wrong
>   with you?! WHAT'S WRONG WITH YOU?!

ELEVEN
                    Mike --

Mike turns around. He races to his bike, hops on and --

Pedals off fast.

                        DUSTIN
            Mike, where are you going?! MIKE?!

But Mike is already gone.

EXT. DIRT ROAD THROUGH WOODS - LATER - NIGHT

Mike bikes through the forest by himself. Fighting tears.
He doesn't look back. He rides faster and faster as...

EXT. ROAD - NIGHT

Joyce stumbles down the road. She's quite far from her house
now; she's shaking, covered in sweat. She looks back over her
shoulder, making sure the monster hasn't followed her, when --

WHOOM! SHE IS SLAMMED BY A BRIGHT LIGHT.

She turns back around to find...

Jonathan's car. Headlights directed right at her.

He pulls to a stop. Climbs out. Races over to her.

                        JONATHAN
            Mom? MOM?? What happened??!

She falls into his arms.

INT. WHEELER HOUSE - LIVING ROOM - NIGHT

Mike enters his house. Breathing hard. A total mess.

Karen is on the couch with Nancy and MR. AND MRS. HOLLAND.
Everyone is talking -- and everyone looks very worried.

Their worry only grows when they see Mike.

                        KAREN
            Mike. What -- what's the matter?

Mike suddenly BURSTS INTO TEARS. Full-on sobbing now.

Karen runs up and holds him tight.

EXT. ROAD - NIGHT

Jonathan and Joyce, meanwhile, are still holding tight to one another, standing in the middle of the empty, lonely street.

We CRANE UP...

In the distance, we see approaching POLICE CARS...

<u>END EPISODE</u>

CHAPTER FOUR:
THE BODY

WRITTEN BY **JUSTIN DOBLE**

EXT. BYERS HOUSE - NIGHT 4

BLUE AND RED LIGHTS strobe the night air.

Police cars (including Hopper's Blazer) are parked outside the Byers'.

JOYCE and JONATHAN lean against Hop's car. Joyce watches the dark house with anxious, bloodshot eyes.

OFFICER CALLAHAN awkwardly attempts comfort.

> OFFICER CALLAHAN
> Don't worry, miss. If something's
> inside there -- they'll find it...

But Joyce isn't listening -- she's too scared.

INT. BYERS HOUSE - LIVING ROOM - NIGHT

HOPPER and OFFICER POWELL move through the house, guns drawn.

Their flashlight beams explore into the dark house. It looks like the place was ransacked: framed photos hang cockeyed on the wall, a coffee table is splintered, a couch on its side.

And then there are the Christmas lights. *Fucking everywhere.*

Hopper and Powell move toward the back wall. We STAY CLOSE on them as they swing their lights at it. And then pause.

They stare, confused.

> OFFICER POWELL
> This the wall she was talkin'
> 'bout, boss?

Hopper nods.

We PAN OVER to the WALL... <u>it looks completely normal</u>.

INT. BYERS HOUSE - LIVING ROOM - MINUTES LATER - NIGHT

TIGHT ON JOYCE as she stares at the wall in disbelief.

Hopper stands beside her as he delivers the heart-breaking news about Will. His voice sounds far away and muffled, like it's deep underwater.

> HOPPER
> (distant)
> ... Trooper saw something last
> night in the water... Sattler
> quarry.
> (MORE)

180

                    HOPPER (CONT'D)
          We're thinking Will fell in three
          nights ago by accident, earth musta
          given way...

The more Hopper speaks, the more his words fade away, until
they are not words at all. Just a HUMMING, UNNERVING DRONE.

                    HOPPER (CONT'D)
               (distant)
          Joyce? Joyce?

She finally turns to Hop. The SOUND snaps back.

                    HOPPER (CONT'D)
          You understand what I said?

Joyce shakes her head. "No." Her voice trembles.

                    JOYCE
          Whoever you found -- it's not my
          son. It's not Will.

Hopper stares at her with heartbroken eyes. Jonathan fights
tears. He's lost his brother... and now he's losing his mom.

                    HOPPER
          Joyce --

                    JOYCE
          You don't understand.
               (beat)
          I talked to him. *Half an hour ago.*

Off Hopper...

INT. BYERS HOUSE - LIVING ROOM - LATER STILL

Joyce throws open the CRAWL SPACE. Shows Hopper inside.

The TANGLE OF LIGHTS is still there. Dark now.

                    JOYCE
               (slightly manic)
          He was talking to me with those --
          those lights.

                    HOPPER
          "Talking"?

                    JOYCE
          One blink for "yes," two for "no."
          I-I think he was hiding in here --
          all along --

                    JONATHAN
     Mom -- stop --

But Joyce keeps going, moves to the OUIJA BOARD on the wall.

                    JOYCE
     ... I made this -- so he could talk
     to me -- I think he was hiding...
     hiding from --
          (she hesitates a moment)
     -- that *thing* ...

                    HOPPER
     The thing that chased you? Same
     thing that came outta the wall?

                    JOYCE
     Yes --

Jonathan walks over. Tries to intervene. *This is enough.*

                    JONATHAN
     Mom, come on, you gotta stop this --

                    JOYCE
     It's after him! He's in danger --
          (back to Hopper, pleading)
     We have to find him.

Hopper tries to be patient, understanding.

                    HOPPER
     And what was this thing -- exactly?
     An animal of some kind, you'd say?

Joyce looks at the wall. Remembering. Her voice shakes.

                    JOYCE
     No. It looked almost human...
     but... it wasn't. It had these...
     long arms... and...
          (beat)
     It didn't have a face...

                    HOPPER
     Didn't have a face?

Jonathan can't take this anymore. He heads down the hall.
WHAM! He SLAMS the door to his room.

Joyce clocks this with worried eyes.

                    HOPPER (CONT'D)
          Look... after Sara -- I *saw her too*.
          Heard her... I didn't know what was
          real... figured out it was... my
          mind... and I knew I had to pack it
          away before I went all the way down
          the hole and couldn't get out...

                    JOYCE
          You're talking about grief. This
          is different.

                    HOPPER
          I'm just saying --

                    JOYCE
          I know what you're saying, Hop.
          And I'm telling you what I saw.
          I'm not crazy --

                    HOPPER
          Not saying you are --

                    JOYCE
          Yes. You are.
              (beat)
          I need you to believe me.

A beat.

                    HOPPER
          Listen. I think you should go down
          to the morgue tomorrow. I think...
          seeing him will give you what you
          need. But tonight -- just... try
          to get some sleep. If you can.

Joyce turns back to that wall.

She's not sleeping tonight. No way.

INT. BYERS HOUSE - JONATHAN'S ROOM - NIGHT

Jonathan lays on his bed. He plays "Atmosphere" by Joy
Division, headphones plugged into his boombox. The SONG
carries over as...

INT./EXT. HOPPER'S BLAZER - BYERS HOUSE - NIGHT

Hopper climbs back into his car, clearly affected by his talk
with Joyce. He is about to drive off -- but then he looks
back at the Byers house with concern. Thinks better of it.

He kicks off the engine and leans back in his seat. As he
settles in, he instinctively touches THE BLUE BRACELET on his
wrist, twirls it. Around and around and...

INT. BYERS HOUSE - HALLWAY - NIGHT

Joyce steps into the hallway. She looks toward Jonathan's
closed door with clear concern. A beat as she decides what
to do -- then she turns and...

EXT. BYERS HOUSE - BACKYARD - NIGHT

Joyce strides out of the back door. Heads into the shed.
She's gone for about five seconds, then re-emerges.

She is now carrying a GIANT FUCKING AXE.

INT. BYERS HOUSE - LIVING ROOM - NIGHT

Joyce sits down on the sofa. Axe at her side.

She looks at the Ouija wall. And waits.

As WE PUSH IN on Joyce...

                    LOCAL REPORTER (PRE-LAP)
              ... Byers' body was found in the
              water of this quarry by state
              police earlier this evening...

INT. WHEELER HOUSE - TELEVISION ROOM - NIGHT

A shocked KAREN and TED watch the LOCAL NEWS from the couch.

                    LOCAL REPORTER (ON TV)
              ... He was discovered by State
              Trooper David O'Bannon...

As the Reporter DRONES ON, Karen fights back tears.

Ted looks at the basement door, concerned.

                    TED
              ... Should I go down there?

Karen shakes her head.

                    KAREN
              Give him space. He'll come to us,
              when he's ready.

INT. WHEELER HOUSE - BASEMENT - NIGHT

Mike lies on the couch in the basement. He is flipping through WILL'S DRAWINGS. His eyes are raw from crying.

Behind him, Eleven plays with the supercomm in her tent.

STATIC HISSES sporadically. CHH. CHH. CHH.

Mike finally can't take it anymore.

>   MIKE
>   Can you please stop that?

Eleven stops for a second. But as soon as Mike looks away --

She resumes playing with the dials. CHH. CHH. CHH.

>   MIKE (CONT'D)
>   Are you deaf?!

Eleven ignores him. CHH. CHH. CHH.

>   MIKE (CONT'D)
>   I thought we were friends, you
>   know? Real friends. But
>   friends... friends tell each other
>   the truth, and they definitely
>   don't lie to each other. You made
>   me think Will was okay, that he was
>   still out there, but he was just...

Mike can't even say the word. "Dead." Shakes his head.

>   MIKE (CONT'D)
>   Maybe you thought you were helping
>   me. But you weren't. You hurt me,
>   do you understand? What you did
>   sucks. Lucas was right about you.
>   All along.

Mike turns back to the drawings. Fighting tears. He flips to a drawing of Will's D&D character, "WILL THE WISE."

As Mike tearfully studies this drawing, we HEAR behind him:

>   WILL'S VOICE (OVER WALKIE)
>   (under static)
>   So if you -- want me o-- your back--

Mike sits up sharply. Did he just hear *Will*?

He whirls around to Eleven.

A SMALL TRAIL OF BLOOD DRIPS down her nose. She extends the
walkie toward him. A VOICE crackles through the speakers:

                    WILL'S VOICE (CONT'D)
               (under static)
          Well -- come on -- let me know --

                    ELEVEN
          ... Will.

Mike leaps to his feet and scrambles over to Eleven, his eyes
gaping wide. They listen together as Will's voice continues.

                    WILL'S VOICE (O.S.)
          Sh-- ould I stay -- or -- should I
          go --

                    MIKE
          WILL?! Will, is that you??! It's
          Mike! Do you copy?! Over.

No answer from Will. Only WARBLING STATIC.

                    MIKE (CONT'D)
          Will?! Are you there?? WILL?!
          Over.

Still nothing. Only static now. They've lost him.

Mike locks eyes with Eleven. Barely able to process this.

                    MIKE (CONT'D)
          Was that... was it... really...?

Eleven nods.

We PUSH IN on Mike, filling with hope, and...

                          MAIN TITLES

EXT. BYERS HOUSE - MORNING 5 - ESTABLISHING

All is quiet outside the Byers house. Almost... too quiet.

INT. BYERS HOUSE - LIVING ROOM - MORNING

Joyce is still on the couch. Still waiting. The axe leans
against the arm of the couch. After a beat, she hears:

                    A VERY DISTANT VOICE (O.S.)
          Mom...

She looks behind her, listening, but the room is completely empty. *Where did that come from?* She turns back and --

SEES WILL. STANDING RIGHT IN FRONT OF HER.

> WILL
> MOM.

INT. BYERS HOUSE - LIVING ROOM - MORNING

Joyce's eyes SNAP OPEN. Suddenly wide awake.

But Will is not standing before her anymore. It's --

Jonathan. Shaking her awake. She was *dreaming*.

> JONATHAN
> Mom. Mom.

She sits up. Her eyes dart to the Ouija wall. All is *quiet*.

> JOYCE
> -- What -- what time is it?

> JONATHAN
> Almost nine. We need to go.

> JOYCE
> Go? Go where?

Jonathan hesitates.

> JONATHAN
> To see Will.

EXT. WHEELER HOUSE - MORNING - ESTABLISHING

Gray clouds gather in the sky.

INT. WHEELER HOUSE - NANCY'S ROOM - MORNING

NANCY stares vacantly into her vanity mirror as she rubs rouge on her cheeks. When she finishes, she rolls up her sleeve. In the mirror's reflection, she examines --

A large BRUISE ON HER ELBOW. Aftermath from her fall in the woods.

The sight of it floods Nancy with fear.

She quickly lowers her sleeve.

INT. WHEELER HOUSE - UPSTAIRS HALLWAY - MORNING

Karen walks up to Mike's room. Knocks gently.

> KAREN
> ... Michael? Can I come in?

A long beat then... Miserable:

> MIKE (O.S.)
> ... Yeah.

INT. WHEELER HOUSE - MIKE'S ROOM - MORNING

She enters. Her face melts at the sight of her son.

He is curled up in bed. His eyes are raw, his hair a mess.

> KAREN
> ... How are you feeling?

> MIKE
> ... I... I don't think I can go to
> school today.

Karen sits next to him on the bed, rubs his shoulders.

> KAREN
> That's fine, sweetie. Whatever you
> want.
> (beat)
> I need to drop off Nance, then I
> was gonna check in on Barb's
> parents... Why don't you grab a
> book or something, come along? We
> can stop by the video store on the
> way back, you can get whatever you
> want -- even R-rated.

Karen smiles softly. But...

> MIKE
> I think... I'd like to just stay
> home... I mean, if that's okay?

> KAREN
> You sure you're going to be alright
> by yourself?

Mike nods. "Yes."

> KAREN (CONT'D)
> If you need anything while I'm out,
> call Dad at work, okay?

Mike nods, "okay." Karen kisses him on the forehead, then
stands and exits the room, shutting the door behind her.

Mike's gloomy demeanor instantly vanishes and he leaps out of
bed. He's not sad, he's on a mission. He full-on Ferris-
Buellered this!

He grabs his walkie off his dresser, hits Talk --

                    MIKE
          Lucas, do you copy? Over.
             (no response)
          Lucas, *c'mon*, I know you're there!

INT. LUCAS' HOUSE - LUCAS'S ROOM - MORNING - INTERCUT

Yup. Lucas is there, all right. He's lying down in bed, on
his side, depressed. He's not even looking at his WALKIE.
He has zero interest in talking to Mike, not today.

                    MIKE'S VOICE (OVER WALKIE)
          This is urgent. I'm serious.
          Over.

Still no response.

                    MIKE
          I'm not going to stop until you
          answer. Lucas. Lucas.
          LucasLucasLucasLucasLucas --

Lucas, irritated, grabs the walkie.

                    LUCAS
          Go away, Mike. I'm not in the
          mood, alright? OVER AND OUT.

                    MIKE
          No, not "out." I'm not messing
          around, okay?! This has to do with
          Will. Over.

Lucas hesitates. His interest piqued just a bit.

                    LUCAS
          What about Will? You mean about
          his funeral? Over.

                    MIKE
          No not his funeral, screw his
          funeral --

                    LUCAS
          What -- ?!

189

                    MIKE
          Just get your ass over here, stat.
          And bring Dustin. Over and <u>out</u>.

The walkie clicks off.

EXT. MORGUE - MORNING - ESTABLISHING

A sign reads: "ROANE COUNTY CORONER."

Hopper's car and Jonathan's car are parked out front.

INT. MORGUE - LOBBY - MORNING

Hopper waits quietly in the lobby. He is alone, save for a
kind-hearted secretary, PATTY, 60s, behind the front counter.

                    PATTY
          ... I feel so bad for that family.
          Poor things.

                    HOPPER
     Mmmm.

                    PATTY
          No one should have to bury their
          child --

Hopper looks away. Patty realizes her error:

                    PATTY (CONT'D)
          Sorry, Chief -- I forgot --

                    HOPPER
          It's alright, Patty. Really.

Hopper glances at a CLOSED DOOR. Getting impatient now.

                    HOPPER (CONT'D)
          What's taking so long?

                    PATTY
          Well. Everything's been a bit
          chaotic around here without Gary.

Hop looks at her. Confused.

                    HOPPER
          "Without Gary?" What're you
          talking about?

                         PATTY
          Thought you knew. Those men from
          State -- they sent Gary home last
          night --

                         HOPPER
          Then who did the autopsy?

Patty shrugs.

                         PATTY
          Someone from State.

Off Hopper...

INT. MORGUE - OBSERVATION ROOM - MORNING

Silence. Joyce and Jonathan stare through a GLASS DIVIDER.

In the glass, we can make out a BLURRED REFLECTION of a
MORGUE ATTENDANT and a GURNEY. A WHITE SHEET conceals a
CHILD'S BODY.

Joyce nods to the attendant. *Okay.* He draws the sheet back.

We don't ever show the body... Instead, we hold VERY TIGHT on
Jonathan and Joyce as each of them have a different reaction:

JONATHAN recoils, sick to his stomach. Tears force their way
out until... he can't take it anymore. He turns, walks off.

JOYCE, meanwhile, studies the body. Scrutinizing it.

She doesn't seem upset at all. She seems... suspicious.

                         JOYCE
                  (to the attendant, meek)
          He -- he had a birthmark on his
          left arm. May I see it?

We STAY TIGHT ON JOYCE as the attendant turns Will's arm.

Off Joyce, studying this...

INT. MORGUE - LOBBY - MORNING

Jonathan sits down next to Hopper. Slumping in his chair.

Hopper notes his pale complexion.

                         HOPPER
          You throw up?

Jonathan nods. Hopper nods, looks away.

                              191

A long beat between them. Then Hopper looks back at him.

                    HOPPER (CONT'D)
          How about your mom?

Jonathan looks at the closed door. *She's still back there...*

                    JONATHAN
          ... I don't know.

                    HOPPER
          All this, with the lights and Will
          and the... thing in the wall...
          How long's it been going on?

                    JONATHAN
          Since that first phone call. She's
          had anxiety problems, you know, in
          the past... but this...
                    (looks away.)
          I -- I don't know... I'm worried it
          could be... I don't know.

                    HOPPER
          Some kind of psychosis, maybe?

Jonathan takes a breath. Not wanting to hear that word.

                    JONATHAN
          It'll be okay. She'll be okay.
          We'll -- figure a way through it.
          My mom... she's... tough.

                    HOPPER
          Yeah. She is.

Jonathan and Hopper share a look. When --

WHOOM! A door flies open and Joyce storms out, moving at a
fast clip. A MORGUE WORKER is hot on her heels, calling out:

                    MORGUE WORKER
          Ma'am! I need you to sign! MA'AM!!

Jonathan watches in shock. Hopper leaps to his feet.

                    HOPPER
          Joyce, hey. Wait a second --

Joyce spins to Hopper.

                    JOYCE
          I don't know what that *thing* is.
          But it's not my kid.

She explodes out of the morgue.

Off Hopper and Jonathan, speechless...

EXT. HIGH SCHOOL - MORNING - ESTABLISHING

Students file into the high school.

EXT. HIGH SCHOOL - BACK OF SCHOOL - MORNING

Steve and Nancy are mid-conversation.

Nancy's voice is low, urgent. Steve is confused.

                    STEVE
          ... I don't understand, you went
          back to *my house*?

                    NANCY
          To look for Barb --

                    STEVE
          Yeah, okay, but -- why didn't you
          just talk to me? That's crazy --

                    NANCY
          I don't know... I was scared --

                    STEVE
          You seriously think --- someone in
          a mask was hanging out in my yard?

                    NANCY
          I don't think it was a mask --

                    STEVE
          But he had no face?

                    NANCY
          I -- I dunno -- I just...
             (Nancy fights tears)
          I have a terrible feeling...

Steve's face suddenly drops, realizing something.

                    STEVE
          ... Oh man. This is bad, this is
          bad.

                    NANCY
          ... What?

                    STEVE
          The cops, they're gonna want to
          talk to all of us now, Tommy H.,
          Carol, everyone at the party --

                    NANCY
          So?

                    STEVE
          My parents are going to *murder* me --

                    NANCY
          Are you serious right now?

                    STEVE
          You don't <u>understand</u>. My dad is a
          grade-A asshole --

                    NANCY
          Barb is *missing*, and... you're
          worried about your dad?

                    STEVE
          Just... when you talk to the
          cops... leave out the beers and
          stuff. It'll just get us trouble
          and none of it's got anything to do
          with Barbara. Okay?

Nancy fights tears. Steve takes her hand.

                    STEVE (CONT'D)
          Hey, hey, I'm sure she's fine,
          alright? She was just upset, like
          you said, and she ran away or
          something --

Nancy yanks her hand away.

                    NANCY
          I... I can't believe you right now.
          I can't believe you.

She strides away. Steve calls after her.

                    STEVE
          Hey, Nancy, wait -- Nancy!

But she's already gone.

EXT. DOWNTOWN - MORNING

Joyce walks home through downtown. Moving fast. Angry.

Jonathan pulls his car alongside her. He calls out the open passenger-side window:

                       JONATHAN
        Mom, come on, get in.

                       JOYCE
        I need to... *think*. You go on home.

                       JONATHAN
        <u>Mom</u>, just get in. Please.

Joyce looks away from Jonathan, picks up her pace.

Jonathan, frustrated, slams the car into park, leaps out, and pursues his mom down the sidewalk. Walking faster, *faster*.

                    JONATHAN (CONT'D)
        Mom, stop -- !

She stops and snaps back --

                       JOYCE
        Jonathan, please, just go home --

                       JONATHAN
        No -- this -- this is not an okay
        time for you to shut down --

                       JOYCE
        Shut down -- ?

                       JONATHAN
        We have to deal with this, we have
        to deal with the funeral --

                       JOYCE
        A funeral? A funeral for *who*? For
        that -- <u>thing</u> in there?

Their argument now begins to draw the attention of a FEW TOWNSPEOPLE. *Rubberneckers.*

                       JONATHAN
        Let me get this straight -- Will,
        that's not his body, because he's
        in the lights, right? And...
        there's -- a *monster* in the wall?
        Do you even HEAR YOURSELF?!

                       JOYCE
        I know how it sounds, I know it
        sounds crazy. It *is* crazy.
                (MORE)

                         JOYCE (CONT'D)
        But I heard him, Jonathan -- I
        talked to him. Will is <u>calling to</u>
        <u>me</u>. He's scared and he's alone and
        I don't care if no one believes me --
        I'm not going to stop looking for
        him. I'm going to find him.
             (beat, firm)
        <u>I'm going to bring him home</u>.

With that, Joyce storms off again. Fighting back tears.

Jonathan shouts after her.

>   JONATHAN
>   Yeah, well, while you're talking to
>   lights, the rest of us are HAVING a
>   funeral for Will. I'll just handle
>   it like I handle everything else --
>   'cause I'm not letting him sit in
>   that damn freezer another day, you
>   hear me MOM?! YOU HEAR ME?!

Once Jonathan stops shouting, calming down, he notices that a
SMALL CROWD is now watching.

>   JONATHAN (CONT'D)
>   Show's over.

He heads back to his car.

PRE-LAP: THE SOUND OF HISSING STATIC.

INT. WHEELER HOUSE - BASEMENT - MORNING

CHHHHHHH. THE SUPERCOMM BLASTS STATIC.

We PULL OUT to REVEAL ELEVEN holding the supercomm.

Mike, DUSTIN, and Lucas crowd around her in a semi-circle.

There is a long beat of tense anticipation and then...

We HEAR SOMETHING cutting thinly through static. It sounds
vaguely like a YOUNG BOY CRYING. *Will?* But it's just there
for a moment, then the crying is SWALLOWED IN STATIC. Gone.

Mike looks at his friends. Expectant.

>   MIKE
>   We keep losing the signal --
>   (excited)
>   But you heard that, right?

Dustin nods. Lucas shakes his head.

>   LUCAS
>   Yeah, I heard a baby.

>   MIKE
>   What?

                    LUCAS
Mike. You've obviously *tapped* into
a baby monitor, probably the
Blackburns' next door.

                    MIKE
Did that sound like a baby to you?
That was Will.

                    LUCAS
Mike --

                    MIKE
Lucas. You don't understand, he
spoke last night -- words. He was
singing that weird song he loves.
El heard him too. Right?

                    ELEVEN
... Right.

                    LUCAS
Oh, well, if the weirdo heard him --

                    DUSTIN
You sure you're on the right channel?

                    MIKE
I don't think the channel matters.
I think... she's somehow channeling
him --

                    DUSTIN
Like Professor X --

                    LUCAS
        (to Dustin)
You actually believe this crap -- ?

                    DUSTIN
I don't know -- I mean, remember
that time Will fell off his bike
and broke his finger? He kinda
sounded like that.

                    LUCAS
Did you guys not see what I saw?
They pulled Will's body out of that
water -- he's dead.

Dustin pales with a sudden bleak realization.

                         198

                              DUSTIN
                    Oh man... maybe it's his ghost...
                    maybe he's haunting us --

                              MIKE
                    It's *not* his ghost.

                              LUCAS
                    How do you know that --

                              MIKE
                    I just do --

                              LUCAS
                    Then what was in that water??

                              MIKE
                    I don't know! All I know is Will's
                    <u>alive</u>. He's out there somewhere.
                    We just have to find him.

Mike looks at the supercomm. It continues to HISS.

                              MIKE (CONT'D)
                    This isn't working. We have to get
                    El to a stronger radio.

It hits Dustin like a lighting bolt.

                              DUSTIN
                    Mr. Clarke's Heathkit ham shack.

Mike nods. *Perfect.* But...

                              LUCAS
                    I'm not risking my life to hear the
                    Blackburn's baby.

                              MIKE
                    What're you talking about?

                              LUCAS
                    I'm talking about the bad people,
                    remember? The ones supposedly
                    after her.

Lucas points a finger gun at Mike. *BANG!*

                              LUCAS (CONT'D)
                    The Heathkit's at *school*. There's
                    no way we get the weirdo there
                    without someone noticing. I mean --
                         (beat)
                    <u>Look at her</u>.

                              199

All eyes fall to Eleven. *The weirdo.*

Off Mike, plan forming...

BEGIN MONTAGE:

INT. WHEELER HOUSE - BASEMENT - DAY - MONTAGE

Dustin and Lucas rummage through the Wheelers' storage.

- Dustin searches through a box of OLD HALLOWEEN COSTUMES.

- Lucas searches through boxes of NANCY'S OLD CLOTHES.

- Dustin digs out a "JEM AND THE HOLOGRAMS" WIG. He tries it on. Lucas makes a face, shakes his head. *Um, no.*

- Lucas holds a pair of GREEN OVERALLS up against his body. Dustin makes a face, shakes his head. *Um, no.*

- Dustin tries on a COSTUME WIG. Lucas nods. *Good.*

- Lucas holds up a LITTLE GIRL'S DRESS. Dustin nods. *Good.*

INT. WHEELER HOUSE - NANCY'S ROOM - DAY - MONTAGE - INTERCUT

Mike putting make-up on Eleven.

- Eleven sits down in front of Nancy's vanity dresser.

- Mike riffles through Nancy's make-up box.

- Mike finds some BLUSH. Okay, that's more like it.

- Eleven flinches as Mike applies the blush. It tickles!

- Mike puts on too much -- she looks like a clown!

- Mike wipes away some blush with tissues. *Better.*

- Mike carefully applies LIP BALM.

- Mike demonstrates puckering his lips.

- Eleven puckers her lips. SMACK!

END MONTAGE.

INT. WHEELER HOUSE - NANCY'S ROOM - LATER - DAY

Mike, Dustin, and Lucas wait on the bed.

Their eyes are all fixed on Nancy's closed bedroom door.

Finally the door inches open and...

<u>Eleven enters</u>. She is now displaying all three elements of her "disguise": THE WIG... THE DRESS... and the MAKE-UP.

The boys stare. With all three of these elements working together, she looks surprisingly... great. *Like a real girl.*

Even Lucas seems impressed.

> DUSTIN
> Wow. She looks...

> MIKE
> *Pretty --*
> (he catches himself)
> -- <u>good</u>.
> (beat)
> You look *pretty* good.

Eleven turns and examines herself in the FULL-LENGTH CLOSET MIRROR. She turns around, checking herself out from all angles. She fights back a flood of emotions. She didn't know she could... look like this.

> ELEVEN
> Pretty... good.

She turns back to our boys. And beams.

EXT. HAWKINS LABS - DAY - ESTABLISHING

Hawkins Labs towers above us. Ominous.

INT. HAWKINS LABS - FREIGHT ELEVATOR

A TEST PILOT rides the elevator.

INT. HAWKINS LABS - RIFT LABORATORY

The Test Pilot steps into the main lab.

TWO TECHS (in HAZMAT SUITS) are waiting for him here.

DIRECTLY AHEAD: <u>THE RIFT</u>. <u>EVEN WORSE NOW</u>. <u>LARGER, GROSSER</u>.

DR. BRENNER, THREE OTHER SCIENTISTS, and a GROUND CONTROLLER (all in Hazmats) watch from the CONTROL ROOM as...

ZZZZT! The technicians wrestle a thick STEEL CABLE out of a POWER WINCH and HOOK it onto a harness on the back of the Test Pilot's suit. They tug on it, making sure it's secure.

One of them gives the Test Pilot a thumbs up. *Ready.*

The Test Pilot nods. Looks to the control room window.

> TEST PILOT
> You boys hear me alright in there?

His VOICE CRACKLES OUT OF A SPEAKER on the control panel.

The Ground Controller answers into a microphone.

> GROUND CONTROLLER
> Loud and clear, Shepard.
> (beat)
> Good luck in there.

The Test Pilot nods. Then turns back to the Rift. He takes a step toward it. Another step. Another. The walk is slow, tense, unbearable. He breathes heavily through his helmet.

He steps up to the Rift. *Now or never.*

He PLUNGES a gloved hand into the Rift, digging it through the outer flesh of the membrane. The surrounding membrane closes up around his arm, enveloping it. This means that neither us, nor the pilot, can see what lies beyond it.

This is a leap of faith. A journey into the unknown.

The Pilot steels himself. Gathering courage. And then...

HE STEPS THROUGH THE RIFT. VANISHING INTO THE *NETHER*.

Off Brenner, exhilarated, terrified...

> ENGLISH TEACHER (PRE-LAP)
> "The brown current ran swiftly out
> of the heart of darkness..."

INT. HIGH SCHOOL - ENGLISH CLASSROOM - DAY

An ENGLISH TEACHER reads from Conrad's *Heart Of Darkness*.

> ENGLISH TEACHER
> "... Bearing us down towards the
> sea with twice the speed of our
> upward progress... and Kurtz's life
> was running swiftly, too, ebbing...

We DOLLY DOWN the aisle to find Nancy. She is looking out the window, lost in her own anxiety, when --

> HIGH SCHOOL PRINCIPAL
> Nancy Wheeler?

Nancy looks up sharply.

The PRINCIPAL is standing in a half-open door.

> HIGH SCHOOL PRINCIPAL (CONT'D)
> If you'll come with me, please?

Off Nancy, heart-in-throat...

INT. HIGH SCHOOL - CAFETERIA - DAY

We are now in the empty cafeteria. We PAN OVER TO FIND...

Nancy sitting across a table from Powell and Callahan.

Sitting at her side: <u>KAREN</u>. Nancy looks miserable. It's one thing to answer questions about the party in front of the cops, but to also answer in front of her mom... *pure torture.*

> OFFICER POWELL
> ... This argument you and Barbara had? What exactly was it about?

> NANCY
> It wasn't really an argument...

Karen gives her daughter a look. *Tell the truth.*

> NANCY (CONT'D)
> Barb just wanted to leave. I didn't. So I told her...
>   (very hard to admit this)
> ... I told her to go home.

> OFFICER POWELL
> Then what?

> NANCY
> Then... I went upstairs, to get on some -- dry clothes.

> OFFICER POWELL
> And the next day, you went back and saw... a bear, you're thinking?

Nancy is terrified at the mention of this.

> NANCY
> I don't know what it was... but I think -- I think maybe it took Barb... You need to check behind Steve's --

203

                    OFFICER CALLAHAN
We did. Nothing's there. No sign
of any bear --

                    OFFICER POWELL
And no car.

                    NANCY
          (completely thrown)
... What...?

                    OFFICER CALLAHAN
The way we figure it, Barbara
must've come back last night, taken
off somewhere.

                    OFFICER POWELL
Has she ever talked about running
off to you? Leaving town, maybe?

                    NANCY
No. Barb wouldn't do that, ever --

                    OFFICER POWELL
She wasn't maybe upset about the
fact that you're spending time with
this boy?
          (checks notes)
Steve Harrington?

                    NANCY
What? No --

                    OFFICER CALLAHAN
Maybe she was jealous -- seeing you
going up to his room and all...

                    NANCY
It wasn't like that --

                    OFFICER CALLAHAN
It wasn't like what?

                    NANCY
Me and Steve -- we're... we're just
friends -- we just talked --

                    OFFICER CALLAHAN
Now... was this before or after you
changed out of your clothes?

Karen tenses up. Very uncomfortable.

Off Nancy, riled up, fighting back tears...

                         204

INT. POLICE STATION - DAY

Hopper stands at the coffee station, mixing a cup.

GARY, 50s, wearing a sweatshirt and jeans, walks in.

Hopper spots him, walks over.

> HOPPER
> Hey there, Gary. Appreciate you
> coming in.

INT. POLICE STATION - BULLPEN - A LITTLE LATER - DAY

ON A SMALL TV, the LOCAL NEWS plays.

> LOCAL REPORTER (ON TV)
> ... We're speaking with State
> Trooper David O'Bannon, who found
> the body...

INT. POLICE STATION - BULLPEN - MOMENTS LATER - DAY

Hop and Gary sit and talk. The TV drones on the cabinet.

> GARY
> ... It was about six of 'em, I'd say.

> HOPPER
> All Staties?

> GARY
> Yessir.

> HOPPER
> They give you any names?

> GARY
> They did. Can't remember for the
> life of me. All I know is: never
> seen that many troopers come with a
> body before.

> HOPPER
> And they told you they'd take care
> of the autopsy?

> GARY
> Claimed jurisdiction -- kicked me
> out. They were polite enough about
> it, but... it all seemed a bit over
> the top to me, considering.

                    HOPPER
          Considering?

                    GARY
          Considering this was Will Byers.
               (beat)
          Not John F. Kennedy.

Hopper takes this in. His gaze drifts to the TV.

On it, STATE TROOPER O'BANNON (who we recognize as the one
who found Will) now speaks to reporters outside the quarry.

                    STATE TROOPER O'BANNON (ON TV)
          ... I was just over here, and I saw
          something red in that water, right
          there, it caught my eye --

Hopper's eyes harden.

EXT. DOWNTOWN - DAY

WHOOSH! Our boys ZIP on their bikes through downtown.

Eleven sits behind Mike, sharing his banana seat, her arms
wrapped around his waist. She looks around the town.

Her eyes wide in awe.

INT. MIDDLE SCHOOL - HALLWAY - DAY

Our boys enter through the back door of the school.

Mike stops them at the precipice of the hallway.

                    MIKE
          Remember. If anyone sees us --
          look sad.

Dustin and Lucas rub their eyes. Eleven mimics them.

Mike nods -- *Exactly.* They continue...

It's empty here. The P.A. system echoes through the wall:

                    SCHOOL P.A. VOICE
          THERE WILL BE AN ASSEMBLY TO HONOR
          WILL BYERS IN THE GYMNASIUM NOW.
          DO NOT GO TO FOURTH PERIOD...

Our kids hurry down the hall, turn a corner, and...

INT. MIDDLE SCHOOL - ADJACENT HALLWAY - A LITTLE LATER

They reach the A.V. Club. *Phew.* They turn the knob but --

                    MIKE
          It's locked.

                    LUCAS
          What?

Lucas tries it. No go. Dustin turns to Eleven.

                    DUSTIN
          Can you open this? With your powers?

Before Eleven can respond...

                    MR. CLARKE (O.S.)
          Boys?

Our boys turn with a start to find MR. CLARKE exiting the
adjacent classroom. His eyes are red from crying.

                    MR. CLARKE (CONT'D)
          Assembly's about to start...

                    MIKE
          We know, we're just -- you know --

                    LUCAS
          Upset.

                    DUSTIN
          Yeah, we're definitely upset.

                    MIKE
          And we needed some... alone time.

                    DUSTIN
          To cry.

                    MR. CLARKE
          Listen... I get it. I do. I know
          how hard this is. But let's just --
          be there for Will, huh? Then...

He digs into his pocket. Tosses Mike a KEY to the A.V. CLUB.

                    MR. CLARKE (CONT'D)
          The Heathkit is all yours for the
          rest of the day.
               (beat)
          What do you say?

The boys share looks. And...

INT. MIDDLE SCHOOL - HALLWAY - MOMENTS LATER - DAY

Mr. Clarke leads our kids to the gymnasium.

He looks at Eleven. Curious.

                    MR. CLARKE
          I don't believe we've met -- what's
          your name?

                    ELEVEN
          Elev--

                    MIKE
          Eleanor. She's my --

                    LUCAS
          Cousin.

                    DUSTIN
          Second cousin.

Lucas shoots him a look. *What the hell?*

                    MIKE
          She's here for Will's funeral.

                    MR. CLARKE
          Ah. Well... Welcome to Hawkins
          Middle, Eleanor. I wish you were
          here under better circumstances...

                    ELEVEN
          Thank... you...

Mr. Clarke is struck by her halting style of speech.

                    MR. CLARKE
          Where are you *from* exactly?

                    ELEVEN
          Bad... place --

                    DUSTIN
          -- *Sweden.*

                    MIKE
          I have lots of Swedish family.

                    DUSTIN
          But she hates it there.

                    LUCAS
          It's cold.

                    DUSTIN
          Subzero.

Mr. Clarke is now very confused. But -- *thank God* -- they
turn the corner and quickly head into the gymnasium...

INT. MIDDLE SCHOOL GYMNASIUM - CONTINUOUS

The gymnasium is PACKED WITH KIDS. Everyone is here already.

They're all sitting on bleachers on one side of the gym. Our
boys' late entrance causes a bit of a scene -- all eyes seem
to fall on our boys and this strange girl who is with them.

So much for passing through unnoticed...

                    DUSTIN
               (low)
          Abort.

Dustin turns to flee, but Lucas yanks him back by his sleeve.

They head up the bleachers.

INT. WHEELER HOUSE - FIRST FLOOR - DAY

Karen chases Nancy into the house. Mid-argument.

                    KAREN
          You lied to the police, Nancy!

                    NANCY
          I <u>didn't lie</u>!

Karen gives her daughter a look.

                    KAREN
          How naive do you think I am? You
          and Steve were just... "talking"?

                    NANCY
          We slept together. Is that what
          you want to know?? Who cares --

                    KAREN
          Who cares?

209

                    NANCY
          Yeah, this is all such bullshit!
          It has nothing to do with Barb and
          she's missing and something awful
          happened to her, I know it, *I know
          it*, and...

Nancy fights back tears.

                    NANCY (CONT'D)
          No one's listening to me.

It breaks Karen's heart to see her daughter like this. She
tries to take her hand, to extend comfort...

                    KAREN
          I'm listening...

                    NANCY
          No, you're not.

                    KAREN
          Nance --

                    NANCY
          Just leave me alone!

Nancy RIPS her hand away.

                    KAREN
          Nancy -- !

And storms up the stairs.

INT. WHEELER HOUSE - NANCY'S ROOM - DAY

Nancy slams the door to her room.

She slumps onto the bed, fighting tears. She digs through
her backpack and pulls out the PHOTOS that Jonathan took at
Steve's party. She lands on the torn PHOTO OF BARBARA ON THE
DIVING BOARD. Barb looks so... alone. *And it's her fault.*

Tears finally start to fall when...

Nancy spots *something* behind Barb. It's on the very edge of
the photo, right where the photo is torn. *The hell is that?*

INT. WHEELER HOUSE - NANCY'S ROOM - SERIES OF QUICK SHOTS

- Nancy digs through her backpack.

- Digs out all the torn pieces of photos.

- Scatters them across her desk.

- Locates the MISSING HALF OF THE PHOTO.

- Lines up the two halves at her desk.

- Mends them with SCOTCH TAPE.

- Swings her desk lamp over the photo.

Nancy's face grows pale as she realizes that a DARK FIGURE is hovering behind Barb. The figure is very blurred. The image was clearly captured while the figure was moving.

But what features we can make out seem... not quite human.

IT IS TOO TALL. ITS LIMBS TOO LONG. ITS FACE TOO FEATURELESS.

Off Nancy, terrified...

INT. HAWKINS LABS - RIFT LAB CONTROL ROOM

Dr. Brenner watches the Rift. Terrified.

He glances at a clock. *It's been too long.*

>   DR. BRENNER
>   Try him again.

The Ground Controller attempts to make contact.

>   GROUND CONTROLLER
>   Shepard, come in. Confirm comm.
>   (no response)
>   Shepard, come in. Confirm comm.

The Ground Controller looks at Brenner. Shakes his head.

Then...

>   TEST PILOT'S VOICE (OVER COMMS)
>   (distorted)
>   Shepard -- con--firm -- over.

Everyone jumps to life. *Holy shit. He's made it.*

Dr. Brenner takes over the microphone.

>   DR. BRENNER
>   ... Shepard. Where are you? Can
>   you describe to us what you see?
>   Over.

                    TEST PILOT'S VOICE
                      (static-y)
             Can't -- our -- hard to --

The Test Pilot's BREATHING QUICKENS. He's panicking. And
that's when we HEAR a NEW SOUND, a sound that clearly does
not belong to our Pilot. Something GUTTURAL. *Otherworldly.*

The scientists aren't familiar with this sound. But we are.

THIS IS OUR MONSTER.

                      DR. BRENNER
             ... Shepard? Do you copy?

                    TEST PILOT'S VOICE
             There's -- some -- thing --

A MONSTROUS SHRIEK SUDDENLY ERUPTS OUT OF THE SPEAKERS.

The lights in the lab FLICKER. Stuttering.

Dr. Brenner calls into the main lab:

                      DR. BRENNER
             Reel him back in. REEL HIM IN!

The techs frantically turn the power winch, reeling the steel
cable back into the lab. ZZZZZZT! The cable coils back one
foot at a time, SLURPING out of the mouth of the Rift. When --

THUNK! The cable catches, going TAUT, and then -- ZZZZZT! IT
YANKS TO THE LEFT! ZZZZT! THEN TO THE RIGHT! ZZZT! THEN
UP! The TEST PILOT'S PAINED SCREAMS echo from the comms as
the cable continues to thrash wildly back and forth until --

THWUMP! The cable crashes to the floor. Going limp.

The Test Pilot's screams come to an ABRUPT END.

Dr. Brenner is stunned. Speechless.

                    GROUND CONTROLLER
             Shepard? Come in. Over.
                      (beat)
             Shepard? Come in. Over.

We hear nothing over the radio anymore.

No breathing. No monster. Only silence.

INT. HAWKINS LABS - RIFT LABORATORY - MOMENTS LATER

ZZZZZZZZT! A Tech reels in the limp cable.

Dr. Brenner and the other scientists are now in the main lab.

They watch in suspense as the cable is drawn out of the Rift, one foot at a time. Finally the last of the cable SLURPS out.

The TEST PILOT is no longer attached to it. *He's gone.*

BUT THE STEEL HOOK IS DRIPPING WITH A FRESH COAT OF BLOOD.

Dr. Brenner, horrified, looks toward the Rift.

It THROBS and PULSES.

Almost... *angry.*

                    MIDDLE SCHOOL PRINCIPAL (PRE-LAP)
                Will Byers' death is an unimaginable
                tragedy...

INT. MIDDLE SCHOOL GYMNASIUM - DAY

The PRINCIPAL speaks to the assembled students with a microphone. A female GRIEF COUNSELOR sits nearby.

                    MIDDLE SCHOOL PRINCIPAL
                ... Will was an *exceptional*
                student, a wonderful friend, to all
                of us. It's impossible to explain
                the hole his loss will leave in our
                community.
                    (motions to grief counselor)
                I'd like to introduce you to Sandy
                Goldberg. She's a local grief
                counselor from...

Mike surveys the crying, grieving crowd.

                    MIKE
                (whispering)
                Look at these fakers.

                    LUCAS
                Most of 'em probably didn't know
                his name till today.

Mike's eyes tick a few rows down and lock onto TROY and JAMES. Unlike their peers, they are not "faking" -- not even attempting to act sad. They're talking, SNICKERING OBNOXIOUSLY.

Mike burns. He notices Eleven clock this.

She eyes his split lip. Putting it together.

>   ELEVEN
>   Mouth breather.

Mike looks away. Burning with embarrassment.

INT. MIDDLE SCHOOL GYMNASIUM - LATER - DAY

The assembly is over. Students file off the bleachers.

Mike walks after Troy. His face red. His heart pounding.

>   MIKE
>   Hey -- hey Troy.

Troy and James pause, turn back to face Mike. Mike's voice
catches a bit. He's very angry -- and very nervous.

>   MIKE (CONT'D)
>   You -- you think this is funny?

>   TROY
>   What'd you say, Wheeler?

Mike glances at Eleven. She watches this exchange intently.

>   MIKE
>   I saw you guys laughing. That's
>   a... a real messed-up thing to do --

>   JAMES
>   Did you not listen to that
>   counselor, Wheeler? Grief shows
>   itself in funny ways --

>   TROY
>   Besides, what's there to be sad
>   about, anyway? Will's in fairyland
>   now, right? Flying around with the
>   other little fairies. All happy
>   and gay!

Troy flaps his arms like wings. James SNICKERS. Satisfied,
the bullies turn to go. Mike fumes. Looks at Eleven. Then
he suddenly strides forward with newfound determination and --

WHOOM! PUSHES TROY. TROY COLLAPSES FACE-FIRST TO THE FLOOR.

The whole school turns to watch in shock. Muffled GASPS FILL
THE GYM.

Troy slowly stands back up. A bit in shock.

                    TROY (CONT'D)
          You're dead, Wheeler! DEAD!

Troy charges Mike. And that's when it happens. He FREEZES.

He can't move. His face contorts... his lower lip
trembles... his eyes fill with tears... *something very weird
is happening to him.* We HEAR a SOUND.

Troy looks down. TILT DOWN: LIQUID stains his crotch,
trailing down his pant-leg. It PUDDLES on the floor.

Troy stares Mike down, fire in his eyes. Until --

GREG MCCORKLE'S VOICE cuts the silence.

                    GREG MCCORKLE
          Troy peed himself!!!

The entire GYM ERUPTS INTO LAUGHTER.

                    DUSTIN
          Holy. Shit.

Mike looks at Eleven. She wipes a drop of blood from her
nose. *She did this.*

The Principal storms over, drawn by the commotion.

                    MIDDLE SCHOOL PRINCIPAL
          Hey, what's going on here?!!

Lucas grabs Mike's sleeve.

                    LUCAS
          C'mon, Mike! Let's go -- LET'S GO!

The kids sprint for THE EXIT, leaving chaos in their wake.

INT. FUNERAL HOME - DISPLAY ROOM - DAY

Sterile quiet. We're looking into the gaping mouth of --

An EMPTY COFFIN.

A FUNERAL DIRECTOR (40, male) is showing it to Jonathan.

                    FUNERAL DIRECTOR
          It's made of softwood with a crepe
          interior... Now, I don't know what
          your budget is, but over here we
          have copper and bronze...

Jonathan listens to the Funeral Director with glazed eyes.
He is only barely absorbing what this man is saying.

Suddenly he notices someone standing across the room:

NANCY. She gives an awkward wave.

INT. FUNERAL HOME - DISPLAY ROOM - MOMENTS LATER - DAY

Jonathan approaches Nancy.

> JONATHAN
> Hey...

> NANCY
> Hey. Your mom -- she said you'd be
> here.
> (beat)
> I'm so... sorry.

Jonathan gives a small nod. *What is there to say in a
situation like this?* Nancy looks away. Suddenly ashamed.

> NANCY (CONT'D)
> I feel -- awful being here --

She looks back at Jonathan. Fighting tears.

> NANCY (CONT'D)
> I just...
> (beat)
> Can we talk for a second?

INT. FUNERAL HOME - HALLWAY - DAY

Jonathan and Nancy sit on a bench in the hallway.

Jonathan is now studying the TAPED-TOGETHER PHOTO OF BARBARA
ON THE DIVING BOARD. His eyes scan the DARK BLURRY FIGURE.

> JONATHAN
> Maybe it's some kind of --
> perspective distortion. But I
> wasn't using a wide angle. I don't
> know. It's weird --

> NANCY
> And you're *sure* you didn't see
> anyone else out there?

> JONATHAN
> No, she was there one second...
> then gone. I figure she bolted.

                    NANCY
          The cops think she ran away. But
          they don't know Barb. She wouldn't
          do that. Never. And...

Nancy grows more scared, more upset as she speaks.

                    NANCY (CONT'D)
          I went back to Steve's, and... I
          thought I saw something. Some...
          weird man... or... I-I don't know
          what it was. And then I saw this...

She meets Jonathan's eyes. He's listening very intently...
but he's not saying anything. Nancy assumes he's just
judging her, same as the cops. She takes the photo back.

                    NANCY (CONT'D)
          I'm sorry... I shouldn't have come
          here -- today -- I'm really sorry.
          Thank you -- for your help.

Nancy pushes to her feet and starts to hurry away when --

                    JONATHAN (O.S.)
          What'd he look like?

Nancy pauses, turns back.

                    NANCY
          What?

                    JONATHAN
          This man you saw -- in the woods.
          What did he look like?

Nancy hesitates. This is... hard to describe.

                    NANCY
          I... I don't know... It's almost
          like... he didn't --

                    JONATHAN
          -- didn't have a face.

Nancy stares. Heart-in-chest.

                    NANCY
          How did you know that?

Off Jonathan...

INT. BYERS HOUSE - LIVING ROOM - DAY

CLUNK! A finger hits a Play button.

WIDEN TO REVEAL: Joyce has set Will's boombox in the center of
the living room. A CASSETTE TAPE begins to roll, PLAYING a
now-familiar song: "Should I Stay or Should I Go" by The
Clash. Joyce cranks the volume. As high as it will go.

She stands up. Slowly looks around the room.

Watching the lights. And the Ouija wall.

> JOYCE
> Come on, baby, come on. I know
> you're out there...

She waits... and waits... and...

INT. MIDDLE SCHOOL - A.V. CLUB ROOM - DAY

CLICK! A BULB FLICKERS TO LIFE as...

Our kids file into the A.V. CLUB. Mike locks the door behind
them. CLICK!

INT. MIDDLE SCHOOL - A.V. CLUB ROOM - MOMENTS LATER - DAY

The kids huddle around Mr. Clarke's HEATHKIT HAM RADIO.

Mike powers it on. Static CRACKLES from the speakers.

Mike swivels the chair to Eleven. She sits. Swivels back
toward the Heathkit. She looks tiny in front of it.

> DUSTIN
> ... Now what?

> MIKE
> She'll find him, right, El?

But Eleven isn't responding. Her mind's elsewhere.

WE SLOWLY PUSH IN on her and...

> DR. BRENNER (PRE-LAP)
> I need to find him...

INT. HAWKINS LABS - SMALL LABORATORY (FLASHBACK)

We are now back in time.

Eleven is sitting at the lab table, electrodes affixed to her head, just like in previous experiments. But this time, instead of a cat or a Coke can in front of her, there is...

A PHOTOGRAPH OF A MAN. THIS IS "TEST SUBJECT ONE."

Dr. Brenner and the OTHER SCIENTISTS observe from behind the glass partition. Brenner speaks into a microphone. His voices crackles over the P.A.

                    DR. BRENNER
               (filtered over P.A.)
          Eleven, can you hear me? The man
          before you. I need you to find
          him.

Eleven seems concerned by this request.

                    ELEVEN
          Hurt -- him -- ?

                    DR. BRENNER
          No. I don't want you to hurt this
          man. I want you to listen to him.

                    ELEVEN
          Listen?

                    DR. BRENNER
          Yes. And I want you to repeat his
          words back to me. Just like those
          old nursery rhymes we used to do.
          Do you think you can do that for me?

Eleven considers. Then nods. "Yes."

INT. HAWKINS LABS - CORRIDOR (FLASHBACK)

We TRACK DOWN the corridor, sweeping past lab room after room until at we reach a room at the end of the hall. This is...

INT. HAWKINS LABS - LAB 205 (FLASHBACK)

The TEST SUBJECT from the photograph sits quietly at a table with a glass of water. A sheet of PAPER is spread out in front of him. He looks like he's about to take a standardized exam.

On the paper: A LIST OF RANDOM WORDS.

                    LABS P.A. SPEAKER VOICE (O.S.)
          Begin.

The Test Subject begins to read the list of words:

                     TEST SUBJECT
          Amulet. Frigid. Binoculars.
          Evacuation...

INT. HAWKINS LABS - SMALL LABORATORY (FLASHBACK)

Eleven closes her eyes. And concentrates.

WE PUSH IN ON HER FACE as she attempts to psychically locate
this man. Her eyes dart back and forth beneath her eyelids.
Slow at first, but getting progressively faster.

                     DR. BRENNER
          Eleven, repeat the words...

But Eleven does not. Her eyes simply continue to dart back
and forth beneath her eyelids, faster and faster until --

The LIGHTS FLICKER and CUT OUT. The room goes DARK. Then --

CHHHHHH! The RADIO in the observation room CRACKLES TO LIFE,
startling Brenner and the scientists. Buried beneath this
wall of STATIC, they hear it... subtle. But there. It's...

The Test Subject's voice:

                     TEST SUBJECT'S VOICE (OVER RADIO)
          ... Orange. Enigma. Valley.
          Profit. Victory. Green...

She's projecting his words through the speakers.

Dr. Brenner listens in awe.

                     SCIENTIST #1
          How is she...?

                     DR. BRENNER
                (very low)
          I don't know.

WE PUSH IN VERY TIGHT ON ELEVEN as her eyes continue to dart
back and forth. Back and forth. Back and --

INT. MIDDLE SCHOOL - A.V. CLUB ROOM - DAY

-- forth. Eleven is now doing the same thing in the A.V. Club.

The kids share looks.

                     MIKE
          She's doing it -- she's finding
          him.

                    DUSTIN
          This is crazy.

                    LUCAS
          Calm down, she just closed her --

WHOOM! THE LIGHTS CUT OUT. PLUNGING THE ROOM INTO BLACKNESS.

The kids startle. *Holy shit.* And that's when they HEAR it:

A STRANGE SOUND EMITS FROM THE RADIO SPEAKERS. IT SOUNDS LIKE
SOME KIND OF OTHERWORLDLY FREQUENCY. THE DIM ORANGE GLOW OF
THE RADIO LIGHTS THE BOYS' FACES AS THEY STARE IN WONDER.

                    DUSTIN
          Holy...

Mike cranks the volume. And that's when we HEAR it...

Whump. Whump. Whump. Some kind of DULL POUNDING.

                    DUSTIN (CONT'D)
               (low)
          What is that...?

Off our boys, scared, listening...

INT. BYERS HOUSE - LIVING ROOM - SAME TIME - DAY

Joyce turns, listening. She HEARS THE SAME SOUND as our
boys, echoing softly beneath the MUSIC. She quickly hits off
the music. Listens: *WHUMP. WHUMP. WHUMP.*

It seems to be emanating from... the wall by the window where
the monster broke through...

Joyce walks up to the wall. Beneath the pounding, she hears
something else. A FAINT VOICE. Barely audible. *But there.*

                    WILL (O.S.)
          M...o...m?!?!

INT. MIDDLE SCHOOL - A.V. CLUB ROOM - DAY

The boys hear Will's voice too, only filtered through static:

                    WILL'S VOICE
               (filtered through static)
          M...o...m?!?!

The boys stare in shock.

                    LUCAS
          ... No way --

                              DUSTIN
                   It's Will... it's really Will!

INT. BYERS HOUSE - LIVING ROOM - CONTINUOUS

Joyce fights back tears.

                              JOYCE
                   ... Will!

She SPRINTS for the door.

EXT. BYERS HOUSE - DAY

Joyce explodes outside. Looks toward the side of the house.

But no one is there.   The yard is empty.

She screams at the top of her lungs.

                              JOYCE
                   WILL?! WILL?!

There is no answer. No one is out here.

INT. BYERS HOUSE - LIVING ROOM - DAY

Joyce races back into the house.

She can still hear his voice coming from behind that wall.

                              WILL (O.S.)
                   M...O...M!

She stares at the wall in total confusion. And then her
instincts kick in. She races forward and begins to peel away
the wallpaper.

INT. MIDDLE SCHOOL - A.V. CLUB ROOM - DAY

Will's tearful voice continues DROPPING IN and OUT as --

The boys shout into the transceiver:

                              MIKE
                   WILL!!

                              LUCAS
                   WILL! IT'S US! ARE YOU THERE?!

                              DUSTIN
                   CAN YOU HEAR US? WE'RE HERE!

There is no response.

                    DUSTIN (CONT'D)
          Why can't he hear us?!

                    MIKE
          I-I don't know --

INT. BYERS HOUSE - LIVING ROOM - DAY

Joyce continues to frantically peel away the wallpaper.

                    JOYCE
          Will -- baby, I'm here! I'm
          coming! Just hold on! HOLD ON!

She tears off more and more wallpaper to uncover...

A SLICK MEMBRANE IN THE MIDDLE OF THE WALL. ITS FIBROUS,
TRANSPARENT SKIN OFFERS A CLOUDY VIEW INTO THE NETHER. A
CHILD'S SILHOUETTE IS ON THE OTHER SIDE. IT'S WILL!!!

                    WILL
               (very muffled)
          MOM!!!

                    JOYCE
          WILL?!

Will presses an open palm to the wall of the membrane.

Joyce is overwhelmed. Tears rush to her eyes.

                    JOYCE (CONT'D)
          WILL!!! WILL!!!! BABY!!!

She reaches out a hand and presses her palm against the
Nether's "window." Her and her child's hands are now
separated by an inch of membrane. So close... *yet so far*.

We suddenly HEAR a STRANGE GUTTURAL SOUND.

Will glances behind him. Terrified.

                    WILL
               (muffled, through tears)
          Mom... it's -- it's coming --

                    JOYCE
          Oh God --

Joyce begins to TEAR at the membrane. Clawing at it with her
nails. But it's thick, like rubber.

She can't get through it. And she's running out of time: The
PLASTER is closing up over the membrane. It's like the
window is <u>sealing up</u>.

She presses her palm against the membrane. Fights tears.

                    JOYCE (CONT'D)
          Where are you, baby?! How -- how
          do I get to you?!

                    WILL
               (muffled)
          I-I don't know -- !

                    JOYCE
          What does it look like? Just tell
          me what it looks like...

INT. MIDDLE SCHOOL - A.V. CLUB ROOM - DAY

The boys continue to listen raptly.

                    WILL'S VOICE (OVER RADIO)
               (filtered)
          Like home -- but it's dark -- so
          dark and empty -- cold -- please
          Mom --

THE GUTTURAL RUMBLE echoes through the receiver. Closer,
louder. The boys hear it. Terrified.

INT. BYERS HOUSE - LIVING ROOM - DAY

Joyce shouts to Will through the membrane.

                    JOYCE
          WILL, BABY. LISTEN TO ME. I
          PROMISE I'M GONNA GET YOU, BUT
          RIGHT NOW -- YOU HAVE TO RUN!

                    WILL
               (muffled)
          MOM, PLEASE --

                    JOYCE
          I WILL FIND YOU BABY! I PROMISE.
          BUT YOU HAVE TO HIDE! <u>NOW</u>!

Will pulls his hand off the membrane "window" just as...

THE WALL CLOSES UP OVER THE MEMBRANE.

INT. MIDDLE SCHOOL - A.V. CLUB ROOM - SAME

ZZZZT-WHOOOOM! The radio SPARKS and EXPLODES INTO FLAMES.

The boys leap back.

> LUCAS
> JESUS!

BEEP! BEEP! BEEP! The FIRE ALARM BLARES loudly, unending.

Dustin grabs a nearby FIRE EXTINGUISHER.

FWOOSH! -- he douses the fire out.

Mike turns to Eleven. His face drops in horror. She doesn't look good. Her body is weak, her face is GHOSTLY WHITE, and she's dripping with sweat. She looks... *sick.*

Mike kneels beside her.

> MIKE
> El?? Are you okay? Can you move?!

She looks at Mike. Opens her eyes. Nods weakly.

Mike turns to the other boys.

> MIKE (CONT'D)
> Help me with her, come on!

They help Eleven onto her feet as...

INT. BYERS HOUSE - LIVING ROOM - DAY

Joyce grabs up the AXE. She lifts it OVER HER HEAD and --

WHACK! Swings it into the wall. The wall dents. Splinters.

She swings again, again and again, going full-on "Jack Torrance" on that bitch. CRAAAASH!! The axe FINALLY SMASHES ALL THE WAY through the PLASTER. She wrenches it free and --

Her face falls. Through the HOLE in the wall she sees...

Her twisting driveway. No Nether. No Will.

EXT. BYERS HOUSE - DAY - CONTINUOUS

WIDEN OUT: Joyce leans on the axe handle, breathless, her small figure perfectly framed by the hole in her wall.

We HOLD on this image a beat and then...

INT. MIDDLE SCHOOL - HALLWAY - DAY

BOOM! The A.V. CLUB DOOR bursts open as...

Mike, Dustin, and Lucas spill out into the hallway, pushing
Eleven on the A.V. cart. They look down a hallway. See a
line of kids filing out. Following the fire drill rules.

                         MIKE
               This way -- !

They race down another hallway.

EXT. TOWN - DUSK 5 - ESTABLISHING

The horizon swallows the sun. Casting long shadows...

EXT. OUTSKIRTS OF TOWN - THE HIDEAWAY BAR - DUSK

A neon sign reads "THE HIDEAWAY."

We're outside a dive bar on the edge of town.

INT. THE HIDEAWAY BAR - DUSK

Hopper sits at the bar, bathed in hot neon light.

He's sipping on whiskey. Out of uniform.

An INDIANA PACERS game plays on a small square television.

Hop finishes his drink, signals a bartender.

                         HOPPER
               Another. And another for my friend
               here.

WIDEN TO REVEAL "his friend": <u>STATE TROOPER O'BANNON</u>. He's
watching the game by himself.

                         O'BANNON
                    (nods at Hop)
               Thanks, man. Appreciate it.

O'Bannon returns his attention to the game.

                         HOPPER
               I'm celebrating. My daughter. She
               won the spelling bee today.

O'Bannon looks back at Hopper. He wants to watch the game but now -- out of politeness -- has to talk to this lonely guy.

                    O'BANNON
          That right?

                    HOPPER
          "Odontalgia." That was the word.
          Know what it means?
               (O'Bannon shakes his head)
          Fancy name for a toothache.

                    O'BANNON
          Huh.

                    HOPPER
          Yeah, she's smart. *Real* smart. No
          idea where she gets it. I've been
          trying to figure it out for years.

O'Bannon smiles politely. The bartender sets their drinks down.

                    O'BANNON
          Your daughter, she got a name?

Hopper's taken aback. Didn't expect the lie to get this far.

                    HOPPER
          What's that?

                    O'BANNON
          Your daughter. What's her name?

                    HOPPER
               (forcing it out)
          Sara. Her name... it's Sara...

                    O'BANNON
               (holds his glass up)
          To Sara.

CLINK! The men hit their glasses, drink. O'Bannon smiles.
Hopper too. But then Hop's smile fades, his brow creasing.

                    HOPPER
          I recognize you? You famous or
          something?

O'Bannon shakes his head. "Nope."

                    O'BANNON
          Maybe you've seen me on TV... I
          found that Byers boy.

Hopper acts surprised.

                    HOPPER
          No kidding. You on the case,
          or...?

                    O'BANNON
              (shakes head)
          Just saw him on my patrol. Dumb
          luck.

Hopper takes another sip of beer. Considers.

                    HOPPER
          That quarry where you found the
          boy. So, that's state run?

                    O'BANNON
          Uh-huh.

A beat. Hopper considers.

                    HOPPER
          That's funny. 'Cause I know for a
          fact the Sattler Company runs it.
          Frank Sattler, decent guy, he's
          still got operational quarries in
          Roane --

                    O'BANNON
          Huh. That right?

                    HOPPER
          Yeah. That's right. So why arc
          you lying to me, man?

O'Bannon looks at Hopper.

                    O'BANNON
          What's your problem, bud?

                    HOPPER
          I don't have a problem. I'm just a
          concerned citizen.

                    O'BANNON
          Yeah, well, stick your nose
          somewhere else, alright? <u>The kid
          is dead</u>. <u>End of story</u>.

O'Bannon tosses down a few bucks, heads for door.

                    O'BANNON (CONT'D)
          Thanks for ruining the game, dick.

Hopper watches him go. Turns to his drink.

He finishes it in one gulp. Slams it down. And...

EXT. THE HIDEAWAY BAR - BACK ALLEY - DUSK

WHAM! Hopper's FISTS fly as he BEATS O'Bannon in an alleyway.

O'Bannon is hurt, weak. They've clearly been at this for some time now. Hopper throws him against the wall. Hard.

Hop takes a beat to catch his breath.

> HOPPER
> Let's try this one more time, huh?
> Who told you to be there? What
> were you doing out there?

O'Bannon doesn't answer.

Hopper raises his hand to start again, but O'Bannon caves --

> O'BANNON
> I DON'T KNOW -- they just -- told
> me to call it in and -- not to let
> anyone get close --

> HOPPER
> Get close to what -- ?

> O'BANNON
> The body --

> HOPPER
> <u>Who</u> told you? N.S.A.? You work
> for Hawkins Lab?

O'Bannon doesn't answer Hopper. Instead, his eyes go wide with fear. Hopper turns and follows his gaze to find...

A DARK SEDAN idling on the street opposite.

Hopper snaps back to O'Bannon.

> HOPPER (CONT'D)
> Who is that?

> O'BANNON
> You're gonna get us both *killed* --

> HOPPER
> <u>Who is that</u>?

O'Bannon stays silent. Hopper shoves him down. And then...

He storms over toward the sedan. All anger.

> HOPPER (CONT'D)
> Hey -- HEY!

SCREECH! The sedan peels away, disappears around a corner.

Hopper looks back at the alley.

O'Bannon is gone.

INT. HIGH SCHOOL - DARKROOM - NIGHT 5

WHOOM! A SCISSOR SLICES THROUGH CARDBOARD. Cuts upward.

We WIDEN to reveal Jonathan and Nancy in the darkroom
development bay, their faces bathed in that red glow.

Jonathan is cutting a small square window into a slab of
cardboard. **A SERIES OF QUICK SHOTS AS:**

- Jonathan carries the cardboard over to an ENLARGER.

- Lays out the photo of Barb.

- Places the cardboard cut-out "window" over the figure

- Hits on a timer for twenty seconds.

- Flips on the enlarger. LIGHT floods DARKNESS.

> NANCY
> ... You're -- ?

> JONATHAN
> Enlarging, brightening.

> NANCY
> Did your mom say anything else --
> where it might have gone...?

Jonathan shakes his head. He hesitates. And then...

> JONATHAN
> Just that it came out of that wall.

Nancy stares. *Could this get any weirder?*

DING! The timer goes off.

INT. HIGH SCHOOL - DARKROOM - MOMENTS LATER

Jonathan tongs the photo into a TRAY OF DEVELOPING FLUID.

The teens stand side by side, watching in suspense as the photo develops in the bath. An IMAGE slowly takes shape.

                    NANCY
          How long does this take?

                    JONATHAN
          Not long.

A beat of silence. *It seems long.*

                    NANCY
          Have you... been doing this awhile?

                    JONATHAN
          What?

                    NANCY
          Photography.

                    JONATHAN
               (small nod)
          I guess I'd rather observe people
          than, you know --

                    NANCY
          -- talk to them.

                    JONATHAN
          I know. It's weird.

                    NANCY
          No --

                    JONATHAN
          It is. It's just, sometimes...
          people don't say what they're really
          thinking, you know? But you capture
          the right moment and... it says
          more. If that makes any sense.

                    NANCY
          Yeah...

                    JONATHAN
          You think I'm full of it.

                    NANCY
          No. No. I guess... I just was
          wondering...
               (MORE)

                        NANCY (CONT'D)
                (beat)
            What was I "saying"?

                        JONATHAN
            What?

                        NANCY
            When you took my picture.

                        JONATHAN
            Oh. You...
                (beat, embarrassed)
            I shouldn't have taken that. I'm
            sorry. I just...

Jonathan trails off. His eyes narrowing. His expression
darkening.

Nancy follows his gaze. Her breath catches.

                        NANCY
            ... That's it...

The image is fully formed now. Behind Barb...

OUR MONSTER. STILL VERY BLURRY, CAUGHT BETWEEN FRAMES -- THE
IMAGE IS FAR TOO UNCLEAR TO SERVE AS PROOF OF THE MONSTER'S
EXISTENCE, BUT *SOMETHING IS THERE*.

The air sucks of the room as our teens stare at this *thing*.

                        NANCY (CONT'D)
            That's... that's what I saw...

Another tense beat. Jonathan can barely breathe.

                        JONATHAN
            My mom... I thought... I thought
            she was crazy...
                (realizing)
            She said... that body wasn't Will.
            That he's alive.

                        NANCY
            If he's alive --

                        JONATHAN
            Barbara.

Out teens latch onto this hope.

                        NANCY
            We have to tell the police.

                    JONATHAN
                 (shakes head)
        My mom already tried. *You* tried.
        It's not like they're suddenly
        going to believe us --

                     NANCY
        We have proof now --

Jonathan pulls the photo out of the bath.

                    JONATHAN
        This -- this isn't proof. It could
        be anything -- they'll think we're
        crazy.

Nancy hesitates. *Knows he's right.*

                     NANCY
        What do we do...?

Off Jonathan, not sure...

EXT. MORGUE - NIGHT

Night outside the morgue. Hop's car parked out front.

INT. MORGUE - LOBBY - NIGHT

Hopper enters. He approaches Patty at the desk.

                    HOPPER
        Hey, girl...

                     PATTY
        Need something, Chief?

                    HOPPER
        Yeah -- my damn hat -- left it back
        there. I'll be right back.

He winks at Patty and continues on his way.

INT. MORGUE - HALLWAY - NIGHT

A STATE TROOPER guards the refrigeration room.

He flips through a paperback of Stephen King's *CUJO.*

                  HOPPER (O.S.)
        Man, I love that book. Nasty mutt.

The Trooper looks up to find Hopper approaching.

                    TROOPER
        Hey -- you can't be back here.

                    HOPPER
        Yeah. I just got off the line with
        O'Bannon -- he wants to see you at
        the station. Some emergency.

                    TROOPER
        The hell are you talking about? I
        don't work with O'Bannon --

                    HOPPER
        Did I say O'Bannon, I meant...
            (knows his gig is up)
        Yeah.

Hopper hesitates a beat. *Change of plans.*

WHAM! HE PUNCHES THE TROOPER.

The Trooper flips back onto the floor. He tries to scramble
back to his feet, but Hopper hits him again. WHAM!

He drops this time. Out cold.

Hopper RIPS the keys off his belt.

INT. MORGUE - REFRIGERATION ROOM - NIGHT

Hopper enters the refrigeration room. Shaking his knuckles.
Ow.

He pulls open a STEEL DOOR, slides a COLD SLAB out, and...

Hopper stares down at the VEILED BODY OF "WILL." He takes a
beat, then throws the sheet back. The sight brings tears to
his eyes. It's Will, all right. But looking closer.
Something is off... Will's bloated, white skin is almost...
polished.

Hop slowly reaches out a hand -- and touches the skin... it
bends inward too easily. Like rubber. *What in the hell?*

Hopper pulls out his ARMY KNIFE, flips the blade out. He
lowers the BLADE to the body... and hesitates, trembling
now... *Is he really going to do this?*... Fuck it...

THUNK! HE PLUNGES THE BLADE INTO THE "BODY'S" ABDOMEN.

He drags the blade lengthwise, like an autopsy incision. He
takes the blade out, uses both hands to pry apart the wound
and --

THERE ARE NO ORGANS OR INNARDS. THE BODY IS HOLLOW. MADE OF PARAFFIN. A TOTAL FAKE.

Off Hopper, pale with shock...

INT. BYERS HOUSE - NIGHT

Moonlight floods through a window, illuminating Joyce. She sits against a far wall, slathered in sweat, exhausted.

WIDEN TO REVEAL: The house has been TORN APART. Every wall has been stripped of its paper and several holes have been chopped into the wall. But there are no more membranes. No more flashing lights. No more Nether. No more Will.

The house is dead.

But then suddenly... BRIGHT HEADLIGHTS cut through the hole in the front wall, briefly lighting up the house.

INT./EXT. BYERS HOUSE - NIGHT

Joyce opens the door.

A PICK-UP TRUCK pulls to a stop in front of the house. The engine cuts off, the lights die, the door opens, and...

LONNIE steps out.

He looks at the holes in the wall. Then at Joyce.

> LONNIE
> ... Babe? Jesus -- the hell
> happened?

Joyce doesn't say anything. She's just so happy to see someone else -- *anyone* else -- that she staggers forward and...

Falls into his arms.

> LONNIE (CONT'D)
> Hey... it's okay... it's okay...
> I'm here now...

As Lonnie holds Joyce in his arms, we PULL AWAY, and...

INT./EXT. HOPPER'S BLAZER & ROAD THROUGH WOODS - NIGHT

Hopper's Blazer pulls to a stop at the edge of the woods.

Hopper climbs out. Calmly walks around to the back of the
car. Pops the trunk. Reaches inside. And removes...

BOLT CUTTERS.

He heads into the woods. Passing a familiar sign:

> RESTRICTED AREA. NO TRESPASSING.
> U.S. GOVERNMENT PROPERTY.

EXT. HAWKINS LABS - FENCE - MOMENTS LATER

Hopper approaches to PERIMETER FENCE to Hawkins Lab.

He positions the bolt cutters against the fence. And...

SNIP!

<u>END EPISODE</u>

CHAPTER FIVE:
THE FLEA AND THE ACROBAT

WRITTEN BY **ALISON TATLOCK**

EXT. HAWKINS LABS - REAR - NIGHT 5

TWO SCIENTISTS exit the back entrance to Hawkins Labs.

PAN TO REVEAL: HOPPER. Hiding behind a column. The second the scientists are out of sight, he slides out and --

Catches the door a split second before it closes.

He slips inside.

INT. HAWKINS LABS - CORRIDOR - NIGHT

Hopper strides through the halls of the facility. On edge.

TWO SCIENTISTS walk his way. Talking urgently.

Hopper ducks down a side corridor. Waits for them to pass.

Then keeps moving.

INT. HAWKINS LABS - QUARANTINED DOOR - NIGHT

Hopper reaches THE QUARANTINED AREA.

This is what he saw last time he was here. CAUTION and RADIATION SIGNS plaster the area.

He unzips the plastic door and --

INT. HAWKINS LABS - QUARANTINED HALLWAY - NIGHT

He heads down the hallway. At the end of this hall lies...

A LARGE STEEL DOOR. He turns the handle. No go.

It's locked. Not only that...

It requires a KEY CARD.

                    SECURITY HEAD (O.S.)
          Hands up. HANDS UP.

Hopper turns. His face drops.

The SECURITY HEAD is approaching him at a fast clip.

And he's not alone. There's another GUARD with him.

Their guns are drawn.

                    HOPPER
          Whoa whoa whoa --

                    SECURITY HEAD
          You forgot all the cameras, bud?
          Hands up, right now --

                    HOPPER
          Whoa, whoa, calm down. Doctor
          Brenner asked for me personally --
          how do you think I got in here?

The Security Head relaxes a bit. Grabs his radio.

                    SECURITY HEAD
          What's your name again?

                    HOPPER
          Jim Hopper. *Chief* Jim Hopper.

The Security Head makes a call on his radio.

                    SECURITY HEAD
          Yeah, I've got Jim Hopper here,
          says he's --

Hopper pulls out his gun and --

                    SECURITY HEAD (CONT'D)
          Hey --

WHACK! PISTOL WHIPS the Security Head.

The other guard moves fast, but Hop is faster and --

WHAM! He slams the other guy up against the wall. Shoves
the muzzle of his gun right to his temple.

He motions to the door.

                    HOPPER
          You got a key card for this thing?

Off the guard...

INT. HAWKINS LABS - QUARANTINED HALLWAY - MOMENTS LATER

Hopper swipes a key card. BEEP.

The steel door opens.

He keeps his gun trained on the guard as he slips into...

INT. HAWKINS LABS - SMALL LABORATORY

Hopper SLAMS the door behind him. Just in the nick of time.

SIRENS begin to blare. SHOUTING VOICES. HEAVY FOOTSTEPS.

Hopper raises his gun, aims it at the keypad, and --

BANG! He FIRES.

INT. BYERS HOUSE - LIVING ROOM - NIGHT

POP! A wine bottle is uncorked.

LONNIE pours TWO GLASSES. Fills them to the brim.

He is sitting on the couch next to JOYCE. She is wearing a
heavy jacket to protect her from the cold air coming from the
shattered wall -- now covered by a TARP.

                    LONNIE
          Drink.

Joyce shakes her head. "No."

                    LONNIE (CONT'D)
          It'll calm your nerves. Help you
          think straight, yeah?

Joyce fights back tears.

                    JOYCE
          I just... don't know what to do.

                    LONNIE
          I know. I know...

                    JOYCE
          This whole time... I could still
          feel him. I knew he was close, I
          knew he was... alive.

Joyce looks at the wall. The tarp flutters in the cold
breeze.

                    JOYCE (CONT'D)
          He was right there -- our hands...
          our hands... they were almost
          touching...
                    (beat)
          But now... I don't feel him
          anymore... it's like...
                    (beat)
          He's gone.

The tarp stops blowing. The wind has calmed now.

Joyce looks back at Lonnie. Finds him looking at her with
sympathetic eyes. And she hates it. *Hates it.*

                    JOYCE (CONT'D)
          Jesus. You're looking at me the
          same way everyone does.

                    LONNIE
          How's that?

                    JOYCE
          Like I'm out of my goddamn mind.

Lonnie considers. He reaches out and takes her hand.

                    LONNIE
          Joyce... I know you don't want to
          hear this... but I think you need
          to seriously consider the
          possibility that all this... it's
          in your head.

Joyce looks away.

                    LONNIE (CONT'D)
          Remember your Aunt Darlene --

                    JOYCE
          This isn't like that --

                    LONNIE
          No? You experience something like
          this... your mind can make things
          up to help you cope, you know? I
          mean, Jesus, there's a funeral
          tomorrow, for *our little boy*...
               (lets that sink in)
          And you're sayin' his body's fake?
          And he's in the wall? How do you
          explain *any* of that? It doesn't
          make any sense. It just doesn't.
               (beat)
          At least... talk to a shrink or, or
          what about Pastor Charles -- ?

                    JOYCE
          They can't help --

                    LONNIE
          Joyce. You just told me yourself
          that Will's gone.
               (MORE)

                              241

LONNIE (CONT'D)
(beat)
What else is there to do?

Joyce considers. *Doesn't know.* She picks up the wine.

And begins to drink.

INT. HAWKINS LABS - SMALL LABORATORY - NIGHT

WHAM! WHAM! WHAM! Guards POUND on the steel door.

The keypad is fried, keeping them out as...

Hopper explores the lab. Sweeps his flashlight around.

HOPPER
Will, you in here?! Will?!

There are white-tiled walls... rooms with observation
windows... EEG and other strange lab equipment. We recognize
this as the place where Eleven was experimented on.

Hopper finds a closed door. Swings it open.

INT. HAWKINS LABS - ELEVEN'S ROOM - NIGHT

Hopper's flashlight falls on a STUFFED ANIMAL ON THE BED.

A *kid* was here. He moves the flashlight to the wall. There
is a CHILD'S DRAWING OF A TALL MAN STANDING WITH A YOUNG
CHILD.

The Tall Man is labeled "Papa." The Child, "11."

Off Hopper, staring, freaked out...

INT. WHEELER HOUSE - BASEMENT - NIGHT

ELEVEN is curled up on the couch. Exhausted and weak.

THE BOYS pace as they try to decipher what Will was saying on
the radio.

MIKE
... Like home... like home... but
dark --

LUCAS
And empty --

MIKE
Empty. And cold -- did he say
cold?

242

                    LUCAS
          I don't know. The stupid radio
          kept going in and out --

                    DUSTIN
               (to himself)
          It's like riddles in the dark.

                    MIKE
          Like home... like home... like his
          house?

                    LUCAS
          Or maybe like Hawkins --

                    ELEVEN
               (low)
          Upside down.

Everyone turns to Eleven.

                    LUCAS
          What'd she say?

                    MIKE
               (realizing)
          Upside down...

                    LUCAS
          What?

                    MIKE
          Upside down!

Mike scrambles over to the DUNGEONS-AND-DRAGONS BOARD.

                    MIKE (CONT'D)
          When El showed us where Will was...
          she flipped the board over,
          remember? *Upside down.*

He flips the board over. The flip side is SOLID BLACK.

                    MIKE (CONT'D)
          Dark. Empty.

Lucas and Dustin share looks.

                    LUCAS
          Do you understand what he's talking
          about?

                    DUSTIN
          No.

                    MIKE
          Guys, come on, just think about it.
          When El took us to find Will, she
          took us to his house, right?

                    LUCAS
          Yeah, and he wasn't there --

                    MIKE
          But what if he was there. What if
          we just couldn't see him. What if
          -- he was on the other side.

Mike flips the game board back to its right side.

                    MIKE (CONT'D)
          What if this is Hawkins...

He flips the board upside down again.

                    MIKE (CONT'D)
          ... and this -- this is where Will
          is.
                    (beat)
          The Upside Down.

The boys share looks.

                    DUSTIN
                    (realizing)
          ... Like the Vale of Shadows...

Mike nods. *Exactly.*

INT. HAWKINS LABS - FREIGHT ELEVATOR CORRIDOR - NIGHT

Hopper races through the hallways, calling out now:

                    HOPPER
          Will? Will?? Can you hear me?!

No answer -- except for SHOUTING coming nearby. Hop turns.
Sees FLASHLIGHTS coming his way. *Guards.* He races forward --

Only to reach a FREIGHT ELEVATOR. *Nowhere to go but down.*

He hits the CALL button.

The metal doors GRIND open and...

INT. WHEELER HOUSE - BASEMENT - NIGHT

WHOOM! The "DUNGEON MASTER HANDBOOK" flies open.

Dustin flips through the pages like a madman until at last he stops on a DRAWING OF A FOGGY AND SINISTER FANTASY WORLD.

The drawing is labeled: THE VALE OF SHADOWS.

Mike and Lucas lean over Dustin as reads:

                    DUSTIN
          "The Vale of Shadows is a dimension
          that is a dark reflection or 'echo'
          of our world..."

INT. HAWKINS LABS - SUB-LEVEL CORRIDOR

WHOOM! The freight elevator doors open.

Hopper steps out into the subterranean corridor. Right away he is struck by the strange atmosphere in here... the wet floor... the sputtering lights... the cracked walls.

He inhales the strange atmosphere. Coughs.

                    HOPPER
          He-hello? WILL?!!

His voice echoes down the tunnel. No answer.

He covers his mouth with his sleeve and keeps moving.

                    DUSTIN (V.O.)
          "... a place of decay and death..."

INT. WHEELER HOUSE - BASEMENT - NIGHT

Dustin continues to read from the passage.

                    DUSTIN
          "... a plane out of phase. A place
          of monsters..."

Dustin looks up. His eyes wide.

                    DUSTIN (CONT'D)
          "... It is right next to you, and
          you don't even see it."

                    MIKE
               (scared)
          An alternate dimension...

                    LUCAS
          But how do we get there?

                    DUSTIN
          You cast shadowwalk --

                    LUCAS
          In *real life*, dummy.

                    DUSTIN
          I know we can't shadowwalk. But
          maybe *she* can.

All eyes turn to Eleven.

                    MIKE
          Do you know how we get there? To
          the Upside Down?

Eleven hesitates. Then shakes her head. "No."

                    DUSTIN
          What do we do?

                    MIKE
          I don't know...

Mike looks back at the D&D manual. At a loss.

We PUSH IN on the illustration of this dark world as...

INT. HAWKINS LABS - RIFT LABORATORY

Hopper slips into the Rift lab. A Lovecraftian nightmare.

                    HOPPER
          Will...? Will?!

His voice sounds hollow, distant. He stumbles, and his cough
is worse now. Being in here unprotected is clearly a bad
idea. But he presses on. Exploring with his flashlight.

He sees the isolation tank. Filled with water...

All those strange, wet growths. And at last...

THE RIFT ITSELF. THROBBING. ALIVE.

Hopper steps up to the Rift. *What the hell?*

He places a hand against it. It pulses outward.

WHOOSH! A SUDDEN BLUR OF MOVEMENT BEHIND HIM.

Hopper spins around. Can't see anything in the fog.

He raises his gun. It trembles weakly in his hand. He can
barely stand now, much less fire a gun properly.

                    HOPPER (CONT'D)
          Wh-who's there?? WHO'S THERE?

He spins to his right. Sees nothing.

To his left. Nothing.

Back around --

A MAN IN A BLACK GAS MASK IS STANDING RIGHT IN FRONT OF HIM.

BEFORE HOPPER CAN REACT -- WHAM! -- A SECOND MAN IN A GAS MASK
GRABS HIM FROM BEHIND AND JAMS A NEEDLE INTO HIS NECK --

HOPPER CRUMPLES TO THE GROUND AND --

<u>ALL GOES BLACK</u>.

                    MAIN TITLES

INT. BYERS HOUSE - NIGHT

JONATHAN steps into the house. He sees --

Lonnie and Joyce. They've almost finished the bottle of
wine.

                    LONNIE
          Hey kid.

Jonathan's face falls.

                    JONATHAN
          What's going on?

                    JOYCE
          Your dad... he's gonna stay here
          tonight... on the couch.

                    LONNIE
          Here as long you need me, okay?
              (beat, sympathetic)
          How you holding up?

Jonathan starts to respond when he notices the TARP hanging
on the wall. He walks over, draws it back to find the HOLE.

He looks back at his mom. Worried.

                    JONATHAN
          What happened?

                    LONNIE
          Don't you worry about that.

Jonathan ignores Lonnie.

                    JONATHAN
          Mom. That thing you saw before,
          did it come back -- ?

Joyce locks eyes with Jonathan. Starts to respond when --

                    LONNIE
          Hey, Jonathan. That's enough.

Jonathan stares at his dad.

                    JONATHAN
          Can we talk? Alone?

INT. BYERS HOUSE - JONATHAN'S ROOM - NIGHT

Jonathan and Lonnie talk in Jonathan's room.

Jonathan is so angry his voice trembles.

                    JONATHAN
          You need to leave --

                    LONNIE
          Hey, hey, I get you're upset. We all
          are. But I need you to listen to me.
          Your mom's sick, *real* sick --

                    JONATHAN
          You being here, you're just making
          things worse. Like always.

                    LONNIE
          Worse? She took down those walls
          with an axe, thought Will was in
          'em, thinks he's talking to her --

                    JONATHAN
          Maybe he was --

                    LONNIE
          This isn't some joke. Your mother
          was half frozen to death when I got
          here -- trembling, scared out of
          her mind. And you start feeding
          these hallucinations of hers -- or
          whatever they are -- you're gonna
          send her right over the edge, you
          hear me?

This hits Jonathan hard. His dad makes some sense here.

                    LONNIE (CONT'D)
          I'm on your side, alright? I'm
          here to help. I'm gonna make
          things better here. For all of us.

                    JONATHAN
          Yeah. Thank God you're here. I
          feel so much better.

Lonnie looks at Jonathan. Hard.

                    LONNIE
          You behave tomorrow, you hear me?
          If not for me -- for your mother.

He motions to the *EVIL DEAD* poster on the wall.

                    LONNIE (CONT'D)
          And take that crap down. It's
          inappropriate.

With that, Lonnie exits. Shuts the door behind him.

Off Jonathan, holding back his anger...

EXT. WHEELER HOUSE - MORNING 6

It's a gray, sad day outside the Wheeler home.

INT. WHEELER HOUSE - MIKE'S ROOM - MORNING

Mike stands in front of a mirror.

TED stands behind him, "helping" him put on a tie.

                    MIKE
          You're choking me, Dad --

                    TED
          Nah. Should be a little tight.

Ted tightens the knot even more. Mike grimaces.

INT. WHEELER HOUSE - NANCY'S ROOM - MORNING

KAREN helps NANCY zip up the back of a pretty dress.

> KAREN
> ... There we go. You look nice,
> sweetie.

Nancy doesn't answer. An awkward beat.

> KAREN (CONT'D)
> ... Anything else? You can borrow
> my black heels if you want -- the
> ones you wore to Cathy's birthday --

> NANCY
> I'm fine. Thanks.

Nancy turns to the mirror. Her mind elsewhere.

EXT. WOODS - MORNING

CHESTER THE DOG wanders alone through the dense woods.

We HINGE with him to REVEAL that he is headed to...

CASTLE BYERS.

INT. CASTLE BYERS - MORNING

Chester enters the fort. It is empty. He crouches down in the middle of Will's belongings. And begins to whine.

We DRIFT OVER to Will's empty bed...

INT. BYERS HOUSE - JONATHAN'S ROOM - MORNING

Jonathan slides on a tie. Has no idea what he's doing.

He finally gives up -- tosses the tie.

INT. BYERS HOUSE - WILL'S ROOM - MORNING

Joyce sits on Will's bed in a striking BLACK DRESS.

Will's MIXTAPE PLAYS on the boombox.

Lonnie enters, squeezes her shoulder.

> LONNIE
> (gentle)
> Come on. Time to go...

Joyce nods. She pushes to her feet. Leaves with Lonnie.

The mixtape reaches its end. CLICK!

EXT. CHURCH CEMETERY - DAY

Grey clouds roll over the LOCAL CHURCH.

A GROUP OF MOURNERS huddle beneath a tented open grave.

PASTOR CHARLES reads from a Bible.

PASTOR CHARLES
"Fear not, for I am with you; be
not dismayed, for I am your God...
I will strengthen you, Yes, I will
help you, I will uphold you with My
righteous right hand..."
(beat)
It's times like these when our faith
is challenged. How, if God is truly
benevolent, could He have taken
someone so young, so innocent, from
us? It would be easy to turn away
from God, but we must remember that
nothing -- not even tragedy -- can
separate us from His love. We are
here today to find comfort in the
truth of Scripture, and to surround
Will and his family with our love,
our faith, and our prayers...

As he speaks, we survey the mourners. There are many
familiar faces, including MR. CLARKE, MR. MELVALD, and
FLORENCE, TED, and KAREN.

We settle on our three boys. All together. Dustin clocks...

JENNIFER HAYES. She's full-on sobbing.

Dustin nudges Mike and Lucas.

DUSTIN
(whispers)
Wait till we tell Will that Jennifer
Hayes was crying at his funeral.

Mike and Lucas chuckle at this. Karen SHUSHES them.

EXT. CHURCH CEMETERY - LATER - DAY

CLOSE ON: Flowers drop on the grave.

The service is now over. Karen and Ted approach the Byers.

KAREN
I'm so sorry -- so sorry.

TED
If there's anything we can do --

LONNIE
Thank you, we appreciate it.

A wave of mourners now comes up to them, offering their
condolences. Lonnie shakes hands, nods, and thanks everyone.

252

He seems extremely gracious. *Too gracious, maybe.* Like he's
playing the part of "Grieving Dad."

Joyce, meanwhile, remains silent, in a total daze.

Her eyes drift over to the coffin resting in the grave. She
stares at it. Trying hard to comprehend what's happened. *Is
Will really gone?* As we PUSH in on that lonely coffin...

We PUSH IN on her face. And suddenly we find ourselves...

INT. BYERS HOUSE - KITCHEN - DAY (FLASHBACK)

Back in time. A peaceful Sunday afternoon not long ago.

Joyce is making up a peanut butter and jelly sandwich.

Will sits at the kitchen counter, putting the finishing touches on a detailed CRAYON DRAWING OF A WIZARD.

Joyce slides him the sandwich.

> JOYCE
> I see "Will the Wise" is back...

Will nods. Yup. Joyce sits down beside him. Studies the drawing.

> JOYCE (CONT'D)
> What's that coming out of his cane?

> WILL
> Fireballs. I couldn't find the red
> crayon, so... that's why it's
> green.

> JOYCE
> What's he need fireballs for? He's
> so wise, can't he just... outsmart
> the bad guys?

> WILL
> Most of the time, yeah, totally.
> But sometimes the bad guys are
> smart too, you know?

> JOYCE
> So he needs fireballs.

> WILL
> Yeah, to burn them to a crisp.
> BOOOM-CCCHHHH! AHHHHHH!

Joyce can't help but smile.

> JOYCE
> Well... I don't know who raised
> you. But I'll get you some new
> crayons. Because it looks like
> he's shooting cabbages.

Will laughs.

EXT. CHURCH CEMETERY - DAY

A tear slips down Joyce's face.

Lonnie takes her hand. Squeezes.

Jonathan sees them holding hands. Fights anger. And --

INT. HOPPER'S TRAILER - LIVING ROOM - DAY

CLOSE ON: HOPPER'S EYES SNAP OPEN.

He jerks awake on the couch. Sits up straight.

He's back in his trailer. Face pale. Slick with sweat.

He looks around. Woozy and disoriented. There are about a
half-dozen TUINAL PILLBOXES scattered across his coffee
table. Even more empty beer bottles. What. The. Fuck.

He rips his gun out of his holster and...

EXT. HOPPER'S TRAILER - DAY

WHOOM! Explodes out of his trailer. Gun raised. Tense.

There's no one out here. He's all alone.

INT. HOPPER'S TRAILER - BATHROOM - DAY

Hopper checks his neck in the mirror.

No sign of being jabbed by a needle.

INT. HOPPER'S TRAILER - LATER - DAY

Hopper now searches his trailer in a paranoid frenzy. We're
talking full-Gene Hackman. A SERIES OF FRANTIC SHOTS as --

- Hopper checks under his sofa cushions. Nothing.

- Smashes his phone receiver. Opens it. Nothing.

- Cuts open the cushions with a razor. Nothing.

- Unscrews the bottom of his phone. Nothing.

- Checks the ceiling fixture in the main room. *And...*

- He's found it. A SMALL LISTENING "BUG."

Off Hopper, paranoia growing...

INT. HAWKINS LABS - AUDIO ROOM - DAY

DR. BRENNER sits in an audio room. Headphones on.

He is listening to a RECORDING of familiar voices...

                    WILL'S VOICE (RECORDING)
                 (filtered through static)
         M...o...m?!?!

                    MIKE'S VOICE
         WILL!!

                    LUCAS'S VOICE
         WILL! IT'S US! ARE YOU THERE?!

                    DUSTIN'S VOICE
         CAN YOU HEAR US? WE'RE HERE!

It's a recording of our boys' communication with Will.

Dr. Brenner looks up at the LEAD AGENT. Nods.

                    DR. BRENNER
         She was there.

Off the Agent...

EXT. CHURCH CEMETERY - DAY

TOWNSPEOPLE file toward the church for the reception.

EXT. CHURCH CEMETERY - MAUSOLEUM - DAY

We find Nancy sitting behind a mausoleum with Jonathan.

Jonathan is showing her a wrinkled map of the town. He
points to three areas on the map MARKED IN RED INK.

                    JONATHAN
         This is where we know for sure it's
         been, right?

                    NANCY
         So that's --

                    JONATHAN
         The woods by Steve's.
            (motions to a second spot)
         That's where they found Will's
         bike.
            (third spot)
         And that -- that's my house.

                    NANCY
         It's all so close --

                              256

                    JONATHAN
          Yeah, exactly. It's like a mile or
          something. This thing, whatever it
          is -- it's not traveling far.

Nancy suddenly realizes what Jonathan's getting at.

                    NANCY
          You want to go out there.

                    JONATHAN
          We might not find anything, but --

                    NANCY
          I found something.

Jonathan nods. *Exactly.*

                    NANCY (CONT'D)
          If we do... see it? Then what?

EXT./INT. LONNIE'S TRUCK - CHURCH CEMETERY - DAY

Jonathan swings open the door to his dad's car. Climbs in.

Nancy stands outside, watching him, anxious, as...

He tries to open the glove compartment. It's locked.

He removes a pocket knife, begins to jimmy the lock.

                    NANCY
          What are you doing?

                    JONATHAN
          Just give me a second.

Jonathan keeps twisting the knife until --

POP. The compartment door opens. Inside...

<u>LONNIE'S .22</u>. *Bingo.*

Jonathan opens the cylinder. Fully loaded. Six rounds.

He snaps the cylinder shut.

Nancy stares.

                    NANCY
          Are you serious?

                    JONATHAN
You want to find this thing and,
what, take another picture? Yell
at it?

Jonathan digs around, finds more ammo boxes. Stuffs them in his jacket pocket.

>NANCY
>This is a terrible idea --

>JONATHAN
>You want to tell someone, go ahead.
>But they won't believe us. You
>know they won't --

>NANCY
>Your mom would.

Jonathan looks up at Nancy. He feels guilty about this, but...

>JONATHAN
>She's been through enough.

>NANCY
>She deserves to know --

>JONATHAN
>Yeah, and we'll tell her. When
>this thing is dead. Okay?

Jonathan climbs out of the car.

>NANCY
>This is all just so...

>JONATHAN
>Crazy?

Nancy looks at Jonathan. Nods.

>NANCY
>Yeah. Crazy.

Jonathan nods. *True.* He SLAMS the door shut. WHAM!

EXT. MIDDLE SCHOOL - DAY

The flag hangs at half-staff. School is in mourning today.

INT. MIDDLE SCHOOL - A.V. CLUB - DAY

The MIDDLE SCHOOL PRINCIPAL leads a "REPAIR MAN" into the A.V. CLUB. This guy seems oddly familiar to us...

                    MIDDLE SCHOOL PRINCIPAL
          I don't know what in the world
          caused it...

                         REPAIR MAN
          Well, let's take a look, huh...?

The Repair Man crouches down by...

THE HAM RADIO. It's fried to a crisp. Dials, speakers
melted. He inspects the machine, the cord, the outlet.

                    MIDDLE SCHOOL PRINCIPAL
          Mr. Clarke says he's never seen
          anything like it.

                         REPAIR MAN
          Mr. Clarke?

                    MIDDLE SCHOOL PRINCIPAL
          He runs our A.V. club.

                         REPAIR MAN
          That right?

                    MIDDLE SCHOOL PRINCIPAL
          Apparently some of the less-
          athletic types go nuts for this
          stuff.

                         REPAIR MAN
          Any kids here at the time?

                    MIDDLE SCHOOL PRINCIPAL
          I don't think so. This seems like
          an electrical problem to me.
          Nothing a kid could do, right?

Off the Repair Man, knowing better...

INT./EXT. POWER & LIGHT VAN - OUTSIDE MIDDLE SCHOOL - DAY

The Repair Man climbs into a familiar "HAWKINS POWER &
LIGHT" VAN.

Sitting in the driver's seat: the LEAD AGENT.

The Agent shifts into DRIVE and...

Speeds away.

INT. CHURCH - RECEPTION AREA - DAY

The most boring reception ever.

Mr. Clarke loads cheese and crackers onto a paper plate.

                    MIKE (O.S.)
          Mr. Clarke?

He turns to find Mike, Dustin, and Lucas.

His face melts. *These poor kids...*

                    MR. CLARKE
          Oh, hey there. How you boys
          holding up?

                    LUCAS
          We're in mourning.

Dustin nibbles on a wafer.

                    DUSTIN
          Aw man, these aren't real Nilla
          Wafers.

Mike pretends Dustin didn't just speak.

                    MIKE
          We were wondering... Do you have
          time to talk?

                    LUCAS
          We have some questions.

                    MIKE
          A lot of questions.

Off Mr. Clarke...

INT. CHURCH - RECEPTION AREA - MOMENTS LATER - DAY

The boys now sit across from Mr. Clarke at a table.

Dustin nibbles on more wafers. *Clearly likes them enough.*

                    MIKE
          ... You know how in *Cosmos,* Carl
          Sagan talked about how there are
          other dimensions? Like beyond our
          world?

                    MR. CLARKE
          Yeah. Sure. Theoretically.

                    MIKE
          Right. Theoretically.

                    LUCAS
          So theoretically -- how would you
          travel there?

Mr. Clarke thinks he now "gets" what this is all about.

                    MR. CLARKE
          You guys have been thinking about
          Hugh Everett's "many worlds"
          interpretation, haven't you?

The boys exchange looks. *Uhhhh...*

                    MR. CLARKE (CONT'D)
          Basically -- there are parallel
          universes. Just like our world,
          but just *infinite variations* of it.
          Which means there's a world out
          there where... none of this tragic
          stuff ever happened --

                    LUCAS
          Yeah, that's not what we're talking
          about.

                    MR. CLARKE
          Oh.

                    DUSTIN
          We're talking about an evil
          dimension, like the Vale of Shadows
          -- do you know the Vale of Shadows?

                    MR. CLARKE
          An echo of the Material Plane,
          where necrotic and shadow magic --

                    MIKE
               (interrupting)
          Yeah, exactly. If it existed, a
          place like the Vale of Shadows --
          how would you travel there?

                    LUCAS
          Theoretically.

                    MR. CLARKE
          Well...

Mr. Clarke considers. Takes out a pen.

He shoves the little bit of food off his paper plate.

                         262

He scribbles on the face of the paper plate -- a very simple
illustration of a stick figure standing on a horizontal line.

                  MR. CLARKE (CONT'D)
         Picture an acrobat, standing on a
         tightrope... Now, the tightrope is
         our dimension. And our dimension
         has rules. You can travel forward,
         or backward --

He moves his pen back and forth along the tightrope.

                  MR. CLARKE (CONT'D)
         But. What if, right next to our
         acrobat, there is...
            (draws a bug on the line)
         A <u>flea</u>. And this flea can travel
         back and forth, just like the
         acrobat. Right?

                  MIKE
         Right.

                  MR. CLARKE
         But here's where things get really
         interesting. The flea can also
         travel this way -- along the side
         of the rope. He can even go...
         <u>underneath the rope</u>.

Mr. Clarke draws an arrow under the rope.

Our boys share looks. Minds blown.

                  LUCAS/MIKE/DUSTIN
         Upside down.

                  MR. CLARKE
         Exactly.

                  MIKE
         But... we're not the flea -- we're
         the acrobat, right?

                  MR. CLARKE
         In this metaphor, yes, we're the
         acrobat --

                  LUCAS
         So we can't move upside down?

                  MR. CLARKE
         No.

                    DUSTIN
          Is there any way for the acrobat
          to... get to the Upside Down?

                    MR. CLARKE
          Well... you'd have to somehow
          create a massive amount of energy
          -- more than humans are currently
          capable of creating, mind you -- to
          open up some kind of tear in time
          and space, and then...

Mr. Clarke folds the paper plate and stabs his pen through
it.

                    MR. CLARKE (CONT'D)
          You create a doorway.

                    DUSTIN
          Like a gate.

                    MR. CLARKE
          Sure. Like a gate. But again,
          this is all --

                    LUCAS
          Theoretical.

Mike considers this for a moment. Struck by something.

                    MIKE
          But... what if this gate already
          existed?

                    MR. CLARKE
          If it did, I think we'd know. It
          would disrupt gravity, the magnetic
          field, our environment. Heck, it
          might even swallow us up whole.
                    (beat)
          Science is neat. But I'm afraid
          it's not very forgiving.

Off our boys, taking this in...

INT. BYERS HOUSE - JOYCE'S ROOM - DAY

Joyce kicks off her shoes. Rips off her tights.

She's getting out of these fucking funeral clothes as fast as
she can. She pulls off her skirt, throws on jeans, when --

There's a KNOCK on the door.

                    JONATHAN (O.S.)
          Mom?

                    JOYCE
          ... Yeah? Come in.

Jonathan enters. Shuts the door behind him.

                    JONATHAN
          Hey, uh...

He sits on the bed beside his mom.

                    JONATHAN (CONT'D)
          I was talking to Eric. At the
          reception. I was thinking about
          staying at his place. I just -- I
          need some time. Away from him...

                    JOYCE
          He's just trying to help.

                    JONATHAN
          ... I know. Just for tonight.
          That's all.

Joyce relents. Nods.

                    JOYCE
          Yeah, of course. Of course.

Jonathan gives her a hug. Holding tight. For all he knows --
this is the last time he'll ever see her.

                    JONATHAN
          I'm sorry.

                    JOYCE
          I told you -- you have nothing to
          be sorry for. So stop saying that.

Jonathan pulls away from his mom. Looks at her.

                    JONATHAN
          If I could -- I -- I'd fix this.
          I'd do anything to bring him back.
          You know that, right?

                    JOYCE
          Yeah, I know.

Jonathan nods, then exits. Shutting the door behind him.

Off Joyce, alone...

EXT. HOPPER'S TRAILER - DAY

A POLICE CAR CRASHES to a stop outside Hopper's trailer.

Powell and Callahan step out.

EXT. HOPPER'S TRAILER - MOMENTS LATER - DAY

Callahan RAPS on the trailer door. Powell at his side.

                    OFFICER CALLAHAN
          Chief, you in there?   Chief?

No answer. Callahan raps again, harder this time, and --

The door swings open to reveal Hopper. He appears borderline
nuts. And it looks like a tornado swept through his trailer.

                    OFFICER POWELL
          Jesus, Chief. You alright -- ?

                    HOPPER
          What are you doing here?

                    OFFICER POWELL
          We tried calling --

                    HOPPER
          Phone's dead.

                    OFFICER CALLAHAN
          Bev Mooney came in all upset. Said
          Dale and Henry were out hunting
          yesterday but never made it back home.

                    OFFICER POWELL
          She thought they were on another
          binger, but now she's not so sure.

                    OFFICER CALLAHAN
          I think with this Will Byers thing,
          everyone's on edge --

                    HOPPER
          Where was this?

                    OFFICER CALLAHAN
          Back at the station --

                    HOPPER
          No. Where were Dale and Henry hunting?

                    OFFICER CALLAHAN
          Out near Kerley --

                    HOPPER
               (to himself)
          Mirkwood.

Powell and Callahan exchange looks.

                    OFFICER POWELL
          What?

                    HOPPER
Nothing. Just go back to the
station. Let me deal with this --

                    OFFICER CALLAHAN
You sure?

                    HOPPER
Leave it.

Hopper is about the shut the door on them when --

                    OFFICER CALLAHAN
Oh hey -- some good news:

Hopper opens the door back up. Impatient.

                    HOPPER
What?

                    OFFICER CALLAHAN
Barbara Holland's car. Seems she
ran away after all. Staties found
it late last night at a bus station.

                    HOPPER
Staties?

                    OFFICER POWELL
Funny, right? They keep doing our
jobs for us.

                    HOPPER
Yeah. Funny.

Hopper SHUTS the door. Firm this time. And...

EXT. HOPPER'S TRAILER - MOMENTS LATER - DAY

Powell and Callahan climb back into their car.

                    OFFICER CALLAHAN
He off his meds again?

                    OFFICER POWELL
He's been spending too much time with
Joyce Byers, that's what I think.

Powell starts the engine. Drives away.

INT. WHEELER HOUSE - BASEMENT - DAY

THUNK! A PENCIL stabs through a folded piece of paper as...

Mike and Lucas replicate Mr. Clarke's lesson for Eleven.

Behind them, Dustin walks in circles with a COMPASS.

>   MIKE
>   (to Eleven)
>   ... It would take a lot of energy
>   to make a gate like this, but...
>   that's gotta be what happened,
>   otherwise how'd Will get there,
>   right?

>   ELEVEN
>   (nods)
>   ... Right.

>   LUCAS
>   What we need to know is: Do you
>   know where The Gate is?

Eleven shakes her head. "No."

Lucas looks suspicious.

>   LUCAS (CONT'D)
>   Then how'd you know about the
>   Upside Down?

Eleven doesn't answer. Her attention is on...

Dustin. Who continues to walk in circles like a madman.

The boys follow her gaze. Watch him for a beat. *Um*...

>   MIKE
>   Dustin. What are you doing?

Dustin just... *keeps* walking in those circles. His eyes
fixed firmly on his compass.

                    MIKE (CONT'D)
          Dustin. *Dustin*.

                    LUCAS
          DUSTIN!

Dustin finally stops. Looks at Mike and Lucas.

                    DUSTIN
          I need to see your compasses.

                    MIKE
          What?

                    DUSTIN
          Your compasses. All of your
          compasses. Right now.

INT. WHEELER HOUSE - BASEMENT - MOMENTS LATER - DAY

A HALF-DOZEN COMPASSES hit the card table.

The needles all point in the exact same direction. *North*.

                    MIKE
          What's exciting about this?

                    DUSTIN
          They're all pointing north, right?

                    LUCAS
          Yeah, so?

                    DUSTIN
          So that's not true north.

                    MIKE
          What do you mean?

                    DUSTIN
          I mean exactly what I just said --
          that's not *true north*.

Mike and Lucas stare. Still confused.

                    DUSTIN (CONT'D)
          Are you both seriously this dense?

Mike and Lucas share looks. Apparently.

                    DUSTIN (CONT'D)
The sun rises in the east --
      (points east)
-- and sets in the west, right?
      (points west)
Which means...
      (points north, a different north
      than the compasses show)
... *That's true* north.

                    MIKE
So the compasses are broken?

                    DUSTIN
Do you even understand how a
compass works?? Do you see a
battery pack on this --

                    MIKE
No --

                    DUSTIN
No, you don't, because it doesn't
need it. Its needle's naturally
drawn to the Earth's magnetic north
pole.

                    LUCAS
So what's wrong with them, then?

                    DUSTIN
That's what I couldn't figure out.
But then I remembered -- you can
change the direction of a compass
with a magnet. If there's the
presence of a more powerful magnetic
field, the needle deflects to that
power. And *then* I remembered what
Mister Clarke said. The Gate would
have so much power --

                    MIKE
      (realizing)
-- it could disrupt the
electromagnetic field --

                    DUSTIN
Exactly.

Our boys are finally getting it.

                    LUCAS
... Meaning if we follow the
compasses north --

                              DUSTIN
                    It should lead us to The Gate.

As our boys share looks, excited...

We turn to Eleven. She has been watching the whole exchange.

But unlike our boys, she looks anything but excited.

She looks... *terrified*.

INT. BYERS HOUSE - LIVING ROOM - DAY

WHAM! A hammer slams into a nail.

WIDEN TO REVEAL: Lonnie hammering a WOOD PLANK over the
GAPING HOLE IN THE WALL.

                              JOYCE (O.S.)
                    What are you doing?

Lonnie turns to find Joyce entering the room. She is now out
of her dress and pulling on some new clothes.

                              LONNIE
                    What do you think I'm doing? You
                    want to freeze to death this
                    winter?

She looks around. Her face falls.

Some of the Christmas lights are down.

                              JOYCE
                    I told you not to take these down --

                              LONNIE
                    They were in the way, babe -- how
                    long you gonna keep those up, I
                    mean, really? Christmas all year?

Joyce ignores them. Begins to quickly re-hang the lights.

Lonnie sighs. Returns to hammering.

                              LONNIE (CONT'D)
                    You know... it really is a shame,
                    what they've done to this family.

                              JOYCE
                    ... What?

                    LONNIE
        The Sattler Company. I stopped by
        their quarry on the way over here.
        Just wanted to see... you know?
        And I couldn't believe it... just
        couldn't believe it. There's no
        fence, no warning signs -- no
        nothing.
              (beat)
        Oughta be held accountable, you ask me.

Lonnie returns to hammering. WHAM! WHAM! WHAM!

Joyce watches him, suspicion rising...

A NAIL drives into the wall and --

INT. BYERS HOUSE - BATHROOM - DAY

WHOOSH! Lonnie showers. Washing off all that sweat.

INT. BYERS HOUSE - LIVING ROOM - DAY

The hole in the wall is now all patched up. We PULL BACK TO
FIND...

Joyce rummaging through Lonnie's DUFFEL BAG. She finds
toothpaste, socks, clothes, shaving cream, cologne, other
expected travel items. But then she finds something else...

A CHEAP BLUE PAMPHLET. It reads:

        A. KOHNER AND ASSOCIATES! LET US FIGHT FOR YOU!

Below, a list of specialties, including:

                    WRONGFUL ACCIDENTS

Off Joyce, anger rising...

EXT. WHEELER HOUSE - GARAGE - DAY

Nancy scours the garage, her backpack strapped on.

She inspects the tools on the wall. Hedge trimmer. Shovel.
Broom. Rake. Finally her eyes lock on:

A WOODEN BASEBALL BAT. IN A SPORTS BUCKET.

She grabs it up. Practices swinging it. Wild.

WHOOSH! WHOOSH! WHOOSH! WHOO--

She almost hits STEVE right in the face!

                         STEVE (O.S.)
               Whoa, whoa, whoa -- !

He backs away, just missing the bat. Nancy startles.

                         NANCY
               ... What are you doing here?

                         STEVE
               What are you doing?

                         NANCY
               Nothing.

                         STEVE
                    (re: bat)
               I hope that's not actually for
               me...

                         NANCY
               What, oh? No. I was just...
               thinking about...
                    (beat)
               ... joining softball.

She tosses the bat back in the bucket.

                    STEVE
        Well, uh... I just wanted to say
        I'm sorry... I mean even before you
        threatened me with that bat.

                    NANCY
        Okay.

                    STEVE
        I panicked. I was being a dick.

                    NANCY
        Yeah. You were.
            (softening)
        Did you get in trouble? With your
        parents?

                    STEVE
        Totally. But so what? Screw them.

Steve hops up on the hood of the Wheelers' car.

                    STEVE (CONT'D)
        Any news about Barbara? Have her
        parents heard from her yet, or...

Nancy shakes her head. "No."

Steve can tell how upset she still is.

                    STEVE (CONT'D)
        Why don't we catch a movie tonight?
        You know, pretend everything's
        normal for a few hours. *All The
        Right Moves* is still playing.

Nancy hesitates.

                    STEVE (CONT'D)
        Come on, it stars your loverboy
        from *Risky Business* --

                    NANCY
        Yeah I know --

                    STEVE
        Carol says I kinda look like him.
        What do you think?

Steve pretends to sing into a microphone.

                              275

                    STEVE (CONT'D)
          "Just take those old records off
          the shelf! I'll sit and listen to
          'em by myself..."

He expects this to earn a laugh from Nancy. At least a
smile. But she remains distant as ever.

                    STEVE (CONT'D)
          No?

                    NANCY
          I just... I don't think I can. I'm
          dealing with all this funeral
          stuff. With my brother. It's been
          hard on him --

                    STEVE
          I'm sure, yeah. Yeah.

                    NANCY
          So...

                    STEVE
          I should leave?

                    NANCY
          Sorry... I'll call you later. Is
          that okay?

                    STEVE
          Yeah yeah -- of course.

Nancy kisses him. Content for now, Steve exits.

                    STEVE (CONT'D)
               (singing to himself)
          "Just take those old records off
          the shelf!"

As soon as he's gone, Nancy picks the bat back up.

She practices swinging again. Harder this time.

WHOOSH! WHOOSH WHOOSH!

INT. BYERS HOUSE - LIVING ROOM - DAY

Joyce and Lonnie are now really going at it. Like old times.

Joyce holds the crumpled pamphlet in her trembling hand.

                    LONNIE
I'm just trying to make something
good out of something bad!! What's
so terrible 'bout that, huh?!

                    JOYCE
You want <u>money</u> --

                    LONNIE
No --

                    JOYCE
Admit it -- that's why you're here.
Not 'cause you care about Will, you
never have --

                    LONNIE
Jesus Christ, Joyce, his funeral was
today, can we not do this right now?!

                    JOYCE
    (shakes head)
I can't believe it -- I can't
believe I fell for this --

                    LONNIE
I'm here to *help*, Joyce.

                    JOYCE
To help -- ?

                         LONNIE
          We could use that money for good --

                         JOYCE
          -- pay off your debts, you mean --

                         LONNIE
          -- pay for Jon to go to college --

                         JOYCE
          Don't. Don't do that --

                         LONNIE
          Do what -- ?

                         JOYCE
          Lie to me.

                         LONNIE
          That's <u>not a lie</u> --

                         JOYCE
          Where does Jonathan want to go?

                         LONNIE
          What?

                         JOYCE
          Where does he want to go to school?

                         LONNIE
          We get that money, anywhere he damn
          pleases --

                         JOYCE
          N.Y.U., Lonnie! N.Y.U.! HE'S
          WANTED TO GO THERE SINCE HE WAS
          SIX!

                         LONNIE
          GREAT, THEN HE GOES TO N.Y.U.!

Joyce walks over to the front door, opens it wide.

                         JOYCE
          Get out.

                         LONNIE
          You need me here --

                         JOYCE
          Haven't needed you for a long time
          now.

                             278

                    LONNIE
          No? Look what happened.

                    JOYCE
          Don't you dare --

                    LONNIE
          Oh come on, Joyce. Just look at
          this place! What do you want me to
          think?! "World's Best Mom"?

Joyce strides over to Lonnie's duffle bag. Starts packing it
up for him. Shoving his clothes inside.

                    JOYCE
          Maybe you're right, maybe I'm crazy,
          out-of-my-mind -- but I'll keep those
          lights up till I die if there's a
          chance Will's still out there.
          Because if he is, God help me...
               (beat)
          I will find him.

WHOOM! She kicks the duffle bag over to Lonnie.

                    JOYCE (CONT'D)
          Now get out of my house.

EXT. FIELD - NEAR FOREST - DAY

BANG! Jonathan FIRES his revolver.

He's trying to hit a ROW OF TIN CANS propped up about fifty
yards away. Misses. He squeezes off some more GUNSHOTS.

Still doesn't hit a single can. *Awful.*

                    NANCY (O.S.)
          You're supposed to hit the cans,
          right?

He turns to find Nancy approaching. She's wears her
backpack, carries the baseball bat.

                    JONATHAN
          Actually, no. See the spaces
          between the cans? I'm aiming for
          those.

                    NANCY
          Ah.

                    JONATHAN
          You ever used a gun before?

                    NANCY
              (uhhh)
         Have you met my parents?

                    JONATHAN
         I haven't used one since I was ten.
         My dad took me hunting on my
         birthday. Made me kill a rabbit.

                    NANCY
         A rabbit?

                    JONATHAN
         He thought it'd make me into more
         of a man or something.
              (beat)
         I cried for a week.

                    NANCY
         Jesus.

                    JONATHAN
         I was a fan of Thumper.

                    NANCY
         I meant your dad.

                    JONATHAN
         Oh. Yeah. He's a nice guy.

Jonathan opens his backpack and takes out a BOX OF BULLETS.
He snaps the cylinder, begins to reload the gun.

                    JONATHAN (CONT'D)
         I suppose he and my mom loved each
         other at one point. I just wasn't
         around for that part.

Jonathan snaps the cylinder shut.

Nancy holds out her hand. Jonathan stares at her.
Surprised. *Okay...* He passes her the revolver.

Nancy takes her time to line up the crosshairs.

                    NANCY
         I don't think my parents ever loved
         each other. It's depressing.

Her finger curls around the trigger.

                    JONATHAN
         Must've married for some reason.

                    NANCY
          My mom was young. My dad was older
          but he had a cushy job, money, came
          from a good family. They bought a
          nice house at the end of a cul-de-
          sac. Started their nuclear family.

                    JONATHAN
          Screw that.

                    NANCY
          Yeah. Screw that.

BANG! Nancy FIRES. GUNFIRE THUNDERS AND --

A CAN BLOWS OFF THE LOG. Bullseye.

The teens share looks. *Damn.*

INT. HOPPER'S TRAILER - LIVING ROOM - DAY

CLOSE ON: A MESSY PILE OF MICROFICHE ARTICLES.

WIDEN TO REVEAL: Hopper sits on the destroyed couch in his
destroyed home. His phone, now haphazardly pieced back
together, sits in front of him atop the articles.

Hopper twists the blue bracelet around his wrist. His
anxiety racing. Finally he makes a rash decision and --

Grabs up the phone. Dials a number. BRRING BRRRING --

A MUFFLED VOICE answers:

                    DIANE'S VOICE (OVER PHONE)
          Hello...?

Hopper is a bit surprised someone is home. Hesitates.

                    HOPPER
          ... Hey...

                    DIANE'S VOICE
          Jim?

                    HOPPER
          Yeah --

                    DIANE'S VOICE
          Why are you calling here, I told you --

                    HOPPER
          I know -- I know -- I just... I
          wanted to hear your voice -- and...
          I wanted to say, you know... even
          after everything that happened, I
          wouldn't take it back, any of it...
          those seven years... they were
          everything to me, and --

                    DIANE'S VOICE
          Have you been drinking?

                    HOPPER
          No, no --

FROM OVER THE PHONE, THE SOUND OF A CRYING BABY INTERRUPTS.

                    DIANE'S VOICE
          Shhh, honey, shhh, it's okay...

Hopper fights back tears.

                    HOPPER
          You know what? I'm sorry. You're
          right. I've been drinking again.

                    DIANE'S VOICE
          Jim --

                    HOPPER
          You take care, Diane. Say hi to
          Bill for me.

                    DIANE'S VOICE
          Are you sure everything's okay -- ?

Hopper hangs up the phone. Takes a deep breath. And...

He grabs up the pile of microfiche articles, throws on his
jacket and hat, and heads for the door. But halfway out --

The PHONE BEGINS TO RING behind him.

Hopper turns to it. Considers.

BBRRRING, BRRRING, BRRRINGRING.

Then he crosses over and --

RIPS OUT THE CORD.

EXT. TRAIN TRACKS - DAY

CLOSE ON: A COMPASS. Its needle points north.

Mike, Lucas, Dustin, and Eleven are marching down an empty train track, wearing their overstuffed mission backpacks.

Dustin and Lucas lead.

> LUCAS
> How much further?

> DUSTIN
> I don't know. This just shows direction, not distance. You really need to learn more about compasses.

> LUCAS
> I'm just saying... how will we know when we get to The Gate -- ?

> DUSTIN
> I think a portal to another dimension will be pretty obvious.

Lucas nods. *Right*. He glances back at Eleven.

She is wiping her nose with her sleeve.

> LUCAS
> You think she's acting weird?

> DUSTIN
> You're asking if the weirdo is acting weird?

> LUCAS
> I mean weirder than normal.

> DUSTIN
> I don't know. Who cares?

We turn our gaze to Eleven. And Lucas is right -- she *is* acting weirder than normal. More hesitant. More *scared*.

She eyes the road ahead with growing trepidation.

> ELEVEN (PRE-LAP)
> How far, Papa?

INT. HAWKINS LABS - ELEVEN'S ROOM (FLASHBACK)

We're back in time. Eleven is sitting on the bed in her prison. Dr. Brenner is at her side. He shows her...

A TELEPHOTO-LENSED PHOTOGRAPH OF AN IMPORTANT-LOOKING MAN.

                    DR. BRENNER
          Much further than we've ever gone
          before.

                    ELEVEN
          The bath?

                    DR. BRENNER
          Yes. Is that okay?

Eleven considers. Then nods.

                    ELEVEN
          Okay.

INT. HAWKINS LABS - INDIGO LABORATORY (FLASHBACK)

CLOSE ON: Eleven's bare feet pad up metal stairs as...

She climbs to the second-floor catwalk of the laboratory.
She is now wearing a SIMPLE FULL-BODY BATHING SUIT. We now
show a MONTAGE OF SHOTS as Eleven gets ready for her "bath":

- TECHNICIANS turn the wheel on the HATCH DOOR atop the
isolation tank. It unlocks. They wrench it open.

- Eleven sits down with her feet dangling in the water.

- The Techs affix EEG electrodes to her head.

- The Techs slide a SCUBA-LIKE GLASS HELMET over her head.

- Eleven is lowered into the tank. Her tiny body floats.

- The Techs close the hatch. Spin the wheel. Locking her
in.

- Eleven looks out the isolation tank's LARGE GLASS VIEWING
WINDOW. Standing directly before her: Dr. Brenner. Only a
layer of glass dividing them. He gives her a friendly wave.

- A TECHNICIAN grabs the tank door handle and --

- Slams the door, shutting Eleven in _DARKNESS_.

EXT. TRAIN TRACKS - DAY

Eleven flinches from the memory. Tugs at Mike's sleeve.

                    ELEVEN
          Mike. Mike.

                    MIKE
          Yeah?

                         284

                    ELEVEN
     Turn back.

                    MIKE
     What? Why?

Eleven hesitates. Wants to tell him something but...

                    ELEVEN
     I'm... tired.

                    MIKE
     I'm sure we're almost there. Just
     a little longer, okay? Come on.

Mike keeps walking. Eleven hangs back a second, then hurries
after Mike -- clearly concerned.

EXT. WOODS - DAY

Our teens walk through the forest. Side by side.

Nancy carries the revolver; Jonathan carries the baseball bat.

                    NANCY
     You never said what I was "saying."

                    JONATHAN
     What?

                    NANCY
     Yesterday. You said I was "saying"
     something. That's why you took my
     picture.

                    JONATHAN
     Oh. Yeah. I don't know... I
     guess... it's...
          (beat, considers)
     I saw this girl, you know, trying
     to be someone else. But for that
     moment, it's like -- you were
     alone. Or thought you were. And
     you could just be yourself --

                    NANCY
     That's such bullshit.

                    JONATHAN
     What?

                    NANCY
          I'm not trying to be someone else.
          Just because I'm with Steve --

                    JONATHAN
          You know what? Forget it. I just
          thought it was a good picture.

They walk in silence for a beat.

                    NANCY
          He's actually a good guy.

                    JONATHAN
          Okay.

                    NANCY
          Yesterday, with the camera -- he's
          not like that at all. He was just
          being... protective --

                    JONATHAN
          That's one word for it.

                    NANCY
          And I guess what you did was okay?

                    JONATHAN
          Never said that --

                    NANCY
          He had *every right* to be pissed --

                    JONATHAN
          Does that mean I have to like him?

                    NANCY
          No --

                    JONATHAN
          Listen -- you shouldn't take this
          so personally. I don't like most
          people. He's in the vast majority.

Nancy just shakes her head. Can't believe this.

                    NANCY
          You know, I was just starting to
          think you were okay.

                    JONATHAN
          Yeah?

                    NANCY
          Yeah. I was thinking: Jonathan
          Byers, he's not a pretentious creep
          like everyone says he is.

                    JONATHAN
          Yeah, well, I was just starting to
          think you were okay. I was
          thinking: Nancy Wheeler, she's not
          just another suburban girl who
          thinks she's rebelling by doing
          exactly what every other suburban
          girl does. Until that phase passes
          and they marry some boring one-time
          jock who now works sales and they
          live out a perfectly boring little
          life at the end of a cul-de-sac,
          exactly like their parents who they
          thought were soooooo depressing,
          but now, hey, they get it.

Nancy stops and stares. Struck by his audacity.

Jonathan keeps on walking.

Nancy bites back her anger, then starts to follow.

EXT. ABANDONED JUNKYARD - DUSK

The sky is darkening. Night just around the corner.

We CRANE DOWN to find our kids walking into an ABANDONED, OVERGROWN JUNKYARD. It's littered with RUSTY CARS and FARM MACHINERY. This place seems almost... post-apocalyptic.

Dustin stares at his compass with growing confusion.

He crashes to a stop.

                       DUSTIN
    ... Oh no.

                       LUCAS
    Oh no? What's oh no?

                       DUSTIN
    We're headed back home.

                       MIKE
    What?!

                       LUCAS
    Are you sure?

                    DUSTIN
               (points west)
          I'm sure. Setting sun, right
          there. We looped right back
          around --

                    LUCAS
          And you're just realizing this now?

                    DUSTIN
          Why is this all on me?!

                    LUCAS
          You're the compass genius!

                    DUSTIN
          What do yours say?

Lucas and Mike pull out their compasses. Check them.

                    MIKE
          North.

                    LUCAS
          North.

                    DUSTIN
          This makes no damn sense.

                    MIKE
          Maybe The Gate moved --

                    DUSTIN
          I don't think it's The Gate. I
          think something else is affecting
          the compasses.

Mike looks around the junkyard.

                    MIKE
          Maybe it's something here.

                    DUSTIN
          Like what? It'd have to be like a
          super-magnet --

                    LUCAS
          It's not a magnet.

Mike and Dustin turn to Lucas. His gaze is fixed on...

Eleven.

                         LUCAS (CONT'D)
              She's been acting weirder than
              normal. If she can slam doors with
              her mind, she can *definitely* screw
              up a compass.

Eleven shrinks under their gaze.

                         MIKE
              Why would she do that?

                         LUCAS
              Because she wants to sabotage the
              mission. Because she's a *traitor*.

Lucas strides over to Eleven.

                         MIKE
              Lucas, what are you doing?

                         LUCAS
                    (to Eleven)
              You did it, didn't you? You don't
              want us to reach The Gate. You
              don't want us to find Will --

                         ELEVEN
              ... No --

                         MIKE
              Lucas, come on, seriously, leave
              her alone --

                         LUCAS
              Admit it!

                         ELEVEN
              No --

                         LUCAS
              ADMIT IT!

Lucas grabs Eleven's arm and turns it over to reveal...

A STAIN OF FRESH BLOOD on her jacket sleeve.

He looks back at Mike. Vindicated.

                         LUCAS (CONT'D)
              Fresh blood. I knew it.

Eleven jerks her arm away from Lucas.

                    MIKE
          Lucas, come on, man --

                    LUCAS
          I saw her wiping her nose on the
          tracks -- she used her powers!

                    MIKE
          Bull! That's old blood. Right, El?

To Mike's surprise, Eleven doesn't answer him.

                    MIKE (CONT'D)
          Right, El?
               (no answer)
          El??

Still no answer. Eleven looks caught. *Guilty*.

She locks eyes with Mike. Fights tears.

                    ELEVEN
               (low)
          Not safe.

Off Mike, shocked by this betrayal...

INT. BYERS HOUSE - DUSK

RAP RAP RAP! Pounding on the front door.

Joyce looks up from the couch.

                    JOYCE
          Lonnie -- GO AWAY!

The KNOCKING continues.

                    JOYCE (CONT'D)
          I swear to God.

Joyce grabs the HAMMER off the floor and --

INT. BYERS HOUSE - MOMENTS LATER - DUSK

Joyce throws open the door. Her face fills with surprise.

It's not Lonnie. <u>It's Hopper</u>.

Before Joyce has a chance to speak, he passes her a note.

It reads: "<u>DON'T SAY ANYTHING</u>"

She looks back up at Hopper. Confused. And...

INT. BYERS HOUSE - LATER - DUSK

CLOSE ON: A PILE OF LIGHT BULBS ON THE TABLE.

Joyce watches dumbfounded as Hopper tears the cover off the
sofa cushion. He's covered in sweat, completely paranoid.
Thanks to him, the house is now even more of a mess than
before... Hard to believe that was even possible. But...

Hopper turns to Joyce. Catches his breath.

>   HOPPER
>   Alright, seems okay. I mean, can't
>   guarantee it, but should be --

>   JOYCE
>   The hell is going on?

>   HOPPER
>   They bugged my place --

>   JOYCE
>   -- What -- ??

>   HOPPER
>   -- bugged my place, put a mic in
>   the light -- I'm onto them and they
>   know it -- figured they might be
>   watching you too --

>   JOYCE
>   *Who* -- ?

>   HOPPER
>   The CIA, the NSA, Department of
>   Energy, I don't know --

>   JOYCE
>   I-I don't understand --

>   HOPPER
>   I went to the morgue, Joyce. Last
>   night. It wasn't him.

>   JOYCE
>   What -- ?

>   HOPPER
>   Will's body. It was a fake.

Joyce takes a second to process this.

Hopper looks at her. Locks eyes. Intense.

                    HOPPER (CONT'D)
          You were right, Joyce. This whole
          time.
               (beat)
          You were right.

Joyce fights back tears. It doesn't matter that Hop seems a
bit crazy. For the first time since this nightmare began...

Someone believes her.

EXT. ABANDONED JUNKYARD - DUSK

Eleven watches in growing apprehension as...

Our boys argue about her ten feet away.

>   LUCAS
>   What did I tell you?? She's been
>   playing us from the beginning --

>   MIKE
>   That's not true! She helped us
>   find Will --

>   LUCAS
>   Find Will?? Find Will?! Where is
>   he, then? I-I don't see him?

>   MIKE
>   You know what I mean --

>   LUCAS
>   No, actually, I don't. Just think
>   about it, Mike! She could've just
>   told us he was in the Upside Down
>   *right away*, instead she's only been
>   talking when she wants to, making
>   us run around like headless
>   chickens --

>   DUSTIN
>   Guys, come on, let's stay calm --

>   LUCAS
>   No! She used us, all of us! She
>   helped just enough to get what she
>   needed: food and a bed, she's like
>   a stray dog --

>   MIKE
>   Screw you, Lucas -- !

>   LUCAS
>   No, screw you, Mike! You're blind,
>   blind because you like that a
>   girl's not grossed out by you. But
>   wake up, man! WAKE! UP! She
>   knows what happened to Will, she's
>   always known, and now she's letting
>   him die in the Upside Down --

                    MIKE
          Shut up -- !

                    LUCAS
          For all we know, it's her fault --

                    MIKE
          SHUT UP --

                    LUCAS
          We keep looking for some monster --
          but did you ever stop to think...
               (beat)
          Maybe she's the monster?

We return our gaze to Eleven. This last blow lands hard.

Eleven fights tears. And suddenly...

INT. HAWKINS LABS - INDIGO LABORATORY (FLASHBACK)

We're back in time again. Eleven is in the tank.

*The world is almost totally dark. We can only make out the
dimmest outline of Eleven. A CACOPHONY OF VOICES overwhelm
us. Overlapping, overrunning each other, multiplying. The
voices are many different ages, many different languages.*

Her eyelids dart back and forth. Faster and faster.

The voices grow in number. More and more.

And --

BLACK VOID (FLASHBACK)

Eleven's eyes SNAP OPEN. There is jarring silence.

She is no longer floating in water. She is standing in...

A BLACK SPACE. It stretches in all directions. Infinite.

*We HEAR a SINGLE VOICE now. RUSSIAN. We SLOWLY DOLLY AROUND
ELEVEN 180 DEGREES TO REVEAL: THE MAN FROM THE PHOTOGRAPH.
He is standing ten feet away, talking animatedly to someone.
Someone we can't see. Someone who is lost in the darkness.*

Eleven walks over to the Russian Man. Stands next to him.

And then she just... listens.

INT. HAWKINS LABS - INDIGO LABORATORY CONTROL ROOM (FLASHBACK)

Dr. Brenner and the scientists listen in awe as...

The RUSSIAN MAN'S VOICE echoes out of the SPEAKERS in the control room. His voice is faint, buried in a bed of static, cutting in and out. But it's there. Most definitely there.

BLACK VOID (FLASHBACK)

Eleven continues to listen to Russian Man. When...

She grows aware of something else. Another NOISE.

It's wet, guttural, terrible. We know this sound -- it's the sound of our monster.

Eleven turns toward the direction of the noise.

INT. HAWKINS LABS - INDIGO LABORATORY CONTROL ROOM (FLASHBACK)

The Russian's VOICE FADES back into STATIC.

In place of his voice, we hear the STRANGE SOUND.

> SCIENTIST
> What is that?

> DR. BRENNER
> I have no idea...

BLACK VOID (FLASHBACK)

Eleven stares into the darkness. Terrified.

The SOUND grows louder. And louder. LOUDER. AND --

Eleven turns and runs away and --

INT. HAWKINS LABS - INDIGO LABORATORY CONTROL ROOM (FLASHBACK)

CHHHHHHH!!!! The sound turns to STATIC on the speakers.

INT. HAWKINS LABS - INDIGO LABORATORY (FLASHBACK)

Eleven's eyes snap open in the tank. Terrified.

She pounds on the tank glass. Desperate to escape.

She opens her mouth and SCREAMS and --

> MIKE (PRE-LAP)
> I SAID SHUT UP!

EXT. ABANDONED JUNKYARD - DUSK

Mike lunges at Lucas, jolting Eleven out of the memory.

He tackles Lucas to the dirty ground. The two boys wrestle.

Eleven watches in growing shock. Crying now.

> ELEVEN
>
> Stop --

They keep fighting. Flailing on the ground.

> ELEVEN (CONT'D)
>
> Stop -- !

Lucas gains the upper hand. He pins Mike to the ground,
climbs on top of him, raises up a fist to punch him, and --

> ELEVEN (CONT'D)
>
> STOP!!!!!!

Eleven shouts at the top of her lungs and suddenly --

WHOOM! Lucas TELEKINETICALLY FLIES through the air and --

WHAM! He SLAMS HARD against a rusted car hood --

He slumps limply to the ground.

Mike and Dustin run to him.

> DUSTIN
>
> JESUS CHRIST!

> MIKE
>
> Lucas, are you alright, Lucas?!

> DUSTIN
>
> Lucas?! LUCAS?!

No response. No movement.

Lucas just lies there on the ground. <u>Unconscious</u>.

Mike snaps to Eleven. There is anger in his eyes.

> MIKE
>
> Why did you do that?! What is
> wrong with you?! WHAT IS WRONG
> WITH YOU?!

Eleven starts to cry. Truly feeling like a monster now.

Mike turns back to Lucas. Shakes him. Panic rising.

> MIKE (CONT'D)
>
> Lucas, get up! Lucas?!

                    DUSTIN
          Lucas, man, come on! LUCAS?!

It doesn't seem like he'll wake. Then, at last...

His eyes flutter open. Mike and Dustin are beyond relieved.

                    MIKE
          Lucas -- you alright?

Lucas doesn't answer. He just sits up against the hood.
Woozy.

                    MIKE (CONT'D)
          Is your head okay? Lucas?!

                    DUSTIN
          How many fingers am I holding up?
               (holds up three)
          How many fingers??

Lucas doesn't answer them. He just slowly and silently
pushes to his feet. He's holding the back of his head.

                    MIKE
          Where did you get hit? Let me see.

Mike tries to see, but Lucas swats him away.

                    LUCAS
          Get off me.

                    MIKE
          Lucas --

                    LUCAS
          GET OFF ME!!!

Lucas turns and storms away from his friends.

                    MIKE
          Lucas, where are you going? Lucas?!

Lucas just walks faster and faster. As he strides out of the
junkyard, holding his injured head, tears begin to fall.

Mike starts to go after him, but Dustin holds him back.

                    DUSTIN
          Let him go, man. Just let him go.

Mike stops. Fighting tears himself now. When...

He realizes someone else is missing.

                    MIKE
          Where's El?

Dustin looks around. Mike's right -- she's nowhere to be
seen.

Mike hurries through the junkyard, searching.

                    MIKE (CONT'D)
          El? El?? Eleven?!

There is no answer.

                    MIKE (CONT'D)
          EL?!?!

Suddenly he stops. He's found something.

ELEVEN'S WIG. It is left on the ground.

As Mike picks up the wig, fighting tears, we SLOWLY CRANE UP
AND AWAY from our boys. They suddenly look very small in
this graveyard of cars and machines. And very... alone.

The group is shattered.

EXT. WOODS - NIGHT 6

Night has now fallen in the forest.

Our teens march in silence. Tension between them now.

Nancy suddenly pauses. Listens. She hears...

A STRANGE WHIMPERING SOUND.

She turns toward the sound. Unsettled.

Jonathan realizes Nancy's not following.

                    JONATHAN
          ... You getting tired?

                    NANCY
          Shut up --

                    JONATHAN
          What -- ?

                    NANCY
          ... I hear something.

Jonathan listens. After a beat, he hears it too.

A STRANGE WHIMPERING SOUND. It's very faint. But there.

EXT. WOODS - CLEARING - NIGHT

Our teens creep through the woods. Tracking the sound.

The WHIMPERING is louder now. *Closer.*

Nancy raises up the gun as they push into a CLEARING.

They freeze. Their faces falling.

>   NANCY
>   ... Oh God.

It's not the monster at all. It's...

A DOE. DYING ON THE GROUND.

Its head cranes a bit and its left front leg drags on the
ground. It's badly hurt. BLOOD POOLING from its body.

Nancy hurries over to it. Kneels down. Sees...

A POOL OF BLOOD SPREADING FROM A GASH IN ITS NECK.

>   NANCY (CONT'D)
>   It's been hit by a car.

Nancy fights tears as she watches the doe struggle.

She looks back at Jonathan.

>   NANCY (CONT'D)
>   We can't just leave it like this.

Jonathan eyes the gun. Nancy hesitates. She knows what she
has to do -- but she clearly doesn't want to.

Jonathan holds out his hand.

>   JONATHAN
>   Let me.

>   NANCY
>   I thought --

>   JONATHAN
>   I'm not nine anymore.

Nancy stands back up and hands the gun off to Jonathan.

He targets the doe's head... hits off the safety... wraps his finger on the trigger... takes a deep breath... and...

WHOOM! THE DOE IS SUDDENLY SUCKED BACKWARD INTO BRUSH.

Nancy SCREAMS -- Jonathan LEAPS BACK.

And just like that -- the doe is gone.

The teens stare. Terrified. Letting this sink in.

Nancy finally speaks. So low it's almost a breath.

                    NANCY
          What was that...?

Jonathan shakes his head. He doesn't know.

He walks over. Pushes through the brush.

He finds no deer on the other side. But there is a TRAIL OF BLOOD FROM WHERE THE DOE WAS DRAGGED. He hoists the gun up and begins to follow it.

                    NANCY (CONT'D)
          Jonathan -- Jonathan --

But he's already gone. Nancy hesitates.

She grabs the baseball bat. Then follows.

EXT. WOODS - NIGHT

CLOSE ON: A TRAIL OF BLOOD ON THE FOREST FLOOR.

Our teens are moving through the woods. Tracking the doe.

The blood trail leads them straight to the base of...

A LARGE, GNARLED TREE. IT MUST BE A THOUSAND YEARS OLD.

The blood trail ends here. Yet... still no sign of the doe.

                    NANCY
               (low)
          Where'd it go?

                    JONATHAN
          I... don't know. You see any more
          blood?

The teens explore the area, searching for blood. They see nothing but dead leaves. As Jonathan continues to search...

Nancy circles back to the tree. Scouring closer. And that's
when she notices: There's something strange about this tree.

She takes out her flashlight and aims it at the tree.

THERE IS A ROTTEN GASH IN THE WOOD. AN OPENING. BLOOD SLIPS
THROUGH THIS GASH. AS IF... THE DOE WAS DRAGGED THOUGH IT.

Nancy kneels down for a closer look, but...

She sees only darkness. *Weird.*

>   NANCY
>   Jonathan?

No answer. He's too far away.

Nancy considers a beat. And then...

She slips off her backpack.

And crawls inside.

INT. TREE - NIGHT

There are wet and throbbing growths in here.

It's disgusting, but Nancy keeps squeezing through until...

EXT. WOODS (NETHER) - NIGHT

Nancy emerges out of the other side.

But it's not the other side she was expecting...

Nancy doesn't know it... but she's inside THE NETHER. We're
still in the forest, yet it's shrouded in a fog... strange
particulates dance in the air... and growths cling to trees.

Her flashlight stutters. On and off. Nancy smacks it. Yet
it continues to stutter. And that's when she HEARS it...

A HORRIBLE GUTTURAL SOUND. SOMEWHERE CLOSE.

She swings the flashlight around and...

Her body goes still. Her face goes white. It's...

THE MONSTER. FEEDING ON THE CARCASS OF THE DOE. ITS FACE IS
BURIED IN ITS OPEN GUT. MAKING A HORRIBLE SUCKING SOUND.

Nancy just watches it for a beat. Too scared to move. Too
scared to scream. She backs up one foot. Two feet. And...

SNAP. A twig SNAPS beneath her shoe.

THE MONSTER LOOKS RIGHT AT NANCY.

ITS FACE PEELS OPEN. A MESS OF FLESH AND BLOOD AND TEETH.

IT SHRIEKS IN ANGER.

EXT. WOODS - NIGHT

Jonathan hears this OTHERWORLDLY SHRIEK. Then NANCY'S SCREAM.

                    JONATHAN
          Nancy?!

He spins toward the sound. Sees no sign of Nancy.

He raises his gun. Races through the woods.

                    JONATHAN (CONT'D)
          Nancy?! NANCY?!!

He spots her backpack by the base of the tree. He grabs it,
whirls around. *What the hell?* Nancy is nowhere to be seen.

It's like she just... vanished. As he continues to search...

We return our gaze to the tree. To the DARK HOLE.

We HOLD on it for a beat. Watching. Waiting.

The hole begins to slowly close...

And...

                    END EPISODE

CHAPTER SIX:
THE MONSTER

WRITTEN BY **JESSIE NICKSON-LOPEZ**

EXT. WOODS - NIGHT 6 CONT'D

WE'RE RIGHT WHERE WE LEFT OFF --

The dark hole in the tree is <u>SLOWLY CLOSING UP</u>.

But JONATHAN doesn't see it. He looks around the woods.
Panic rising. To him, it seems like Nancy has simply...

<u>Vanished</u>.

>   JONATHAN
>   NANCY?!! NANCY?!

EXT. WOODS (NETHER) - NIGHT

NANCY backs away from THE MONSTER. Faster. Faster.

And then she turns -- and runs.

Her eyes dart through the fog. Looking for Jonathan.

For the tree. For signs of life. For *something*.

>   NANCY
>   Jonathan?! JONATHAN?! WHERE ARE
>   YOU?!

There is no answer. She keeps racing around. But every
direction she turns, she finds only more dead trees, more
dense fog. *Where the hell is she*?!

EXT. WOODS - NIGHT

Jonathan continues to shout.

>   JONATHAN
>   Nancy?! NANCY?! NANCY?!

EXT. WOODS (NETHER) - NIGHT

His MUFFLED VOICE ECHOES into the Nether. Very, very low.

But... it's *just* loud enough that Nancy hears it.

>   NANCY
>   JONATHAN?! JONATHAN! I'M RIGHT
>   HERE! WHERE ARE YOU?! JONATHAN!

EXT. WOODS - NIGHT

Jonathan HEARS her distant voice.

                         JONATHAN
          I'M RIGHT HERE, FOLLOW MY VOICE!
          JUST FOLLOW MY VOICE!

EXT. WOODS (NETHER) - NIGHT

Nancy starts to do just that when --

A SHAPE MOVES IN THE FOG. THE MONSTER. STALKING HER.

She ducks behind a slimy tree. Holding her breath as...

The MONSTER slinks *right past her.* Fog ripples in its wake.
It's hard to make out much... but we see enough... long
arms... long fingers... the flesh of its face moves... *alive.*
And, of course, we HEAR its awful, guttural, wet *BREATHING.*

Nancy holds her mouth, *doing her best not to scream.*

She can still HEAR JONATHAN, calling in the distance. His
voice is closer now. It sounds like it's coming from...

THE LARGE AND GNARLED TREE. TEN YARDS AWAY.

The hole she came through is still there.

Only now it's closing. More and more.

Nancy doesn't want to leave her hiding spot. But it's only a
matter of time before the hole is completely closed and she's
trapped in this hell forever. So she takes a breath. And --

Makes a break for it.

EXT. WOODS - NIGHT

Jonathan's voice is getting hoarse now:

                         JONATHAN
          NANCY?! CAN YOU HEAR ME?! FOLLOW
          MY VOICE!

He suddenly silences. Hearing something. Sounds like...

A SCREAM. *What the hell?* He tracks the noise...

To the base of the gnarled tree. He finally sees the hole.
Closing up.

                         JONATHAN (CONT'D)
          Nancy -- ?

WHAM! A HAND SUDDENLY LEAPS OUT OF THE HOLE. SLAMMING TO
EARTH.

Jonathan leaps back in terror until he realizes --

<u>The hand belongs to Nancy.</u> <u>Dragging herself through the hole.</u>

                    JONATHAN (CONT'D)
          NANCY!

He drops to the ground, grabs her hand, and starts to pull
her out. But the tree is closing in on her, the wet growths
pressing against her body like the most disgusting vice ever.

Nancy SCREAMS in pain. Jonathan pulls. Harder, harder, and --

WHOOMP! She's pulled out of the hole just as IT SEALS UP.

Nancy is shaking, smothered in mud and strange mucus.

She doesn't know how to act. Doesn't know what to do. She
just falls into Jonathan's arms. As he holds her tight...

Jonathan looks in horror at the tree.

The opening is now GONE.

Like it never was.

                    MAIN TITLES

EXT. NEIGHBORHOOD - NIGHT

A calm, quiet night in the neighborhood.

VROOM! A BMW suddenly speeds past us.

INT./EXT. STEVE'S CAR - NEIGHBORHOOD - NIGHT

STEVE drives. TOMMY H. rides shotgun.

CAROL sits in the back. Smacking her gum. Irritated.

                    CAROL
          I just don't understand why we're
          coming out here -- she obviously
          doesn't want to talk to you --

                    STEVE
          That's not it --

                    CAROL
          Oh, really? Because no girl would
          ever blow off King Steve --

                    STEVE
          No, because she was acting weird.
          Something's wrong --

                    CAROL
          So... you're worried about her?

                    STEVE
          What??

Steve plays this off. But Carol sees right through it.

                    CAROL
          Awwww. You are!! You totally are!
          You're worried about her!! Steve
          has a heart!!

                    TOMMY H.
          Stevey's in looooove --

                    STEVE
          Shut up --

                    CAROL
          Who knew --

                    STEVE
          Shut. Up.

Steve pulls to a stop. He's reached...

THE WHEELER CUL-DE-SAC. Carol leans out the window.

                    CAROL
          So this is it? The princess's
          castle?

                    STEVE
               (ignores her)
          I'll just be a minute.

EXT. WHEELER HOUSE - NIGHT

Steve scales the side of the house. His usual routine.

EXT. WHEELER HOUSE - ROOF OUTSIDE NANCY'S ROOM - NIGHT

Steve walks up to her window. And freezes. His face falls.

Nancy is here, sitting on the bed. And she's not alone...

Someone surprising is sitting next to her, comforting her...

Jonathan Byers.

                         309

We PUSH IN ON STEVE, his eyes burning, and...

INT. BYERS HOUSE - LIVING ROOM - NIGHT

We DRIFT across the living room...

The MICROFICHE ARTICLES are scattered on the coffee table.

>   JOYCE (O.S.)
>   ... Let's walk through it again.

INT. BYERS HOUSE - KITCHEN - NIGHT

JOYCE smokes. Her anxiety racing. HOPPER sits beside her at
the kitchen table, on edge.

>   HOPPER
>   I told you everything I saw --

>   JOYCE
>   I want you to tell me again --

>   HOPPER
>   Downstairs or upstairs --

>   JOYCE
>   Upstairs --

>   HOPPER
>   There was some lab... where they
>   must do experiments -- then at the
>   end of a hall -- that kid's room --

>   JOYCE
>   How do you know it was a kid's room?

>   HOPPER
>   It was more of a prison --

>   JOYCE
>   How did you know it was a kid's?

>   HOPPER
>   I told you -- 'cause of the stuffed
>   animal, the size of the bed, the
>   drawing --

>   JOYCE
>   You never told me about a drawing.

                    HOPPER
          There was a kid's drawing on the
          wall. Two figures, an adult and
          child holding hands. It said
          "eleven," I think --

                    JOYCE
          Eleven -- ?

                    HOPPER
          The eleventh drawing or something --

                    JOYCE
          Was it good?

                    HOPPER
          What?

                    JOYCE
          This drawing. Was it good or bad?

                    HOPPER
          It was a kid's drawing, Joyce,
          stick figures --

That's all Joyce needs to hear. She strides over to the
fridge, rips Will's drawing off the refrigerator and...

Slides it over to Hopper.

                    JOYCE
          Then Will didn't draw it.

Hopper stares at this drawing. Suddenly -- it hits him.

He shoves away from the table and...

INT. BYERS HOUSE - LIVING ROOM - MOMENTS LATER - NIGHT

Hopper riffles through the microfiche articles. Frantic.

                    HOPPER
          Earl. The night Benny died, he saw
          a kid with a shaved head, with
          Benny. He said it might've been
          Will, *after* I pressed him, at first
          he didn't think so --

                    JOYCE
          So it wasn't him.

                    HOPPER
          I don't know. Maybe not.

Hopper lands on the PHOTO OF TERRY IVES. Passes it to Joyce.

>   HOPPER (CONT'D)
>   This woman -- Terry Ives. She
>   claims she lost her kid, a
>   daughter, Jane. She sued Brenner,
>   the government, it went nowhere, of
>   course, but...
>   (beat)
>   What if this whole time I thought I
>   was looking for Will...

He looks up at Joyce.

>   HOPPER (CONT'D)
>   ... I've been chasing some other kid?

Off Joyce...

INT. WHEELER HOUSE - UPSTAIRS BATHROOM - NIGHT

WHOOSH! Water rushes down Nancy's face as she showers.

Strange mucus pools by her feet, swirling down the drain.

INT. WHEELER HOUSE - NANCY'S ROOM - NIGHT

Jonathan unfurls a sleeping bag on the floor.

He looks up as Nancy enters. She's wearing her pajamas and
her hair is soaking wet, clinging to her. She looks better
now that she's clean... but her face is still pale with shock.

>   JONATHAN
>   Better?

Nancy gives a small nod.

>   JONATHAN (CONT'D)
>   (motions to sleeping bag)
>   ... Is this okay? I found it in
>   the closet -- I mean... I can go
>   home -- I just... I figured --

>   NANCY
>   Yeah, no. I don't... I don't want
>   to be alone. Do you?

>   JONATHAN
>   No. No.

Nancy climbs into her bed. Lies down on the covers.

Jonathan lies down in his sleeping bag.

Neither of them close their eyes.

A long beat. Then:

>   NANCY
>   ... Can you just get up here?

Jonathan hesitates. Climbs up onto the bed.

Nancy keeps a pillow between them.

>   JONATHAN
>   You want the lights off or --

>   NANCY
>   On.

>   JONATHAN
>   Yeah.

Another beat.

>   JONATHAN (CONT'D)
>   It can't get us here.

>   NANCY
>   We don't know that.

Jonathan hesitates. He reaches out his hand and curls it
around the grip of the revolver, tucked beneath his pillow.

As our teens lie there, a foot apart, eyes open...

We slowly PULL AWAY from them...

They seem very small in here. Very *alone*.

EXT. WHEELER HOUSE - DAWN 7

The sun rises outside the Wheeler house.

INT. WHEELER HOUSE - BASEMENT - DAWN

MIKE lies on the couch. Very alone.

His eyes are fixed on the basement door, waiting for Eleven.

And from the looks of him... he's been waiting all night.

He turns to look at her tent. It's empty. Sad.

He walks over to it. Fights tears. And --

<u>TEARS IT DOWN</u>.

EXT. RURAL ROAD - PAY PHONE - MORNING

Joyce's car is parked on a road alongside...

A LONELY PAY PHONE. ALL BY ITSELF OUT HERE.

Hopper is in the booth. Mid-call.

> HOPPER
> ... Yeah, yeah. "Ives." "Terry
> Ives." That's with a "Y."
> (beat)
> Yeah, I got a pen.

Hopper scribbles an address onto his palm.

> HOPPER (CONT'D)
> I appreciate this, Frank,
> sincerely. Tell the boys hey for
> me, alright?

He hangs up. DING.

INT./EXT. JOYCE'S CAR - RURAL ROAD - MOMENTS LATER - MORNING

Hopper slides back into the car. Joyce sits passenger.

She looks at him -- hopeful.

> JOYCE
> You got it?

Hopper holds up his palm. *Damn straight.*

VROOM! The car PEELS OFF. Kicking up dirt. And...

INT. WHEELER HOUSE - NANCY'S ROOM - MORNING

Jonathan wakes. He sits up. Groggy.

Nancy is wide awake. She sits cross-legged on the end of the
bed. There is a PILE OF BIOLOGY TEXTBOOKS AND ENCYCLOPEDIAS
all around her. It looks like she's cramming for an exam.

> JONATHAN
> Hey.

> NANCY
> ... Hey.

Jonathan sits up. He looks at the books. They are open to
pages about animals. *Predators.*

                    JONATHAN
              ... Couldn't sleep?

Nancy shakes her head.

                      NANCY
              ... Every time I close my eyes...
              I keep seeing... that thing...

A beat as Jonathan takes this in.

                    NANCY (CONT'D)
              I think that... wherever I was...
              that place... it *lives there*...
              and it was feeding in there...
              feeding on that deer...

Her eyes fill with tears. Her voice trembles.

                    NANCY (CONT'D)
              And that means... if Will,
              Barbara...

Her voice trails off. The thought is just too awful to put
into words. The tears begin to fall.

                    JONATHAN
              My mom's talked with Will... If
              he's alive, then there's a chance
              Barbara is too --

                      NANCY
              But that means she's trapped... in
              that place... that awful place.

Nancy looks up. Firm. Certain.

                    NANCY (CONT'D)
              We have to find it again.

A hard beat as Jonathan takes this in.

                    JONATHAN
              You want to go back out there?

                      NANCY
              Maybe we don't have to.

Nancy slides Jonathan a BOOK ON PREDATORS. We see a few
GRUESOME IMAGES OF ANIMALS ATTACKING THEIR PREY. Nancy --
the good student that she is -- has highlighted a few
passages.

                    NANCY (CONT'D)
When I saw it... it was feeding on
that deer. Meaning it's a
predator, right?

                    JONATHAN
... Right.

                    NANCY
It seems to hunt at night, like a
coyote, or a lion. But it doesn't
hunt in a pack like them -- it's
always alone. Like a bear. And...
          (beat)
Remember that night at Steve's...
when you took those pictures...
when Barbara cut herself?

                    JONATHAN
Yeah.

                    NANCY
She was bleeding. When I went
back... her bandage, it was in the
pool. The same place she went
missing.
          (he nods)
And then last night... that deer --

                    JONATHAN
          (realizing)
-- was bleeding too.

Nancy nods. *Exactly*. She now slides Jonathan a BOOK ON
SHARKS. It's open on a terrifying image of a shark leaping
out of the water to eat a seal.

                    NANCY
Sharks can detect blood at <u>one part
per million</u>. That's *one drop* of
blood in a million. They can smell
it from a quarter mile away --

                    JONATHAN
You think it can detect blood --

                    NANCY
It's just a theory.

Jonathan considers.

                    JONATHAN
We could test it.

A beat. Nancy nods. *She knows.*

> JONATHAN (CONT'D)
> But if it works...

> NANCY
> At least we'll know it's coming.

A beat as the idea of this sinks in. And then --

THE DOOR HANDLE TO NANCY'S ROOM SUDDENLY JOSTLES UP AND DOWN.

Nancy and Jonathan startle. They instinctively grab hands.

> KAREN (O.S.)
> Are you up, honey?

The tension deflates. *It's just Karen.*

> NANCY
> Yeah -- I'm getting dressed --

> KAREN (O.S.)
> I made some blueberry pancakes --

> NANCY
> I -- I'll be down in a second.

As Karen's FOOTSTEPS recede, the two teens suddenly realize
that they're holding hands. They quickly let go, pull away.

An awkward beat. Then...

> JONATHAN
> Your mom doesn't knock?

Nancy smiles a bit, breaking the tension, and --

EXT. SMALL HOUSE - DAY

WHAP! WHAP! WHAP! Knuckles RAP on a door.

WIDEN TO REVEAL: "CONNIE FRAZIER," the agent who killed
Benny, standing outside an unfamiliar house. After a beat,
the door swings open to reveal...

MR. CLARKE.

> CONNIE
> Scott Clarke?

> MR. CLARKE
> ... Yes...?

                    CONNIE
        The same Scott Clarke who teaches
        science and A.V. at Hawkins Middle?

                    MR. CLARKE
        The very same --

                    CONNIE
        Oh, wonderful.

Connie flashes a warm smile.

INT. MR. CLARKE'S HOUSE - LIVING ROOM - DAY

Connie now sits across from Mr. Clarke in his living room.

If one of our boys had a salary, and owned a house, it'd look
like this. Movie posters and science books and miniatures and
models and all the latest toys. Total nerd heaven in here.

Connie passes Mr. Clarke a FRIENDLY PAMPHLET which reads:

                "INDIANA A.V. CLUB!"

                    CONNIE
        ... And we're making a newsletter
        that we'll send out monthly. It'll
        showcase all the latest equipment,
        as well as how-to articles, which
        the kids write themselves.

                    MR. CLARKE
        Oh wow --

                    CONNIE
        What we're really trying to do,
        Mr. Clarke --

                    MR. CLARKE
        Please, call me Scott --

                    CONNIE
        Scott. What we're trying to do
        here, Scott, is connect kids from
        all over the state, and give them
        the support and encouragement to
        pursue careers in technology. We
        just... we feel like these are the
        kinds of kids that will make
        Indiana proud.

                    MR. CLARKE
        I agree, yes -- *completely.*

                              CONNIE
                    So... do you have some kids you
                    think would like to participate?

Mr. Clarke smiles.

                              MR. CLARKE
                    Oh -- I have a few in mind.

EXT. WHEELER HOUSE - DAY

A tire WHOOSHES past us as...

DUSTIN bikes up to the Wheeler house.

                              MIKE (PRE-LAP)
                    ... I just -- can't believe she
                    didn't come back...

INT. WHEELER HOUSE - BASEMENT - DAY

ANGLE ON: Eleven's dismantled tent.

PAN TO FIND: Mike pacing back and forth across the basement,
his mind racing, while Dustin tries to keep him calm.

                              DUSTIN
                    She's gotta be close --

                              MIKE
                    She said it wasn't safe. She just
                    messed up the compasses because she
                    was trying to protect us. She
                    didn't betray us --

                              DUSTIN
                    Mike, calm down --

                              MIKE
                    I shouldn't have yelled at her -- I
                    NEVER should have done that --

                              DUSTIN
                    This isn't your fault --

                              MIKE
                    Yeah, it's Lucas's.

                              DUSTIN
                    It wasn't his fault, either.

                              MIKE
                         (incredulous)
                    "It wasn't his fault" -- ?!

                    DUSTIN
No --

                    MIKE
You're saying he wasn't WAY out of
line -- ?

                    DUSTIN
Totally, but so were you --

                    MIKE
What -- ?

                    DUSTIN
-- and so was Eleven --

                    MIKE
Oh give me a break --

                    DUSTIN
Give ME a break. All three of you
were being total assholes. I was
the only reasonable one. But
bottom line is: You pushed first.
And you know the rule: Draw first
blood --

                    MIKE
No. *Forget it.* I'm not shaking
his hand --

                    DUSTIN
You're *shaking* his hand.

                    MIKE
No I'm not --

                    DUSTIN
It's not a discussion. It's the
rule of law. Obey or you're
banished from the party.
     (off Mike)
You want to be banished -- ?

                    MIKE
No.

                    DUSTIN
Good.

Dustin stands up. Grabs up his backpack and slips it on.

Dustin heads for the door.

> MIKE
> Where are we going?

> DUSTIN
> Where do you think? To get Lucas.
> And then we're going to find
> Eleven.

He tosses Mike his backpack. Mike catches it.

INT. HAWKINS LABS - ELEVEN'S ROOM (FLASHBACK)

*WHOOM! ELEVEN's eyes snap open to the SOUND OF A DOOR
UNLOCKING.*

*WIDEN TO REVEAL: She's in her doll-like bedroom at Hawkins
Labs, back in her hospital gown. The ultimate nightmare...*

DR. BRENNER enters. He sits down beside her.

He takes one of her hands.

> DR. BRENNER
> *This is a special day for us. Do
> you know why?*

Eleven shakes her head. "No."

> DR. BRENNER (CONT'D)
> *Because today, we make history.*
> (beat)
> *Today -- we make contact.*

EXT. WOODS - FALLEN TREE - DAY

Eleven JERKS awake. She was only dreaming.

She's curled up under a fallen tree. Deep in the forest.

She crawls out. She's covered in leaves and twigs... there
is dried blood under her nose... her crumpled wig beside her.

She looks primal, *feral,* like when we first met her.

EXT. WOODS - POND - DAY

CLOSE ON: Eleven's dirty Converses slop in the mud as...

She walks up to a pond. Alone in the woods.

She kneels by the pond and looks down at her reflection. She places the wig onto her head, adjusts it. But it doesn't look right -- crumpled, uneven. She doesn't look "pretty" anymore. She looks... like a *monster.*

She tosses the wig aside... narrows her eyes... and --

SPLASH! IN A BURST OF TELEKINETIC ENERGY, WATER RIPPLES OUTWARD, LIKE A HEAVY ROCK WAS THROWN, SHATTERING HER REFLECTION. BIRDS *SCATTER* --

We CUT WIDE: She's GONE. The only sign of her: her wig.

INT. WHEELER HOUSE - KITCHEN - DAY

THUNK! A KNIFE slices into a fluffy blueberry pancake as...

KAREN cuts pancakes for HOLLY. Holly has a flap of pancake in her mouth, but she's not eating it, she just moves it around while making noises.

> KAREN
> Sweetie, swallow the pancake.

TED is reading the paper.

> TED
> Where's Nancy? I thought she was
> coming down?

> KAREN
> She is. She was. I don't know.

Holly continues to move the pancake around in her mouth.

Karen has had enough. She shoves away from the table and --

INT. WHEELER HOUSE - UPSTAIRS - DAY

Karen charges up the steps.

> KAREN
> Nancy?! What's taking so long?

There is no answer.

> KAREN (CONT'D)
> Nancy?!

Karen rattles the handle to her room. It's locked.

> KAREN (CONT'D)
> Nancy -- come on...

Karen considers. *Screw it.* She removes a hair clip and thrusts it into the lock. POP! The door unlocks and...

INT. WHEELER HOUSE - NANCY'S ROOM - CONTINUOUS - DAY

Karen barges into Nancy's room. Her face falls as she sees:

No one is here. The bed is covered in books on predators, the bedroom window is open, an unrolled sleeping bag is on the floor.

Off Karen...

EXT. LUCAS'S HOUSE - DAY

DING DONG! Dustin rings the doorbell to Lucas's house.

Mike stands a bit behind him. Looking none too happy.

LUCAS answers the door. Not happy to see Mike either.

                    LUCAS
          ... What do you want?

Mike hesitates. Dustin elbows him.

                    MIKE
          I drew first blood. So...

Mike holds out his hand. Offering it.

Lucas stares at his hand. Considering. And...

INT. LUCAS'S HOUSE - LIVING ROOM - DAY

Lucas paces in the living room. Back and forth. Back and forth.

Dustin and Mike wait. Their patience is wearing thin.

Lucas finally stops. Turns to Mike and Dustin.

                    LUCAS
          Okay -- I'll shake.

Mike holds out his hand again.

                    LUCAS (CONT'D)
          On one condition: We forget the
          weirdo, and go straight to The
          Gate.

Mike pulls his hand away.

                        MIKE
          Then the deal's off.

                        LUCAS
          Fine --

                        MIKE
          Fine --

                        DUSTIN
          No, no, not fine! Guys,
          seriously?! Have you totally
          forgotten what happened on the
          Bloodstone Pass?!

Mike and Lucas stare. *They clearly have.*

                        DUSTIN (CONT'D)
          We couldn't agree on which path to
          take so we split up our party and
          those trolls took us out one by one
          and it all went to shit. By
          nightfall, we were all disabled!
          We stick together, no matter what --

                        LUCAS
          Yeah, I agree. But, this is the
          party, *right here*, in this room --

                        MIKE
          El's one of us now --

                        LUCAS
          Um, no, she's not, not even close,
          she never will be, she's a liar, a
          traitor -- !

                        MIKE
          She was just trying to keep us safe!
          She didn't mean to hurt you -- it
          was *an accident* --

                        LUCAS
          An accident -- ?!

                        DUSTIN
          Even if wasn't an accident, admit
          it, it was also a little awesome --

                        LUCAS
          Awesome -- ??

                              324

                    DUSTIN
          She threw you in the air with her
          mind!

                    LUCAS
          I could've been killed -- !

                    MIKE
          Which is exactly why we *need* her --

                    LUCAS
          What -- ?!

                    MIKE
          She's a weapon! You seriously want
          to fight the Demogorgon with your
          Wrist-Rocket? It'd be like R2-D2
          going to fight Darth Vader.
                    (beat)
          We're no use to Will if we're dead.

Lucas hesitates. Wavering. Mike has a point here. But...

                    LUCAS
          If you two want to waste your time
          looking for a traitor, go ahead.
          But I'm not spending any more time
          on her. No way. I'm going to The
          Gate.
                    (beat)
          I'm going to find Will.

Off Mike and Dustin, defeated...

EXT. WINKY'S GROCERY STORE - PARKING LOT - DAY

CLOSE ON: TWO DIRTY CONVERSES STEP OUT OF THE FOREST.

We BOOM UP to find Eleven. She is standing outside --

WINKY'S GROCERY STORE.

She watches customers stream out of the store. It's the
weekend, so the store is very busy right now. *Too busy.*

She heads for the store anyway.

INT. WINKY'S GROCERY STORE - DAY

WHOOSH! Automatic doors slide open as --

Eleven strides into the store. She looks very out of place.
The weirdo. Customers turn and stare at her as she passes
them by. A lot of shared looks, a lot of whispering.

A concerned mother pulls her toddler away.

As Eleven strides past the gawkers...

> DR. BRENNER (PRE-LAP)
> It's okay, Eleven. These are all
> friends...

INT. HAWKINS LABS - INDIGO LABORATORY (FLASHBACK)

Dr. Brenner leads Eleven into the lab. Holding her hand.

*The lab today is now filled with many more people than
normal. There are the usual SCIENTISTS and LAB TECHS,
including SCIENTIST #1 and the ELEVATOR SCIENTIST (#101), but
also now a cadre of important-looking MEN IN SUITS.*

Everyone is staring at Eleven.

She is noticeably unsettled by all this attention.

> DR. BRENNER
> *... They're just here to watch.*
> *Don't focus on them.*
> *(taps her head)*
> *Stay in here. Like before.*

> *ELEVEN*
> *Yes, Papa.*

INT. HAWKINS LABS - INDIGO LAB - MOMENTS LATER (FLASHBACK)

WHOOM! TECHNICIANS wrench open the isolation tank door.

*As the techs affix the EEG electrodes to her head,
Dr. Brenner kneels by Eleven. Speaks calmly. Quietly.*

> DR. BRENNER
> *Now remember -- whatever it is, it*
> *can't hurt you. Not from here. So*
> *don't be frightened of it.*

Eleven looks at him. Unsure.

> DR. BRENNER (CONT'D)
> *It is calling to you because it*
> *wants you. It is reaching out to*
> *you. So don't turn away from it*
> *this time. I want you to find it.*
> *Do you understand?*

A beat as Eleven considers. Then:

                        ELEVEN
          Yes.

We now move into a barrage of VIOLENT, RAPID SHOTS as...

- The tech slides the SCUBA-LIKE GLASS HELMET over her head.

- Eleven plummets into the water.

- The hatch door slams shut, locks.

- The observation door shuts.

- Eleven's eyes close and...

BLACK VOID (FLASHBACK)

Eleven's eyes snap open. She is in the VOID OF DARKNESS.

A voice echoes through the abyss:

                    GROCERY MANAGER (PRE-LAP)
          Are you lost?

INT. WINKY'S GROCERY STORE - DAY

A GROCERY MANAGER, 30s, approaches Eleven.

                    GROCERY MANAGER
          ... Is your mom here? Your dad?

Eleven stares at the manager.

                        ELEVEN
          Mouth breather.

She continues past him, wandering up to a LARGE FRIDGE.

She slides open the door and removes a BOX OF EGGOS. Then
another box. Then another. She stacks them up in her arms.

A FEMALE CLERK walks up to the Manager.

                    FEMALE CLERK
          What should we do?

                    GROCERY MANAGER
          ... Call the police.

The Clerk hurries off toward a phone as...

Eleven strides for the exit. Stacked Eggo boxes in her arms.

                    GROCERY MANAGER (CONT'D)
          Excuse me?! Young lady? Where do
          you think you're going with that?!

Eleven ignores him. Picks up the pace.

She blows right past the checkout.

                    GROCERY MANAGER (CONT'D)
          You have to pay for those -- !!

Eleven races through the sliding glass doors!

                    GROCERY MANAGER (CONT'D)
          HEY -- stop right there! THIEF!

The Manager races after Eleven, sprinting now. But just as
he reaches the doors, Eleven narrows her eyes and --

WHOOM! The doors SLAM SHUT in his face so hard that --

THE GLASS EXPLODES.

EXT. WINKY'S GROCERY STORE - PARKING LOT - DAY

SHOUTING and CHAOS ECHO in the parking lot as...

Eleven calmly walks away. Eggos safely in her arms.

Fresh blood drips from her nose.

INT/EXT. JOYCE'S CAR - FARM ROAD - DAY

WHOOSH! Joyce's car speeds down a lonely farm road.

They're in the middle of nowhere right now. Just rows of
farmland on every side of them. Corn fields, etc.

Hopper hangs a right, pulling onto a dirt driveway.

They pass a mailbox which reads: "IVES."

EXT. IVES FARM - DAY

The car parks outside a TWO-STORY FARMHOUSE.

EXT. IVES FARMHOUSE - DAY

DING DONG! Hopper rings the doorbell.

The door creaks open to reveal a WOMAN, late 30s. This is --

                    BECKY
          Can I help you?

                           328

                    HOPPER
          Uh, yeah, we're looking for Terry
          Ives. She live here?

                    BECKY
          Who's asking?

                    HOPPER
          Hawkins Chief of Police.

Becky looks him over.

                    BECKY
          You don't look like police.

Hopper digs out his badge, holds it up. Becky examines it.

She seems... very confused by all this.

                    BECKY (CONT'D)
          And you want to speak to my sister?

                    HOPPER
          If your sister's Terry Ives, then
          yeah, we do.

                    BECKY
          What about?

                    HOPPER
          We just have a few questions.

                    BECKY
          What about?

                    JOYCE
          Her daughter.

Becky is taken aback. She was *not* expecting this.

She regains her composure.

                    BECKY
          You're wasting your time.

She starts to close the door, but Joyce catches it.

                    JOYCE
          <u>Please</u>. My son is missing. Maybe
          you've seen on the news -- his name
          is Will... Will Byers --

She pulls out the flyer and shows it to Becky.

Becky looks at it. Softening a bit, but...

> BECKY
> I'm sorry for your son. I am. But
> I don't see how this has anything
> to do with Terry --

> JOYCE (CONT'D)
> Her daughter, Jane. We think maybe
> the same people who took her also
> took Will --

> BECKY
> No. That's not possible.

She goes to shut the door again, firmer, but --

Joyce catches the door again. Even *firmer.*

> JOYCE
> Please... even if it's not, I -- I
> need her to tell me.
> (fierce)
> Please.

Becky looks at Joyce. She can see that *this woman's not
giving up.* She looks back into the house.

At last, she sighs. Then relents.

> BECKY
> You can come in. But if you need
> Terry to tell you anything, you're
> about five years too late.

She opens the door the rest of the way.

Hopper and Joyce exchange a look. *The hell does that mean?*

INT. IVES FARMHOUSE - LIVING ROOM - DAY

Becky leads Hopper and Joyce into the living room.

They find TERRY IVES, early 40s but worn beyond her years,
sitting in a rocking chair, watching *Family Feud.* She wears
pajamas and slippers.

> BECKY
> Terry? You have some visitors.

Terry slowly turns and looks up at her "visitors." But she
doesn't seem to register them. Just looks *right through
them.* Her eyes are glassy, like a doll. No life to them.

Hopper and Joyce exchange looks.

                    HOPPER
          What's wrong with her?

Joyce shoots Hopper a look. *Quiet.*

She kneels down by Terry. Gentle.

                    JOYCE
          Terry? My name's Joyce. We'd like
          to ask you some questions about
          your daughter. Jane.

Terry blinks at the mention of Jane.

                    JOYCE (CONT'D)
          We wanted to know -- when was she
          taken?

No answer.

                    HOPPER
          What's your relationship with
          Doctor Brenner?

No answer.

                    JOYCE
               (no answer)
          See -- my son's missing -- he's been
          missing for almost a week now --

Joyce starts to remove the flyer to show Terry, but...

Terry abruptly turns away, returning her attention to the
show. She rocks gently back and forth.

                    BECKY
          Like I said... you're wasting your
          time.

Joyce looks up at Hop. At a loss.

INT. LUCAS'S HOUSE - LUCAS'S ROOM - DAY

WHOOM! Lucas shoves supplies into his backpack.

Flashlights, walkie-talkie, compass.

EXT. LUCAS'S HOUSE - DAY

Lucas pedals away down his driveway.

As he does, he notices a REPAIR VAN parked across from Mike's house. The side of the van reads, in bold letters:

HAWKINS POWER & LIGHT

A "REPAIR MAN" steps out. This is the same Ham radio Repair Man (from episode #105). He sees Lucas, waves.

Lucas waves back. And then, thinking nothing of it --

He continues on his way.

> DUSTIN (PRE-LAP)
> This is weird without Lucas.

EXT. STREET - DAY

Mike and Dustin bike down a street.

> MIKE
> He should've shaken my hand.

> DUSTIN
> He's just jealous.

> MIKE
> What are you talking about?

> DUSTIN
> Sometimes your total obliviousness
> blows my mind.

Mike stares. Looking, well, oblivious.

Dustin sighs. He can't believe he has to explain this.

> DUSTIN (CONT'D)
> He's your best friend, right?

> MIKE
> What? I mean -- I don't know --

> DUSTIN
> It's fine -- I get it. I didn't
> move here till the fourth grade and
> Lucas has the advantage of living
> right next door, but none of that
> matters. What matters is -- you
> guys are best friends, then this
> girl shows up and starts living in
> your basement and all you want to
> do is pay attention to her--

                    MIKE
          -- That's not true --

                    DUSTIN
          -- Yes it is and you know it and he
          knows it, but no one says anything
          until you both yell and punch each
          other like goblins with
          intelligence scores of zero and...
                    (beat)
          ... now everything is weird.

The boys bike in silence for another beat. Then:

                    MIKE
          He's not my best friend.

                    DUSTIN
          Yeah, right --

                    MIKE
          I mean he is. But so are you. So
          is Will.

                    DUSTIN
          You can't have more than one best
          friend.

                    MIKE
          Says who?

                    DUSTIN
          Says logic.

                    MIKE
          Well, I call "bull" on your logic.
          Because you're my best friend too.

Dustin shakes his head. But... this clearly means the world
to him. Then his eyes go wide as he sees something up ahead.

                    DUSTIN
          Whoa.

Mike and Dustin pull to a stop. Stare.

REVERSE ANGLE TO REVEAL: WINKY'S GROCERY STORE. A POLICE CAR
is now parked out front, roof lights flashing, and a CROWD OF
GAWKERS standing by the SHATTERED GLASS. The Grocery Manager
holds up his hands, showing OFFICERS CALLAHAN and POWELL the
height of the girl.

                    DUSTIN (CONT'D)
          You don't think -- ?

                         MIKE
            Uh. Definitely.

The manager points in the direction she ran off.

Mike and Dustin share looks. *Bingo.*

They bike off in that direction. Galvanized.

As they explode into the woods...

We cut to an EXTREME WIDE SHOT TO REVEAL:

A BLURRED SHAPE WATCHING THEM FROM THE ADJACENT WOODS.

Is it Eleven? The shape darts out of frame.

INT. IVES FARMHOUSE - LIVING ROOM - DAY

Terry Ives continues to watch *Family Feud*.

She rocks back and forth in her chair. Her eyes glazed.

                         BECKY (O.S.)
            ... She was part of some study, in
            college --

INT. IVES FARMHOUSE - KITCHEN - DAY

Becky is seated across a table from Joyce and Hopper.

She drags a camel.

                         HOPPER
            MKUltra?

                         BECKY
            Yeah that's the one. Started in
            the fifties. By the time Terry got
            involved, it was supposed to be
            ramping down, but... the drugs were
            just getting crazier. Messed her
            up good. It wasn't too bad at
            first, but it got worse over time,
            and now...
                (glances at Terry)
            ... here we are...

                         HOPPER
            This was the CIA who ran this?

Becky can't help but smile.

                    BECKY
          You and Terry would've gotten
          along. "The Man" with a capital
          "M" -- same guys who killed Kennedy
          and King, am I right?

Becky takes another drag of her cigarette.

                    BECKY (CONT'D)
          Truth is, it was a bunch of hippie
          professors taking government money.
          They'd pay a couple hundred bucks
          to people like my sister, then give
          'em drugs -- psychedelics. LSD,
          mostly. Then they'd have her strip
          naked and get into these isolation
          tanks.

                    JOYCE
          Isolation tanks...?

                    BECKY
          Big old bath tubs, basically, with
          salt water in 'em, so you float in
          there. You lose any sense of...
          sense. Feel nothing, see nothing.
          They wanted to "expand the
          boundaries of the mind." Real
          hippie crap. My sister was into
          it. It's not like they forced her
          to do it or something.
               (beat)
          Thing is, she didn't know she was
          pregnant at the time --

                    JOYCE
          Jane.

Becky nods. "Yup."

                    JOYCE (CONT'D)
          Do you have any pictures of her?

                    BECKY
          Of *Jane*?
               (Joyce nods)
          I don't think you understand.
          Terry miscarried in the third
          trimester.

Off Hopper and Joyce...

INT. IVES FARMHOUSE - JANE'S ROOM - DAY

Becky leads Hopper and Joyce into a room in the back.

There is a crib here complete with a mobile, pink walls, cute toys -- the perfect home for a newborn. It looks clean, well kept up. Only: there is no child here. *Never was.*

> BECKY
> She keeps this up -- been doing it
> for twelve years now.

Hopper spins the mobile. Brahm's Lullaby begins. Eerie.

> BECKY (CONT'D)
> Terry -- she pretends like Jane's
> real. Like she's gonna come home
> someday. Says she's special --
> born with "abilities" --

> JOYCE
> Abilities?

> BECKY
> You read any Stephen King?

Joyce and Hopper share a look. Becky smiles.

> BECKY (CONT'D)
> You guys look actually scared or
> something. It's all make-believe --

> JOYCE
> What kind of abilities?

> BECKY
> Telepathy, telekinesis -- you know,
> doing shit with your mind. That's
> why the "big bad Man" stole Jane
> away, see? Her baby's a *weapon*,
> off fighting the commies.

Becky takes a drag, shakes her head at the absurdity of this.

> BECKY (CONT'D)
> The doctors all say it's a coping
> mechanism or something. To deal
> with the guilt of it, you know?

                    JOYCE
          You don't think she could be
          telling the truth?

Becky gives Joyce look. Uhhhhh...

                    JOYCE (CONT'D)
               (clarifying)
          About having had a kid?

                    BECKY
          No birth certificate, nothing from
          the hospital, doctor and nurses all
          confirm she miscarried --

                    HOPPER
          And no indications it might've been
          covered up?

Becky just smiles. Takes another drag.

                    BECKY
          Like I say, you and Terry would've
          gotten along.

The mobile stops spinning. The lullaby ends. And...

EXT. WOODS - DAY

CLOSE ON: A compass needle points NORTH as...

Lucas pushes his bike through the woods.

EXT. COUNTRY ROAD - FENCE - DAY

Lucas emerges onto a country road. He crashes to a halt.

                    LUCAS
          Oh man...

Before him, a METAL FENCE blocks his way. It stretches in
every direction, vanishing into the woods. No way past.

A familiar sign reads:

               RESTRICTED AREA. NO TRESPASSING.
               U.S. GOVERNMENT PROPERTY.

Lucas looks down at his compass. The needle points straight
ahead. Straight on the other side of that giant fence.

Lucas looks around. Annoyed. Then...

He starts to walk around the fence...

This is going to take some time.

INT. OUTDOOR SUPPLY AND HUNT - DAY

CLOSE ON: THE JAWS OF A BEAR.

It's mounted on the wall of a local hunting store.

Jonathan and Nancy move through the aisles with a shopping cart. A SERIES OF QUICK SHOTS as they toss supplies in:

Gasoline... lighter fluid... nails... barbed wire...

And last but certainly not least:

A GIANT-ASS BEAR TRAP.

INT. OUTDOOR SUPPLY - REGISTER - MOMENTS LATER - DAY

Jonathan and Nancy drop everything at the register.

                    JONATHAN
          And four boxes of twenty-twos.

The HUNTING STORE OWNER stares at them. Suspicious.

                    HUNTING STORE OWNER
          What you kids doin' with all this?

Jonathan and Nancy share a quick look.

                    NANCY
          Monster hunting.

The Store Owner stares at her. Then chuckles. *Good one.*

He begins to ring them up.

EXT. OUTDOOR SUPPLY PARKING LOT - DAY

Jonathan and Nancy toss their "weapons" into the trunk of Jonathan's car.

                    JONATHAN
          "Monster hunting"?

Nancy shrugs. Can't help but smile a little.

                    NANCY
          Last week... I was shopping for a
          new top Steve might like. It took
          me and Barb all weekend.
                    (MORE)

338

                    NANCY (CONT'D)
          It seemed like life or death, you
          know? And now...

                    JONATHAN
          You're shopping for bear traps with
          Jonathan Byers.

                    NANCY
          Yeah.

Jonathan slams the trunk. They head for the car doors.

                    JONATHAN
          What's the weirder part? Me or the
          bear trap?

                    NANCY
          You. Definitely you.

HOONNNKK!! A LOUD CAR HORN BLASTS. Our teens turn to find --

A high school boy, REED, hanging out the window of a speeding
car.

                    REED
          Hey Nance!! I can't wait to see
          your movie!

The car PEELS OFF. LAUGHTER TRAILS in its wake.

Nancy and Jonathan stare. Taken aback.

                    JONATHAN
          ... What the hell was that?

                    NANCY
          I -- I don't know.

Nancy looks back in the direction the car came from. Her
eyes narrow, her expression darkens. We don't know what
she's looking at, not yet, but whatever it is shocks her.

She begins to walk toward it. Moving fast.

                    JONATHAN
          Where are you going? Nancy?
          Nancy?!

But Nancy ignores him. Just keeps walking.

As her pace quickens, tears welling in her eyes...

                            339

EXT. DOWNTOWN - MOVIE THEATER - DAY

Nancy races up the sidewalk. Stops. Breathing hard.

REVERSE ANGLE: The movie theater marquee. The official
letters read:

ALL THE RIGHT MOVES

But directly beneath, in red spray paint, someone has added:

STARRING NANCY "THE SLUT" WHEELER

Jonathan comes up behind Nancy. Takes in the marquee.

> JONATHAN
> Jesus...

Nancy's eyes dart around. She sees a THEATER MANAGER talking
to an exasperated TICKET TEARER. Townspeople looking at the
sign. Talking, whispering, gawking. Cars speed by. People
stare out windows. Everyone is seeing this. *Everyone*.

Nancy's panic mounts. And that's when she hears it --

LAUGHTER. We know this laughter. And so does Nancy.

It's TOMMY H. His AWFUL, MEAN-SPIRITED CACKLE.

It's coming from around the back of the theater.

She strides toward the laughter.

> JONATHAN (CONT'D)
> Nancy -- Nancy -- !

But she is already gone.

EXT. MOVIE THEATER - BACK ALLEYWAY - DAY

Nancy strides down the alley behind the theater.

Sure enough, she finds Tommy H. here, spray-painting the wall.
And he's not alone. He's with Carol, NICOLE, and...

Steve. Nancy's heart almost stops at the sight of him.

Steve clocks her. He looks away. Angry. Ashamed?

The others, however, seem *delighted* she's here.

> CAROL
> Hey there, princess!

> TOMMY H.
> Uh oh, she looks upset.

341

Nancy strides over to the teens. But she's not even looking
at Tommy H. and Carol. Her eyes are fixed on one person and
one person only: Steve. She walks right up to him and --

WHAP! Slaps him. So hard his face snaps sideways.

                    CAROL
          OHHHH!!!

                    TOMMY H.
          Damn!

Nancy's glares at Steve. Her eyes glisten with tears.

                    NANCY
          What is wrong with you?!

                    STEVE
          What is wrong with YOU?! I was
          worried about you -- actually
          worried about you, you believe
          that?!

                    NANCY
          What are you talking about -- ?!

                    CAROL
          Wouldn't lie if I was you. You
          don't want to be known as a lying
          slut, now do you?

As Nancy's confusion grows, Tommy H.'s eyes narrow.

                    TOMMY H.
          Speak of the devil.

Nancy follows his gaze to find...

Jonathan. Headed their way.

It suddenly clicks for Nancy. She turns back to Steve.

                    NANCY
          You came by last night?

                    CAROL
          DING-DING-DING! Does she get a
          prize?

                    NANCY
          I don't know what you saw but it
          wasn't like that --

                         STEVE
              Oh, so you just let him in your
              room to, what, study?

                         TOMMY H.
              For another pervy photo session?

                         NANCY
              We were just...

                         STEVE
              Just what? Finish that sentence.
              Finish that sentence.

Nancy hesitates. Not sure how to.

                         STEVE (CONT'D)
              Go to hell, Nancy.

Nancy stares at Steve. Confused and hurt. *Really hurt.*

                         JONATHAN
              Come on, Nancy, let's go. They're
              not worth it --

He takes Nancy's hand and pulls her away.

                         STEVE
              I gotta say, Byers, I'm impressed.
              I always took you for a queer.
              Guess you're just a screw-up.

Jonathan doesn't take the bait. He and Nancy just continue
to walk away. But Steve doesn't let go. Calls after him:

                         STEVE (CONT'D)
              After all, runs in your family,
              right? Bunch of screw-ups in that
              house. Not surprised what happened
              to your brother.

Now this -- *this* gets to Jonathan. He stops, turns back.

Nancy squeezes his hand tight. Pulls him.

                         NANCY
              Jonathan, leave it --

But Jonathan can't. He tears free of Nancy's hold and --

Strides back over to Steve.

                              343

                              STEVE
          I'm sorry, man, just tellin' the
          truth. The Byers are a disgrace to
          this town, everyone knows it --

WHAM! Jonathan SUCKER-PUNCHES Steve. HARD. He goes down.

GASPS erupt from the crowd.

Steve touches his lip. It's bleeding. He looks back up at
Jonathan. Burning with anger. Then he RUSHES Jonathan and
TACKLES him to the ground. And suddenly the two boys are
going at it. This is a *real* fight. No holds barred. Messy.

Steve is stronger, but Jonathan has a RAGE that has been
building inside him a while now. WHAM! He lands a PUNCH.

Tommy comes to help out but Steve wants no help, shoves him
back.

                              STEVE (CONT'D)
          GET AWAY!

Tommy does. Jonathan swings again at Steve, but misses, and --

WHAM! Steve hits Jonathan square in the face with a right
hook. It infuriates Jonathan. WHAM! Jonathan fires back.
HARD. Again. HARDER. And --

WHUMP! Steve flips back onto the ground. Dazed. Jonathan
climbs on top of him and begins to BEAT HIS FACE IN. He
looks crazy -- almost rabid. All the anger and pain coming
out in a flash of violence. When --

WOOO WOOOOOP! POLICE SIRENS SUDDENLY WAIL.

Nancy whirls to find a POLICE CRUISER SCREECHING TO A HALT AT
THE END OF THE ALLEY. Callahan and Powell leap out.

As they race toward the teens, Jonathan continues to pound on
Steve. He's so wound up he can't stop. Carol freaks at the
sight of the cops, pulls Tommy H. away --

                              CAROL
          We gotta go!!

As Nancy tries to call Jonathan off --

                              NANCY
          JONATHAN -- !

WHAM! Jonathan hits Steve.

                         NANCY (CONT'D)
          STOP -- !

WHAM! Again. Powell and Callahan arrive and --

WHOOM! Callahan tries to haul Jonathan off Steve, but --

WHAM! Jonathan's errant elbow slams Callahan in the nose.

Callahan stumbles back, but Powell grabs hold tight --

                    OFFICER POWELL
          HEY -- STOP! STOP, KID -- !

WHOOM! Powell hauls him over toward the brick wall as --

Tommy H. and Carol wrench Steve to his feet and hobble off --

                    TOMMY H.
          C'MON -- GO, GO, GO!

As Steve and his cronies escape around a corner --

Callahan and Powell restrain Jonathan. Callahan pulls out
HANDCUFFS and whips them around his wrists. CLICK-SNAP!

Off Nancy, in shock...

INT. IVES FARMHOUSE - JANE'S ROOM - DAY

Joyce and Hopper sift through Terry's items.

They look through old articles, pictures, etc.

                    JOYCE
          This must've been before she was
          pregnant...

Joyce passes Hopper a faded photograph of a group of young
people, including YOUNG TERRY, standing in a UNIVERSITY
HOSPITAL. They are all smiling. Beside them, we see --

A YOUNG DOCTOR BRENNER.

Hopper taps Brenner.

                    HOPPER
          That's him. Martin Brenner.

Joyce reads the caption.

JOYCE
"Doctor Martin Brenner, associate
professor, abnormal psychology..."

HOPPER
It all connects -- it's gotta be
her. *Gotta be.* Terry gets
pregnant, Jane's born -- she's
taken by Brenner for whatever the
hell he's doing down there. She
escapes -- winds up at Benny's --
maybe she's hungry. Benny tries to
protect her -- bad idea.

JOYCE
This was Monday?
   (Hopper nods)
Then where's she been for five
days?

HOPPER
That's the thing. This girl --
she's got no hair -- been cooped up
in some asylum her whole life...

JOYCE
Someone should have seen her.

Hopper nods. *Exactly.*

HOPPER
But if anyone knows what happened
to Will --

JOYCE
We have to find her.

Hopper looks back up at the empty crib. And we CUT TO:

EXT. WOODS - LOG - DAY

Eleven. She sits alone in woods. Eating an Eggo.

There are crumbs from Eggos all over the ground, as well as a
few open boxes. She's clearly been at this for awhile now.

Suddenly -- she stops eating. Her head jerks up.

She hears something. VOICES off in the distance. They are
hard to hear at first. But they're getting LOUDER. CLOSER.

It sounds almost like... Mike and Dustin.

                    MIKE'S & DUSTIN'S VOICES
              (very distant)
          Eleven?! EL?!

EXT. WOODS - DAY

Sure enough, it is them. They're pushing their bikes through
the woods, calling out at the tops of their little lungs:

                    MIKE/DUSTIN
          Eleven?! EL?! EL??!!

Mike suddenly pauses.

                    MIKE
          You hear that?

                    DUSTIN
          What?

Dustin listens. Sure enough, he HEARS something now too:

RUSTLING FOLIAGE. Our boys turn toward the sound.

They see a FAINT SHAPE moving toward them through foliage.

Mike hurries toward the movement. Excited.

                    MIKE
          El -- ?? EL?!

The shape emerges. Mike goes dead cold. It's not Eleven.

It's TROY AND JAMES.

                    TROY
          Hey there, Frogface.

                    JAMES
          Toothless.

SWOOSH! Troy flicks open a SWITCHBLADE.

Our boys' faces go pale.

                    MIKE
          GO -- GO !!

Mike and Dustin drop their bikes -- and run --

                    JAMES
          DAMMIT!

347

The bullies chase after them.

<u>The RACE IS ON</u>.

INT. IVES FARMHOUSE - LIVING ROOM - DAY

APPLAUSE fills the air as the *Family Feud* credits roll.

WIDEN TO REVEAL: Becky leading Hop and Joyce to the front
door. Hop gives her a thankful nod as she opens the door.

                    HOPPER
          Thanks again for your time --
          appreciate it.

                    BECKY
          Sorry I couldn't be of more help.

                    HOPPER
     Mm.

Hopper slips on his hat and heads out onto the porch. Joyce
starts to follow, when --

                    BECKY
          Hey. Good luck. Finding your son.

Joyce gives her a small nod. Her gaze then shifts to Terry.
Rocking back and forth in her chair. Mumbling to herself.

Crazy. Sad. *Lonely.*

Off Joyce...

INT./EXT. JOYCE'S CAR - IVES FARM - DAY

Joyce climbs into the car.

Hopper turns the keys when he notices Joyce. She looks
upset.

                    HOPPER
          ... Hey.

Joyce snaps out of it, looks at him.

                    JOYCE
          ... What?

                    HOPPER
          We're going to find him.

348

                         JOYCE
               Like Terry found her daughter?

Joyce takes out a cigarette. It trembles as she lights it.

                         HOPPER
               We're close --

                         JOYCE
               Twelve years, _twelve years_ she's
               been looking for her --

                         HOPPER
               And she was at Benny's less than
               five days ago. That means we've
               got a chance, yeah?

Joyce look away. Takes a drag. Not feeling any better.

                         HOPPER (CONT'D)
               You know what I'd give? For a
               chance? You know what I'd give?

Joyce looks at Hopper. At the intensity in his eyes.

A beat. Then --

CHHHHHHHHH! The radio blasts to life.

                         OFFICER CALLAHAN'S VOICE (OVER RADIO)
               Chief, you there? Chief --

Hopper grabs the radio. Hits it on.

                         HOPPER
               What?

                         OFFICER CALLAHAN'S VOICE
               A fight broke out here and --

                         HOPPER
               Cal -- I don't have time --

                         OFFICER CALLAHAN'S VOICE
               It's Jonathan Byers. You haven't
               seen Joyce, have you -- ?

Hopper and Joyce share a look and...

EXT. WOODS - FENCE - DAY

CRACK! Branches SNAP underfoot as Lucas reaches an edge of the fence. He turns the corner, walks about twenty feet...

And pulls out his COMPASS. Opens it. Looks at the NEEDLE.

Lucas's face falls...

Because the needle is pointing not straight ahead, but back over that giant fucking fence. <u>Suddenly it hits Lucas</u>:

<u>The Gate is somewhere inside</u>.

Lucas scans the fence. Twenty feet tall. Razor wire on top.

His eyes search the nearby woods, lock on:

AN OLD ELM TREE.

EXT. QUARRY ROAD - DAY

WHOOSH! Mike and Dustin race down a steep hill.

They crash to a halt. Their eyes shooting wide. Troy is running right for them. He's cut them off.

They race away.

EXT. QUARRY SIDE - DAY

Mike and Dustin race deeper into the quarry.

> DUSTIN
> Aggg, I have a cramp --

> MIKE
> Just keep going, keep going!!

> DUSTIN
> SHIT!

They suddenly slam to a stop.

REVERSE ANGLE: <u>JAMES IS RUNNING TOWARD THEM FROM THE BOTTOM</u>.

Our boys swivel around. But --

<u>TROY IS RUNNING TOWARD THEM FROM THE OTHER DIRECTION</u>.

Mike's eyes dart, panicked, searching for an escape route.
But there are only two other impossible directions: a cliff
wall straight up; and a cliff's edge and steep drop to the
water below.

They're surrounded. Trapped.

The bullies catch up to them.

Mike breathes hard from the chase. Dustin holds his stomach.

Mike grabs up a ROCK, Dustin grabs a STICK.

                    MIKE
          Don't come any closer!!

The bullies come closer.

Mike hurls the rock. It whizzes past James.

                    JAMES
          Nice throw, numbnuts --

Dustin charges forward with a courageous WAR CRY, swinging
his stick at Troy, but Troy grabs him, easily disarming him,
putting him in a choke hold.

                    DUSTIN
          GET OFF -- GET OFF ME -- !

                    MIKE
          LET HIM GO -- !

Mike charges to Dustin's rescue but --

Troy presses his switchblade up to Dustin's neck.

                    TROY
          STAY BACK OR I CUT HIM!

Mike goes pale. Holy shit. This just got real. *Too real.*

                    MIKE
          What do you want...?!

                    TROY
          I want to know how you did it!

                    MIKE
          How I did what??

                    TROY
          I know you did something to me, some
          nerdy science shit to make me do that --

                              351

                        MIKE
            You mean pee your pants?

Troy clenches his teeth. *Yes.*

                        DUSTIN
            Our friend has superpowers and she
            squeezed your tiny bladder with her
            mind --

Troy slides the knife up to Dustin's mouth, shutting him up.

                        TROY
            I think maybe I should save
            Toothless here a trip to the
            dentist, help him lose the rest of
            his baby teeth. What do you say,
            James?

                        JAMES
            I say that's a helluva idea.

Dustin is so scared now he begins to sob.

                        MIKE
            LET HIM GO!! LET HIM GO!

                        TROY
            I'll let him go, sure. But
            first... it's your turn.

                        MIKE
            My turn to what -- ??

                        TROY
            Wet yourself.

                        MIKE
            ... What -- ?

Troy motions to the edge of the quarry.

                        TROY
            Jump. Or Toothless here gets an
            early trip to the dentist.

Troy digs the knife into Dustin's mouth. Dustin cries.

Mike holds up his hands.

                        MIKE
            Okay, okay! Just hold on! HOLD ON!

                             352

Mike walks over to the cliff and looks down. It's a
dizzying, vertiginous drop to the water below. No way he
survives this.

He looks back at Dustin. Dustin shouts through tears.

                    DUSTIN
          DON'T -- MIKE -- DON'T -- I DON'T
          NEED MY BABY TEETH -- I DON'T -- !

Mike turns back to the cliff. Gathering courage.

                    JAMES
               (low)
          Troy, I don't know if this is a
          good idea, man --

                    DUSTIN
               (muffled)
          MIKE -- DON'T --

Mike takes a deep breath...

                    TROY
          Dentist's office opens in five --

Mike takes a step closer to the cliff...

                    TROY (CONT'D)
               -- four --

Another step...

                    TROY (CONT'D)
               -- three --

Another...

                    TROY (CONT'D)
               -- two --

Mike closes his eyes...

                    DUSTIN
               (muffled)
          MIIIKKE -- !

And...

<u>MIKE STEPS OFF THE EDGE.</u>   <u>VANISHING OVER THE LIP.</u>

A beat of terrible silence.

James and Troy race to the edge.

                         353

They look down. Their eyes shoot wide with shock.

WE NOW CUT TO AN EXTREME WIDE SHOT TO REVEAL THAT:

MIKE IS HOVERING MID-AIR BENEATH THE LIP OF THE QUARRY. JUST
HANGING ABOVE THE WATER. HIS LEGS KICK LIKE CRAZY. *HOLLLLY
SHIT*. AND THEN, SLOWLY, HE BEGINS TO RISE BACK UP THE CLIFF
EDGE, AS IF DRAWN BY AN INVISIBLE HAND. HE'S SLOWLY CARRIED
BACK OVER ONTO DRY LAND. HOVERS FOR A SECOND. AND THEN...

WHOOOMP! HE DROPS. LIKE A PUPPET WITH ITS STRINGS SNIPPED.

He crashes to the earth. Hard. Dust billows.

The bullies stare. Too stunned to speak.

A SMALL FIGURE approaches. It's...

ELEVEN. PALE. DIRTY. BLOOD STREAMS OUT OF HER NOSTRILS.

She strides toward the bullies. Intense. Angry.

WHOOSH! An invisible force knocks James on his ass.

THEN Troy's arm suddenly twists unnaturally to the right and --

SNAP! We HEAR the CRUNCH OF BONE as his arm breaks.

Troy drops the knife and WAILS in pain.

Eleven glares at him.

                    ELEVEN
          Go.

Troy SOBS like a little baby as he and James turn heel and --

Run like hell.

                    DUSTIN
          THAT'S RIGHT, YOU BETTER RUN.
          SHE'S OUR FRIEND AND SHE'S
          CRAAAZY!!! YOU COME BACK HERE,
          SHE'LL KILL YOU!!! YOU HEAR ME?!!
          SHE'LL KILL YOU, YOU
          SONSOFBITCHES!!

Mike looks at Eleven. Filled with relief. But then...

WHOMP! Eleven collapses to the ground.

                    MIKE
          El?! EL? Are you okay??

Mike and Dustin kneel by Eleven.

She's still conscious, but weak, pale. A stream of blood
spills out her nose and ears. Mike cradles her head in his
arms.

She looks up at him with tear-stained eyes. Her eyes flutter.

                    ELEVEN
          Mike -- I'm -- sorry --

                    MIKE
          Sorry? What are you sorry for?

Eleven fights back more tears and...

BLACK VOID (FLASHBACK)

We're suddenly back in the VOID OF DARKNESS.

ELEVEN HEARS the GUTTURAL SOUND she heard the other day.

*But this time she doesn't turn back. She walks toward the
sound. Gradually, out of the darkness, "it" emerges:*

*OUR MONSTER. Its slick white skin stands out starkly against
the blackness. It is hunched on the ground, turned away from
us. Its back heaves, horribly, as it feeds on some kind of
FLESHY ALIEN EGG-SACK. The sack spews a strange yellow liquid.*

Eleven tenses. Terrified of this thing before her.

But... then she remembers her orders: "Don't be afraid."

*She keeps walking. Until she is close enough to touch the
monster. It still doesn't notice her. Just keeps eating.*

Then slowly... very slowly... Eleven reaches out a hand.

CLOSE ON: Her finger touches its pale, withered flesh.

THE MONSTER SUDDENLY SNAPS ITS HEAD AROUND --

ITS FLESH PEELS OPEN --

IT SHRIEKS --

AND --

INT. ISOLATION TANK (FLASHBACK)

Eleven SCREAMS.

Blood streams out her nose and ears.

INT. HAWKINS LABS - INDIGO LABORATORY CONTROL ROOM (FLASHBACK)

Dr. Brenner and the scientists react in horror as --

THE MONSTER'S EAR-SPLITTING SHRIEK ERUPTS OUT OF EVERY SPEAKER IN THE ROOM. THE EEG MACHINES GO HAYWIRE AND THE LIGHTS IN THE LABORATORY FLICKER WILDLY.

INT. HAWKINS LABS - INDIGO LABORATORY (FLASHBACK)

We see GLIMPSES OF HORROR in the stuttering light:

- A CRACK races across the floor of the lab...

- Spreading up the side of the wall where...

- THE RIFT FORMS IN THE WALL.

> ELEVEN (PRE-LAP)
> ... The Gate...

EXT. QUARRY SIDE - DAY

A tear slips down Eleven's cheek.

> ELEVEN
> ... Lucas -- he -- he was right.
> (beat)
> I opened it.
> (beat)
> I'm... the monster.

Mike shakes his head. Fighting back tears.

> MIKE
> No -- no. You're not the monster.
> You saved me, El. *You saved me...*

He pulls Eleven up off the ground and into his arms, holding her close, not letting her go. Not again, not ever. She hugs him back. A beat and then...

Dustin comes up and joins the hug!

As our three friends hug...

We slowly DRIFT BACK OVER the majestic quarry.

EXT. POLICE STATION - DAY - ESTABLISHING

The American flag flutters outside the station.

Powell's cruiser and Jonathan's car are parked out front.

356

INT. POLICE STATION - KITCHEN - DAY

FWOOM! A fridge door swings open.

FLORENCE reaches inside and removes some SOME ICE CUBES,
which she proceeds to wrap in a rag. *Making an ice pack.*

Nancy hovers behind her. Awkward -- and on edge.

                    NANCY
          You think... we'll be out of here
          soon?

                    FLORENCE
          You. Yes. Him, no. He assaulted
          an officer.

                    NANCY
          How long will you keep him?

                    FLORENCE
          You and your boyfriend got big
          plans, do you?

                    NANCY
          He's... not my boyfriend.

Florence gives her a look.

                    FLORENCE
          I think you better tell him that.

                    NANCY
          What?

                    FLORENCE
          Only love makes you that crazy,
          sweetheart. And that damn stupid.

Florence passes Nancy the ice pack.

INT. POLICE STATION - BULLPEN - DAY

Jonathan sits handcuffed in the back of the bullpen.

Nearby, Callahan types up a report.

                    NANCY
          ... Found some ice.

Jonathan looks up to find Nancy. Approaching with the ice
pack.

                         JONATHAN
              Thanks.

Nancy sits down beside him and begins to gently ice his
cheek. She's a bit... awkward about it. And he clocks this.

                         JONATHAN (CONT'D)
              ... Everything alright?

                         NANCY
              Yeah. Everything's... fine.

Off Nancy, blushing...

EXT. WOODS - TREE TOP & HAWKINS LABS - DAY

WHOOM! HANDS grasp a thick branch from underneath as...

Lucas hauls himself up onto the upper branch of the elm tree.

He unzips his bag and removes his dad's 'NAM BINOCULARS.

Lucas raises them to his face. Looks out.

A SERIES OF PANNING BINOCULAR POV SHOTS:

- We see the lab building with its enormous RADAR TOWERS.

- The M.P. SOLDIER at the checkpoint, letting in sedans.

- THE BACK DOOR to the lab, guarded by three M.P.s.

- FOUR VANS parked near the back door. Their sides read:

                    HAWKINS POWER & LIGHT

Lucas lowers the binoculars. Mind racing. *It can't be.*

He raises the binoculars again. As he locks once more on the
Power & Light vans, we CUT to:

EXT. WHEELER HOUSE - VAN - DAY

The Hawkins Power & Light van parked outside of the Wheelers.

INT. POWER & LIGHT VAN - DAY

The "Repair Man" (from #105) is listening to the surveillance
equipment when suddenly --

He sits up in his seat, spotting something. THROUGH THE
WINDSHIELD: Mike, Eleven, and Dustin in the distance. Headed
this way.

He grabs up his walkie and makes a call and...

INT. HAWKINS LABS - ARMORY - DAY

WHOOM! A GUN is ripped off the wall. Then another.

AGENTS in Power & Light outfits are removing TRANQUILIZER GUNS from the wall. They load darts into chambers. Moving fast.

EXT. HAWKINS LABS - DAY

Dr. Brenner explodes out of the lab. Trench coat billowing.

And he's not alone. All other agents (including LEAD AGENT and Connie) and about two-dozen disguised military police are with him.

A SERIES OF QUICK SHOTS as --

Brenner and the others climb into Power & Light vans.

Doors SLAM shut.

As the vans SQUEAL away...

EXT. WOODS - TREE TOP & HAWKINS LABS - DAY

BINOCULAR POV: The vans race away from the lab, kicking up a whirlwind of dust. As they leave the gate and exit view...

Lucas lowers the binoculars. His face ghost white.

We PUSH IN on him and...

EXT. WHEELER HOUSE - DAY

Mike, Eleven, and Dustin head back into the basement.

They head inside the house. Unaware.

The door closes shut. And...

<u>END EPISODE</u>

CHAPTER SEVEN:
THE BATHTUB

WRITTEN BY **JUSTIN DOBLE**

INT. WHEELER HOUSE - BASEMENT BATHROOM - DAY 7 CONT'D

WHOOSH! A RAG wipes across pale, dirty skin.

WIDEN TO REVEAL: <u>MIKE is cleaning ELEVEN</u>.

She sits next to him on the edge of the bathroom counter.

Mike wipes the last of the dirt off her face.

                    MIKE
          That's better.

Eleven slowly turns and looks back at herself in the mirror.
She studies herself. Touches her short hair. She clearly
misses her wig.

                    MIKE (CONT'D)
          You don't need it.

                    ELEVEN
          Still... pretty...?

Mike doesn't hold back this time:

                    MIKE
          Yeah. Pretty. Really pretty.

Eleven turns back to Mike. An emotional moment here as these
two kids look at one another. They're physically closer now
than they've ever been before... their faces just a few
inches away.

                    MIKE (CONT'D)
          ... El?

                    ELEVEN
          Yes?

                    MIKE
          I'm... happy you're home.

                    ELEVEN
          ... Me too.

Another beat. Mike's heart beats fast. His breath quickens.

TIME SEEMS TO SLOW DOWN and the SOUND FADES AWAY and...

<u>Mike starts to lean in</u>. Is he going to kiss Eleven???

Just as his face draws near --

WHOOM! THE BATHROOM DOOR FLIES OPEN.

It's DUSTIN. *Of course it's Dustin.*

>   DUSTIN
>   Guys --

>   MIKE
>   (annoyed)
>   What -- ?

>   DUSTIN
>   It's Lucas. I think he's in
>   trouble.

INT. WHEELER HOUSE - BASEMENT - DAY

Mike and Eleven hurry out of the bathroom.

Dustin leads them over to his supercomm. HISSING STATIC.

>   DUSTIN
>   He said he was going to The Gate,
>   remember? What if he found it?

Sure enough, we can HEAR LUCAS'S VOICE coming out of the
receiver. At least... we *think* it's Lucas. The signal is
terrible... so terrible it's impossible to understand what
he's saying. But we can tell that he's clearly SHOUTING.

>   MIKE
>   What's he saying -- ?

>   DUSTIN
>   I don't know -- he's out of range --

Mike picks up the supercomm:

>   MIKE
>   Lucas. If you copy, slow down --
>   we can't understand you...

Off this, we make a SHARP CUT and --

EXT. COUNTRY ROAD - DAY - INTERCUT

Suddenly we're flying HIGH SPEED DOWN THE ROAD with LUCAS!

He's pedaling for his FUCKING LIFE. Practically FLYING DOWN
THIS ROAD. He's pouring sweat, been at this for a while now.

He screams into the supercomm:

                    LUCAS
        -- YES I COPY!! DO YOU!?!! THEY
        KNOW ABOUT ELEVEN! THEY'RE
        COMING!! ALL OF THEM -- YOU HAVE
        TO GET OUT OF THERE!! GET OUT!!
        THE BAD MEN ARE COMING!!! YOU HEAR
        ME?! THE BAD MEN ARE COMING!!

INT. WHEELER HOUSE - BASEMENT - DAY

Our boys hear him -- they just can't *understand him*.

                    DUSTIN
        "Mad hen?" Does that mean anything
        to you?

Mike's eyes shoot wide with realization.

                    MIKE
        "Bad men" -- *bad men*.

Off Dustin, ohhh shit...

INT. WHEELER HOUSE - FIRST FLOOR - DAY

WHOOM! Mike and Dustin bound upstairs. They race into --

INT. WHEELER HOUSE - LIVING ROOM - CONTINUOUS

They peer out the front windows of the house. They see the
"HAWKINS POWER & LIGHT" VAN parked at the end of the cul-de-
sac.

The "REPAIR MAN" who waved at Lucas is still in there.

Our boys eye him. Suspicious.

                    MIKE
        What's that guy doing?

                    DUSTIN
        You don't think...?

INT. WHEELER HOUSE - KITCHEN - DAY

KAREN paces on the phone. Worried.

                    KAREN
        ... I just know her and Steve have
        been spending some time together --
        and --

Mike barges in. Interrupting:

                         MIKE
          Mom --

                         KAREN
                    (ignoring Mike)
          Well, is Steve home, could you ask
          him -- ?

                         MIKE (O.S.)
          Mom?!

                         KAREN
                    (into phone)
          I'm sorry, h-hold on --

Karen cups the phone receiver to her shoulder, turns to Mike.

                         KAREN (CONT'D)
          Mike, I'm on the phone, I've told
          you --

                         MIKE
          Did you schedule any repairs -- ?

                         KAREN
                    (wtf)
          What -- ?

                         MIKE
          Is anyone supposed to do any
          repairs on the house -- ?!

INT. WHEELER HOUSE - LIVING ROOM - DAY

Dustin is still watching the van out the window when...

THREE MORE "POWER & LIGHT" VANS PULL INTO THE CUL-DE-SAC.

Inside: MORE "REPAIR MEN." Their eyes are on the house.

Suddenly one of them locks eyes with Dustin.

Dustin shuts the curtains. *Holy shit.*

INT. WHEELER HOUSE - KITCHEN - MOMENTS LATER

Dustin explodes into the kitchen. Mike and Karen are now
arguing.

                         KAREN
          I don't understand -- is something
          wrong with the house? Do I need to
          call someone?

                    MIKE
          No I just need to know if --

                    DUSTIN
          Mike -- !

                    MIKE
          One second -- !

                    DUSTIN
          MIKE -- !!

Mike finally looks back at Dustin. And then it hits him.

Dustin is scared. Like -- *really scared*.

                    DUSTIN (CONT'D)
          We have to go. RIGHT NOW.

And just like that Dustin is off and running, scampering back
down into the basement. Mike starts to race after him. But
then, at the last second, he stops and turns back to his mom.

                    MIKE
          If anyone asks where I am, I left
          the country.

                    KAREN
          What -- ?!

Mike races into the basement.

EXT. WHEELER HOUSE - BACKYARD/DRIVEWAY - DAY

The basement door flies open.

The boys and Eleven race out. Dustin puts on a ridiculous-
looking WALKIE-TALKIE HEADSET as they grab their bikes off
the grass and begin to quickly push them up to the driveway.

They begin to climb onto their bikes when they spot --

DR. BRENNER and THREE "REPAIR MEN" striding down the driveway.
Eleven locks eyes with Dr. Brenner. TIME SEEMS TO SLOW DOWN
as "father" and "daughter" hold the other's gaze. This is the
first time they've seen each other since the escape.

                    DR. BRENNER
          Eleven.

WE PUSH IN ON ELEVEN and then...

She looks away from him, wraps her arms around Mike, and --

                    DUSTIN
          GO GO GO -- !!!!!

WHOOSH! They bike through the gate in the backyard fence.

Off Brenner, watching them leave...

EXT. FIELD WITH POWER LINES - DAY

WHOOSH! The kids race through the next-door-neighbor's yard.

Dustin's headset antenna wobbles like crazy.

                    DUSTIN
          Ohmygodohmygodohmygodohmy--

EXT. NEIGHBORHOOD - CUL-DE-SAC - DAY

Dr. Brenner and the agents leap back into vans. Before the
doors even shut --

The vans SCREECH off in pursuit of our kids.

EXT. NEIGHBORHOOD - ROAD #1 - DAY

The boys hop a curb onto a neighborhood street. LUCAS'S
VOICE blasts through Dustin's walkie headset. Clearer now:

                    LUCAS'S VOICE (OVER WALKIE)
          Dustin -- Dustin -- you copy ?!

                    DUSTIN
          Lucas -- ! They're on us --

                    LUCAS'S VOICE
          Where are you -- ?!

                    DUSTIN
          Cornwallis --

                    LUCAS'S VOICE
          Meet me at Elm and Cherry --

                    DUSTIN
          Copy -- !
               (beat)
          Elm and Cherry!!

Mike and Dustin take a sharp turn, veering off the road --

EXT. NEIGHBORHOOD - ROAD #2 - MOMENTS LATER - DAY

They swerve onto another neighborhood street.

Mike looks to his right. TWO "POWER & LIGHT" VANS race
toward them.

> DUSTIN
>> SHIT!

> MIKE
> This way -- !

Mike leads them up onto a driveway and --

EXT. STRANGER'S BACKYARD - DAY - CONTINUOUS

-- into a stranger's backyard.

TWO HAPPY LITTLE GIRLS are jumping rope.

> DUSTIN
> OUTTA THE WAY!!!

The girls leap out of the way as our kids race past them.

The girls stare -- slack-jawed as...

EXT. NEIGHBORHOOD - ROAD #3 - DAY

WHOOM! The boys hop onto another road.

LUCAS bikes up to them. The boys all SCREECH to a stop as
they reach one another. They take a beat to catch their
breath.

> LUCAS
> Where are they?

> MIKE
> I -- I don't know --

> DUSTIN
> ... I think we lost them --

SCREECH! Two VANS suddenly speed out behind them. *Nope.*

> MIKE
> GOGOGOGOGOGOOOOOO!!

They pedal away as fast as they can. Mike looks behind him,
panicked. The vans are gaining on them. This is a race they
aren't going to win.

> DUSTIN
>> SHIT!

Mike looks back at the road ahead. His eyes shoot wide.

A VAN IS BARRELING TOWARD THEM AT FULL SPEED.

IT'S GOING TO CRASH RIGHT INTO THEM!

We PUSH IN on ELEVEN as she hones in on the van and --

WHOOOM! THE APPROACHING VAN IS RIPPED FROM THE GROUND BY HER
TELEKINETIC ENERGY AND TOSSED OVER THEM. IT CRASHES ONTO THE
PAVEMENT BEHIND THEM AND ROLLS. A CRUMPLED MESS.

THE OTHER VANS SWERVE TO A HALT IN FRONT OF THE CRASHED VAN.

BLOCKED.

The boys pedal away. They eye Eleven. In awe.

Blood spills down her nose.

> DUSTIN (CONT'D)
> (low)
> Superpowers.

They bike off the road and race into the forest.

Dr. Brenner exits his van and watches Eleven escape once again.

We PUSH IN on him as his frustration rises and...

EXT. ABANDONED JUNKYARD - DAY

We SLOWLY CRANE DOWN from the sky as...

The boys and Eleven bike into the junkyard. It's quiet here.
Safe. They've escaped the agents. At least for now.

Mike helps Eleven off the banana seat. She's weak, pale.

> MIKE
> Are you okay?!

Eleven nods. She wipes some blood from her nose and mouth.

> DUSTIN
> Holy shit, did you guys see what
> she did to that van -- ??

> MIKE
> No, Dustin, we missed it.

Mike helps Eleven onto the ground to rest.

> DUSTIN
> I mean, that was... that was...

                    LUCAS
          Awesome.   It was awesome.

Everyone looks at Lucas. A bit surprised by this admission.

Lucas walks over to Eleven and kneels down beside her. He
locks eyes with her. An emotional beat between them here.

                    LUCAS (CONT'D)
          Everything I said before... about
          you being a traitor and stuff.
          I... I was wrong.
               (beat)
          I'm sorry.

A beat as Eleven takes this in. Her eyes well with tears.

                    ELEVEN
          Friends... friends don't lie.
               (beat)
          I'm... sorry. Too.

Another beat. Then...

                    MIKE
          ... Me too.

Lucas looks at Mike. Then holds out his hand.

Mike eyes it for a beat.

And then shakes it.

                    MAIN TITLES

EXT. POLICE STATION - DAY

An American flag FLUTTERS in the sky.

Slowly TILT DOWN to reveal the police station.

SCREECH! Joyce's car suddenly swerves into the lot.

INT. POLICE STATION - ENTRANCE - DAY

WHOOM! JOYCE and HOPPER BURST into the station.

They stride past FLORENCE and into...

INT. POLICE STATION - BULLPEN - DAY

JONATHAN is at a desk. Still handcuffed. He's still on edge
from the fight.

OFFICER CALLAHAN stands beside him, a bruise now on his
cheek. Further behind them, NANCY is with OFFICER POWELL.

Joyce takes all this in, totally confused.

> JOYCE
> Jonathan -- *Jesus* -- what
> happened?! What happened?!

> JONATHAN
> I'm fine --

Her voice catches as she notices his handcuffs --

She turns to Callahan.

> JOYCE
> Why is he handcuffed -- ??

> OFFICER CALLAHAN
> Your boy assaulted an officer,
> that's why --

> JOYCE
> Take them off --

> OFFICER CALLAHAN
> I'm afraid I can't do that --

> JOYCE
> Take them off.

Callahan looks at Hopper for help but --

He's not getting any.

> HOPPER
> You heard her. Take them off.

> OFFICER POWELL
> Chief -- I get everyone's emotional
> here, but... there's something you
> need to see.

Off Hopper, confused...

EXT. POLICE STATION - DAY

FROM BLACK: the trunk hinges open. We're looking up at
Hopper, Callahan, and Powell. They stare down into the trunk.

REVERSE to REVEAL -- the trunk is filled with weapons: the
bear trap, knives, hammers, a gun, bullets, etc. From their
hunting expedition.

Off Hopper, shocked and confused...

INT. WHEELER HOUSE - BASEMENT - DAY

Karen hurries down into the basement. Worried.

> KAREN
> Mike? Michael?!

She looks around. He's not here.

But then she notices something:

ELEVEN'S MAKESHIFT TENT. TORN DOWN BY MIKE. PIECES ON THE FLOOR.

She kneels down and inspects the mess. She finds the sleeping bag, the pillow, and...

A FEW STRANDS OF BLONDE HAIR. *What the -- ?*

DING DONG! The DOORBELL RINGS upstairs.

INT. WHEELER HOUSE - FOYER - DAY

TED trudges to the door.

DING DONG! The doorbell rings again. DING DONG!

> TED
> Hold your horses...

Ted opens the door. His face falls.

REVERSE ANGLE TO REVEAL: DR. BRENNER, CONNIE, LEAD AGENT, and a HALF-DOZEN AGENTS standing on the front porch.

> CONNIE
> Mister Wheeler?

> TED
> Yes...?

Connie flashes an N.S.A. badge.

Behind Ted, Karen steps into view. Her eyes go wide.

INT. POLICE STATION - BULLPEN - DAY

Hopper bursts into the bullpen carrying a heavy box.

He drops it on the desk in front of Jonathan and Joyce and Nancy. Joyce stares at it in confusion. Inside the box: THE TEENS' MONSTER-HUNTING "WEAPONS" -- BULLETS, GASOLINE, AND...

THE GIANT FUCKING BEAR TRAP.

> JOYCE
> What is this?

> HOPPER
> Ask your son. We found it in his
> car.

> JOYCE
> What -- ?

> JONATHAN
> Why are you going through my car?

> HOPPER
> Does that seem like the right
> question to ask right now?
>> (beat)
> We need to talk. My office. Right
> now.

Jonathan hesitates. Looks at Nancy. Then back to Hopper.

> JONATHAN
> ... You won't believe me.

Hopper shares a loaded look with Joyce.

> HOPPER
> Give me a try.

INT. WHEELER HOUSE - LIVING ROOM/KITCHEN - DAY

Agents fan out across the Wheeler house.

A few agents walk upstairs... Brenner and others head into
the basement... Others rummage through the living room,
tearing through the house, scouring for signs of Eleven.

INT. WHEELER HOUSE - BASEMENT - DAY

Dr. Brenner and other agents search the basement.

Lead Agent looks inside the tent.

Dr. Brenner unfurls a "Benny's Burgers" T-shirt.

> KAREN (PRE-LAP)
> I... I don't understand...

INT. WHEELER HOUSE - DINING ROOM - DAY

Karen, Ted, and HOLLY are now sitting directly across from Connie in the dining room. Holly watches the agents search the house with a mixture of befuddlement and amusement.

Karen stares at the photo of Eleven.

Her voice is quiet. Shaky.

                    KAREN
          You think my son's been... been
          <u>hiding</u> this girl?

                    TED
          What happened to her hair?

                    CONNIE
          We just need to know if you've seen
          her in the past week.

                    KAREN
          No, no --

                    TED
          Absolutely not. Our son? With a
          girl?

Ted shakes his head. Slides the photo back over.

                    TED (CONT'D)
          Believe me, if our son had some
          girl sleeping in our home, we'd
          know about it.
               (to Karen)
          Wouldn't we?

Karen hesitates. Not so sure...

She takes the photograph again.

                    KAREN
          This... girl... What has she done?

                    CONNIE
          I'm afraid I can't answer that.

                    KAREN
               (incredulous)
          You can't *answer that* -- ?

                    TED
          Is she Russian -- ?

                         KAREN
          You can't treat us like this --

                         CONNIE
          Ma'am. I need you to stay calm --

                         KAREN
          Calm? *Calm?*

Karen fights tears. Her voice trembles she's so upset.

                         KAREN (CONT'D)
          You come into my house -- you --
          you tell me my son is hiding some
          girl -- God knows why -- and that
          he's in danger -- but you won't
          tell me why -- and you expect me to
          what?! Just -- stay calm?!

Karen is crying now. Connie stares, unsure how to deal with
this, when ANOTHER VOICE now interjects. Calmer, stronger.

                         DR. BRENNER (O.S.)
          I understand this is upsetting...

Karen and Ted look up to find Dr. Brenner. He sits down.

                         DR. BRENNER (CONT'D)
          ... And I'm sorry we can't tell you
          more. But I can tell you that your
          son, Michael... is in very real
          danger.

Karen looks terrified. Dr. Brenner reaches out and takes her
hand. Comforting her.

                         DR. BRENNER (CONT'D)
          But we can help him, we will help
          him. You have my word. But we can
          only do that if you trust me.
                    (beat)
          Will you trust me?

Karen gives a small nod. "Yes."

                         DR. BRENNER (CONT'D)
          Good. Now: Do you have any idea
          where your son might have gone?

Off Karen...

EXT. ABANDONED JUNKYARD - DAY

CLOSE: A stick is dragged across the dirt, drawing a line.

                         LUCAS
          This is Randolph, right? The fence
          starts here and goes all the way
          around --

He continues to draw a giant circle in the dirt. Sketching
out the perimeter of the Hawkins Labs fence. Then he grabs a
rusty tin can and drops it in the middle of his "fence."

                         LUCAS (CONT'D)
          And the lab is right there. The
          Gate's gotta be in there somewhere.
          It's gotta be.

                         DUSTIN
          Who owns Hawkins Labs -- ?

                         LUCAS
          The sign said Department of Energy.

                         DUSTIN
          Department of Energy? What does
          that mean?

                         MIKE
          It means it's government. *Military.*

                         DUSTIN
          Then why does it say "Energy" -- ?

                         MIKE
          Trust me, it's military, my dad's
          told me before --

                         LUCAS
          Mike's right, there were soldiers
          out front --

                         DUSTIN
          Do they make light bulbs or
          something -- ?

                         MIKE
          No -- weapons. To fight the
          Russians and commies and stuff.

All eyes turn to Eleven. *Suddenly it's starting to click.*

                         LUCAS
          Weapons...

                         DUSTIN
          Oh Jesus. This is bad.

                    LUCAS
          Really bad. The place is like a
          fortress. And now they're looking
          for us... we'll never get within a
          mile of it now.

                    DUSTIN
          What do we do?

                    MIKE
          I don't know. But we can't go
          home.
               (beat)
          We're fugitives now.

This fact hits our boys hard. No one knows what to do. They
just let the reality of the situation sink in. When...

                    DUSTIN
          Hey guys, do you hear that?

Mike and Lucas listen. HEAR it too. Distant. *But there*.

WHO-WHO-WHO-WHO. CHOPPING AIR.

All eyes go to the sky. Way off in the distance --

<u>A FEW MILITARY HELICOPTERS</u>. <u>HEADED THIS WAY</u>.

We DOLLY IN on our kids, their eyes wide as saucers, and...

INT. ABANDONED BUS - JUNKYARD - MOMENTS LATER - DAY

The kids scramble into an OLD ABANDONED BUS.

They duck down behind rusty seats, listening in suspense to
the SOUND OF THE CHOPPERS. LOUDER now. The whole bus
SHUDDERS as the choppers pass overhead. Dust rains from the
ceiling.

Quiet settles in as the sound of the choppers recedes.

The boys share shocked looks. No one speaks at first. No
one knows what to say. Until finally Dustin sums it up:

                    DUSTIN
               ... Mental.

INT. POLICE STATION - HOPPER'S OFFICE - DAY

CLOSE ON: THE BLURRY PHOTOGRAPH OF THE MONSTER.

Joyce looks at it. Heart-in-throat.

She passes it to Hopper. *Jesus Christ.*

> HOPPER
> ... And you think blood draws this
> thing?

> JONATHAN
> We don't know --

> NANCY
> It's just a theory.

Jonathan glances at his mom. She's upset. *Really* upset.

INT. POLICE STATION - HALLWAY - A BIT LATER - DAY

Jonathan and his mom argue in the hallway.

> JONATHAN
> I'm sorry Mom --

> JOYCE
> Sorry -- you're sorry? That's not
> good enough, Jonathan. *That's not
> even close.*

> JONATHAN
> I thought I could save him, I <u>still
> do</u> --

> JOYCE
> You told me you were with Eric, you
> <u>lied to me</u> --

> JONATHAN
> I know --

> JOYCE
> And if this thing took you too?
> You risked your life, Nancy's --

> JONATHAN
> I'm sorry --

> JOYCE
> This isn't on you, this isn't yours
> to fix alone, you act like you're
> alone in the world, and you're not,
> you're not alone --

> JONATHAN
> I know, I know --

                    JOYCE
         Dammit Jonathan! DAMMIT!

She pushes him. He doesn't budge. She pushes him again.
And then... mother and son fall into an embrace. Hold each
other tight. Together at last. Their bond strong. When --

They HEAR COMMOTION and SHOUTING coming from downstairs.

Hopper steps out of the office. Looks toward the noise.

                    HOPPER
              (to Joyce and Jonathan)
         Stay here.

INT. POLICE STATION - BULLPEN - DAY

Hopper strides into the bullpen.

He finds an ANGRY, PREPPY-LOOKING MOM shouting at Callahan
and Powell. She is spitting mad, her face red as a tomato.

TROY is at her side, his right arm in a cast.

This is TROY'S MOM.

                    TROY'S MOM
              I WANT AN APOLOGY -- !

                    OFFICER CALLAHAN
         Ma'am, I need you to calm down --

                    TROY'S MOM
         What is your name, Deputy -- ?!

                    OFFICER CALLAHAN
         Officer --

                    TROY'S MOM
         NAME AND BADGE NUMBER --

                    HOPPER
         HEY! What's going on?

Troy's Mom turns to Hopper.

                    TROY'S MOM
         These men are humiliating my son!

                    OFFICER CALLAHAN
         Hey now, that's not true --

                    OFFICER POWELL
         There was some fight, Chief --

                    TROY'S MOM
          A psychotic child broke his arm --

                  OFFICER CALLAHAN
          A *little* girl --

                    TROY'S MOM
          That tone! Did you hear that tone?!

                  OFFICER CALLAHAN
          Just stating a fact, ma'am --

                     HOPPER
          Yeah, okay, I don't have time for
          this -- take a statement and get
          her out of here. *Now.*

Hop starts to walk away. As Hopper makes his way out of the
bullpen, Powell begins to casually ask Troy some questions:

                  OFFICER POWELL
          So -- kid, this girl, what'd she
          look like?

                      TROY
          Like a freak, she had no hair and
          she was bleeding from her nose --

Just as Hop's *about* to exit the bullpen, the words "no hair"
stop him dead in his tracks.

He strides back over to Troy.

                     HOPPER
          What'd you just say?

                      TROY
          I said she's a freak --

                     HOPPER
          No. Her hair, what about her hair?

                      TROY
          Her head's shaved, she doesn't even
          look like a girl. And...

Troy hesitates. It looks like he's about to break down into
sobs.

                     HOPPER
          And *what?*

                    TROY'S MOM
          Tell the man, Troy.

                        380

                    TROY
          She can... do things.

                         HOPPER
          Things? What kind of things?

                    TROY
          Like make you fly.
                    (beat, low)
          And piss yourself.

                         OFFICER POWELL
          What -- ?

Hopper shuts Powell up with an outstretched hand.

                         HOPPER
               Was she alone?

Troy shakes his head.

                    TROY
          She always hangs out with those
          losers.

A beat as Hopper processes this.

                         HOPPER
          ... What losers?

EXT. LOCAL GAS STATION - DAY

Steve's car idles outside a LOCAL GAS STATION.

STEVE and CAROL lean up against the car. TOMMY H. exits the
gas station carrying a bag of ice, aspirin, some water.

He tosses it all to Steve.

                    TOMMY H.
          You owe me a dollar twenty.

Steve doesn't respond. He just silently pops the aspirin and
presses the ice up against his swollen eye-socket.

                    TOMMY H. (CONT'D)
          Don't worry. He'll need more than
          ice when we're finished with him.

                    CAROL
          Yeah, if the creep ever gets out --
          the cops should just lock him up
          forever. You see that look on his
          face?

                              381

Carol makes a scrunched "angry" face.

                    TOMMY H.
          Probably had that same look when he
          killed his brother.

Carol mock shivers.

                    CAROL
          Oh God, I just had an image of him
          making that face while he and Nancy
          were...

Tommy H. bursts out laughing. Steve does not.

                    STEVE
          Carol, for once in your life, watch
          your damn mouth --

                    CAROL
          What -- ?

                    TOMMY H.
          What's your problem, man?

                    STEVE
          You're both assholes, that's my
          problem.

Tommy stares at Steve. Can't believe what he just heard.

But Steve isn't joking. This isn't the Steve we know.

                    TOMMY H.
          Are you serious right now, man?

                    STEVE
          Yeah, I'm serious. You shouldn't
          have done that --

                    TOMMY H.
          Done what -- ?

                    STEVE
          You know what --

                    TOMMY H.
          You mean call her out for what she
          is? That's funny, 'cause I don't
          remember you asking me to stop --

                    STEVE
          Yeah I should have put that spray
          paint down your throat --

                         CAROL
          What the hell, Steve -- ?!

                         STEVE
          Neither of you ever liked her, you
          know, because she's not miserable
          like you. She actually *cares* about
          other people --

                         CAROL
          The slut with a heart of gold --

                         STEVE
          I thought I told you to watch your
          mouth --

                         TOMMY H.
          HEY!

Tommy grabs Steve by the collar of his shirt and --

WHAM! Throws him against the car.

                         TOMMY H. (CONT'D)
          I don't know what's gotten into
          you, man. But you don't talk to
          her that way --

                         STEVE
          Get out of my face --

Steve shoves Tommy back but -- WHAM! Tommy slams him right
back, harder this time, pinning him up against the door of
the car.

                         TOMMY H.
          Or what? *Or what?* You want to
          fight me now, too, that it?

Tommy leans right into Steve. Inches away.

                         TOMMY H. (CONT'D)
          Because you couldn't beat *Jonathan
          Byers*. So I wouldn't recommend it.

A tense stand-off. The tension grows and grows between our
two teen boys until finally...

Steve shoves Tommy away and climbs into his car.

                    TOMMY H. (CONT'D)
          That's right, bitch, run away.
          She's turned you into a weak little
          pussy, you hear me? You hear me,
          Harrington?!

Steve SQUEALS AWAY. Leaving his friends behind.

INT. WHEELER HOUSE - BASEMENT - DAY

WHAM! THE DUNGEONS AND DRAGONS MANUAL is slammed into a box.

Agents are packing up the Wheeler basement.

EXT. WHEELER HOUSE - DAY

Agents carry boxes down the front steps.

As they load up the boxes, we suddenly CUT TO:

EXT. NEIGHBORHOOD - NEARBY - DAY

We are now viewing the action from a few hundred yards away.

The CAMERA PANS over to reveal Hopper, Joyce, Jonathan, and
Nancy. They are all seated inside Jonathan's car --
observing this ominous sight from afar.

INT. JONATHAN'S CAR - NEIGHBORHOOD - DAY - CONTINUOUS

Nancy is understandably *freaked.*

                    NANCY
          I have to go home --

                    HOPPER
          You can't --

                    NANCY
          My mom, my dad --

                    HOPPER
          They'll be okay --

But Nancy isn't listening to him. She's in a panic. She
throws off her seatbelt and leaps out of the car.

EXT. NEIGHBORHOOD - NEARBY - DAY - CONTINUOUS

Nancy starts to head toward her house but --

Hopper grabs her by the arm. Pulls her back.

                    HOPPER
          Hey hey --

                    NANCY
          Let go, LET GO -- !

                    HOPPER
          HEY! HEY! Listen to me. *Listen to
          me*. The last thing we need is them
          knowing you're mixed up in this too,
          that doesn't help anyone --

                    NANCY
          But Mike --

                    HOPPER
          I don't think they've found him.
          Not yet, at least.

                    NANCY
          What -- ?

                    HOPPER
          You see that?

Hopper motions to the sky. A few miles away, Nancy can see
the DISTANT SHAPE of a MILITARY HELICOPTER. Hovering over
the treeline of Hawkins. *Searching*.

Nancy can barely process this.

                    NANCY
          For *Mike* -- ?

                    HOPPER
          Get in the car --

                    NANCY
          This is insane --

                    HOPPER
          In the damn car.

INT. JONATHAN'S CAR - NEIGHBORHOOD - DAY - MOMENTS LATER

WHAM! Doors slam as Hop and Nancy get back into the car.

Hopper kicks on the engine. Looks back at Nancy.

                    HOPPER
          We need to find them before they do
          -- Do you have any idea where he
          might have gone?

                    NANCY
          No, I --

                    HOPPER
          I need you to think --

                    NANCY
          I-I don't know -- we don't talk
          much -- I mean -- lately --

                    JOYCE
          Does he have another friend he
          might go to, a hiding place, or --

                    NANCY
          I -- I don't know --

                    JONATHAN (O.S.)
          I might.

All eyes turn to Jonathan. Surprised.

                    HOPPER
          What?

                    JONATHAN
          I don't know where he is, but --
               (beat)
          I might know how to ask him.

Hopper and Joyce share a look.

EXT. BYERS HOUSE - DAY

SCREEEECH! Jonathan's car slams to a stop in the Byers
driveway.

INT. BYERS HOUSE - DAY

Joyce, Hopper, Jonathan, and Nancy stride into the house.

Nancy pauses as she takes in the house for the first time.
The tangle of Christmas lights. The torn wallpaper. *A mess.*

                    NANCY
          Whoa. What happened in -- ?

She abruptly stops talking as she realizes no one's listening
to her -- they're all headed down the hallway, moving fast.

Nancy hurries after them.

INT. BYERS HOUSE - WILL'S ROOM - DAY

The group strides into Will's room. Crowding the small space.

Jonathan shoves aside the mess of lamps, clearing his way to Will's desk. He fumbles through the drawers. On edge.

>   JONATHAN
>   I -- I don't see it --

>   JOYCE
>   It's here. It has to be here.

Joyce drops to her knees and peers under his bed. Shoves aside a mess of toys and wrinkled clothes and --

>   JOYCE (CONT'D)
>   Got it.

She unearths: WILL'S SUPERCOMM.

INT. ABANDONED BUS - DAY

Mike, Dustin, Lucas, and Eleven continue to hide in the bus, alone and scared, when suddenly we HEAR a very muffled:

>   FILTERED VOICE
>   (muffled)
>   Mike, are you there? Mike?

The boys share looks --

>   DUSTIN
>   Did you guys hear that -- ?

>   FILTERED VOICE
>   (muffled)
>   Mike? Mike?! It's me --

Mike digs through his backpack until he finds his supercomm. They can we hear the voice is loud and clear. It's...

>   NANCY'S VOICE (OVER WALKIE)
>   If you're there, you need to
>   answer. Please answer.

>   LUCAS
>   Is that your sister?

Mikes stares. Dumbfounded. *What. In. The. Fuck.*

INT. BYERS HOUSE - WILL'S ROOM - DAY

Nancy talks into the supercomm.

>   NANCY
>   This is an *emergency*.   Do you copy?
>   Mike -- do you copy?!

INT. ABANDONED BUS - DAY

The boys exchange more dumbfounded looks.

>   DUSTIN
>   ... Okay, that's really weird.

Lucas reaches for the supercomm, but Mike stops him.

>   MIKE
>   Don't answer.

>   LUCAS
>   She said it's an *emergency* --

>   MIKE
>   What if it's a trick?

>   LUCAS
>   It's YOUR SISTER, Mike!

>   MIKE
>   Yeah, what if the bad people
>   kidnapped her? What if they're
>   forcing her to do it?

>   DUSTIN
>   (realizing)
>   ... Like Lando Calrissian.
>   (to Mike)
>   *Don't answer.*

INT. BYERS HOUSE - WILL'S ROOM - DAY

Nancy shakes her head.   "No go."

Hopper grabs the walkie from Nancy. Gives it a try.

>   HOPPER
>   Hey kid, it's the chief. If you're
>   there: <u>pick up</u>. We know you're not
>   safe. We know about the girl.

EXT. ABANDONED JUNKYARD - DAY

The kids stare at the walkie in growing confusion.

                    LUCAS
         Why is she with him -- ?!

                    DUSTIN
         How the hell does he -- ?

                    HOPPER'S VOICE (OVER WALKIE)
               (filtered)
         We can help. We can protect you.
         But you need to pick up if you're
         there. Do you copy? Over.

The kids exchange looks. Unsure what to do. And...

INT. BYERS HOUSE - WILL'S ROOM - DAY

Hopper waits for a response. But...

Only silence.

He lowers the walkie.

                    HOPPER
         Anyone got any other ideas?

Jonathan and Nancy shake their heads. At a loss. When --

                    MIKE'S VOICE (OVER WALKIE)
              Copy.

All eyes go back to the walkie.

INT. ABANDONED BUS - DAY

Mike speaks into the walkie. The kids hover around him.

                    MIKE
         It's Mike. I'm here.
              (beat)
         We're here.

INT. BYERS HOUSE - WILL'S ROOM - DAY

Off adults and teens, hope growing, we CUT TO...

EXT. MOVIE THEATER - DAY

CLOSE ON: A RAG scrubs red paint.

WIDEN TO REVEAL: A MOVIE THEATER MANAGER, 40s, cleaning up
the "NANCY 'THE SLUT' WHEELER" graffiti.

                    STEVE (O.S.)
         Need a hand...?

The Manager looks down to find Steve walking toward him.

The Manager eyes Steve's bruised, swollen face.

> MOVIE THEATER MANAGER
> You have something to do with all
> this?

Steve doesn't answer. Doesn't have to.

> STEVE
> I just... I want to help.

The Movie Theater Manager considers. Then:

He climbs down the ladder. And passes Steve the rag.

> MOVIE THEATER MANAGER
> All yours.

Steve climbs the ladder...

And begins to clean the graffiti.

INT. WHEELER HOUSE - LIVING ROOM - DAY

A distraught Karen watches out the window as...

Brenner and Connie climb into sedans. Returning to the
search.

A few agents remain in the house. One has unscrewed the
kitchen phone receiver, and is wiring in a new component.

Karen fights tears. Keeps her voice low.

> KAREN
> They just expect us to sit here --
> like prisoners? We should be
> looking for him --

> TED
> We have to trust them. This is our
> *government,* Karen. They're on our
> side.

Karen hesitates. Watches the sedans drive away.

> KAREN
> That man gave me the creeps.

She turns to Ted. Suddenly realizing something.

                    KAREN (CONT'D)
          Nancy. You don't think she's...
          involved in this too, do you?

                    TED
          Nancy? *With Mike?* No no no.

Karen looks back out the window. Worried.

In THE KITCHEN behind them, Holly waddles up to the agent who
is tapping the phone.

INT. WHEELER HOUSE - KITCHEN - CONTINUOUS

Holly holds up a STUFFED-ANIMAL PIG.

                    PHONE-TAPPING AGENT
          For me?

Holly nods. The Agent smiles. Charmed by this little girl.
He kneels down and reaches out to take the pig, but --

Karen swoops in and picks Holly up.

                    KAREN
          Come on, Holly, let's go upstairs.
          Let the man do his work.

As they head off... the Agent is left alone with an
apologetic Ted.

                    TED
          She's just a bit... emotional.
             (awkward beat)
          So this girl. With the shaved head --
          is she Russian?

The Agent ignores him. Returns to tapping the phone.

INT. ABANDONED BUS - DAY

The kids are hiding in the abandoned bus.

Dustin is pacing. Lucas's leg bounces. Everyone on edge.

                    MIKE
          Would you stop pacing?!

                    DUSTIN
          It's been way too long -- maybe
          you're right. Maybe it's a trap and
          the bad men are coming to get us --

LUCAS

It's not a trap. Why would the
chief turn us in? Nancy, maybe,
but the chief -- ?

                    DUSTIN
          Lando Calrissian --

                    LUCAS
          Would you shut up about Lando --

                    DUSTIN
          I just don't feel good about this,
          I don't feel good about this --

                    LUCAS
          When do you ever feel good about
          anything -- ?

Suddenly: the SOUND of an APPROACHING CAR ENGINE.

The boys exchange looks and race to the window.

Their faces drop.

REVERSE ANGLE TO REVEAL:

IT'S NOT HOPPER. IT'S A PAIR OF GOVERNMENT SEDANS.

A FEW AGENTS step out.

But they haven't spotted our kids. At least not yet. Our
kids scramble away from the window and duck behind seats.

They're breathing hard. Panicked.

                    DUSTIN
          Lando --

                    LUCAS
          Did they see us -- ?

                    MIKE
          Both of you -- SHUT UP!

EXT. ABANDONED JUNKYARD - MOMENTS LATER - DAY

The agents fan out across the junkyard.

We TRACK ONE OF THE AGENTS as he makes his way past the bus.
It seems like he is going to walk right past the bus without
stopping. *Phew.* But then at the last second he notices...

BIKE TRACKS IN THE DIRT. LEADING TO THE BUS.

The Agent draws his tranquilizer gun...

Creeps over to the bus...

Steps up to the door...

And...

<u>WHACK</u>! <u>A GUN CLOCKS HIM ACROSS THE BACK OF THE HEAD</u>.

He goes down. Hard. And...

INT. ABANDONED BUS - DAY

The bus CREAKS and MOANS as --

<u>Hopper steps inside</u>. <u>Standing tall</u>.

Our kids peek out from behind their seats.

Hopper locks eyes with them. With Eleven. Then:

                    HOPPER
            Come on, let's go.

Our kids stare at Hop in a bit of shock.

                  HOPPER (CONT'D)
        LET'S GO!

The kids finally jolt to action. They grab their bikes.

                  HOPPER (CONT'D)
        Leave the damn bikes -- !

They drop the bikes, which go CLATTERING to the floor and --

EXT. BYERS HOUSE - NIGHT 7

Darkness falls outside the Byers house.

INT. BYERS HOUSE - NIGHT

Silence. Stillness.

MOONLIGHT cuts through the windows, illuminating the space.

Joyce, Jonathan, and Nancy sit on the couch in silence. They stare off, nervously waiting for Hopper's return. Suddenly:

BRIGHT HEADLIGHTS sweep the room. Lighting their faces.

As they all stand as one --

EXT. BYERS HOUSE - NIGHT

Hopper's Blazer parks at the edge of the dirt driveway.
Hopper, the boys, and Eleven spill out. They head for the
house. Mike stops in his tracks, confused, when he sees...

Joyce and Jonathan exit the house. And behind them...

Nancy. Fraught with worry.

She SPRINTS down the stairs and throws her arms around Mike.
Choking back tears. Relieved.

Mike is a little startled by this show of emotion. He
awkwardly hugs her back.

> NANCY
> Mike, God -- I was so scared --

> MIKE
> Yeah... uh... me too...

As she pulls away, Joyce and Jonathan arrive behind them,
joining the group. OUR MUSIC SWELLS as they all take each
other in. The adults, teens, and kids. Together at last.

But after a moment, Nancy's eyes find Eleven. They narrow...

> NANCY
> Is that my dress?

Off Eleven...

INT. BYERS HOUSE - LIVING ROOM - LATER - NIGHT

We slowly DRIFT into the living room to find...

Joyce, Hopper, Jonathan, and Nancy squeezed on the couch.

Mike, Dustin, Lucas, and Eleven kneel opposite, their knobby
knees buried in the carpet. On the table between them, Mike
has drawn the ACROBAT AND FLEA ILLUSTRATION (from #105).

> MIKE
> ... Okay, so, in this example,
> we're the acrobat and... Will and
> Barbara -- and that monster,
> they're this flea... And this is
> the Upside Down... where Will is
> hiding. Mister Clarke said the only
> way to access this place would be
> through a rip in time and space --

                              DUSTIN
             -- a <u>Gate</u> --

                              LUCAS
             -- which we tracked to Hawkins Lab --

                              DUSTIN
             -- with our compasses.

The boys look up at the adults and teens, who are taking this
information in. Or maybe a better way to put it is: *absorbing
it*. Dustin, of course, feels the need to explain further:

                         DUSTIN (CONT'D)
                    The Gate has a strong
                    electromagnetic field, and that
                    changes the directions of the
                    compass' needle --

Hopper ignores Dustin. Turns to Eleven.

                              HOPPER
                    This Gate... is it underground?

                              ELEVEN
             ... Yes.

                              HOPPER
                    Near a large water tank --

                              ELEVEN
             ... Yes...

The boys share looks -- *Holy shit*.

                              DUSTIN
                    How'd you know all that?

                              MIKE
                         (realizing)
                    He's seen it.

Hopper doesn't say anything. But it's clear he has.

Joyce kneels down by Eleven.

                              JOYCE
                    We need to know where Will is. Can
                    you find him again? Talk to him?
                    Inside that... place?

                              ELEVEN
                    The Upside Down?

                               396

Joyce nods.

                    JOYCE
          Yes. The Upside Down.

Eleven studies Joyce for a moment. And then... she nods.

Joyce's eyes fill with tears. <u>Hope</u>.

                    NANCY
          And my friend, Barbara? Can you
          find her too?

Off Eleven, considering...

PRE-LAP: CHHHHHHHH! -- A LOUD BURST OF WALKIE STATIC...

INT. BYERS HOUSE - KITCHEN - LATER - NIGHT

CLOSE: We're looking STRAIGHT DOWN on the PHOTO OF BARBARA ON
THE DIVING BOARD that Nancy and Jonathan developed earlier.

We DRIFT OVER to WILL'S SUPERCOMM next to it. BLARING
STATIC.

PULL OUT TO REVEAL the adults, teens, and kids sitting in a
circle around the kitchen table, waiting and watching as...

ELEVEN concentrates in front of Will's supercomm...

She closes her eyes and...

WE SLOWLY PUSH IN ON HER FACE as she tries to locate Will and
Barbara in the Nether. Her eyes dart back and forth under
her eyelids. Slow at first, but faster and faster, until --

TSSST! THE COMM CRACKLES, ABOUT TO CONNECT --

TCHTCHT! LIGHTS SPUTTER, STROBING OFF, THEN ON, AND --

CHHH! SUPERCOMM BLASTS STATIC. <u>THE CONNECTION IS LOST</u>.

Eleven opens her eyes. Scans the expectant faces.

She fights tears. Frustrated.

                    ELEVEN
          I'm... sorry.

                    JOYCE
          What's wrong-- ?

                    ELEVEN
          I -- I can't find them...

Off worried faces...

INT. BYERS HOUSE - BATHROOM - NIGHT

WHOOSH! Water POURS from the faucet.

Eleven stands in front of the sink. She splashes her face as
she fights off tears. Her failure has clearly taken a toll.

After a moment, she gets her bearings. She dries her face
with a towel. She studies herself in the mirror. And
then...

Her face falls. Her eyes lock onto something in the MIRROR'S
REFLECTION. Like she's had some kind of GRAND REVELATION.
Only now do we RACK FOCUS on what she is STARING at...

THE BATHTUB.

As Eleven turns and goes to it, knowing something we don't...

                    MIKE (PRE-LAP)
          Whenever she uses her powers, she
          gets weak...

INT. BYERS HOUSE - LIVING ROOM - NIGHT

The adults, teens, and boys sit around the coffee table now.
None of them exactly sure what to make of what just happened.

The boys are explaining the nature of Eleven's powers...

                    DUSTIN
          The more energy she uses, the more
          tired she gets --

                    LUCAS
          And she flipped a car earlier --

                    DUSTIN
          -- It was awesome --

                    MIKE
          But she's drained --

                    DUSTIN
          -- like a bad battery.

The adults and teens share looks.

                    JOYCE
          How do we make her better?

                    MIKE
          We don't. We just have to wait.
          And try again --

                    NANCY
               (worried)
          How long?

Mike hesitates. Not sure. A small, meek voice interjects:

                    ELEVEN
          ... Bath...

Everyone turns. Eleven is standing in the bathroom doorway.

                    JOYCE
          What...?

                    ELEVEN
          I can find them. In the bathtub.

                    MIKE
          I -- I don't understand --

We PUSH IN CLOSE on JOYCE. As she gradually realizes...

                    JOYCE
          I think I might.

INT. MR. CLARKE'S HOUSE - LIVING ROOM - NIGHT

A HIGH-PITCHED SCREAM PIERCES THE AIR.

Mr. Clarke and his scared girlfriend, JEN (30s), are watching
THE EXORCIST on VHS. Regan projectile vomits THICK GREEN
VOMIT all over Father Merrin. Jen reacts in horror --

                    JEN
          Oh God, Oh God, nononono --

She buries her face in Mr. Clarke's shoulder.

Mr. Clarke squeezes her hand. Reassuring her.

                    MR. CLARKE
          Hey. You know how they did that?
          You know what that is?

                    JEN
          What?

                    MR. CLARKE
          Pea soup. They used *pea soup* for
          the vomit.

                         JEN
              Really?

                         MR. CLARKE
              Really.

Jen smiles. Feeling calmer. When --

BRRRRIIIINNNG!!! The TELEPHONE SCREAMS TO LIFE. Jen JUMPS.
Mr. Clarke checks his watch. Gets up to answer the phone.

                         MR. CLARKE (CONT'D)
              What in the world --

                         JEN
              Should I pause it?

                         MR. CLARKE
                    (shakes head)
              I'm sure it's just a wrong number.

He answers the phone.

                         MR. CLARKE (CONT'D)
              ... Hello?

INT. BYERS HOUSE - KITCHEN TABLE - NIGHT - INTERCUT

Dustin is on the other end of the telephone.

The adults, teens, and kids stand around. Waiting,
listening.

                         DUSTIN
              Mister Clarke? It's Dustin.

Mr. Clarke is now very confused.

                         MR. CLARKE
              Dustin? Is everything okay?

                         DUSTIN
              Yeah, I just -- I have a science
              question.

                         MR. CLARKE
                    (ummmm)
              It's almost ten on Saturday, why
              don't we --

                              400

                    DUSTIN
               (ignoring him)
          Do you know anything about sensory
          deprivation tanks? Specifically --
          how to build one?

Mr. Clarke is now even *more* confused.

                    MR. CLARKE
          Sensory deprivation...? What --
          what's this for?

                    DUSTIN
          ... Fun?

                    MR. CLARKE
          Okay. Well. How about we meet up
          Monday after school to discuss?

                    DUSTIN
          You always say we should never stop
          being curious. To always open any
          Curiosity Door we find.

                    MR. CLARKE
          Dustin --

                    DUSTIN
          Why are you keeping this Curiosity
          Door locked?

Mr. Clarke can't argue against himself. Finally breaks:

                    MR. CLARKE
          You got something to write with?

INT. BYERS HOUSE - KITCHEN - A FEW MINUTES LATER - NIGHT

Dustin sits at the table with the phone still to his ear. He
writes furiously in a notebook. Joyce and Hopper still
hover.

Dustin listens to Mr. Clarke on the other end. And then --

                    DUSTIN
          Right. Yup. Okay.
               (he listens, writes)
          Uh-huh, yeah...
               (listens more, writes)
          How much...?
               (listens)
          Okay, yeah --
               (listens)
          We'll be careful -- definitely.

Dustin hangs up the phone. Everyone looks at him. Waiting.

                        DUSTIN (CONT'D)
          (to Joyce)
      The kiddie pool we bobbed for
      apples in? You still have it?

                        JOYCE
      I... I think so.

Dustin considers.

                        DUSTIN
      Okay. Good. Then we just need
      salt. Lots of salt.

                        HOPPER
      What's "lots" mean?

Dustin consults his notes. Then back up.

                        DUSTIN
      Fifteen hundred pounds.

Everyone stares. Stunned.

                        NANCY
      ... Where do we get that much salt?

Off Hop, an idea brewing...

EXT. MIDDLE SCHOOL - NIGHT

We TILT DOWN from the Hawkins school water tower to find...

Hopper's Blazer and Jonathan's car pulling to a stop outside
the school.

EXT. MIDDLE SCHOOL - NIGHT

WHAM! Jonathan tosses a ROAD-SALT BAG onto a PLATFORM CART.

Hopper and Jonathan are pulling ROAD-SALT BAGS from a LARGE
STOCKPILE.

Jonathan shares a look with Hopper. Realizing something.

                        JONATHAN
      It's not supposed to snow next
      week, is it?

                        HOPPER
      Worst case -- no school.

                    JONATHAN
          Right.

A moment of silence as they load more salt. Then:

                    JONATHAN (CONT'D)
          Even if we find where Will is --
          what do we do about that... thing
          in there --

                    HOPPER
          First of all, "we" don't do
          anything. You're getting nowhere
          near this. Your mother's been
          through enough --

                    JONATHAN
          But --

                    HOPPER
          I'll get him back, kid. I need you
          to trust me on that, alright? I'll
          get him back.

Hopper returns to gathering salt. Jonathan hesitates a beat.
Not feeling so confident. He grabs up more salt.

He tosses another bag onto the cart. WHAM!

INT. MIDDLE SCHOOL - GYMNASIUM - NIGHT

Dustin and Lucas drag a KIDDIE POOL into the gym.

They struggle to unfold it. It keeps collapsing on itself.

                    DUSTIN
          How does this even work?

                    LUCAS
          Just hold up that side --

It collapses again.

                    DUSTIN
          Sonofabitch!

EXT. MIDDLE SCHOOL MAINTENANCE SHED - NIGHT

WHAM! Nancy wrenches on a MAINTENANCE SHED near the baseball
field. It's locked with a PAD LOCK. Won't budge.

As Mike tries to pry it open, Nancy grabs up a ROCK.

                         NANCY
               Out of the way.

                         MIKE
               What -- ?

Nancy raises the rock and slams it into the PAD LOCK and --

CRASH! THE PAD LOCK SNAPS.

Nancy throws open the door and barges inside. Mike stares.
Impressed. This is a side of his sister he's never seen.

He hurries in after her.

INT. MIDDLE SCHOOL MAINTENANCE SHED - NIGHT

The inside of the shed brims with MAINTENANCE SUPPLIES.

Nancy finds a STACK OF COILED GARDEN HOSES. *Bingo.*

Brother and sister toss them into a WHEELBARROW...

EXT. MIDDLE SCHOOL - MOMENTS LATER - NIGHT

CLOSE ON: A RUBBER WHEEL cuts waves through grass as...

Mike and Nancy together push a wheelbarrow full of GARDEN
HOSES toward school. The silence finally gets to Nancy:

                         NANCY
               What did she even eat?

                         MIKE
               What?

                         NANCY
               Eleven.

                         MIKE
               Oh. Leftovers. Candy. Eggos.
                    (beat)
               She really likes Eggos.

Nancy takes this in. It's all so... *insane.*

                         NANCY
               I knew you were acting weird. I
               just... I thought it was because of
               Will.

                         MIKE
               I knew you were acting weird, too.
               I thought it was because of Steve.

They walk in silence for another beat. Then Nancy pauses.

> NANCY
> Hey.

Mike pauses, looks at her.

> NANCY (CONT'D)
> No more secrets, okay? From now on
> -- we tell each other everything.

> MIKE
> Okay.
> (beat, considering)
> Do you like Jonathan now?

> NANCY
> What? No. It's not... like that.
> (beat)
> Do you like Eleven?

> MIKE
> ... No. Gross.

Brother and sister stare, sizing one another up. After a
beat, they continue pushing the wheelbarrow into the school.

The door SLAPS shut behind them.

INT. MIDDLE SCHOOL - MR. CLARKE'S CLASSROOM - NIGHT

WHOOM! A storage closet FLIES open as --

Joyce rifles through Mr. Clarke's science equipment closet.

She finds SAFETY GOGGLES and a ROLL OF DUCT TAPE.

INT. MIDDLE SCHOOL - MR. CLARKE'S CLASSROOM - MOMENTS LATER

She tapes STRIPS OF DUCT TAPE over the lens of the GOGGLES.

Eleven watches her. Curious.

> JOYCE
> This will keep it dark for you.
> Just like your bathtub.

Eleven nods. She takes the goggles. Studying them.

> JOYCE (CONT'D)
> You're a very brave girl. Very
> brave. You do know that, right?

Eleven doesn't say anything. Doesn't think so.

Joyce reaches out and gently takes her hand.

> JOYCE (CONT'D)
> Everything you've done... for my
> boy... for Will... for my family...
> thank you.

Eleven gives a small nod.

> JOYCE (CONT'D)
> I'll be right with you this whole
> time. If it ever gets too scary...
> in that place... you just let me
> know -- okay?

> ELEVEN
> ... Yes.

Another beat.

> JOYCE
> Are you ready?

Another beat. Then Eleven nods.

> ELEVEN
> Ready.

INT. MIDDLE SCHOOL - BATHROOM/GYMNASIUM - NIGHT - MONTAGE

We now move into a FASTER MONTAGE as our group combines all
the elements to create the bathtub:

- Nancy connects two hoses to water spigots in the bathroom.
HOT and COLD (ONE RED, ONE BLUE).

- Mike drags the hoses across the gym.

- Mike drops the hoses into the now-unfolded kiddie pool.

- Nancy switches on the faucets. Red and blue.

- WHOOSH! Hot and cold water begins to fill up the pool.

- Lucas uses a THERMOMETER to gauge the temperature.

> LUCAS
> (SHOUTING)
> WARMER...

- Nancy turns up the RED SPIGOT.

- WHOOSH! Warm water spills into the pool.

                              LUCAS (CONT'D)
                        (SHOUTING)
                    COLDER...

- Nancy turns up the BLUE SPIGOT.

- WHOOSH! Cold water spills into the pool.

- Lucas measures the temperature again.

                              LUCAS (CONT'D)
                    RIGHT THERE!

- RIP! Hopper and Jonathan tear open ROAD-SALT BAGS.

- Salt pours into the water, bag after bag. It DISSOLVES.

- Dustin drops a BRICK into the pool. It sinks. Not
floating.

- Hopper and Jonathan pour MORE SALT in. Bag after bag.

- Dustin watches as: THE BRICK FLOATS.

- Will's SUPERCOMM is propped on an A.V. CART by the pool.

- Mike flips Will's SUPERCOMM to "ON." STATIC HISSES.

- Eleven, still in her dress, passes her watch to Mike, takes
off her shoes, and then places her DUCT-TAPED GOGGLES on,
covering her eyes in darkness. On this striking image, we...

END OUR MONTAGE.

INT. MIDDLE SCHOOL - GYMNASIUM - MOMENTS LATER - NIGHT

Two TINY FEET pad into the pool. We PULL OUT to reveal...

Mike and Joyce are helping a duct-tape-goggled Eleven into
the kiddie pool. Once she's in, she blindly wades her way
out to the middle. And then, with the help of Joyce and
Hopper, she LIES DOWN. Looking upwards. She exhales and...

FLOATS. Suddenly --

WHOOM! The lights cut out. *It's working*. Hopper and Joyce
step away from the pool, joining the others around the rim of
the pool.

We CUT TO A HIGH OVERHEAD SHOT looking down on Eleven in the
pool. We begin to gently... ever so gently... CRANE DOWN
toward her. As we draw ever closer to her face, the
SOUNDSCAPE gradually FADES and the SOUND of her HEARTBEAT
TAKES OVER...

We MOVE IN to her goggled eyes and then...

BLACK VOID

We pull away from Eleven's eyes to find ourselves...

In the VOID OF DARKNESS.

Eleven is now standing up. Alone. Surrounded by
nothingness.

She takes a few hesitant steps, searching for something.
Anything. But even her footsteps make no noise. It's
unnerving. Until...

Eleven hears a STRANGE, THROBBING SOUND. It is WET and
PULSATING and IMPOSSIBLE TO PLACE. Eleven steps toward it.

She soon notices SOMETHING in the distance. It looks like a
PERSON. Lying on their side. Facing away. Eleven draws
near.

Only when she's on top of THE SHAPE does she recognize it:

                    ELEVEN
          Barb...

INT. MIDDLE SCHOOL - GYMNASIUM - INSIDE THE POOL - NIGHT

Eleven's speaks quietly in the pool, mimicking her words in
THE VOID:

                    ELEVEN
          ... Barbara?

Nancy leans in. Her eyes wide.

BLACK VOID

Eleven's BARE FEET approach THE FIGURE.

BARBARA isn't moving... isn't responding... isn't breathing.
Eleven slowly moves to BARBARA'S FRONT and we now see why:

BARBARA IS COVERED IN NETHER GROWTHS: THROBBING, GROTESQUE
VINES GROW OUT FROM THE SHELL OF HER BODY; HER EYES STARE
BACK, LIFELESS. LIKE GLAZED MARBLES. AND THEN SUDDENLY --

A SPIDER CRAWLS OUT OF HER HALF-OPEN MOUTH.

Eleven RECOILS BACK in HORROR and --

INT. MIDDLE SCHOOL - GYMNASIUM - NIGHT

Eleven's breaths QUICKENS. She SHAKES. The water RIPPLES. The lights flicker.

Everyone shares looks. <u>Worried</u>.

> NANCY
> What's happening -- ?

> MIKE
> I don't know --

> NANCY
> Barbara -- is she okay? Is she okay?!

BLACK VOID

Eleven stumbles back through the BLACKNESS. Getting away from the horrible sight as fast as she can. Panicking. Fighting tears.

> ELEVEN
> Gone, gone, gone, gone...

INT. MIDDLE SCHOOL - GYMNASIUM - NIGHT

> ELEVEN
> <u>Gone, gone</u>...

Everyone shares terrified looks as --

We PUSH IN on Nancy. Her eyes fill with tears, with shock, as it hits her. *Barb is dead.* She covers her mouth with her hand.

Jonathan takes her hand. She holds it. Tears falling.

BLACK VOID

Eleven looks around the darkness in terror.

She can HEAR STRANGE SOUNDS all around her. *Is the monster close?* Her breathing grows faster. And faster.

SHE IS FULL-ON PANICKING NOW.

INT. MIDDLE SCHOOL - GYMNASIUM - NIGHT

Eleven SHAKES IN THE REAL WORLD. Her nose drips BLOOD.

Everyone watches, unsure of what to do.

We PUSH IN ON JOYCE as she makes a decision. She reaches
into the water, grabs Eleven's hand, and squeezes it tight.

She begins to talk in a quiet, comforting voice.

> JOYCE
> Don't be afraid. I'm here...

BLACK VOID

JOYCE'S VOICE reaches Eleven in the void. Echoing.

Faint. But there. Definitely there.

> JOYCE'S VOICE
> (filtered)
> I'm here... I'm right here with you.

Eleven closes her eyes. Calming herself.

INT. MIDDLE SCHOOL - GYMNASIUM - NIGHT

Eleven's breathing slows. Returning to normal.

Everyone shares relieved looks. *It worked.*

BLACK VOID

Eleven is now calm. Her heartbeat, breathing back to normal.

She opens her eyes again. And now she sees:

A STRUCTURE IN THE DISTANCE. Decrepit, rudimentary.

A CHILD'S FORT. *WILL'S FORT*.

Eleven heads toward it --

EXT. WILL'S FORT (BLACK VOID) - MOMENTS LATER

Eleven reaches it. Familiar signs read:

> "CASTLE BYERS." "ALL FRIENDS WELCOME."

Eleven reads the sign -- quietly murmuring the words aloud.

> ELEVEN
> Castle...

INT. MIDDLE SCHOOL - GYMNASIUM - NIGHT

Eleven's voice echoes across the water. Low. But audible.

> ELEVEN
> *... Castle Byers...*

Joyce and Jonathan share a look. *They know where this is.*

EXT. WILL'S FORT (BLACK VOID)

Eleven stares at the words on the sign: "ALL FRIENDS WELCOME."

Her eyes go to the fort. There is nothing welcoming about it.

Its stick walls are smothered in those awful pulsing growths,
that disgusting, caul-like skin. There is no mistaking where
this fort is. It is inside the Nether.

Eleven takes a breath. And enters.

INT. WILL'S FORT (BLACK VOID)

She stops. Her eyes grow wide.

WILL is in here.

He is lying on side, curled up in a ball. Just like Barbara.

Is he dead? Eleven kneels by him. Only up this close, she
sees that he is breathing. *But only barely.* His breaths are
short, labored, wheezy. His eyes mere slits. His skin ghost
white. He's not dead. But we get the distinct sense that --

It's only a matter of time.

                    ELEVEN
          Will...?

INT. MIDDLE SCHOOL - GYMNASIUM - NIGHT

Eleven speaks in the pool.

                    ELEVEN
          ... Will?

Joyce's breath catches. She fights tears.

                    JOYCE
          Tell him we're coming for him...
          Tell him Mom is coming for him...

INT. WILL'S FORT (BLACK VOID)

Eleven places a hand on Will's frail body. Repeats:

                    ELEVEN
          Your mom is coming for you.
              (no answer)
          Will, can you hear me? She's
          coming --

At last, Will's eyes blink open. He takes a wheezy gasp.

His voice is weak, frail...

                    WILL
          Hur... hu-rry...

INT. MIDDLE SCHOOL - GYMNASIUM - NIGHT

This chilling cry for help crackles out of the supercomm.

                    WILL'S VOICE (OVER WALKIE)
              (filtered)
          ... Hu-rry...

Joyce pales. Her voice shakes.

                    JOYCE
          Tell him... tell him to stay
          strong... to keep fighting... Just
          hold on a little longer...

BLACK VOID

                    ELEVEN
          Just... hold on... a little
          longer... just hold on --

But as Eleven says this: The fort BEGINS TO DISAPPEAR. Incrementally eaten away by THE VOID OF BLACKNESS WHICH SURROUNDS IT. First the ceiling, then the walls, then floor.

And then Will himself is --

SWALLOWED IN DARKNESS.

INT. MIDDLE SCHOOL - GYMNASIUM - NIGHT

CHHHH! The SUPERCOMM CUTS OUT and BLASTS STATIC.

THE LIGHTS FLICKER BACK ON AND --

FWOOM! Eleven JOLTS out of the water, sputtering. She is breathing heavy, sobbing. Blood POURS from her nose.

Joyce pulls her to the edge of the pool, wraps her arms around her.

> JOYCE
> It's okay, shhh, shhh... It's
> okay...

As she begins to rock Eleven back and forth, comforting her, we SLOWLY CRANE AWAY from them... the opposite way we started the sequence, rising high above the pool... up and up and...

INT. MIDDLE SCHOOL - GYMNASIUM - LATER - NIGHT

It's a little later now.

Mike, Dustin, and Lucas are now hovering over Eleven, drying her with a towel. She sits on the bleachers, still SHAKEN.

Nancy is gone...

Back by the pool, Hopper speaks to Jonathan and Joyce.

> HOPPER
> This fort? Where is it?

> JOYCE
> In the woods behind our house.

> JONATHAN
> He used to go there, to hide, to
> feel safe --

Hopper doesn't waste another second.

He strides for the door.

413

EXT. MIDDLE SCHOOL - NIGHT

WHOOM! Hopper bursts out of the school. Moving fast.

Joyce and Jonathan are hot on his heels. Hopper feels them
following, spins around. Knows what they're doing.

                    HOPPER
          Go back inside --

                    JOYCE
          Go to hell, Hop.

                    HOPPER
          Anything happens to me in there --
          if I don't make it --

                    JOYCE
          Then I'll go alone. You stay here.
          How about that?

Hopper stares. She's got a wild, fierce look in his eyes.

                    JOYCE (CONT'D)
          He's my son, Hop. *My son.*

Hopper doesn't even bother arguing for another second. This
is a battle he won't win. He gives a small nod and then heads
for the Blazer. But Joyce doesn't follow him. Not yet.

She turns back to Jonathan.

                    JOYCE (CONT'D)
          I need you to stay, watch over the
          kids --

                    JONATHAN
          I can help --

                    JOYCE
          Jonathan. For me.

Hopper is getting impatient by the car.

                    HOPPER
          Joyce.

Joyce pulls Jonathan into a hug.

She fights tears.

                    JOYCE
          I'll be back soon, okay?
               (beat)
          With Will.

Jonathan fights tears. He doesn't want to let her go, but...

At last he does.

Joyce climbs into the Blazer. The second her door shuts --

SCREEECH! IT SPEEDS AWAY.

Off Jonathan, feeling small, helpless...

INT. MIDDLE SCHOOL - HALLWAY - NIGHT

Nancy is slouched on the ground in the middle of the hallway.

Her eyes are red. She's clearly been crying for some time.
But it seems like everything is now drained out of her. No
more tears left. And so she just stares straight ahead.

Jonathan walks up to her. Doesn't say anything. Just sits
down quietly beside her. They sit in silence for a beat.

At last, Nancy speaks. Her voice is very low.

                    NANCY
          We have to go back to the station.

                    JONATHAN
          ... What?

                    NANCY
          Your mom and Hopper... they're just
          walking into that place like bait.
          That thing... it's still in
          there...
               (beat)
          We can't just sit here while it
          gets them too. We can't.

                    JONATHAN
          You still want to draw it out --

Nancy locks eyes with Jonathan. Her eyes determined. *Angry.*

                    NANCY
          I want to finish what we started.
               (beat)
          I want to <u>kill it</u>.

Off Jonathan...

416

EXT. COUNTRY ROAD - FENCE - NIGHT

WHOOM! Hopper swings open the Blazer's back window.

Hop removes his BOLT CUTTER from the back.

Joyce eyes it.

>   JOYCE
>   This is it -- this is your plan?

>   HOPPER
>   It worked before.

>   JOYCE
>   Did it?

Hopper turns to her. Firm.

                    HOPPER
          Hey -- you want to do this? I need
          you to trust me.

With that, he walks away from her and over to the fence.

He clamps the cutters down on some chain link. And...

SNIP!

INT. POLICE STATION - BULLPEN - NIGHT

A POLICE OFFICER, his legs kicked up on his desk, listens to
OLDIES on the radio while playing solitaire. He is the only
one here. We RACK FOCUS behind him to reveal --

Jonathan and Nancy sneaking into the police station.

INT. POLICE STATION - HOPPER'S OFFICE - NIGHT

Jonathan and Nancy sneak into Hopper's office.

Jonathan picks up his BOX OF SUPPLIES -- gun, gasoline, bear
trap. Right where Hopper last left it. As they hurry out --

INT. POLICE STATION - HALLWAY - NIGHT

Jonathan stops, considers, and grabs up --

A FIRE EXTINGUISHER.

EXT. HAWKINS LABS - BACK ENTRANCE - NIGHT

Silence.

Hopper and Joyce head for the back entrance -- the same way
Hopper broke in before. Hopper scans the area. Sees no one.

He waves Joyce forward.

But just as they reach the back door --

FWHOOM! SPOTLIGHTS FIRE UP THE NIGHT SKY LIKE THE SUN.

Hopper and Joyce wince. Blinded. Barely able to make out...

TWO DOZEN M.P. OFFICERS APPROACHING FROM EVERY DIRECTION.

They have their semi-automatic rifles leveled on Hopper and
Joyce, closing the distance between them. Fast. Imposing.

Joyce gives Hopper a look.

                              JOYCE
                    Trust you -- ?

Hopper doesn't even look at her.

                              HOPPER
                         (low)
                    Put up your hands. And let me do
                    the talking.

Hopper raises up his hands. Joyce hesitates, then follows suit.

We PULL AWAY FROM THEM as the M.P.s draw CLOSER and CLOSER --

Until we RISE OVERHEAD, and this dark visage BECOMES...

INT. WILL'S FORT (THE NETHER)

We DRIFT across the wall of a familiar fort.

We see a line of Will's drawings on the wall. Only something
is wrong with these drawings. They're decayed and covered in
growths and slime. It doesn't take long for us to realize...

We're in the NETHER.

We SLOWLY PAN off the pictures to reveal...

WILL.

He lies on the floor. Crumpled in a ball. He hasn't moved
since his encounter with Eleven. Only now he is alone and
scared. He SINGS quietly, trying to drive away the fear...

                              WILL
                    IF I GO THERE WILL BE TROUBLE...
                    AN' IF I STAY IT WILL BE DOUBLE...
                    SO COME ON AND LET ME KNOW --

Suddenly, a GUTTURAL ROAR ECHOES through the fort. CLOSE.

FOOTSTEPS break branches outside. Getting CLOSER. LOUDER.

We see the faintest stutter of MOVEMENT through gaps in the
wood walls.

Will's breathing QUICKENS. But he can't move. Can't run.

The GUTTURAL ROAR and FOOTSTEPS grow CLOSER and CLOSER and --

BOOM! The wall EXPLODES open. Wood SPLINTERS and --

                         END EPISODE

CHAPTER EIGHT:
THE UPSIDE DOWN

WRITTEN BY **THE DUFFER BROTHERS**
STORY BY PAUL DICHTER

EXT. HAWKINS LABS - NIGHT 7 CONT'D

FADE UP on the night sky. Dark clouds swallow the stars.

We TILT DOWN to reveal Hawkins Labs, sitting alone in a dense woods. We HOLD on it for a beat. Then...

INT. HAWKINS LABS - HOLDING ROOM - NIGHT

THWACK! A PAIR OF HANDCUFFS thrash against metal.

WIDEN TO REVEAL: JOYCE is in a holding room at the lab, handcuffed to a metal chair, alone.

JOYCE
HEY! LET ME OUT OF HERE! HEY!

She yanks on the cuffs harder and harder and --

Gives up. It's no use. Just when all seems lost --

She looks up at the door. Listening. She can HEAR APPROACHING FOOTFALLS. The JANGLE OF KEYS IN THE LOCK. Then at last...

The door opens with a HEAVY METAL GROAN to reveal...

<u>DR. BRENNER</u>. A tense moment here as Joyce and Brenner take in one another for the first time. Joyce is finally face-to-face with the man responsible for all this pain, all this suffering. She fights back anger. It's so intense that, for once, she finds herself at a loss for words...

Dr. Brenner takes a seat opposite her. Speaks calmly.

DR. BRENNER
Your son. We know you've been in
contact with him --

JOYCE
Where's Hopper?

DR. BRENNER
When and how did you first make
contact?

JOYCE
<u>WHERE IS HE</u> --

DR. BRENNER
Six.

Joyce stares. *What?*

422

                    DR. BRENNER (CONT'D)
          -- Six people were taken in the
          past week.
               (beat)
          This... thing that took your son.
          We don't understand it. But its
          behavior is predictable. Like any
          other animal, it feeds. It will
          take more sons, more daughters.
               (beat)
          I want to save them. I want to
          save your son. But I can't do it --
          not if I don't understand it.
               (beat)
          Not without your help.

Joyce gives this man the stare of fucking death.

                         JOYCE
          My help?

Her rage builds. Tears well in her eyes.

                    JOYCE (CONT'D)
          You take my boy away from me... you
          leave him in that place to die...
          You -- you fake his death -- we had
          his funeral -- and now -- now you
          want my help?

She SPITS IN HIS FACE.

                    JOYCE (CONT'D)
          Go to hell.

Dr. Brenner stares. Slowly wipes away the spit. And...

INT. HAWKINS LABS - LAB ROOM - NIGHT

ZZZZZAPP! A POWERFUL SURGE OF ELECTRICITY JOLTS HOPPER.

He drops to the floor. Hard. He's not looking very good.
His face is pale. His eyes red. His breathing shallow.

The HEAD OF SECURITY holds a SHOCK STICK, doing the dirty
work as CONNIE and the LEAD AGENT ask him questions.

                    LEAD AGENT
          What do you know -- ?

                    HOPPER
          Did I stutter? I told you: everything --

WHAM! The Security Head SHOCKS Hopper again.

This one gets him bad. He doubles over and THROWS UP.

                    CONNIE
          What do you know?

Hopper looks back up. Wipes his mouth.

                    HOPPER
          I know you experiment on kidnapped
          little kids -- whose parents'
          brains you turned to mush -- I know
          you took things too far and messed
          up in a big way, I mean you really
          messed up big time, didn't you?
          And I know you've been trying to
          clean up your mess, killing Benny
          Hammond, faking Will Byers' death,
          making it look like that girl ran
          off --
                    (spits)
          Like I said, *everything* --

                    LEAD AGENT
          Who have you been working with?

                    HOPPER
          No one. But I gave it all up to my
          buddy at the *Times*. He's gonna
          blow this whole thing wide open --

WHOOM! The Security Head SHOCKS Hopper again.

Hopper goes down. Hard. His consciousness flags.

Security Head kneels beside him.

                    SECURITY HEAD
          You're just a junky. A small-town
          cop who had a really bad week --
          and took one too many pills this
          time.

He grabs Hopper and props him up on a chair. Then... he
opens a case to reveal a <u>LARGE SYRINGE</u> and a <u>SMALL GLASS</u>
<u>BOTTLE FILLED WITH LIQUID</u>.

He begins to fill the syringe with the liquid.

Hopper eyes it. Wary.

                    CONNIE
          It was a mistake coming back here.

                    HOPPER
          No. It wasn't.
               (off Connie)
          You're going to let me and Joyce
          go. You're going to give us
          anything we need. We're going to
          find her kid and bring him back.
          And then -- then we're all going to
          forget any of this ever happened.

The Lead Agent and Connie share looks. Amused.

                    CONNIE
          Is that right?

Hopper stares. He's not amused. He's <u>deadly serious</u>.

                    HOPPER
          Yeah. <u>That's right</u>.

INT. MIDDLE SCHOOL - GYMNASIUM - NIGHT

Silence. We DRIFT past the kiddie pool to find...

Our BOYS still with ELEVEN by the bleachers. Eleven is
looking better now, but still tired. Not yet "charged."

Mike checks his calculator watch. Looks toward the doors.

He's concerned.

EXT. MIDDLE SCHOOL - ENTRANCE OUTSIDE GYMNASIUM - NIGHT

Mike heads outside.

                    MIKE
          Nancy? Nancy? Jonathan?

His face falls. The parking lot is empty.

<u>Jonathan's car is gone</u>.

INT. MIDDLE SCHOOL - GYMNASIUM - NIGHT

Mike heads back into the gym. *Very* concerned now.

                    MIKE
          They're gone --

                    LUCAS
          What?

                    MIKE
          Nancy and Jonathan -- his car's
          gone --

                    DUSTIN
          They're probably just sucking face
          somewhere --

                    LUCAS
          Gross --

                    MIKE
          No. No way.

                    DUSTIN
          Did they go with the chief?

                    MIKE
          I don't know --

                    ELEVEN
          No.

Everyone turns to Eleven. Mike walks over to them.

                    MIKE
          What? Did you see them? Do you
          know where they went?

Eleven hesitates. No more lying.

                    ELEVEN
          Yes.

                    MIKE
          Where -- where did they go?

A hard beat. Then:

                    ELEVEN
          ... Demogorgon.

Off Mike and the boys, terrified...

EXT. BYERS HOUSE - NIGHT

SCREECH! Jonathan's car SLAMS to a stop in the driveway.

EXT. BYERS HOUSE - MOMENTS LATER - NIGHT

JONATHAN pops the trunk.

He removes the BOX OF MONSTER-HUNTING WEAPONS AND SUPPLIES.

INT. BYERS HOUSE - VARIOUS - NIGHT

We move into a MONTAGE as Jonathan and NANCY set up "traps."

- They plug the Christmas bulbs back in.

- They dump the box of weapons on the living room floor. Share a look. *Here we go...*

- Nancy loads the revolver. Snaps the cylinder shut.

- Jonathan hammers NAILS into the baseball bat. Creating a MAKESHIFT MACE.

- Jonathan and Nancy screw the Christmas lights back in.

- Jonathan grabs a ZIPPO LIGHTER. Tests it. The flame is steady.

- Nancy floods the hallway with gasoline. She makes a TRAIL OF GASOLINE leading from the hallway to Will's bedroom.

- Jonathan and Nancy work together to secure the bear trap into the middle of the hallway. Nancy holds it down while Jonathan hammers a massive metal STAKE into the floor.

We didn't realize this poor house could become any more of a disaster. We were wrong. Because this is <u>next-level disaster</u>.

They continue to hammer the trap in.

WHAM! WHAM! WHAM! WH--

INT. HAWKINS LABS - HOPPER'S CELL - NIGHT

SNAP! A BOLT UNLOCKS as a cell door swings open.

Dr. Brenner steps inside. He finds Hopper sitting alone, looking like shit, of course -- but somehow calm. Confident.

Brenner doesn't waste a second. Urgent.

                DR. BRENNER
     Where is she?

                HOPPER
     I need your word. No one else
     knows about this. And the kids --
     those boys -- you leave them alone.
         (beat)
     You guarantee me that -- and I'll
     tell you.
         (beat)
         (MORE)

                    HOPPER (CONT'D)
    I'll tell you where your little
    science experiment is.

Off Brenner...

INT. HAWKINS LABS - JOYCE'S CELL - NIGHT

Joyce sits in her cell. Fuming. Fiery. When --

The door opens. To her surprise -- Hopper is there. He's flanked by M.P.s. Joyce tenses as the M.P.s stride toward her and...

CLICK-SNAP! They remove her handcuffs.

She looks at Hop, stunned.

INT. HAWKINS LABS - HALLWAY - NIGHT

Joyce and Hop walk down a long hallway. M.P.s escorting them.

Their voices are low, intense.

> JOYCE
> I don't understand --

> HOPPER
> We came to an understanding --

> JOYCE
> What -- ?

Hopper keeps his voice down.

> HOPPER
> Everything that happened here --
> anything that happens from here on
> out -- we don't talk about it. You
> want to save Will -- this place, it
> had nothing do with it. That's the
> deal. You understand?

Joyce hesitates. Then nods. She knows this isn't adding up, but there's no time for more questions. Whatever the hell Hopper did -- whatever the hell he said -- it *worked*.

As they continue forward, Hopper's face darkens.

INT. MIDDLE SCHOOL - GYMNASIUM - NIGHT

CLOSE ON: Eleven, watching the boys argue in the gymnasium.

> MIKE
> We can't just wait around!

                    LUCAS
          Mike, in case you forgot, we're
          still fugitives, the bad men are
          looking for us --

                    DUSTIN
          Yeah, and we don't even know where
          your sister went --

                    MIKE
          Eleven can locate her --

                    DUSTIN
          Mike -- look at her.

Mike looks at Eleven. Still very weak. *Not yet charged...*

                    DUSTIN (CONT'D)
          I say we stick to the chief's plan --

                    LUCAS
          Exactly. We stay here. And we
          keep El out of sight. We keep her
          safe. That's the most important
          thing, remember?

Dustin nods. Mike can't deny this. But... he also can't
hide his concern for Nancy.

                    LUCAS (CONT'D)
          She has Jonathan with her, too.
          She'll be okay.

                    DUSTIN
          Yeah and she's kind of a badass
          now.

On that note, Dustin starts to walk away.

Mike is a bit flustered.

                    MIKE
          Where are you going? You just said
          we were sticking to the plan!

                    DUSTIN
          I am -- I'm just going to get some
          chocolate pudding. I'm telling
          you, Lunch Lady Phyllis hoards that
          shit --

                    MIKE
          Are you serious?!

                                  DUSTIN
                         El needs to be recharged!

Lucas gives Mike a look, then follows after Dustin...

Off Mike, frustrated...

INT. BYERS HOUSE - HALLWAY - NIGHT

WHAM! Jonathan slams the last stake into the bear trap.

He tugs on the bear trap. Makes sure it's secure. It is.

INT. BYERS HOUSE - MOMENTS LATER

He places his foot on the flat spring. Loosening the trap.

INT. BYERS HOUSE - MOMENTS LATER

WHEEEEE... Metal GROANS as Jonathan and Nancy lower the
metal jaws to the floor. Then, very carefully, Jonathan ties
the end of a loose SMILEY-FACE YO-YO to one of the open jaws.
He takes his foot off the spring and slowly backpedals away
from the bear trap, pulling the yo-yo back down the hall
into...

INT. BYERS HOUSE - WILL'S ROOM - NIGHT

Jonathan sets down the yo-yo in the middle of the room.

INT. BYERS HOUSE - KITCHEN - NIGHT

WHOOM! Jonathan flings open a kitchen drawer. Grabs --

A PAIR OF SHARP KITCHEN KNIVES.

Nancy flings open another drawer. Removes GAUZE BANDAGES.

INT. BYERS HOUSE - LIVING ROOM - NIGHT

Jonathan and Nancy stand in the middle of the destroyed
living room, each holding one of the sharp knives.

They're both scared shitless.

                         JONATHAN
                 Remember --

                         NANCY
                 Straight to Will's room. And --

                         JONATHAN
                 -- don't step in the trap.

                    NANCY
          Wait until the yo-yo moves.

                   JONATHAN
          Then --

Jonathan flicks the Zippo. *FWOOSH.*

Nancy nods. *Okay.* The plan is clear. All set.

They place the sharp blades of the knives against their open
palms. *They're going to cut themselves.* Right here. Right
now. They share an intense look.

                   JONATHAN (CONT'D)
          You ready?

                    NANCY
          Ready.

                   JONATHAN
          On three.

Nancy nods.

                   JONATHAN (CONT'D)
               (beat)
          One.
               (beat)
          Two.

Jonathan hesitates. Looks at Nancy.

                   JONATHAN (CONT'D)
          You don't have to do this --

                    NANCY
          Stop talking.

                   JONATHAN
          I'm just saying --

                    NANCY
          <u>Three</u>.

THWUNK! THE TEENS draw the knives across their palms.

Their faces grimace in pain as --

FRESH BLOOD SPLATTERS the floorboards.

INT. HAWKINS LABS - HAZMAT ROOM - NIGHT

A TECHNICIAN passes Hopper and Joyce...

MILITARIZED HAZMAT SUITS.

                    HOPPER
          ... What's this for?

                    TECHNICIAN
          Protection. The atmosphere is
          toxic.

Worried looks between Hop and Joyce.

                    JOYCE
          Will -- my son -- he's in there --

The technician hesitates. He doesn't say anything. *What is
there to say?* He just continues to hand out equipment.

Hopper begins to put on the suit. Looks at Joyce.

                    HOPPER
               (to Joyce)
          Put it on.

Joyce hesitates a beat. Then begins to dress.

INT. HAWKINS LABS - HALLWAY - NIGHT

WHOOM! The elevator GROANS OPEN.

Joyce and Hop step out into the fog-and-spore-choked hallway.
Wearing their militarized hazmat suits. Hopper now wields a
semi-automatic military weapon, and Joyce has an EXTRA GAS
MASK clipped to her belt. We might not understand "why" yet --
but this is for Will.

They stare straight ahead. Silent. And then start moving
deeper into the hallway --

EXT. HAWKINS LABS - NIGHT

WHOOM! The main doors to Hawkins Labs fly open.

Brenner strides out. His trench coat billows. A STREAM OF
AGENTS (including Connie and Lead Agent) follow close behind
him, armed with TRANQUILIZER GUNS AND TRANQUILIZER RIFLES.

They are mid-conversation --

                    DR. BRENNER
          You wanted them gone, didn't you?

                    CONNIE
          And if they find the boy?

                    DR. BRENNER
          ... They won't.

They climb into a row of parked sedans and military vehicles.

As the caravan PEELS out of the lab, *headed for Eleven...*

INT. HAWKINS LABS - RIFT LABORATORY

Joyce and Hopper enter the Rift Lab, *headed for Will...*

Joyce takes in this nightmare. She's struck with terror, awe. THE RIFT has grown even more since the last time we saw it -- overtaking the room -- and spores choke the air.

Joyce and Hopper step up to it. And stop. Their BREATHING picks up. HEAVY and FILTERED by their suit respirators.

And then, without a word... Hopper pushes through the THROBBING MEMBRANE... Joyce watches him for a beat.

And then, she, too, bravely steps forward.

The Rift closes up behind them.

And just like that...

They're gone.

                    MAIN TITLES

EXT. HAWKINS LABS (THE NETHER) - NIGHT

Hawkins Labs looms in the distance.

Only... it's not the Hawkins Labs we know. It's shrouded in fog. Decaying, covered in growths. *We're in the Nether.*

We CRANE DOWN to find --

Hopper and Joyce. Barely visible through the fog. No one speaks. No one dares. Their BREATHING, fearful and heavy, is the only sound here.

With every step, Joyce's breathing grows faster.

Hopper turns to her.

                    HOPPER
          Keep your breathing steady. In and
          out. In and out.

Joyce nods. Hopper watches as she focuses on her breathing.

In and out. In and out. In and --

EXT. PARK - SUNNY DAY (FLASHBACK)

WHOOSH! Hopper is sprinting through sun-lit park land.

He's frantically looking for someone. Finally --

*He finds his target: a cute FIVE-YEAR-OLD LITTLE GIRL! She's
giddily racing away from him in a princess dress. This is
SARA HOPPER. He rips her into his arms, swings her around.*

*Sara screams in delight. DIANE, Hopper's wife, watches with
amusement as Hopper assumes the voice of a DIMWITTED TROLL:*

> HOPPER
> HUMAN FOOD. TROLL LIKE PRINCESS!
> TAKE BACK TO CAVE TO EAT!

*Hop throws her over his shoulder and begins to carry her
away.*

> HOPPER (CONT'D)
> ROASTED PRINCESS WITH GRAVY AND
> PAPRIKA!! TROLL FAVORITE FOOD!

Sara kicks and flails in his arms.

> SARA
> No no no no no!!

*She giggles and screams and kicks, loving this playtime with
her dad, when suddenly her giggles dissolve into a PAROXYSM
OF WHEEZING. She can't breathe. Asthma?*

Hopper sets her down and Diane hurries to their side.

*Hop's troll act falls away. He's now just a concerned
parent. A <u>scared one</u>.*

> HOPPER
> Hey -- hey. Baby. Breathe.
> Breathe.

> DIANE
> What happened?!

> HOPPER
> I -- I don't know.

He lays a hand on Sara's chest.

                    HOPPER (CONT'D)
          Slow down. Slow down. Breathe
          deep. Breathe deep. With me...
          With me...

He pulls her close to him. Helps her breathe.

HOPPER (CONT'D)
In. And out. Like this... like
this...

Sara begins to breathe more slowly. In rhythm with her dad.

In and out. In and out. In and...

EXT. HAWKINS LABS & WOODS (THE NETHER) - NIGHT

... Out. Joyce finally gets her breathing under control as...

Hop and Joyce press forward. Joyce leads the way.

REVERSE ANGLE TO REVEAL: <u>THEY ARE HEADED INTO THE FOREST</u>.

It looks like death in there. Like hell. Scary as shit.

They enter the forest. But we don't follow. Instead, we
watch as they recede into the forest. Before long, they
are...

<u>Lost in fog and shadow.</u>

EXT. BYERS HOUSE - NIGHT

Laundry flutters in the moonlight.

INT. BYERS HOUSE - LIVING ROOM - NIGHT

We focus on a POOL OF BLOOD. Smeared across the wood floor.

WE SLOWLY DOLLY PAST THE BLOOD TO FIND...

Nancy and Jonathan at the couch. Their weapons -- the gun
and the spiked bat -- are laid out on the table before them.

Nancy's hand wound is now wrapped in layers of gauze... the
gauze is stained pink from where the blood has leaked through
the layers. She is now busily working to wrap Jonathan's
wound.

As they work, they glance nervously around the empty room.
Waiting for a sign of the monster. Every CREAK and GROAN of
this house sets them -- and us -- on edge.

                    NANCY
Did you hear that?

                    JONATHAN
That's just the wind. The lights.
My mom, she said the lights... speak
when it comes...

                         NANCY
          Speak?

                        JONATHAN
          Blink.
               (motions to Christmas lights)
          Think of them as... alarms.

Nancy relaxes. *A little.* She returns to wrapping his hand.

                         NANCY
          Is it too tight -- ?

                        JONATHAN
          No. That's good. Thanks.

Nancy nods. She starts to take her hand away -- but Jonathan
keeps holding it. Their fingers intertwine.

                     JONATHAN (CONT'D)
          Nancy?

                         NANCY
          ... Yeah?

Jonathan hesitates. Doesn't know what to say.

He starts to pull his hand away, but this time Nancy doesn't
let go of it. The two teens look at one another. Their
hearts are racing. Time seems to stand still. And then...

BAM BAM BAM BAM! A LOUD NOISE SHATTERS THE MOMENT.

The teens startle. But --

BAM BAM BAM! It's just KNOCKING. Someone is here. *Who the
hell?*

Nancy opens her mouth to speak, but Jonathan holds up his
hand. *Don't answer.* The KNOCKING persists. Then, a voice:

                      STEVE (O.S.)
          Jonathan, man, you there? It's
          Steve. I just... I want to talk.

Jonathan and Nancy share a look. *Are you fucking kidding?*

BAM BAM BAM! Steve continues to knock.

Jonathan looks at Nancy -- urgent.

INT./EXT. BYERS HOUSE - MOMENTS LATER - NIGHT

Nancy cracks open the door, just enough so that STEVE can see her -- but not into the house. Steve looks terrible, his face even more swollen than the last time we saw him. He's a far cry from the swaggering Steve we met in episode one.

He's only mildly surprised to see Nancy.

                    NANCY
          Steve --

                    STEVE
           Nancy --

                    NANCY
          Listen to me. You <u>need to leave</u> --

                    STEVE
          I'm not trying to start anything,
          alright --

                    NANCY
          I don't care about any of that --
          you need to leave... <u>RIGHT NOW</u> --

She starts to shut the door, but Steve holds it open.

                    STEVE
          I -- I messed up... okay? Okay?!
          And I want -- I need --- I <u>need</u> to
          make this right, okay? I just want --

Steve suddenly silences. He's noticed something: her BANDAGED HAND which holds the door open. Fresh blood oozes through the gauze, dripping down the side of the door.

                    STEVE (CONT'D)
          ... What happened to your hand?

                    NANCY
          Nothing, an accident --

She tries to shut the door again, but Steve holds it open.

His sadness has now turned to concern.

                    STEVE
          What's going on -- ?

                    NANCY
          Nothing --

                    STEVE
          Did he do this to you -- ?

                    NANCY
          No -- NO --

Steve forces open the door and --

                    NANCY (CONT'D)
          STEVE -- !

He SHOVES PAST HER into the house.

INT. BYERS HOUSE - LIVING ROOM - NIGHT

Steve crashes to a stop. His eyes shoot wide as he sees --

The Christmas lights, the mashed walls, the bullets, the
spiked bat, the blood smeared on the floor, Jonathan with his
own cut hand, the bloody knives on the table --

It hits him all at once like a tidal wave of insanity.

He can barely process it. Scratch that -- can't process it.

                    STEVE
          What the f--

Jonathan charges up to him.

                    JONATHAN
          YOU have to get out of here -- !

                    STEVE
          What -- what is all this -- ?!
               (whiffing gasoline)
          What is that smell -- ?! Is that
          gas?

Nancy suddenly removes her gun and --

Aims it at Steve.

                    NANCY
          Steve. Get out.

All color drains out of Steve.

                    STEVE
          Whoa whoa whoa -- WHAT?!

                    NANCY
          You have five seconds to get out of
          here --

                    STEVE
          WHAT IS THIS?!

                    NANCY
          I'm doing this for you --

                    STEVE
          IS THIS A JOKE --?!

                    JONATHAN
          Nancy --

                    NANCY
          Three --

                    STEVE
          WHOA WHOA WHOA --

                    JONATHAN
          NANCY --

                    NANCY
          Two --

                    JONATHAN
          NANCY!!!!!

Nancy finally turns to look at Jonathan. He looks absolutely
terrified. And that's when she realizes: The lights behind
them on the wall have begun to FLICKER. On and off. On and
off. Going completely haywire. *The alarms.*

                    NANCY
          Where is it -- ?

                    JONATHAN
          I don't know --

                    STEVE
          Where is what?!!

Jonathan and Nancy look around the house, panicked, turning
360 degrees as Christmas lights continue to flicker like
some kind of twisted light show --

                    STEVE (CONT'D)
          What is this -- ?!

Jonathan looks up --

Nancy follows his gaze --

TO THE CEILING. THE PLASTER BEGINS TO BULGE OUTWARD AND --

                           441

WHOOM! A MONSTROUS HAND BURSTS THROUGH AND THEN A HEAD AND --

BANG! Nancy FIRES at the monster. Once, twice, and --

>   JONATHAN
>   GO! GO!

Nancy takes off toward Will's room --

Steve stands slack, frozen in terror, when -

Jonathan GRABS Steve and forcibly drags him away.

INT. BYERS HOUSE - HALLWAY - CONTINUOUS

The CHRISTMAS LIGHTS FLICKER LIKE CRAZY as --

Our teens race down the hallway.

>   JONATHAN
>   JUMP!

The teens LEAP over the bear trap as...

INT. BYERS HOUSE - LIVING ROOM - NIGHT

WHOOM! THE MONSTER DROPS into the living room with a ROAR.

INT. BYERS HOUSE - WILL'S ROOM - NIGHT

WHOOM!! The teens slam the door to Will's room.

Steve is now hyperventilating.

>   STEVE
>   What the hell was that what the hell
>   was that WHAT THE HELL WAS -- ?!!!

>   NANCY
>   SHUT UP!

GUTTURAL SHRIEKS ECHO FROM THE LIVING ROOM.

Nancy looks to the door, eyes wide, gun trained on it, while
Jonathan FLICKS the ZIPPO -- a SMALL FLAME sparks to life.

But he doesn't drop it on the gas. Not yet. His eyes watch --

THE SMILEY-FACE YO-YO. Waiting for it to move.

He waits. And waits. And...

>   NANCY (CONT'D)
>   What's it doing -- ?

                         JONATHAN
                    I don't know --

Steve whimpers.

Nancy looks up at the door. Listens intently.

The sounds of the monster have ended.

                         NANCY
                      (whispering)
                    Do you hear anything?

They listen some more. Jonathan shakes his head. "No."

INT. BYERS HOUSE - HALLWAY - MOMENTS LATER

CREEEEAAAAAAAAAAAK. Will's door inches open.

Jonathan slowly steps out. He's got his SPIKED BAT in one
hand and the Zippo in the other, ready to throw.

He looks around. Quiet. We now CUT VERY WIDE TO REVEAL:

An empty hallway. The bear trap wide open.

The monster is gone.

We PUSH IN ON JONATHAN, as it sinks in that the plan failed,
then...

INT. WOODS (THE NETHER) - NIGHT

CLOSE ON: WHITE BOOTS SMASHING THROUGH WET GROUND as...

Hopper and Joyce march through the Nether woods.

Strange growths swell on trees. Making odd NOISES.

Hopper notices something. It looks like a flower. That same
fleshy egg-sack Eleven saw the monster eating in episode
#106. It moves and throbs, makes a strange GURGLING sound,
spewing that odd yellow liquid. As Hopper takes this in --

Joyce spots a shape in the distance. We don't see anything
at first. But then the fog parts...

IT'S A FAMILIAR WOODEN STRUCTURE. TORN AMERICAN FLAG OUT
FRONT.

CASTLE BYERS.

                         JOYCE
                    WILL?!!

                          443

INT./EXT. CASTLE BYERS (THE NETHER) - MOMENTS LATER - NIGHT

Joyce races to the "castle." But as she nears...

Her face darkens. A look of horror washes over her.

The fort has been DESTROYED. It looks like a bomb went off in here. Wood and toys and marbles scattered everywhere. The friendly hand-painted sign, "ALL FRIENDS WELCOME," lies on the ground. Totally splintered.

And Will... Will is nowhere to be seen.

Joyce looks around in a panic.

Her panic rises, her breathing increases.

> JOYCE
> Will...?!! Will?!!

But there is no answer. No sign of him.

He's gone.

> JOYCE (CONT'D)
> WILL -- ????!!!

As Joyce continues to shout for her son, Hopper kneels down and examines the fort. There is goo here. Some blood, too. It is clear that this "thing" was here. Drag marks cut through the dirt. The horror of what happened slowly begins to take shape. *Will was taken...*

Hopper picks up a STUFFED-ANIMAL LION.

It, too, is shredded. Stuffing everywhere.

We PUSH IN on Hopper and --

INT. HOSPITAL (NYC) - SARA'S ROOM - DAY (FLASHBACK)

Suddenly we're back in time again. Sara holds a stuffed-animal tiger.

WIDEN TO REVEAL: She lies on a New York City hospital bed, undergoing chemotherapy. An IV tube slips down her arm, her head is bald, and she wears a hospital gown. Her look is very reminiscent of Eleven when we first met her...

Hopper and Diane sit across from her. Hopper is reading from Anne of Green Gables. His voice sounds very distant, very far away...

                    HOPPER
          *"Isn't it splendid to think of all
          the things there are to find out
          about? It just makes me feel glad
          to be alive -- it's such an
          interesting world. It wouldn't be
          half so interesting if we know all
          about everything, would it?"*

As Sara listens, rapt...

INT. HOSPITAL (NYC) - STAIRWELL - DAY (FLASHBACK)

Hopper stands alone in the hospital stairwell.

After a beat, he slumps down to his knees.

EXTREME WIDE SHOT: He seems very small. Very alone.

INT./EXT. CASTLE BYERS (THE NETHER) - NIGHT

Joyce SCREAMS across the dark and empty Nether:

                    JOYCE
          WILL! WILL!

Hopper snaps out of his dark reverie. Pushes to his feet.

And joins Joyce:

                    HOPPER
          WILL! WILL!

Their VOICES ECHO out across the forest. It's dark, choked
with spores, and foggy. You can't see more than ten feet.

Will could be anywhere.

INT. BYERS HOUSE - LIVING ROOM - NIGHT

Nancy and Jonathan creep into the living room.

Their weapons are raised. But the monster's not out here.

                    JONATHAN
          HEY! WHERE ARE YOU?! HEY!

Jonathan's calls are greeted with silence.

Steve is, of course, still freaking out. His voice trembles.

                    STEVE
          This is crazy -- this, this is
          crazy --

Steve races for the phone, but Nancy grabs it away and --

RIPS IT OUT OF THE WALL.

> STEVE (CONT'D)
> What the hell is wrong with you?!
> Are you insane?!

Nancy just gives him a look. Fierce. And...

> NANCY
> It's going to come back. So you
> should leave. Right now.

Off Steve...

EXT. BYERS HOUSE - NIGHT

Steve scrambles out of the house.

His eyes dart around. Terrified. Laundry billows on the
clothes line. Dense fog shrouds the driveway. STRANGE
SOUNDS echo across the darkness. Is it just the wind? Or
something else?

Steve finally reaches his BMW. Unlocks it. But...

Then he stops. Looks back toward the house.

He's noticed something:

THE LIGHTS INSIDE ARE BLINKING AGAIN.

Off Steve...

INT. BYERS HOUSE - LIVING ROOM - NIGHT

Sure enough, the "alarms" are going nuts. Light Show, Part 2.

We MOVE 360 DEGREES around Nancy and Jonathan as they spin
around in horror... weapons at the ready... eyes peeled...

> JONATHAN
> (low)
> Where are you, where are you -- ?

We continue to spin around and around and then --

WHOOM! THE LIGHTS ALL GO OUT. We can't see anything
anymore. But we HEAR it. It's close.

Then: a SILHOUETTED SHAPE rises behind Jonathan. It's
exactly what happened to his brother. The rest happens FAST:

                          NANCY
              Jonathan!!

-- Jonathan spins. Sees it. Too late.

-- THE MONSTER strikes Jonathan.

-- Jonathan crashes to the ground.

-- The spiked bat goes flying from his hand.

-- The monster leaps on top of him.

-- ITS FACE PEELS OPEN. A SUCKING PIT OF TEETH AND BLOOD.

-- It bends down to FEED ON JONATHAN -- inches away -- and --

-- BANG!! A BULLET HOLE blows through the monster's flesh.

-- It SHRIEKS in pain. Its head snaps. Looks at --

-- Nancy. Standing tall. Gun pointed at its ugly face.

                      NANCY (CONT'D)
              GO TO HELL YOU SONOFA--

THE MONSTER SCREAMS AND LUNGES FOR NANCY.

BANG! BANG!! BANG!!! Nancy FIRES, again and again and
again, unloading her cylinder into this thing's hideous,
gaping maw. But the bullets aren't stopping it. Aren't even
slowing it.

IT LUNGES AT HER... SCREECHING... INCHES AWAY WHEN --

WHAM!! THE SPIKED BAT COMES OUT OF NOWHERE AND STUNS IT!

REVERSE ANGLE TO REVEAL: IT'S STEVE. HE'S GOT THE BAT.

STEVE RAISES BACK THE BAT AND SLUGS THE MONSTER AGAIN.

WHAM! AGAIN!

WHAM! AGAIN.

WHAM! BLOOD FLIES AS THE MONSTER STAGGERS BACK INTO...

INT. BYERS HOUSE - HALLWAY - CONTINUOUS

KA-SNAP! THE JAWS OF THE BEAR TRAP COME CRASHING DOWN ON THE
MONSTER'S LOWER LEFT LEG -- SHATTERING ITS BONES -- IT
SHRIEKS IN PAIN --

INT. BYERS HOUSE - WILL'S ROOM - NIGHT

The smiley-face yo-yo flies forward as --

INT. BYERS HOUSE - HALLWAY - NIGHT

THE MONSTER TRIES TO WRITHE FREE BUT CAN'T. <u>IT'S TRAPPED.</u>

                    NANCY
       NOW!

Jonathan scrambles to his feet, flicks on his Zippo, and --

HURLS IT AT THE GASOLINE-SOAKED FLOOR.

A TRAIL OF FLAMES rushes down the hallway and then --

FWOOOM!!! <u>THE MONSTER ERUPTS IN FLAMES. BURNING ALIVE.</u>

<u>IT RELEASES A HORRIBLY LOUD SCREAM OF PAIN.</u>

EXT. FOREST (THE NETHER) - NIGHT

Its SCREAM is so loud that --

Joyce and Hopper HEAR it in the woods.

Their panicked eyes dart around. They see nothing but fog.

Yet... THE SOUND OF THE MONSTER SCREAMING persists. *It's close.*

                    HOPPER
      Come on!

They hurry toward the sound as...

INT. BYERS HOUSE - HALLWAY - NIGHT

Fire and smoke chokes the Byers hallway.

Jonathan grabs the fire extinguisher and --

FWOOOSH! He sprays it at the fire. White chemicals go everywhere, suffocating the fire. And then, at last...

The fire dies out. The smoke gradually dissipates to reveal...

THE BEAR TRAP. Pieces of smoking, charred flesh fill its jagged jaws. <u>But the monster itself isn't there. It's gone.</u>

                    NANCY
    ... Where is it?

                         JONATHAN
            It has to be dead. It has to be...

But the teens seem uncertain...

EXT. BYERS HOUSE (THE NETHER) - BACKYARD - NIGHT

Joyce and Hopper emerge out of the Nether woods and...

Enter the BACKYARD OF THE BYERS HOUSE now. It is decayed
and covered in growths. *Netherized.*

INT. BYERS HOUSE (THE NETHER) - LIVING ROOM - NIGHT

Joyce and Hopper head into the house. The walls and
furniture are covered in those awful growths. Stranger
still, the Christmas lights emit a PULSING STRANGE GLOW here
in the Nether. It's almost as if... we can SEE their
magnetic fields.

                         JOYCE
            Will -- ?!

As Joyce and Hopper move across the living room, their bodies
sweep through the glow of the magnetic fields and...

INT. BYERS HOUSE - LIVING ROOM - NIGHT

Jonathan and Nancy watch in terror as --

BLINKING LIGHTS MOVE THROUGH THE HOUSE. The lights travel
from the living room... to the kitchen... to the hallway...

Our teens raise their weapons, terrified. But little do they
know, this is not the monster this time -- this is...

INT. BYERS HOUSE (THE NETHER) - HALLWAY - NIGHT

Hopper and Joyce.

Hopper crouches in the hallway, aims his flashlight at the
floor. There is no sign of Will here -- but he has found
something else.

FRESH BLOOD AND BURNT MONSTER FLESH.

He looks back at Joyce.

                         HOPPER
            It was here. It was hurt...

His flashlight tracks the BLOOD TRAIL... It leads away from
the bear trap and out of the house.

He follows it.

INT. BYERS HOUSE - LIVING ROOM - NIGHT

Jonathan, Nancy, and Steve watch the blinking lights as they move out of the living room.

INT. BYERS HOUSE (THE NETHER) - LIVING ROOM - NIGHT

Hopper tracks the blood out the front door of the house.

Joyce starts to follow when she HEARS GHOSTLY VOICES:

>   GHOSTLY JONATHAN VOICE
>   ... Where is it going...?

>   GHOSTLY NANCY VOICE
>   ... I don't know...

Joyce looks back at the empty living room. Confused.

>   JOYCE
>   Jonathan -- ?

INT. BYERS HOUSE - LIVING ROOM - NIGHT

Jonathan freezes. It's almost as if... he can feel her.

>   JONATHAN
>   ... Mom?

INT. BYERS HOUSE (THE NETHER) - LIVING ROOM - NIGHT

Joyce stands in the same room -- beside her son, in a parallel universe.

Hopper pauses in the doorway, turns back.

>   HOPPER
>   Joyce -- we need to hurry.

Joyce hesitates -- then follows Hop out of the house.

EXT. BYERS HOUSE - PORCH - NIGHT

The teens step out onto the front porch. They watch helplessly as, a hundred yards away, the yard lamp flickers.

>   NANCY
>   ... Where's it going?

>   JONATHAN
>   I don't think that's the monster.

NANCY
You think...?

Jonathan nods. Nancy doesn't respond. Doesn't know how to.

We now CUT TO AN EXTREME WIDE SHOT of our three teens,
standing on the porch, exhausted... scared... alone...

INT. MIDDLE SCHOOL - CAFETERIA PANTRY - NIGHT

Lucas and Dustin forage for food in the cafeteria pantry.

Dustin throws open cupboards like a madman. He finds a STASH
OF CHOCOLATE PUDDING. Hundreds of little plastic cups fill
the entire cabinet.

DUSTIN
I knew she hoarded it, I knew it!
Such a liar -- always saying she's
out -- a bald-faced liar!

He calls into the cafeteria as loud as he can:

DUSTIN (CONT'D)
MIKE I FOUND THE PUDDING!!!

INT. MIDDLE SCHOOL - CAFETERIA - NIGHT

Mike and Eleven are in the cafeteria.

MIKE
OKAY!!!!!!

Mike turns back to Eleven.

MIKE (CONT'D)
Are you feeling any better?

Eleven shrugs. *A little.*

ELEVEN
What's "putting?"

MIKE
Pudding. It's like chocolate goo
that you eat with a spoon.
    (off Eleven, grossed out)
Don't worry. When this is all
over, you don't have to just eat
junk food and leftovers like a dog
anymore. My mom, she's a pretty
awesome cook. She can make
whatever you like.

                    ELEVEN
          Eggos?

                    MIKE
          Well, yeah, Eggos -- but, you know,
          real food, too. See, I was
          thinking... Once this is all over
          and Will's back and you're not a
          secret anymore, my parents can get
          you an actual bed for the basement.
          Or you can have my room if you want
          and I'll take the basement, since
          I'm down there all the time, anyway.

Eleven considers this. We can tell this means a lot to her.
But a part of her... a part of her is not sure she believes
this will actually happen. Or *can* happen.

                    MIKE (CONT'D)
          My point is: they'll take care of
          you. They'll be your new parents.
          And Nancy, she'll be like your
          sister.

                    ELEVEN
          Will you... be like my brother?

                    MIKE
          What?! No -- no!

                    ELEVEN
          Why "no"?

                    MIKE
          Because -- because it's different.

                    ELEVEN
          Why?

                    MIKE
          I mean -- I guess it's not.

Mike looks away. Embarrassed.

                    MIKE (CONT'D)
          It's stupid.

                    ELEVEN
          ... Mike...

                    MIKE
          Yeah?

                              452

                    ELEVEN
          Friends don't lie.

                    MIKE
               (shit, she got him)
          I was just... I don't know. I was
          thinking -- maybe we could go to
          the Snow Ball together --

                    ELEVEN
          Snow Ball --

                    MIKE
          It's like the cheesy school dance,
          where you dance and stuff to music,
          in the gym. I mean, I've never
          been. But I know you can't go to
          the Snow Ball with your sister --

                    ELEVEN
          No?

                    MIKE
          No! I mean you can, but it'd be
          really weird. You go to school
          dances with someone that... you
          know...

Eleven shakes her head. "No." She *doesn't* know.

                    MIKE (CONT'D)
          Someone you... *like*...

                    ELEVEN
          A friend.

                    MIKE
          No! Not a friend. A... a...

Screw it. Mike suddenly and promptly leans in and ---

<u>KISSES ELEVEN</u>!

There. He did it!

Eleven pulls back. Surprised. Her face is flushed bright
red. So is his. Before either of them can say anything...

BRIGHT HEADLIGHTS sweep across the glass windows of the
cafeteria. *Someone* is here.

Mike fills with hope.

                    MIKE (CONT'D)
         Nancy. Stay here, I'll be right
         back -- !

Mike races out of the cafeteria.

EXT. MIDDLE SCHOOL - PARKING LOT - NIGHT

Mike crashes to a stop outside. His eyes shoot wide.

REVERSE ANGLE TO REVEAL: THE LARGE CARAVAN OF SEDANS AND
MILITARY VEHICLES PULLING INTO THE SCHOOL PARKING LOT. DOORS
FLY OPEN AND AGENTS SPILL OUT OF THE CARS.

Brenner leads the way.

They're headed into the gym. They don't see Mike. Not yet.

INT. MIDDLE SCHOOL - CAFETERIA - MOMENTS LATER - NIGHT

A GIANT TRAY OF PUDDING CUPS crash onto the table.

Dustin and Lucas are proudly displaying their collection.

Eleven picks up a cup and studies it. Curious.

                    DUSTIN
         This will charge your battery right
         up, I'm telling you.

He starts to peel open a top when --

                    MIKE
         Guys -- guys!

Mike scrambles over to them.

His face is white. His eyes saucer-wide.

                    LUCAS
         ... What is it?

Off Mike, breathing hard...

INT. MIDDLE SCHOOL - NIGHT - SERIES OF QUICK SHOTS

WHAM! Doors FLY OPEN as agents FAN OUT through the school.

- Checking the GYMNASIUM.

- SWEEPING through two hallways.

- SLAMMING into the A.V. Club and a classroom with military
precision.

INT. MIDDLE SCHOOL - CAFETERIA - NIGHT

A TEAM OF AGENTS sweeps into the cafeteria.

A HUNDRED AND TWENTY-EIGHT pudding cups sit on the table.
What the hell? They sweep their flashlights around.

The cafeteria is empty.

INT. MIDDLE SCHOOL - HALLWAY - MOMENTS LATER

Our gang of kids sneak down a dark hallway. Keeping quiet.

>   LUCAS
>   How did they find us -- ??

>   MIKE
>   I don't know -- but they knew we
>   were in the gym --

>   DUSTIN
>   Lando...

Lucas and Mike share looks. *Holy shit. He might be right.*

Up ahead: The EXIT door. But just as they near it --

WHOOM! The door FLIES OPEN and TWO AGENTS MOVE IN.

>   MIKE
>   GO -- !

The kids turn on their heels and race back down the hallway.

INT. MIDDLE SCHOOL - HALLWAY - MOMENTS LATER STILL

They scramble back around a corner but --

FOUR MORE AGENTS (INCLUDING CONNIE) MOVE TOWARD THEM FROM THIS
DIRECTION. THEY PICK UP THE PACE WHEN THEY SEE THEM.

THE KIDS GASP AND SPIN BACK AROUND BUT --

THOSE OTHER AGENTS ARE BEHIND THEM NOW.

THEY'RE TRAPPED.

Connie and the agents raise their tranquilizer weapons, when --

THEY SUDDENLY FREEZE IN PLACE. THEIR FACES CONTORT... LIKE
THEY'RE TRYING TO MOVE BUT THEY CAN'T. THEIR MUSCLES BEGIN
TO BULGE AROUND THEIR NECKS.

We PUSH IN on Eleven. She's doing her thing. *Big time.*

CLOSE ON: AGENTS' FINGERS UNCURL OFF TRIGGERS. GUNS CLATTER
TO THE FLOOR. THEN BLOOD STARTS TO POUR OUT OF THEIR NOSES.
THEN OUT OF THEIR EARS. THEN OUT OF THEIR EYES. THEN --

WHUMP! Connie folds to the ground. WHUMP! Then another
agent folds. WHUMP! Another. WHUMPWHUMPWHUMPWHUMPWHUMP!

ONE BY ONE THEY ALL DROP TO THE FLOOR LIKE BOWLING PINS.

The boys turn to Eleven, in awe, but --

WHUMP!! ELEVEN DROPS TO THE GROUND TOO. LIMP AS A RAG DOLL.

Mike kneels beside her.

                    MIKE
          El -- ?? El -- ?

But Eleven can't hear him. This isn't like before. Her skin
is colorless. Blood spills from her nose and mouth. Her eyes
are closed. She's totally lost consciousness. She looks more
than drained this time. *She looks like she's dying.*

                    MIKE (CONT'D)
          Something's wrong --

                    DUSTIN
          She's drained --

                    MIKE
          No, she won't wake up! EL! EL!

Off Mike, panic growing...

INT. DOWNTOWN HAWKINS (THE NETHER) - NIGHT

WHOOSH! A flashlight beam highlights BLOOD on pavement.

Joyce and Hop continue to follow the blood trail.

All around them, STRANGE SHAPES begin to emerge out of the
dense fog. HUGE SHAPES. As the shapes draw closer, we
realize... they are in fact buildings. *Familiar* buildings.

A DRUGSTORE. A MOVIE THEATER. A FURNITURE STORE.

                    JOYCE
          My God...

WE ARE IN DOWNTOWN HAWKINS. Only it's nothing like the
downtown we know.

The buildings are suffocated in growths, and all of the lights
from the town (street signs, street lights, etc.) emit that
strange electromagnetic glow.

Hopper and Joyce appear very small here. And <u>very alone</u>.

They track the blood down Main Street...

Moving under the street lights...

Until at last they stop at...

<u>THE HAWKINS PUBLIC LIBRARY. THE HEART OF OUR TOWN AND THE
HEART OF THIS NIGHTMARE. IT'S SQUIRMING WITH GROWTH AND CAUL-
LIKE MUCUS. IT LOOKS MUCH WORSE THAN ALL THE OTHER
BUILDINGS.</u>

The blood trail SLITHERS up the staircase and through the
doors, which are cracked open... as if inviting them in.

A GUTTURAL GROAN rumbles from somewhere within.

Hopper and Joyce share a look.

And press forward.

INT. PUBLIC LIBRARY (THE NETHER) - NIGHT

CREEEEAK. The library door GROANS open. Hopper and Joyce
enter the library. Their flashlights cut through the fog.

EVERY INCH OF THIS PLACE IS COVERED IN GROWTHS AND MUCUS.

Hopper and Joyce are on edge. This thing... it's got to be
in here. But then Hopper notices something. Kneels down...

The BLOOD TRAIL has dried up.

                    JOYCE
          ... Where is it?

Hopper looks around. Sweeps his flashlight. On edge.

                    HOPPER
          I don't know.

Off Joyce, frightened...

INT. MIDDLE SCHOOL - HALLWAY - NIGHT

Mike feels Eleven's pulse. Panicked.

                    MIKE
          I can barely feel anything --

                    LUCAS
          We have to get out of here -- !

The boys start to pick her up, when --

                    DR. BRENNER (O.S.)
               Leave her.

The boys turn. It's...

DR. BRENNER. CALMLY WALKING THEIR WAY.

He's with Lead Agent and his team of agents.

                    DR. BRENNER (CONT'D)
               Step away from the girl.

But the boys don't step away. *Hell no.* Instead, they move
closer, forming a close circle around their fallen friend.

                    MIKE
               No. You want her, you have to kill
               us first.

                    DUSTIN
               That's right!

                    LUCAS
               Eat shit!!

The agents aren't intimidated. A few sweep in from behind
and GRAB OUR BOYS, restraining them, pulling them away from
Eleven.

                    DUSTIN
               Get off of me!

                    LUCAS
               LET GO!!

                    MIKE
               NO!!! No!! El!! EL!!

The boys KICK and SCREAM and STRUGGLE MIGHTILY, trying to get
out of the agents' grasp, but the agents are much too strong.

Dr. Brenner kneels by Eleven. Being this close to her after
all this time is very emotional for him.

                    DR. BRENNER
               Eleven. Can you hear me?

Eleven's eyes flutter open. Conscious. Barely.

```
                    ELEVEN
          ... Pa...pa...

Dr. Brenner smiles through tears.

                    DR. BRENNER
          Yes.  It's me.  It's your Papa.
          I'm here now.  I'm here.

He reaches down and touches her face.  Her whole body is
trembling and her face is drenched in blood and sweat.

                    DR. BRENNER (CONT'D)
          Shhhh, shhh, shhh.  You're sick.
          You're sick.  But I'm going to make
          you better.  I'm going to take you
          back home.  Where I can take care
          of you again.  Where we can make
          all of this better.  So no one else
          gets hurt.

He holds out his hand.  Waiting.

Eleven fights back tears.  Her gaze shifts back to Mike,
flailing in the agent's arms.  Then back to Brenner.

She withdraws her hand.  And manages one word:

                    ELEVEN
          ... Bad...

Brenner flinches as if he was slapped.

                    MIKE
          LEAVE HER ALONE!  LEAVE HER ALONE
          YOU BASTARD!

Dr. Brenner fights back tears, ignores the shouting, then
reaches down to pick Eleven up... gently placing his hands
under her back... and that's when it happens...

FW-FWOOM!  THE LIGHTS IN THE HALLWAY BEGIN TO FLICKER.

Dr. Brenner pauses.  The agents look around.  Confused.

Mike is the first to realize:

                    MIKE (CONT'D)
               (low)
          ... Blood...

                    LUCAS
          ... What...?
```

                    MIKE
          ... <u>blood</u>...

WE GLIDE PAST THE INJURED AGENTS, MOVING THROUGH THE POOL OF
BLOOD THEY LEFT ON THE FLOOR. WE CONTINUE TO MOVE UP TO...

THE WALL AT THE END OF THE HALLWAY, WHERE THE BEAR-CUB PAW IS
PAINTED. THE WALL BULGES OUTWARD AS THE MONSTER BEGINS TO
BREAK THROUGH THE CEMENT. THE MONSTER IS DIFFERENT NOW. ITS
SKIN IS SHRIVELED AND CHARRED AND SLICK WITH BLOOD.

IT'S SCARIER NOW THAN BEFORE. AND ANGRIER. *MUCH* ANGRIER.

Our boys stare at the monster in awe, horror.

                    DUSTIN
               (low)
          ... The Demogorgon.

WHOOM! THE OVERHEAD LIGHTS SUDDENLY GO OUT AND...

<u>WE ARE PLUNGED INTO DARKNESS</u>.

<u>SCREAMS FILL THE DARKNESS</u>. <u>SCREAMS OF AGENTS</u>. <u>SCREAMS OF</u>
<u>OUR MONSTER</u>. <u>TERRIBLE THINGS ARE HAPPENING IN THIS DARKNESS</u>.

<u>THE LIGHTS SPUTTER BACK ON FOR US TO WITNESS GLIMPSES OF</u>
<u>HORROR: AGENTS FIRING THEIR AUTOMATIC WEAPONS. SCREAMING IN</u>
<u>HORROR. THE MONSTER ROARING IN ANGER. AND FINALLY</u> --

<u>DR. BRENNER AS HE IS DRAGGED BACKWARD ACROSS THE BLOOD-</u>
<u>SLICK HALLWAY. HE VANISHES AROUND THE CORNER WITH A SCREAM</u>.

The remaining agents release our boys. And run to help.

In the chaos, the boys grab hold of Eleven --

<u>And run</u>.

INT. PUBLIC LIBRARY (THE NETHER) - BASEMENT - NIGHT

CREEEEEEEAK. Heavy boots creep down steps as...

Hopper and Joyce make their way into the LIBRARY BASEMENT.

Their faces pale. This is a place of horror.

The BASEMENT FLOOR IS ABSOLUTELY LITTERED WITH DEAD BODIES.
We recognize a few of them -- the TEST PILOT, the ELEVATOR
SCIENTIST from #101 Teaser... and, of course, BARB. All of
their dead bodies have been overtaken by those horrible
Nether growths.

<u>THIS PLACE IS A GRAVEYARD</u>.

Joyce fights tears. *If Will is here, that might mean...*

The thought is too much to take.

She moves forward in a panic.

                    JOYCE
        WILL?! WILL?!! WILL?!!

Her flashlight lands on a TANGLED MESS OF GROWTHS AND VINES
ON THE FAR BASEMENT WALL. It looks like a GROTESQUE SPIDER'S
WEB. The whole thing throbs, up and down, up and down, like
it's breathing.

Joyce and Hop sweep their flashlights across the web. They
find a tangled DEER, unmoving, and...

A SMALL HAND. *A BOY'S HAND.*

                    JOYCE (CONT'D)
        Will... ?!

Hopper and Joyce frantically pull the tendrils away.

A MOP OF BLACK HAIR PEEKS FROM UNDER THE STUFF.

They pull more and more until finally a face comes through.

IT'S WILL. WET. PALE. FRAIL. EYES CLOSED.

WORSE STILL -- A WET TENDRIL SNAKES DOWN HIS OPEN THROAT.
It's like he's got some sort of living snake down his throat,
feeding him. It's awful.

Hopper stares in horror.

INT. HOSPITAL (NYC) - SARA'S ROOM - DAY (FLASHBACK)

A QUICK FLASH OF SARA WITH A LIFE-SUPPORT TUBE IN HER MOUTH.

INT. PUBLIC LIBRARY (THE NETHER) - BASEMENT - NIGHT

                    JOYCE
        Oh my God, oh my God -- !

Hopper acts fast. He reaches into Will's mouth --

AND STARTS PULLING THE TENDRIL OUT OF HIS THROAT.

HE PULLS MORE OF IT OUT. AND MORE OF IT. AND MORE.

How deep does this fucking go?? Finally --

SHHTWWWWWICK! HE FINALLY REACHES THE END. The tendril
THROBS and WRITHES in his hands. It's *alive*. Disgusting.

                    HOPPER
          Jesus -- !

Hopper SLAMS the awful thing to the ground and --

SHOOTS IT TO DEATH. BANGBANGBANG -- !

INT. MIDDLE SCHOOL - HALLWAYS - NIGHT

The boys race through the hallways. Lights flicker like mad.

GUNFIRE and SCREAMS reverberate through the darkness.

It's a maze of madness. Of horror.

They turn a corner. See a SOLDIER FIRING his rifle like mad
at something off-screen. We HEAR the ROAR OF THE MONSTER.

                    MIKE
          This way -- this way!!

Mike leads them into --

INT. MIDDLE SCHOOL - MR. CLARKE'S CLASSROOM - NIGHT

Our boys carry the unconscious Eleven into the classroom.

Lucas SLAMS the door behind them and locks it as...

Mike and Dustin lay El down on a science table.

                    MIKE
          El, El -- can you hear me?! El!

Her eyes flag. No response.

Mike holds Eleven's hand. Squeezes.

                    MIKE (CONT'D)
          Keep your eyes open, okay? He's
          gone now. The bad man's gone. You
          just have to hold on, okay? We'll
          be home soon. And my mom will get
          you your bed. And you can eat as
          many Eggos as you want. And we can
          go to the Snow Ball...

                    ELEVEN
          ... Promise...

Mike nods.

                    MIKE
          Promise...

Both kids fight back tears. When --

A TERRIFYING SHRIEK SUDDENLY CUTS THROUGH THE AIR.

The boys turn toward the door. SCREAMING and GUNFIRE as
MUZZLE FLASHES light up the hallway. It's like a war zone
out there. Lucas pulls out his Wrist-Rocket when...

SILENCE. The fighting ends.

Our kids watch the door. Tense. Terrified...

                    DUSTIN
          Is it -- dead -- ?

Before any of our boys have a chance to respond --

WHOOM! THE DOOR EXPLODES OPEN AND CRASHES TO THE FLOOR.

THE MONSTER LURCHES INTO THE CLASSROOM. IT'S HERE!

THE LIGHTS STROBE LIKE MAD AS THE MONSTER TURNS TO FACE OUR
BOYS, GIVING US MOMENTARY GLIMPSES OF ITS TERRIBLE BURNED
FACE.

IT LETS OUT A HORRIBLE SHRIEK.

                    DUSTIN (CONT'D)
          LUCAS -- WRIST-ROCKET!!!!

The boys leap into action. Dustin passes Lucas a rock and --

WHOOM! Lucas fires. The rock bounces off the monster.

Mike passes Lucas another rock. Load, fire.

BOOM! He hits the monster again. BOOM! And again. BOOM!
And again. But with each hit, the monster presses forward.

                    LUCAS
          It's not working!!!

                    MIKE
          HIT HIM AGAIN!

                    DUSTIN
          MONSTER KILLER!

Dustin tosses him the LARGE ROCK they found on the
playground.

Lucas loads it, fires, and --

WHOOM! THE MONSTER FLIES BACK AGAINST THE FAR WALL. PINNED.

Our boys stare at Lucas. Holy shit -- it worked! Then...

Eleven strides past our boys. That was no rock. It was *her*.

Something about her seems different. Her eyes are blood red.
Her skin is ghost white. Her ears and nose spilling blood.

She hardly looks human anymore.

She strides toward the monster.

                    MIKE
          Eleven... stop -- !

Mike races to stop her but --

WHOOM! He's TELEKINETICALLY KNOCKED BACKWARD. Skids to the
wall.

Eleven walks right up to the pinned creature. At long last,
she is face to face with this monster she unleashed.

She looks from the creature back to Mike. Tears fill her
eyes.

                    ELEVEN
          Good night. Mike.

She turns back to the monster and places a small hand to the
monster's pale chest. It WAILS in extreme pain. *Eleven is
tearing this thing apart with her mind*. But it's not going
down without a fight. It reaches out and --

Coils its long fingers around her neck. CHOKING ELEVEN.

Mike pushes to his feet. Weak. Scared.

                    MIKE
          EL!

El glares at the monster. Summons the last of her strength.

                    ELEVEN
               (barely audible)
          No. More.

She slows her breathing... closes her eyes... and...

A TERRIBLE TINNITUS SOUND FILLS THE AIR.

Mike stops in his tracks and covers his ears. Dustin and
Lucas do the same. The sound is so loud it hurts.

THE TINNITUS SOUND GROWS LOUDER...

THE MONSTER BEGINS TO DISINTEGRATE...

LAYERS OF SKIN BEGIN TO PEEL OFF...

THEY FLOAT LIKE LITTLE PIECES OF ASH...

IT LOOSENS ITS GRIP... RELEASES A FINAL SCREAM... AND...

BOOOOOOOOM!!! ITS ENTIRE BODY DISINTEGRATES INTO A THOUSAND
PIECES. THE ROOM FILLS WITH A WHITE CLOUD OF ITS ASHEN SKIN.

The boys shield their eyes.

The white ash dissipates gradually to reveal that...

The monster is now gone. But...

So is Eleven.

Mike stumbles forward. Looks around. Panic growing.

                    MIKE
          EL??   EL?!!

His calls are met with silence.

Tears fill his eyes.

                    MIKE (CONT'D)
          EL?!! Where are you?!!!
          EL?!!!!!!!

Off Mike, at a loss, stunned...

INT. PUBLIC LIBRARY (THE NETHER) - BASEMENT - NIGHT

THWACK! Will is finally torn free of the "web."

Hopper and Joyce lay his body onto the wet ground. He is covered in strange mucus, his eyes closed, his body limp.

He looks dead.

> JOYCE
> Will -- !

Fuck it. Joyce RIPS off her helmet. It comes off with a HISS of depressurization. She presses an ear on his chest.

> JOYCE (CONT'D)
> He's not breathing --

Hopper rips off his helmet. Listens too.

Sure enough: <u>Nothing</u>.

Hopper places the heel of his left hand in the center of Will's little chest.

> JOYCE (CONT'D)
> No -- no -- NO -- WILL! -- WILL!

She starts to shake him. Hopper grabs her. Firm.

> HOPPER
> Joyce, listen to me -- LISTEN -- I
> need you to tilt his head back and
> lift his chin -- !

She does this. Hopper now starts doing CHEST COMPRESSIONS.

He counts aloud and talks to Joyce at the same time.

> HOPPER (CONT'D)
> Alright, now when I tell you --
> *four, five, six* -- you're going to
> pinch his nostrils shut -- *ten,
> eleven* -- and you're going to
> breathe into his mouth -- *fifteen,
> sixteen* -- twice -- *eighteen,
> nineteen* -- one second -- *twenty-
> one* -- then pause -- *twenty-three,
> twenty-four* -- then one second --
> *twenty-five, twenty-six, twenty-
> seven, twenty-eight, twenty-nine,
> thirty* --

He stops the compressions. Sharply:

> HOPPER (CONT'D)
> (sharply)
> Now, Joyce. NOW!

Joyce, trembling, leans down and BLOWS AIR INTO WILL'S MOUTH.

Hopper watches his chest. Watching for movement. Praying that it will rise and fall. But <u>nothing</u>. He looks back at Joyce.

> HOPPER (CONT'D)
> Again!

She BLOWS AGAIN. Hop looks back at Will's chest -- NOTHING.

> HOPPER (CONT'D)
> Come on, kid, come on!

Hopper starts compressions again.

> HOPPER (CONT'D)
> One, two, three, four, five, six...

He continues to count to thirty as Joyce squeezes his hand.

She whispers through tears.

> JOYCE
> Will. It's me, it's me. It's your
> mom. I love you, you hear me,
> baby, I love you, I love you more
> than anything in the world and I'm
> not leaving here without you, you
> hear me?!

As Hopper continues his compressions, heaving, suddenly...

INT. HOSPITAL (NYC) - SARA'S ROOM - DAY (FLASHBACK)

We're back in time again. A terrified, helpless Hopper looks on as a cluster of NURSES and DOCTORS work to resuscitate his daughter, Sara. We can't even see her -- just the people hard at work around her. Diane is overwhelmed. As we SLOWLY PUSH IN ON HOPPER...

INT. PUBLIC LIBRARY (THE NETHER) - BASEMENT - NIGHT

We SLOWLY PUSH IN ON Joyce...

> JOYCE
> I'M NOT LEAVING HERE WITHOUT YOU,
> BABY, SO YOU NEED TO WAKE UP, YOU
> HEAR ME, YOU NEED TO WAKE UP!

INT. HOSPITAL (NYC) - SARA'S ROOM - DAY (FLASHBACK)

We reach a TIGHT CLOSE-UP ON HOPPER just as...

BEEEEEEEEPPP... the EEG flatlines and --

INT. PUBLIC LIBRARY (THE NETHER) - BASEMENT - NIGHT

Hopper pounds Will's chest one more time, harder, and --

GASP! <u>WILL SUDDENLY AND VIOLENTLY JOLTS TO LIFE.</u>

<u>CHOKING, GASPING, BUT BREATHING!</u>

<u>MUCUS SPITS OUT OF HIS MOUTH.</u>

Joyce is sobbing now.

> JOYCE
> That's it, that's it, that's it!

Joyce removes the EXTRA GAS MASK and slides it over her son's head. Will breathes in the fresh air for the first time in a long time.

> JOYCE (CONT'D)
> That's it, breathe it in, keep
> breathing --

Joyce pulls her son into her arms, SOBBING WITH RELIEF. He shivers in her arms. He is wrecked, exhausted, and frail.

But he's okay... <u>HE'S ALIVE.</u>

Will finally speaks. His voice is weak, thin.

> WILL
> (soft)
> Mom...

Joyce laughs with joy at the sound of his voice.

> JOYCE
> Yeah, baby, it's me... it's me...

As Hopper watches mother and son hold one another, reunited, something in him breaks, some long-ago-built wall, and he lets himself feel it. Relief, sadness, joy, all of it.

Overwhelmed, he begins to cry. Joyce takes his hand.

Off the three of them, laughing and crying and holding each other...

EXT. MIDDLE SCHOOL - NIGHT

RED AND BLUE LIGHTS flash in the night. Police cars, ambulances, fire trucks -- it's CHAOS at the school.

A familiar Country Squire BARRELS into the parking lot.

KAREN AND TED BURST OUT OF THE CAR and rush the school...

Past Lucas, being held tight by his kneeling FATHER...

Past Dustin, his MOM and DAD on either side, crying...

Until at last they reach Mike. He's wrapped in a blanket, sitting on the back of an ambulance.

> KAREN
> MICHAEL!! OH MY GOD, MICHAEL!!

Mike bursts into tears as Karen wraps him into an embrace.

> KAREN (CONT'D)
> Hey, shhh, hey, shhhhh...

Mike breaks down into sobs.

We slowly CRANE UP AND AWAY.

> FADE OUT.

OVER DARKNESS, PRE-LAP the SOUNDS of a hospital room as we --

INT. HAWKINS HOSPITAL - WILL'S ROOM - NIGHT

FADE UP to the REASSURING WHIR OF MACHINES. *Beep, beep, beep.*

Will lies tucked into a hospital bed. Several IV tubes snake down into his wrist, providing his body with fluids.

After a few long beats, he blinks awake. The world is blurry at first, but gradually it comes into focus, revealing...

His brother and his mom sitting next to him.

Joyce smiles gently.

> JOYCE
> Hey, baby...

Will looks around, momentarily disoriented.

                    WILL
               (weak)
          ... Where...?

                    JONATHAN
          You're home now. You're safe.

Will turns to look at Jonathan. Blinks.

                    WILL
          ... Jonathan...

Jonathan smiles.

                    JONATHAN
          Yeah, yeah, it's me. We missed
          you, buddy. God, we missed you.

Jonathan leans in. Brushes some of Will's hair. Tearing up.

Will notices the bandage on his hand.

                    WILL
          ... Are you okay...?

                    JONATHAN
          Oh. That... that's just a cut.
          It's nothing.
               (beat)
          You're worried about my hand...

Jonathan laughs a bit through his tears. Moved by the
kindness of his brother. He wipes his tears as he remembers:

                    JONATHAN (CONT'D)
          Oh hey. Hey. We've brought you
          some stuff. So you don't get bored
          in here...

Jonathan grabs up a cardboard box and passes it to Will.
It's filled with a TREASURE TROVE OF COMICS, a WALKMAN,
TOYS... a boy's dream collection.

                    JONATHAN (CONT'D)
               (re: Walkman)
          I made you a new mixtape. Stuff I
          think maybe you'll really like.

                    WILL
          Cool.

                        JONATHAN
          Yeah. Cool.

Jonathan smiles through his tears.

INT. HAWKINS HOSPITAL - WAITING ROOM - NIGHT

We SURVEY the rest of the gang, all cramped in the waiting
room:

There's Mike, Dustin, Lucas, Nancy, Hopper, Steve, Karen, Ted,
Lucas's parents, Dustin's parents. Dustin and Lucas are both
asleep. Dustin has his head resting on Lucas's shoulder.

Mike, however, is awake. Lost in thought. When...

He HEARS FOOTSTEPS APPROACHING. He looks up to find...

Jonathan walking into the room. Jonathan doesn't say
anything. He just gives a small nod.

Mike leaps to his feet. Shakes Dustin and Lucas.

                        MIKE
          Guys, he's up. He's up.

Lucas startles awake -- and sees that Dustin is sleeping on
him. Gross! Dustin is grossed out too. But there's no time
for antics -- Mike is already racing away to greet Will.

Dustin and Lucas scramble after them.

INT. HAWKINS HOSPITAL - WILL'S ROOM - NIGHT

WHOOM! The boys explode into Will's room.

They race to his side. Give him hugs, high-fives.

                        LUCAS
          BYERS!

                        JONATHAN
          Hey -- go easy on him -- !

                        LUCAS
          You won't believe what happened
          when you were gone, man -- !

                        DUSTIN
          ... Stuff you wouldn't *believe* --

                        LUCAS
          You had a funeral!

                    DUSTIN
          Jennifer Hayes was crying at it!

                    WILL
          What -- ??

                    LUCAS
               (ignoring Lucas)
          And Troy *peed* himself...

                    DUSTIN
          In front of the whole school!

Will laughs at this. But his laugh leads into a cough.

The boys quiet down. Share looks. The intensity of what
Will must have gone through in there really hits them here.

                    MIKE
          ... You okay?

Will nods. Looks at Mike.

                    WILL
               (quietly)
          It got me. The Demogorgon.

                    MIKE
          We know. But it's okay now. It's
          gone now. We... we made a new
          friend. And...
               (beat)
          She stopped it.
               (beat)
          She saved us.

Mike smiles through his tears.

                    DUSTIN
          Yeah, her name's Eleven --

                    WILL
          Like the number?

                    LUCAS
          But we call her "El" for short --

                    DUSTIN
          She's basically a wizard --

                    LUCAS
          She had superpowers --

```
                    MIKE
         More like Yoda --

                   DUSTIN
         Yeah and she flipped a car and --
```

As our boys rattle on and on, telling Will about their
adventures...

We FOCUS our attention on Nancy, who is watching from the
doorway. She's happy to see Will back, to see the joy, but
she wishes Barbara could be here too. *Could smile again too.*

After a beat, Nancy quietly exits the room. Jonathan
notices. Watches her go. Then he turns back to his brother.

EXT. HAWKINS HOSPITAL - NIGHT

Hopper walks out of the hospital. Lights a cigarette.

It's been a long day. A long fucking week. He trudges
across the parking lot to his Blazer when --

A SEDAN PULLS UP BEHIND HIM.

He turns as...

A MAN DRESSED IN A SUIT steps out. And then...

OPENS THE BACK DOOR OF A SEDAN.

Hopper looks at them. Considers. He tosses his cigarette.

Then, to our surprise, he climbs in.

THE BLACK SEDAN DRIVES OFF.

As the sedan recedes into the darkness...

We SLOWLY TILT UP TO FIND:

A BLACK CLOUDLESS SKY FULL OF TWINKLING STARS...

                                        DISSOLVE TO:

EXT. WHEELER HOUSE - NIGHT 8

A WINTER NIGHT SKY.

Superimpose title: ONE MONTH LATER.

We TILT DOWN to the Wheeler house, dressed in Christmas
lights. There's a sprinkling of fresh snow on the ground.

```
                MIKE (PRE-LAP)
... Something is coming...
something angry... hungry for your
blood...
```

INT. WHEELER HOUSE - BASEMENT - NIGHT

The boys play DUNGEONS & DRAGONS.

Mike, Will, and Lucas are back at the card table. The boys listen intensely to Mike, who peers out from behind his Dungeon Master notebook.

                    WILL
          What is it -- ?!

                    DUSTIN
          It's the thessalmonster, I'm
          telling you --

                    LUCAS
          -- It's not the thessalmonster --

                    DUSTIN
          I'm telling you, it's --

WHAM! Mike slams a TERRIFYING CREATURE onto the board.

                    MIKE
          -- THE THESSALMONSTER!

                    DUSTIN
          Dammit --

                    MIKE
          It ROARS in anger. Will -- your
          action!

Everyone turns to Will.

                    LUCAS
          Fireball him!

Will looks at Dustin, expecting disagreement, but this time --

Dustin <u>agrees</u>. Nodding.

                    DUSTIN
          <u>Fireball the sonofabitch.</u>

Will nods. Fuckin'-A. He takes the dice. Shakes it. And...

<u>Rolls</u>. The dice scatter to a stop on the table. It's a...

                    DUSTIN (CONT'D)
          FOURTEEN!

                    LUCAS
          BOOM!

                    MIKE
          DIRECT HIT! Will the Wise's
          fireball hits the thessalmonster --
          it lets out a PAINFUL --
               (Mike SCREECHES)
          -- it stumbles back and then --
               (he slaps the table)
          -- it crashes to the floor -- its
          clawed hand reaches for you one
          last time -- and -- and -- and...

Mike "dies" in the most dramatic way possible.

The boys go NUTS, CHEERING WILDLY. Dustin runs a victory lap
around the basement. Lucas gives Will a high-five. Mike
waits for them to settle down, then...

                    MIKE (CONT'D)
          Lucas cuts off its ten heads with
          his sword, and Dustin places them
          into his Bag of Holding. You carry
          the heads out of the dungeon,
          victorious, and present them to
          King Tristan. He thanks you for
          your bravery and service --

                    DUSTIN
          Whoa whoa whoa -- that's not it, is
          it?!

                    MIKE
          No, there's a medal ceremony and --

                    DUSTIN
          A medal ceremony?! WHAT are you
          talking about?!

                    LUCAS
          Yeah, that campaign was way too short --

                    WILL
          Yeah -- !

                    MIKE
          It was TEN HOURS -- !

                    DUSTIN
          But it makes no sense --

                    MIKE
          It makes *sense* -- !

                    DUSTIN
          What about the Lost Knight -- ??

                         LUCAS
               And the Proud Princess -- ??

                         WILL
               And those weird flowers in the cave -- !

Before Mike has a chance to answer --

                         JONATHAN (O.S.)
                    Ooph! What is that smell??

Our boys look up to find Jonathan bounding down the steps.

                         JONATHAN (CONT'D)
               Have you guys been playing games,
               or just farting all day --

The boys laugh.

                         LUCAS
               Just Dustin. He sharted.

Dustin punches Lucas. Lucas punches him back.

Jonathan walks up to Will, rubs his head.

                         JONATHAN
                    Come on, time to go, buddy.

                         WILL
                    'Kay.

Will grabs his backpack and follows Jonathan upstairs. As
they exit, Dustin and Lucas continue to slap one another.

                         DUSTIN
                    Stop it -- !

                         LUCAS
               You stop it -- !

                         DUSTIN
                    HEY!

Dustin grabs Lucas and starts giving him a noogie. Lucas
lets out a high-pitched scream. Mike smiles.

But then his smile fades as his gaze shifts to...

The tent. He's put it back up. The supercomm sits on a
pillow. Waiting -- *for Eleven.*

INT. WHEELER HOUSE - KITCHEN - NIGHT

Jonathan and Will head through the kitchen, where...

Karen is busy cooking a Christmas Eve feast.

>   KAREN
>   Hey boys -- wish your mom "Merry
>   Christmas" for me, okay?

>   WILL   JONATHAN
> Yeah.   Yeah.

INT. WHEELER HOUSE - FOYER - NIGHT

The Byers brothers head for the door, when --

>   NANCY (O.S.)
>   Hey, wait up --

Jonathan turns to find Nancy hurrying down the steps toward
him. She carries a medium-sized Christmas present. She
passes it to Jonathan.

>   NANCY (CONT'D)
>   Merry Christmas.

Jonathan is a bit caught off-guard.

>   JONATHAN
>   Oh, thanks -- God, now I feel bad,
>   I didn't --

>   NANCY
>   No, no. It's... not really a present.

Jonathan looks down at it. Confused. Sure looks like one.

>   NANCY (CONT'D)
>   It's just... you'll see.

She leans in and kisses him sweetly on the cheek.

INT./EXT. JONATHAN'S CAR & WHEELER HOUSE - NIGHT

Jonathan and Will climb into his car.

As Jonathan revs the engine --

>   WILL
>   Can I open it?

>   JONATHAN
>   Yeah, sure. Go ahead.

Will unwraps the present. Plucks out --

A BEAUTIFUL NEW 35mm CAMERA.

> WILL
> Whoa... Pretty cool.

Jonathan looks at the camera.

> JONATHAN
> Yeah. Pretty cool.

Jonathan kicks the car into drive. And speeds away.

INT. WHEELER HOUSE - TV ROOM - NIGHT

Ted sleeps on his La-Z-Boy. A BOWL OF POPCORN in his lap.

Nancy crosses into the room. She sits on the sofa next to...

Steve. He's wearing a Christmas sweater.

> STEVE
> You give it to him?

> NANCY
> Yeah.

Steve and Nancy now CLASP HANDS as they settle in to watch
A CHARLIE BROWN CHRISTMAS on their "huge" 22-inch TV.

MATCH CUT TO:

INT. POLICE STATION - BULLPEN - NIGHT

A CHARLIE BROWN CHRISTMAS playing on the police station TV.

WE DOLLY OVER FROM THE TV, past a bulletin board, where
pinned news articles give a little bit of detail on the
cover-up. We read a few key headlines:

"The Boy Who Came Back to Life"

"Coroner Arrested for Falsifying Autopsy"

"Hawkins Lab Locked Down After Bacterial Mold Outbreak"

"More Heads Roll in Ongoing State Trooper Scandal"

We CONTINUE PAST the bulletin board to find:

A SMALL OFFICE CHRISTMAS PARTY in full swing. CALLAHAN and
POWELL and FLORENCE and a FEW OTHER OFFICERS are here,
drinking punch and having a grand old time.

We find Hopper by himself at the food table.

He scrapes food into a Tupperware container.

> OFFICER POWELL
> Leaving already, Chief -- ?

> HOPPER
> You think I actually wanted to come
> to this thing? I was just hungry --

> OFFICER CALLAHAN
> That's the spirit --

> HOPPER
> Hey. Your wife doesn't have time
> to cook for me, you know what I'm
> saying?

Powell cackles.

As Hopper heads for the exit, Tupperware in hand, Florence grabs a cigarette dangling out his mouth. Snuffs it out.

> FLORENCE
> Merry Christmas, Hop.

> HOPPER
> Mm.

INT./EXT. HOPPER'S BLAZER & COUNTRY ROAD - NIGHT

Hopper's Blazer pulls off onto the shoulder.

Hopper steps out of the car. He's in the middle of nowhere, adjacent to the woods. He glances around. Nobody's watching.

He takes the Tupperware out of the car.

EXT. WOODS - A FEW MINUTES LATER - NIGHT

Deep in the woods now. Hopper walks through snow until he comes upon a WOODEN BOX ANCHORED TO THE GROUND.

It's pretty well concealed in some underbrush. The snow around it is untouched.

Hopper opens the box and places the Tupperware inside.

Then he remembers something.

He reaches into his pocket and removes: <u>AN EGGO WAFFLE</u>.

He places the waffle into the Tupperware. And then...

He shuts the wooden box. As he walks away, we HOLD ON THE STRANGE BOX, listening to Hop's FOOTSTEPS CRUNCHING AWAY...

EXT. BYERS HOUSE - NIGHT

No Christmas lights, but a warm glow through the windows...

INT. BYERS HOUSE - LIVING ROOM/DINING ROOM - NIGHT

Presents are piled under a Christmas tree (decorated with popcorn instead of the usual lights). CHESTER THE DOG rests peacefully in front of the pile. He watches as --

Will picks up a GREEN PRESENT -- the largest. He shakes the present, trying to decipher what is hidden within...

We DOLLY PAST him to...

The DINING ROOM, which has now been cleared of junk. A new table is here as well, where Joyce is placing an impressive-looking dinner. A lot of time clearly went into this meal.

Jonathan snaps pictures with his new camera.

> JOYCE
> What are you doing?

> JONATHAN
> Documenting --

> JOYCE
> Why?

> JONATHAN
> It looks great?

> JOYCE
> Yeah, well, it's not. I overcooked
> the beans, and the mashed potatoes
> are all watery, and --

> JONATHAN
> Mom.

> JOYCE
> Yeah.

> JONATHAN
> It's gonna be great.

Jonathan snaps a photo of her. Joyce shoots him a look as...

Will comes bounding over.

                         WILL
               It's *definitely* an Atari.

                         JOYCE
               What?

                         WILL
               The green present. It's an Atari.
               I felt Dustin's today and it's the
               exact same weight.

                         JOYCE
               Oh yeah? And where the hell do you
               think we have the money for an
               Atari, huh? After all the repairs
               on this place --

                         WILL
               I don't know --

                         JOYCE
               Well, sorry to disappoint, but it's
               a big fat Cabbage Patch Kid.
               Because that's what snoopers
               deserve. Now --

She slaps food on his plate.

                         JOYCE (CONT'D)
               Eat.

Will abruptly pushes away from the table.

                         JOYCE (CONT'D)
               I said enough snooping --

                         WILL
               I forgot to wash my hands. I'll --
               I'll be right back --

Will hurries away. Joyce sighs. Continues to dish out food.

INT. BYERS HOUSE - BATHROOM - NIGHT

SHHHHHHH. Water gushes from the faucet.

But Will doesn't wash his hands. Instead, he leans over the
sink and gags. Once, twice, and --

THWUNK! He coughs up a SMALL WET GROWTH. It slops into the
sink. He quickly washes it down the drain.

Then he looks up at his reflection in the mirror.

<u>He looks scared</u>.

THE LIGHTS SUDDENLY FLICKER AND -- WHOOSH! SUDDENLY
EVERYTHING GOES DARK AND FOGGY. <u>WE'RE IN THE NETHER</u>. THE
BATHROOM IS COVERED IN THOSE AWFUL GROWTHS AND PARTICULATES
FALL FROM THE CEILING. THIS HORRIFIC IMAGE LASTS FOR JUST AN
INSTANT AND THEN --

BAM! THE LIGHTS COME BACK ON AND --

<u>EVERYTHING IS BACK TO NORMAL</u>.

Will hits off the water.

INT. BYERS HOUSE - KITCHEN - NIGHT

Will sits back down at the table.

Joyce looks at Will. Something seems off.

                    JOYCE
          You okay?

Will considers. Nods.

                    WILL
          Yeah. I'm okay.

He starts to eat. CHRISTMAS MUSIC PLAYS through the house.

WE SLOWLY PULL AWAY as our reunited family eats dinner.

                              FADE TO BLACK.

                    <u>END OF SEASON</u>